DIRECTORY OF LIBRARY AUTOMATION SOFTWARE, SYSTEMS, AND SERVICES

DIRECTORY OF LIBRARY AUTOMATION SOFTWARE, SYSTEMS, AND SERVICES

1993 EDITION

PAMELA R. CIBBARELLI

COMPILER AND EDITOR

PUBLISHED BY

LEARNED INFORMATION, INC.

MEDFORD, NJ

Learned Information, Inc.
143 Old Marlton Pike
Medford, NJ 08055

(609) 654-6266

Copyright 1993
Learned Information, Inc.
ISBN: 0-938734-65-2

Price for the 1993 edition is $79.00.
Cover Design: Sandy Brock

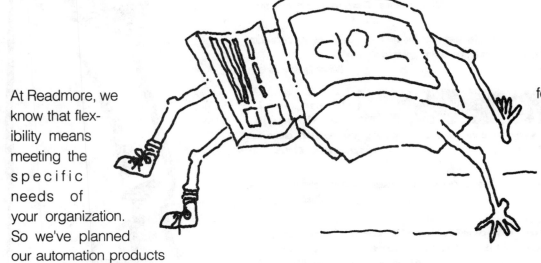

TABLE OF CONTENTS

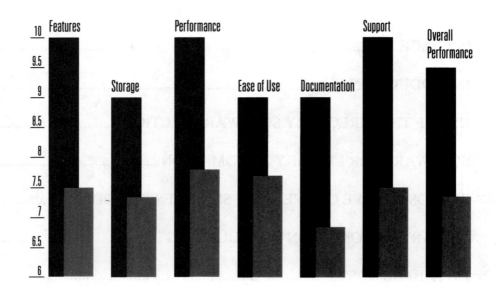

PREFACE

This 1993 edition of the *Directory of Library Automation Software, Systems, and Services* is a continuation of *Directory of Information Management Software for Libraries, Information Centers, Record Centers*. Learned Information, Inc. acquired the rights to the publication in 1992 from Pacific Information, Inc. Pamela R. Cibbarelli, who has been co-editor of the publication since it began in 1983, continues as the editor.

The title of the publication has been changed from *Directory of Information Management Software for Libraries, Information Centers, Record Centers* to *Directory of Library Automation Software, Systems, and Services* to provide specific emphasis on library automation, and to reflect its expanded coverage Previous editions included only software products. This edition introduces the inclusion of library automation systems and services. Although the publication will continue to provide references to many products systems and services of interest to records managers, the criteria for inclusion is the relevance of the product or service to the library automation marketplace.

Extensive diligence has gone into the compilation of this Directory to ensure the inclusion of the most current and accurate information. Information has been requested from each software supplier and the majority of suppliers verified copy.

Special thanks are owed to those who worked in creating this edition of the Directory. To Tom Hogan for trusting. To Richard Zeiler for helping to get the project underway. To Trish Sanders who worried at all the right times. To Carleton Morgan for lighting the path. To Michael Johnson for combining working, learning, and healing in a most delightful way. To Geneva Johnson Ackley for a trip down memory lane with happy thoughts of Ken Plate, Ed Kazlauskas, Carol Tenopir, & Jerry Lundeen. Thank you all.

The Directory of Library Automation Software, Systems, and Services began in 1980 as Pamela Cibbarelli and Carol Tenopir began to offer seminars on software packages to the library and information community. These were held in various cities as one and two-day seminars and as pre-conference workshops for the American Society for Information Science, the Medical Library Association, and CLASS. The first edition of the Directory was created in response to numerous requests from individuals and organizations for the materials and handouts from these seminars. Seminars on library automation are again available through CIBBARELLI'S.

In the first edition of the Directory (1983), 55 software packages were described in detail. The volume of new software products and changes to existing software warranted a 1984 supplement. The 1985-1986 edition described over 85 software packages. The 1987-1988 edition described over 175 packages. The 1989-1990 edition included more than 200 packages. In the 1993 edition, 240 software packages are described in detail, and a section of the Directory provides brief references to other packages for which there has been either name changes, removal of the product from the marketplace, or simply no response from the software supplier to enable the editor to confirm product information.

Comments, suggestions, changes, and additions are invited by the editor to assist in making future updates as accurate and helpful as possible. Contact Pamela R. Cibbarelli, Cibbarelli's, 416 Main Street #82, Huntington Beach, CA 92648. Telephone 714-969-8358; Fax 714-960-5454; Internet PCibbarelli@Fullerton.edu.

INTRODUCTION

PURPOSE

This publication provides a survey of library automation software, systems, and services. It includes basic information to locate and compare available options for library automation based on various criteria such as hardware requirements, operating systems, components and applications, and price. The Directory presents the information pertinent to begin a comparative study of the available automation alternatives. It also provides the necessary contact information to allow further investigation.

SOFTWARE

There are thousands of software packages on the market; therefore, it has been necessary to develop a set of criteria for inclusion of software packages in the Directory. These criteria are as follows:

1. The package must be targeted to the library market place. This includes those packages specifically tailored, for example, to a special library, as well as general purpose packages which have the capability of handling information management applications.

2. There must be current installations of the package in libraries, i.e., the package must be developed beyond the initial design and development stages.

3. Software packages are limited to those currently marketed and with installations in North America. North American packages installed elsewhere are often noted in the "sampling of current clients" section found with each software description.

4. Only commercially available software packages are included. Thus excluded are online union catalog systems such as the University of California's MELVYL. Many libraries and corporations create their own software and do not release it commercially.

RETROSPECTIVE CONVERSION SERVICES

This section is new to the Directory. It includes vendors who process bibliographic information to provide records for use in automated retrieval systems for libraries.

LIBRARY AUTOMATION CONSULTANTS

This section is new to the Directory. It includes profiles of the services provided by consultants who specialize in the automation of library services.

DATABASE HOSTS

Included in this section, also new to the Directory, are the online services which provide access to online databases through computer modems. There are many such services with a variety of database products. Included here are only those services which provide databases of interest to the automation of libraries.

CD-ROM DISTRIBUTORS

This section provides contact information for agencies which focus on the sales of CD-ROM products and services to libraries.

MEETINGS & CONFERENCES

A list of meetings and conferences, which will include sessions focused specifically on library automation during 1993 and 1994, is included along with date of the meeting and city.

BRIEF INFO

To provide users of the Directory the most complete information possible about the commercially available library automation software packages, the Directory also includes a section BRIEF INFO which provides mention of software about which sufficient information was not available to include a full description in the main section of this Directory. For most of these packages, suppliers simply did not respond to multiple requests for information. For some, suppliers indicated the software is no longer available. For others, the software name has been replaced with a new product name.

LIBRARY AUTOMATION PUBLICATIONS

RECENT LIBRARY AUTOMATION BOOKS - bibliographic citations are provided to recently published materials related to library automation.

LIBRARY AUTOMATION SERIALS - citations, frequency, and pricing information is provided for journals which focus on library automation.

INDEX

A single alphabetical index is provided at the end of the Directory which refers the user to specific sections of the Directory. This index combines access by company name, software, service, hardware, and components.

USE OF THE DIRECTORY SOFTWARE SECTION

The descriptions of software are arranged alphabetically by the name of the software package. Under each package there is a consistent set of descriptive information. This includes the following:

NAME OF SOFTWARE PACKAGE:

NAME OF COMPANY DISTRIBUTING SOFTWARE PACKAGE:
> Company
> Address
> Telephone Number
> Contact's name

HARDWARE:
Computers on which the software operates.

SYSTEM REQUIREMENTS:
Operating system; number and size of required disks, tape drives; amount of main memory required.

PROGRAMMING LANGUAGE:
The computer languages in which the software was written, e.g., COBOL, FORTRAN.

COMPONENTS & APPLICATIONS:
The capabilities most frequently required of software for information management applications include:

ACQUISITIONS - Provides access to information about materials which have been ordered, but have not yet been received and processed for circulation. Standard information from acquisitions files includes:
> author
> title
> publisher
> publisher's address
> requestor
> price
> edition or date of publication
> ISBN or ISSN

CATALOG (BATCH) - Provides a computer generated listing of the items in the collection in a print format including paper, microfiche, catalog cards.

CATALOG (ONLINE) - Provides an online computer-based system to query for information by authors, titles, subjects, etc.

CATALOGING - Provides computer-based routines to provide descriptive cataloging of materials in the collection.

CD-ROM INTERFACE - Software has interface with CD-ROM applications.

CIRCULATION - Provides access to "check-out" files for materials in the collection. Circulation files include as a minimum:
> - date checked out
> - name of borrower
> - item identification

FORMATTING BIBLIOGRAPHIES - With the advent of extensive automation of bibliographic collections and online searching of commercial databases coinciding, some suppliers have developed software with the ability to format bibliographic citations in a variety of standard formats, such as *MLA Style Sheet, Chicago Manual of Style, Turabian's*. These packages permit the user to select the bibliographic citations and bibliographic style preferred for inclusion with research papers and other publications.

INDEX OF KEYWORDS - Similar to, but simpler than the thesaurus, the index provides an alphabetic listing of all terms used in a specific field; it often includes frequency of occurrence.

INTER-LIBRARY LOAN - Provides a system for loaning materials from one collection to another agency. As a minimum, ILL systems track:
> - item loaned
> - borrowing agency
> - fees (if any)
> - date of loan

MEDIA BOOKING - Media centers (sometimes stand alone units, but more often a branch of the library or information center) schedule the loan of audio visual materials. The information contained in media booking applications includes as a minimum:
> type of equipment
> date of loan (often time of day)
> date due (often time of day)
> borrower

RESERVE ROOM - This component is especially important in an academic setting where a professor may require many students to read specific items in a period of time too short for standard loan periods to apply.

SERIALS - Providing ordering, check-in, and claim routines for publications, such as periodicals, which are issued in successive parts.

THESAURUS - Providing a list of acceptable terms for specified fields such as subject. Full thesaurus capabilities provide term validation and hierarchies providing the relationship of one term to another, e.g., broader terms, used-for terms, narrower terms.

UPDATING MODES:
After a database is created, and there are more records to add or modify, updating is done in one of the following modes:

BATCH UPDATE - Modifications and additions are entered into a file for later integration into the computer database

DYNAMIC UPDATE - Modifications are done real time, online, with the modifications to the database taking place immediately and the modified record fully accessible immediately.

FEATURES:

BOOLEAN LOGIC SEARCHABLE - Boolean logic operators provide the ability to combine search terms. Possible operators include AND, OR, NOT, XOR, GREATER THAN, EQUAL TO, and LESS THAN.

FULL TEXT SEARCHABLE - Provides the capability to search for any word appearing in the database, or in specified fields of the database.

RECORD FIELDS - Indicates the maximum number of fields available for the description of each item in the collection. Examples of fields includes: author, title, subject, call number, ISBN, publisher, etc.

RECORD SIZE - Indicates the maximum number of characters or bytes available per record for the descriptive cataloging of the materials in the collection.

STATISTICAL & MATH CAPABILITIES - Indicates if the software provides the ability to add, subtract, divide, or multiply. Also, if the the software automatically compiles or can be easily programmed to provide database statistics.

WHOLESALE CHANGE CAPABILITY - When modifying an existing database, several records may need to have the same modifications made, e.g., change CEMENT to CONCRETE. Wholesale changes provide the ability to enter a single command for a specific change and all records to be modified are altered from the single command.

SUPPORT:

This section describes the additional services in support of the software available from the supplier.

APPLICATION CONSULTING - Is consulting available from the supplier for using the software for specific applications?

MAINTENANCE AND UPDATES - Is software maintenance available? Is there an additional fee for maintenance?

TIME SHARE AVAILABLE - Is it possible to use the software through time share access to a supplier's computer without having to purchase and operate a computer in-house?

USER TRAINING - Is training provided for the personnel who will be using the software?

RECOMMENDED FOR:

This section indicates to what vertical market sector the supplier has developed the package. Because the requirements of software may differ significantly depending upon its intended audience, this section indicates to whom the supplier sells the majority of its software:

CORPORATE & GOVT LIBRARIES - Also known as Special Libraries. This software tends to be developed to handle many types of materials including books, documents, drawings, etc.

MEDIA CENTER MANAGEMENT - Collections of audio visual materials and the equipment required for their use, e.g., films, tapes, CDs, projectors, etc.

PUBLIC LIBRARIES - Government supported institutions which provide the management and loan of library materials to the public.

RECORDS & FILES MANAGEMENT - Information centers and records centers manage a broad variety of materials in addition to books and periodicals, e.g., company records of contracts, personnel, proposals, emergency procedures, operations manuals, etc.

SCHOOL LIBRARIES - Libraries for educational institutions from preschool through high school.

UNIVERSITY LIBRARIES - Libraries on college and university campuses.

INSTALLATIONS:

To assist user's of this Directory in their evaluation of the supplier's of the software, the following information has been included:

INITIAL INSTALLATION DATE - When was the software first installed at a user site and considered fully operable?

TOTAL NUMBER OF INSTALLED SITES - This section indicates how many copies of the software package have been installed in client locations.

SAMPLING OF CURRENT CLIENTS - Provides the names of a few of the locations currently using this software.

PUBLISHED REVIEWS & ARTICLES:

Citations are provided to articles appearing in trade literature describing or evaluating the software. Most of these citations were provided by the suppliers. By reading the articles cited, it may be possible to evaluate the software more fully.

PRICE:

The pricing information is as detailed as possible from the information supplied by the vendors. If a demo disk is available, it is often mentioned in this section.

SUPPLIER'S COMMENTS:

Suppliers are invited to describe their software packages in this section. For many packages suppliers provided text. For some others, excerpts were made from supplier's literature or ads to assist the reader of the Directory to understand the scope and intent of the packages.

SOFTWARE FOR
LIBRARY AUTOMATION

A-V HANDLER

Data Trek, Inc.
5838 Edison Place
Carlsbad, CA 92008
(619) 431-8400 or (800) 876-5484;   Fax (619) 431-8448
Contact: Kimberly Gates

Hardware: Apple, IBM PC Compatibles

System Requirements: MS/DOS; 640K minimum; available for local area networks

Programming Language: dBASE III

Components & Applications:

acquisitions	no	catalog (batch)	yes
catalog (online)	no	cataloging	yes
CD-ROM interface	no	circulation	yes
formatting bibliographies	no	index of keywords	no
inter-library loan	no	interface for MARC records	no
media booking	yes	reserve room	no
serials	no	thesaurus	no

Updating Modes:

batch update	no	dynamic update	yes

Features:

Boolean logic searchable	no	full text searchable	no
record fields	predefined	record size	unlimited
statistical & math capabilities	yes	wholesale change capability	no

Support:

application consulting	yes	maintenance and updates	yes
time share available	no	user training	yes

Recommended for:

Corporate & govt libraries	yes	Media center management	yes
Public libraries	yes	Records & files management	no
School libraries	yes	University libraries	yes

Installations:

Initial installation date	1985	Total number of installed sites	50 plus
Sampling of current clients:	no info		

Price: $2,450 for software and manual; $30 for manuals; $50 for demo disk; $500 for maintenance agreement. Additionally , several training options are available upon request.

Supplier's comments: The Audio Visual Handler Module provides media cataloging, vendor file maintenance, rental film control, booking file control, and equipment inventory control. It can also be used with the **Manager Series.**

A/V IMAGE

Library Systems and Services, Inc.
200 Orchard Ridge Drive
Gaithersburg, MD 20878
301-975-9800 or 800-638-8725
Attn: Marketing

Hardware: IBM compatibles; one or more floppy drives and one hard drive; 640K memory, & CD-ROM drive

System Requirements: DOS

Programming Language: Microsoft "C"

Components & Applications:

acquisitions	yes	catalog (batch)	yes
catalog (online)	yes	cataloging	yes
CD-ROM interface	yes	circulation	no
formatting bibliographies	no	index of keywords	yes
inter-library loan	no	interface for MARC records	yes
media booking	no	reserve room	no
serials	no	thesaurus	no

Updating Modes:

batch update	yes	dynamic update	no

Features:

Boolean logic searchable	yes	full text searchable	no
record fields	MARC format	record size	MARC format
statistical & math capabilities	no	wholesale change capability	no

Support:

application consulting	yes	maintenance and updates	yes
time share available	no	user training	no

Recommended for:

Corporate & govt libraries	yes	Media center management	yes
Public libraries	yes	Records & files management	no
School libraries	yes	University libraries	yes

Installations:

Initial installation date	1992	Total number of installed sites	new

Sampling of current clients:

Published reviews & articles:

Price: $895 annually

Supplier's comments: A/V image is a truly comprehensive cataloging tool for non-print materials. It provides access to over 600,000 MARC records for Music, Maps, A/V Materials, Sound Recordings, Special Instructional Materials and Kits. A/V image is compatible with ULTRACAT™, Bibliofile™, and SuperCAT™.

ACCESSION CONTROL V.2

Right On Programs
755-F New York Avenue
Huntington, NY 11743
(516) 424-7777   FAX (516) 424-7207

Hardware: IBM & compatibles; Apple series

System Requirements: MS-DOS

Programming Language: Turbo Pascal

Components & Applications:

acquisitions	yes	catalog (batch)	no
catalog (online)	no	cataloging	no
CD-ROM interface	no	circulation	no
formatting bibliographies	no	index of keywords	no
inter-library loan	no	interface for MARC records	no
media booking	no	reserve room	no
serials	no	thesaurus	no

Updating Modes:

batch update	no	dynamic update	yes

Features:

Boolean logic searchable	no	full text searchable	no
record fields	no info	record size	no info
statistical & math capabilities	yes	wholesale change capability	no

Support:

application consulting	yes	maintenance and updates	yes
time share available	no	user training	no

Recommended for:

Corporate & govt libraries	yes	Media center management	yes
Public libraries	yes	Records & files management	no
School libraries	yes	University libraries	yes

Installations:

Initial installation date	1992	Total number of installed sites	1400
Sampling of current clients: no info			

Price: $129

Supplier's comments: This new version of the software will still do all the things it did before and more:
   1) go back and edit every entry
   2) choose and enter any accession number you want
   3) use up to an eight-digit accession number
   4) search and print to screen or printer by author, title, accession number or date accessioned
   5) search using upper or lower case and wild card characters
   6) print out all books accessioned between specific dates and the computer will total number of books and total cost of those books

ACQ ACQUISITIONS SYSTEM

JES Library Automation Consulting Services, Inc.
#104-221 Blue Mountain Street
Coquitlam, BC, V3K 4H3 Canada
604-939-6775; fax 604-939-9970
Contact: Peter Smode

Hardware: DEC VAX

System Requirements: VAX/VMS

Programming Language: VAX BASIC

Components & Applications:

acquisitions	yes	catalog (batch)	no
catalog (online)	yes	cataloging	yes
CD-ROM interface	no	circulation	n/a
formatting bibliographies	n/a	index of keywords	yes
inter-library loan	n/a	interface for MARC records	no
media booking	n/a	reserve room	n/a
serials	no	thesaurus	no

Updating Modes:

batch update	yes	dynamic update	yes

Features:

Boolean logic searchable	yes	full text searchable	no
record fields	17	record size	2000
statistical & math capabilities	yes	wholesale change capability	no

Support:

application consulting	yes	maintenance and updates	yes
time share available	no	user training	yes

Recommended for:

Corporate & govt libraries	yes	Media center management	no
Public libraries	yes	Records & files management	no
School libraries	yes	University libraries	yes

Installations:

Initial installation date	1991	Total number of installed sites	2

Sampling of current clients: Burnaby Public Library (BC); Prince George Public Library (BC).

Published reviews & articles:

Price: $10,000 to $20,000 (software only), depending upon system size, options, etc. Turn-key systems (with hardware) are available as well. Custom pricing information is available upon request.

Supplier's comments: While able to support academic users as well, ACQ is especially well-suited for public libraries. Support for selection lists (to be used by library selection committees or supervisory personnel) and batch order approval improve the efficiency and accuracy of the ordering process.

Designed as a multi-user system, users from any terminal may inquire or update the database at any time. Interfaces to and from our ULISYS library system ties the ACQ database and main library catalogue together. Public specifications are available for those who may wish to write their own interface to inquire into the ACQ system.

ACQ is a solid system that will form the base of our further development work. BISAC interfaces will be in production use by the end of 1993 and other enhancements are pending.

ACQUIRE

Baker & Taylor
652 E. Main Street
P.O. Box 6920
Bridgewater, NJ 08807-0920
(800) 526-3811   (201) 722-8000

Hardware: IBM PC

System Requirements: MS-DOS

Programming Language: no info

Components & Applications:

acquisitions	yes	catalog (batch)	no
catalog (online)	no	cataloging	no
CD-ROM interface	no	circulation	no
formatting bibliographies	no	index of keywords	no
inter-library loan	no	interface for MARC records	no
media booking	no	reserve room	no
serials	no	thesaurus	no

Updating Modes:

batch update	no	dynamic update	yes

Features:

Boolean logic searchable	no	full text searchable	no
record fields	no info	record size	no info
statistical & math capabilities	yes	wholesale change capability	no

Support:

application consulting	no	maintenance and updates	yes
time share available	no	user training	yes

Recommended for:

Corporate & govt libraries	yes	Media center management	no
Public libraries	yes	Records & files management	no
School libraries	yes	University libraries	yes

Installations:

Initial installation date	1985	Total number of installed sites	no info
Sampling of current clients:	no info		

Price: free

Supplier's comments: The Acquire system utilizes the personal computer to facilitate quick and precise book ordering. It increases the efficiency of the acquisitions workflow by eliminating many of the manual tasks like typing and mail handling. It helps expedite book selection and collection development by providing the most exact picture of your current on-order file. And it supplies instant feedback on inventory, so book orders can be placed with accuracy and realistic expectations. You will know immediately which titles will be shipped, back ordered or cancelled.

All the user needs is an IBM or compatible computer and Hayes compatible modem. To place an order, the ISBN or title/author and quantity are entered on the personal computer. Dialing the toll-free number sends the order directly to Baker & Taylor.

The Acquire electronic book ordering service is completely free of charge. Significant savings on both postage and labor costs also result in further library economy. But the ultimate result is the extra staff time available to serve your library users.

ACQUISITION MANAGER

Professional Software, Inc.
21 Forest Avenue
Glen Ridge, NJ 07028
201-748-7658

Hardware: IBM compatibles

System Requirements: 256K RAM, DOS

Programming Language:

Components & Applications:

acquisitions	yes	catalog (batch)	no
catalog (online)	see Online Catalog	cataloging	see Circ. Manager
CD-ROM interface	no	circulation	no
formatting bibliographies	no	index of keywords	no
inter-library loan	no	interface for MARC records	no
media booking	no	reserve room	no
serials	see Serial Control System	thesaurus	no

Updating Modes:

batch update	no	dynamic update	yes

Features:

Boolean logic searchable	no	full text searchable	no
record fields	no info	record size	no info
statistical & math capabilities	no	wholesale change capability	no

Support:

application consulting	no	maintenance and updates	yes
time share available	no	user training	no

Recommended for:

Corporate & govt libraries	yes	Media center management	no
Public libraries	yes	Records & files management	no
School libraries	yes	University libraries	yes

Installations:

Initial installation date	1985	Total number of installed sites	no info
Sampling of current clients: no info			

Published reviews & articles:

Price: $495   Check in, Claiming, Subscription Management
$ 60   Demo package

Supplier's comments: The Acquisition Manager addresses all aspects of library acquisitions including:
• Book selection
• Placement of orders and requisitions
• Recording of receipts, returns & cancellations
• Tracking of overdue items
• Fund control/analysis
• Listing of recent acquisitions by subject or by department

ACQUISITIONS MANAGER

Right On Programs
755-F New York Avenue
Huntington, NY 11743
(516) 424-7777   FAX (516) 424-7207

Hardware: IBM & compatibles; Apple series

System Requirements: MS-DOS

Programming Language: Turbo Pascal

Components & Applications:

acquisitions	yes	catalog (batch)	no
catalog (online)	no	cataloging	no
CD-ROM interface	no	circulation	no
formatting bibliographies	no	index of keywords	no
inter-lilrary loan	no	interface for MARC records	no
media booking	no	reserve room	no
serials	no	thesaurus	no

Updating Modes:

batch update	no	dynamic update	yes

Features:

Boolean logic searchabl	no	full text searchable	no
record fields	no info	record size	no info
statistical & math capabilities	yes	wholesale change capability	no

Support:

application consulting	yes	maintenance and updates	yes
time share available	no	user training	no

Recommended for:

Corporate & govt libraries	yes	Media center management	yes
Public libraries	yes	Records & files management	yes
School libraries	yes	University libraries	yes

Installations:

Initial installation date	1991	Total number of installed sites	1200+
Sampling of current clients: no info			

Price: $169

Supplier's comments: This easy to learn and use program allows the user to encumber the price and to change that price when the item is received. The user can check how much money has been allocated and how much is left in each budget code. Allows user to charge purchase to specific account and to add shipping and handling if and when necessary.

Enter supplier once and call back by ID later. Program is easy to learn and use with no bulky manual.

Network version also available.

ACTIVE RECORDS SOFTWARE

Automated Records Management
23011 Moulton Parkway, Suite J-10
Laguna Hills, CA 92653
(714) 855-8780   FAX (714) 855-9078

Hardware: IBM/PC, XT, AT, PS/2 and most IBM compatibles

System Requirements: MS DOS

Programming Language: dBase III Plus and compiled using Foxbase

Components & Applications:

acquisitions	no	catalog (batch)	no
catalog (online)	yes	cataloging	no
CD-ROM interface	no	circulation	no
formatting bibliographies	no	index of keywords	no
inter-library loan	no	interface for MARC records	no
media booking	no	reserve room	no
serials	no	thesaurus	no

Updating Modes:

batch update	no	dynamic update	yes

Features:

Boolean logic searchable	no	full text searchable	yes
record fields	no info	record size	no info
statistical & math capabilities	no	wholesale change capability	no

Support:

application consulting	yes	maintenance and updates	yes
time share available	no	user training	yes

Recommended for:

Corporate & govt libraries	no	Media center management	no
Public libraries	no	Records & files management	yes
School libraries	no	University libraries	no

Installations:

Initial installation date	1989	Total number of installed site	50
Sampling of current clients:	no info		

Price: $695 single user
$1195 multi-user

Supplier's comments: This software manages and tracks active records. Every department within your company must manage their file records (contract files, project files, employee files, etc.) until they are no longer needed; then, the files are boxed and sent to the Record Center or off-site to a Commercial Storage Facility. This software provides for identifying and tracking files during their life within the Department.

The $695 price includes the ARMS Retention Management Software usually sold separately for $249.00.

ADVANCE

Geac Computer Corporation
11 Allstate Parkway
Markham, Ontario
CANADA L3R 9T8
(416) 475-0525

Hardware: Data General, IBM RS6000, DEC, Motorola, Pyramid, C.Itoh, Fujitsu, Ultimate, Honeywell, ICON

System Requirements: UNIX compatible platforms

Programming Language: Compiled BASIC

Components & Applications:

acquisitions	yes	catalog (batch)	yes
catalog (online)	yes	cataloging	yes
CD-ROM interface	yes	circulation	yes
formatting bibliographies	yes	index of keywords	yes
inter-library loan	yes	interface for MARC records	yes
media booking	yes	reserve room	yes
serials	yes	thesaurus	yes

Updating Modes:

batch update	yes	dynamic update	yes

Features:

Boolean logic searchable	yes	full text searchable	yes
record fields	MARC format	record size	MARC format
statistical & math capabilities	yes	wholesale change capability	yes

Support:

application consulting	yes	maintenance and updates	yes
time share available	yes	user training	yes

Recommended for:

Corporate & govt libraries	yes	Media center management	no
Public libraries	yes	Records & files management	yes
School libraries	yes	University libraries	yes

Installations:

Initial installation date	1984	Total number of installed sites	75

Sampling of current clients: House of Lords (UK), Central European University (Czech), Texas Woman's University (US), Greater Victoria Public Library (CAN), San Francisco State University (US), Royal Northern College of Music (UK), University College of Northern Victoria (Aus), Direction du Livre et de la Lecture (FR), Centre National de cooperation de Bibliotheques Publiques (FR), California State University (Fresno, US), Olivet Nazarene University (US).

Published reviews & articles:

Price: Contact vendor as pricing depends on configuration.

Supplier's comments: The Geac ADVANCE Integrated Library System is a comprehensive, Unix-based, online system easily tailorable to meet the needs of a wide range of libraries and information centers. ADVANCE is a functionally rich library automation solution designed with efficiency, growth and portability in mind.

Files are updatable in real time, and updates are immediately available to all users. Extensive security procedures protect both data and transactions from unauthorized access. ADVANCE was designed from the outset to be a fully integrated system. Continuously growing to meet the changing needs of the international library community, ADVANCE functions include: Online Public Catalogue, Acquisitions, Cataloging and Authority Control, Serials, Control, Circulation, Journal Citation Databases, Inventory Control, Materials, Booking, Shut-In or Homebound Patrons, Gateway, BISAC Electronic ordering and receipts.

AGILE III

Auto-Graphics, Inc.
3201 Temple Avenue
Pomona, CA 91768-3200
Contact: Sales/Marketing Dept.
(714) 595-7204; (800) 776-6939

Hardware: Terminals - IBM PC compatible; modem

System Requirements: Turnkey system

Programming Language: Not applicable

Components & Applications:

acquisitions	no	catalog (batch)	yes
catalog (online)	no	cataloging	yes
CD-ROM interface	no	circulation	no
formatting bibliographies	no	index of keywords	no
inter-library loan	yes	interface for MARC records	yes
media booking	no	reserve room	no
serials	no	thesaurus	no

Updating Modes:

batch update	yes	dynamic update	yes

Features:

Boolean logic searchable	yes	full text searchable	no
record fields	MARC format	record size	MARC format
statistical & math capabilities	no	wholesale change capability	no

Support:

application consulting	yes	maintenance and updates	yes
time share available	yes	user training	yes

Recommended for:

Corporate & govt libraries	yes	Media center management	no
Public libraries	yes	Records & files management	yes
School libraries	yes	University libraries	yes

Installations:

Initial installation date	1981	Total number of installed sites	45+

Sampling of current clients: Maryland Statewide Network (cataloging and interlibrary loan); Sacramento City-County Library; Tennessee State Library and regional library centers; Gaston-Lincoln Public Library.

Price: Varies, depending on dedicated vs. dial access.

Supplier's comments: AGILE III is an online database management system and bibliographic utility supporting online cataloging and interlibrary loan. A shared resource approach provides access to MARC records as well as individual customer and regional databases for retrospective conversion, current acquisitions cataloging, interlibrary loan and upgrading of brief circulation records to full MARC. Dedicated line via US Sprint or dial access to AGILE III is available.

Other Auto-Graphics products include: IMPACT™ CD-ROM Public Access Catalogs, COM catalogs, circulation load files, database upgrades, authority control, subject guides, spin-off catalogs such as large type, foreign language, etc. The IMPACT Small Library Management System (IMPACT/SLiMS) is a PC-based integrated system for smaller libraries (less than 40,000 volumes).

AIS-COMPUTERIZED RECORDS MANAGEMENT SYSTEM

Assured Information Systems, Inc.
P.O. Box 947
Chadds Ford, PA 19317
(215) 459-0711
Contact: Ray Carden

Hardware: IBM PC and compatibles

System Requirements: PC-DOS/MS-DOS

Programming Language: Nantucket Clipper

Components & Applications:

acquisitions	no	catalog (batch)	yes
catalog (online)	yes	cataloging	yes
CD-ROM interface	no	circulation	no
formatting bibliographies	no	index of keywords	yes
inter-library loan	no	interface for MARC records	no
media booking	yes	reserve room	no
serials	no	thesaurus	no

Updating Modes:

batch update	yes	dynamic update	yes

Features:

Boolean logic searchable	yes	full text searchable	yes
record fields	fixed	record size	various
statistical & math capabilities	yes	wholesale change capability	yes

Support:

application consulting	no	maintenance and updates	yes
time share available	no	user training	yes

Recommended for:

Corporate & govt libraries	no	Media center management	no
Public libraries	no	Records & files management	yes
School libraries	no	University libraries	no

Installations:

Initial installation date	1985	Total number of installed site	73

Sampling of current clients: Library of Congress; Union Carbide; American Institute of CPA's; American Life Insurance Co.; ARAMCO Services Co.; City of Atlanta; CONOCO Inc; E.I. DuPont; General Dynamics; Hoffman LaRoche; Mount Sinai Hospital; Pima County (AZ); San Diego Gas and Electric; Smith Kline & French Laboratories; Alcan Smelters and Chemicals, Ltd.; American Savings Bank; Bank of California; Home Federal Savings & Loan

Price: Single User $ 7,500
           Multi-User $10,000

Supplier's comments: The software manages records retention and record centers. Included are automated assignment of box locations, automated destruction, box contents indexing, request processing, records out-of-file monitoring, litigation support, vital records control, active records inventory, media management, cost allocation, keyword retrieval and many other features.

ALEXANDRIA 3.0

COMPanion
3755 Evelyn Drive
Salt Lake City, UT 84124
801-278-6439 or 800-347-6439
FAX 801-278-7789
Contact: Dawn Collins

Hardware: Macintosh

System Requirements: 6.01 or newer

Programming Language:

Components & Applications:

acquisitions	yes	catalog (batch)	no
catalog (online)	yes	cataloging	yes
CD-ROM interface	yes	circulation	yes
formatting bibliographies	no	index of keywords	yes
inter-library loan	no	interface for MARC records	yes
media booking	yes	reserve room	no
serials	yes	thesaurus	no

Updating Modes:

batch update	no	dynamic update	yes

Features:

Boolean logic searchable	yes	full text searchable	yes
record fields	MARC format	record size	MARC format
statistical & math capabilities	yes	wholesale change capability	yes

Support:

application consulting	no	maintenance and updates	yes
time share available	no	user training	yes

Recommended for:

Corporate & govt libraries	yes	Media center management	yes
Public libraries	yes	Records & files management	yes
School libraries	yes	University libraries	yes

Installations:

Initial installation date	1987	Total number of installed sites	3,000

Sampling of current clients: Schools 80%; University/Special 10%; Business 10%.

Published reviews & articles:
Apple Library Users Guide, January 1992
Apple Library Users Guide, October 1992

Price: $999 Circulation only; up to $4000 site license for all components.

Supplier's comments: Let us show you how to free yourself from routine chores that gobble up your most precious resource - time. Call and ask for the Alexandria interactive demonstration disk and you'll see how the ease of Macintosh combined with the power of Alexandria can change the way you run your library.

With Alexandria, library staff can manage circulation and the catalog, teachers and students can browse the collection from classroom workstations, researchers can produce bibliographies and anyone can find up-to-date catalog information at easy-to-use library-based workstations. Best of all, you can give everyone information that is accurate up to the minute, because Alexandria stores all data in a single source file that's updated instantly with each transaction.

Alexandria tackles jobs you'd never ask of your card catalog. Find titles that haven't circulated for the last two years. Print overdue notices and sort them by homeroom - automatically. Find an item on a reading list. Is it in stock? When is it due back? And, what's more, you'll find these answers instantly.

ALLIANCE PLUS

Follett Software Company
809 North Front Street
McHenry, IL 60050-5589
(815) 344-8700 or (800) 323-3397
FAX (815) 344-8774
Contact: Joy Danley

Hardware: IBM PC or compatible; CD-ROM drive (ISO 9660 format compatible); 20MB hard disk drive recommended

System Requirements: 640K RAM; MS-DOS 3.3 or higher, Microsoft Extensions 2.2 or higher

Programming Language: C

Components & Applications:

acquisitions	no	catalog (batch)	no
catalog (online)	no	cataloging	no
CD-ROM interface	yes	circulation	no
formatting bibliographies	no	index of keywords	no
inter-library loan	no	interface for MARC records	yes
media booking	no	reserve room	no
serials	no	thesaurus	no

Updating Modes:

batch update	yes	dynamic update	yes

Features:

Boolean logic searchable	no	full text searchable	no
record fields	no info	record size	no info
statistical & math capabilities	no	wholesale change capability	no

Support:

application consulting	no	maintenance and updates	yes
time share available	no	user training	yes

Recommended for:

Corporate & govt libraries	no	Media center management	no
Public libraries	no	Records & files management	no
School libraries	yes	University libraries	no

Installations:

Initial installation date	1989	Total number of installed sites	1500+

Sampling of current clients: References available.

Published reviews & articles:

Price: $250/application software
         $350/single CD-ROM disc
         $450/quarterly CD-ROM discs

Supplier's comments: Alliance Plus consists of application software and a specialized CD-ROM database, based on Library of Congress MARC records. The CD contains book, audio-visual, and serial records spanning years from 1901 to present. Many of which have been enhanced with: reading levels, interest levels, review sources, annotations, and LC, LC Children's and Sears subject headings. This product is a tool for library cataloging, etc. CardMaster Plus also works with the Alliance Plus CD-ROM MARC Database.

ANSWERING QUESTIONS LIBRARY STYLE

Learnco Inc.
Box L
Exeter, NH 03833
800-542-0026
Contact: J.H. Smith

Hardware: Apple II

System Requirements: 48 K, one disk drive

Programming Language: BASIC/Assembly

Support:

application consulting	no	maintenance and updates	yes
time share available	no	user training	no

Recommended for:

Corporate & govt libraries	no	Media center management	no
Public libraries	yes	Records & files management	no
School libraries	yes	University libraries	no

Installations:

Initial installation date	Nov 1982	Total number of installed sites	3000
Sampling of current clients:			

Published reviews & articles:

Price: $39.95

Supplier's comments: Answering Questions Library Style is a simulation of getting library information from non-reference sources: narrowing down the topic, using the card catalog to find the right book, using the index to get the right page, finding the information. Includes a student question book.

Editor's note: This is a special package for teaching library skills; therefore, it does not include the usual list of components and applications.

ASKSAM

Asksam Systems
PO Box 1428
Perry, FL 32347
800-800-1997 or 904-584-6590
Fax 904-584-7481
Contact: Tonya Mosley

Hardware: IBM PC or compatibles

System Requirements: DOS, 384K RAM

Programming Language: C

Components & Applications:

acquisitions	yes	catalog (batch)	yes
catalog (online)	yes	cataloging	yes
CD-ROM interface	no	circulation	yes
formatting bibliographies	yes	index of keywords	yes
inter-library loan	no	interface for MARC records	no
media booking	no	reserve room	no
serials	no	thesaurus	no

Updating Modes:

batch update	yes	dynamic update	yes

Features:

Boolean logic searchable	yes	full text searchable	yes
record fields	need info	record size	need info
statistical & math capabilities	yes	wholesale change capability	yes

Support:

application consulting	yes	maintenance and updates	yes
time share available	no	user training	yes

Recommended for:

Corporate & govt libraries	yes	Media center management	yes
Public libraries	yes	Records & files management	yes
School libraries	yes	University libraries	yes

Installations:

Initial installation date	1985	Total number of installed sites	40,000+

Sampling of current clients: Corpus Christi State University Library; Madison Public Library; Utah State University Merrill Library; Los Angeles County Public Library; New York Public Library; Del Mar College Library; National Institute of Health Library; U.S. General Accounting Office Library.

Published reviews & articles:
Pruett, Nancy, "Using askSAM to Manage Files of Bibliographic References." *Online*, July 1987.
Talley, Marcia and Virginia McNitt. *Automating a Library with askSam*. Meckler Publishing.
"Solutions Focus, Editors Choice for Free-Form Database Managers." *Byte Magazine*, June 1992.
"Readers Choice Award Runner-Up for Personal Information Manager." *Byte Magazine*, JunSe 1992.

Price: $ 395 - askSam version 5.1 single user
         $ 1,095 - askSam version 5.1 network 5 user
         $ 100 - additional network users (each)

Supplier's comments: askSam is an information manager combining database, word processing and text retrieval functions. It is this combination of functions that make askSam unique. askSam requires no structure. Like a text retrieval program, you can search through your entire information for a specific word or phrase. If your data is structured, askSam acts like a database and outputs fields, sorts data, performs arithmetic, and creates reports. askSam's hypertext function makes it easy to structure and search your information.

Combining these capabilities, askSam can interweave structured data with free-form text and offers you a tool to manage nearly any type of information including, names and addresses, research, bibliographical data, card catalogs, legal texts, meeting notes, letters, and even structured database applications.

THE ASSISTANT

INLEX, Inc.
P.O. Box 1349
Monterey, CA 93942
(800) 553-1202 (outside CA)   (408) 646-8600 (CA)
FAX (408) 646-0651
Contact: Marketing Dept.

Hardware: IBM PC or compatible

System Requirements: 10 MB hard disk, 640K RAM, DOS Version 3.1 or later

Programming Language: C

Components & Applications:

acquisitions	yes	catalog (batch)	yes
catalog (online)	yes	cataloging	yes
CD-ROM interface	no	circulation	yes
formatting bibliographies	no	index of keywords	yes
inter-library loan	no	interface for MARC records	yes
media booking	no	reserve room	no
serials	yes	thesaurus	yes

Updating Modes:

batch update	no	dynamic update	yes

Features:

Boolean logic searchable	yes	full text searchable	yes within key fields
record fields	variable	record size	variable
statistical & math capabilities	yes	wholesale change capability	yes

Support:

application consulting	yes	maintenance and updates	yes
time share available	no	user training	yes

Recommended for:

Corporate & govt libraries	yes	Media center management	no
Public libraries	yes	Records & files management	no
School libraries	yes	University libraries	no

Installations:

Initial installation date	1985	Total number of installed sites	no info

Sampling of current clients: Chase Manhattan Bank, Chesebrough-Pond's, Inc., Deloitte and Touche, MCI Communications, Moody's Investors Service, Novell, Skadden Arps, FDA Medical Library, US Customs Service, Andrews University, Hill College, Maine State Library, Bell Communications Research, Edison Electric Institute.

Published reviews & articles:
"The Assistant in a Law Library", *Automatome*, Vol. 10, No.3/4, Summer/Fall, 1991.
"The Assistant" Test Report, *Library Technology Reports,* March-April, 1990.

Price: $900 - $12,000 plus maintenance; demo disks are available

Supplier's comments: The ASSISTANT is an integrated library automation system designed for small to medium-sized libraries. Based on a modular concept where each functional system can operate independently or in conjunction with one another, you need only invest in those modules which you require. The software is composed of five modules: on/line public access catalog, cataloging, acquisitions/accounting, circulation, and serials control. The modules can be purchased separately or in any combination.

The ASSISTANT was written for the IBM PC/XT/AT or compatible and runs on standard local area networks. The LAN version utilizes the record locking and file protection capabilities of a true LAN.

AUTHEX PLUS

Reference Press
P.O. Box 70
Teeswater, Ontario, Canada N0G 2S0
Contact: George Ripley
(519) 392-6634

Hardware: IBM PC, XT, AT, PS/2, Compaq 386 and most compatibles

System Requirements: 256K memory; 2 diskette drives; MS-DOS 2.0 and up

Programming Language: Microsoft compiled BASIC

Components & Applications:

acquisitions	no	catalog (batch)	no
catalog (online)	no	cataloging	no
CD-ROM interface	no	circulation	no
formatting bibliographies	no	index of keywords	no
inter-library loan	no	interface for MARC records	no
media booking	no	reserve room	no
serials	yes	thesaurus	no

Updating Modes:

batch update	no	dynamic update	yes

Features:

Boolean logic searchable	yes	full text searchable	no
record fields	maximum of 16	record size	8192 bytes
statistical & math capabilities	no	wholesale change capability	yes

Support:

application consulting	no	maintenance and updates	yes
time share available	no	user training	yes

Recommended for:

Corporate & govt libraries	yes	Media center management	no
Public libraries	yes	Records & files management	no
School libraries	no	University libraries	yes

Installations:

Initial installation date	1984	Total number of installed sites	200
Sampling of current clients:	no info		

Price: $125.00 (U.S.) software and documentation $ 30.00 demonstration disk $ 15.00 user guide

Supplier's comments: AUTHEX Plus is an improved version of the AUTHEX periodical indexing package developed by Reference Press in 1984. It combines the ease-of-use, simplicity and reasonable price of the original software with a better user interface, expanded capacity and greater flexibility.

By design, AUTHEX Plus remains a professional indexing system, capable of producing sophisticated journal indexes to exacting specifications. By extension, this software can be used effectively for a variety of work, from maintaining patron databases in small libraries to compiling bibliographies and annotated lists. AUTHEX provides a range of tools to assist in building and manipulating databases , including discretionary global editing, on-line retrieval in specified fields, context-sensitive help screens, easily accessible accents and diacritics and normalized sorting of numbers and leading articles. Database files utilize variable-length records, and for practical purposes there is no limit to file size or to the number of records you can store. An on-line authority file can store subjects and names, along with associated cross-references, and permits the generation of topical indexes with multiple levels of sub-headings and automatic cross-referencing.

AUTOMATED LIBRARY SYSTEM

Foundation for Library Research, Inc.
2764 U.S. 35 South
Southside, WV 25187
(304) 675-4350

Hardware: IBM or 100% compatible

System Requirements: 640K; DOS 3.3; minimum 20 MB hard drive; graphics printer, color monitor

Programming Language: dBase III Plus compiled

Components & Applications:

acquisitions	no	catalog (batch)	yes
catalog (online)	yes	cataloging	yes
CD-ROM interface	no	circulation	yes
formatting bibliographies	no	index of keywords	no
inter-library loan	no	interface for MARC records	yes
media booking	no	reserve room	yes
serials	possible	thesaurus	no

Updating Modes:

batch update	yes	dynamic update	yes

Features:

Boolean logic searchable	no	full text searchable	no
record fields	13 fixed length fields	record size	fixed length
statistical & math capabilities	no	wholesale change capability	no

Support:

application consulting	yes	maintenance and updates	yes
time share available	no	user training	yes

Recommended for:

Corporate & govt libraries	yes	Media center management	yes
Public libraries	yes	Records & files management	no
School libraries	yes	University libraries	yes

Installations:

Initial installation date	1983	Total number of installed sites	100 plus

Sampling of current clients: Ravenswood High School, WV; Woodrow Wilson (Beckley WV); Washington State Community College (Marietta OH); Jackson High School (OH)

Published reviews & articles:

Graham, Judy. "Automated Library System", *CMC News*, Spring 1984, p.2.

Graham, Judy. "My Micro Chased the Blues Away." *School Library Journal*, February 1983, p. 23-26.

McKean, Robert C. "High School Library Uses Microcomputer." *Educational Leadership*, April 1982, p. 559.

Williamson, Judy Graham. "Automated Library System." *West Virginia Educational Media Yearbook 1984*, p. 6.

Monroe C. Gutman Library, *Microcomputer Directory: Applications in Educational Settings*, Harvard University Graduate School of Education, 2d ed., 1982, p. 296.

1983 Classroom Computer News Directory of Educational Computing Resources, p. 118.

Case Studies: Microcomputers in Libraries, Knowledge Industry Publications, Inc., February 1984.

Practical Guide to Computers in Education, Intentional Educations, 1984.

Nolan, Jeanne M., editor. *Micro Software Evaluations*. Nolan Information Management Services, 1984, p. 13.

"There Was an Easier Way." *State Ed.*, November 1981, p.3.

Stover, Sue. "Libraries Join Trend Toward Computers." *Raleigh County Schools News and Views*, November 1984, p. 3-4.

LaRue, James. "Software for Libraries." *Wilson Library Bulletin*. March 1987, p. 60-61.

LaRue, James. "Microcomputing" *Wilson Library Bulletin*. February 1991, p. 106-108.

Price: $995 for the complete system
Multi-user and bar code software options for $500.

AUTOMATED LIBRARY SYSTEM continued

Supplier's comments: Many libraries are using Automated Library System for card catalog searches, bibliographies, overdue notices, fines, circulation, reserve lists, cataloging, circulation analysis, item status, patron status fine receipts and accounting, authority lists, inventory by accession number and by call number, patron lists, audio-visual, total volumes available lists, barcoding, multi-user terminals, and many more functions.

The same program will welcome patrons of all ages to use the card catalog and bibliography functions; clerical staff to circulate all types of print and non-print materials; and the librarian to oversee all of these functions plus coordinate all areas of library management.

The integrated software cost is $995. The user also has the option to add the barcode circulation programs and the portable inventory program for $300. The networking option is available for $300 regardless of the number of terminals installed. Both options can be purchased at one time for a combined price of $500.

The ALS software is marketed by a non-profit corporation, which was created to assist libraries and library students to enter the world of automation with ease.

AUTOMATED LIBRARY SYSTEM

Project Simu-School
8160 San Cristobal
Dallas, TX 75218
Contact: Bill Dunklau
(214) 327-6914

Hardware: IBM PC-XT or above

System Requirements: Hard disk

Programming Language: C

Components & Applications:

acquisitions	yes	catalog (batch)	yes
catalog (online)	yes	cataloging	yes
CD-ROM interface	no	circulation	yes
formatting bibliographies	no	index of keywords	yes
inter-library loan	no	interface for MARC records	no
media booking	no	reserve room	no
serials	no	thesaurus	no

Updating Modes:

batch update	yes	dynamic update	yes

Features:

Boolean logic searchable	no	full text searchable	no
record fields	maximum of 41	record size	title-50;author-40; subject-20
statistical & math capabilities	yes, limited	wholesale change capability	no

Support:

application consulting	yes	maintenance and updates	yes
time share available	yes	user training	yes

Recommended for:

Corporate & govt libraries	no	Media center management	no
Public libraries	no	Records & files management	no
School libraries	yes	University libraries	no

Installations:

Initial installation date	1983	Total number of installed sites	no info
Sampling of current clients:	no info		

Costs: $3,000 for software
Will quote on multi-terminal, networked, and multi-library installations.

Supplier's comments: The Automated Library System (ALS) is a full-function, computer-based system for libraries with acquisitions numbering 5,000 to 50,000 or more. The system is easy to use, with a menu-driven format.

The electronic catalog allows searching by title, author, or subject. It also allows "browsing" of adjacently shelved books without changing search type or search text.The catalog saves you steps by telling you whether the book is on the shelf or checked out. If checked out, it tells the due date.

Circulation features include: verification of identity by returning name when given student number; blocking loan if either overdue books or outstanding fine exists for student; retrieval by accession number; total or partial fine payment and recording of new outstanding balance (if any).

Circulation, management, inventory, overdue notice, volumes added, and other reports are included.

Authors of this software system are willing to work with librarians to adapt the program to handle local library procedures or grant requirements. Grant application assistance is available, generally at no charge.

Technical support is by telephone, with no charge for first year.

AVANT CARDS

Addison Public Library
235 N. Kennedy Drive
Addison, IL 60101-2499
708-543-3617

Hardware: Apple IIe, IBM compatibles

System Requirements: Apple IIe - DOS 3.3, 64K memory, 80 column text card, 2 disk drives; IBM -128 K memory, 2 disk drives, async communications adapter card for serial printer

Programming Language: no info

Components & Applications:

acquisitions	no	catalog (batch)	yes
catalog (online)	no	cataloging	no
CD-ROM interface	no	circulation	no
formatting bibliographies	no	index of keywords	no
inter-library loan	no	interface for MARC records	no
media booking	no	reserve room	no
serials	no	thesaurus	no

Updating Modes:

batch update	no	dynamic update	yes

Features:

Boolean logic searchable	no	full text searchable	no
record fields	50 fixed	record size	3000 characters
statistical & math capabilities	no	wholesale change capability	no

Support:

application consulting	yes	maintenance and updates	yes
time share available	no	user training	yes

Recommended for:

Corporate & govt libraries	yes	Media center management	no
Public libraries	yes	Records & files management	yes
School libraries	yes	University libraries	no

Installations:

Initial installation date	1983	Total number of installed sites	200+
Sampling of current clients:	no info		

Published reviews & articles:

Price: $250 one-time license fee

Supplier's comments: Avant CARDS is a collection of computer programs designed to aid technical services personnel in the preparation of cards for a manual catalog in libraries of any size. The core of the package consists of a data entry program, a program which generates printouts for proofreading purposes, a label printing program, and a card printing program. In addition, there are programs to help set up formatting of cards and labels, printing ranges, and choosing printers. All of these programs operate under menu control.

The program is completely documented in a 100 page manual and help is just a phone call away.

BACS

Washington University School of Medicine Library
660 S. Euclid Avenue
St. Louis, MO 63110
(314) 362-7080
Contact: Ms. Betsy Kelly

Hardware: DEC PDP 11-40 (or any configuration supporting standard MUMPS)

System Requirements: MUMPS Operating Language

Programming Language: MUMPS

Components & Applications:

acquisitions	yes	catalog (batch)	no
catalog (online)	yes	cataloging	yes
CD-ROM interface	no	circulation	yes
formatting bibliographies	no	index of keywords	yes
inter-library loan	yes	interface for MARC records	yes
media booking	no	reserve room	no
serials	yes	thesaurus	no

Updating Modes:

batch update	yes	dynamic update	yes

Features:

Boolean logic searchable	yes	full text searchable	yes
record fields	MARC format	record size	MARC format
statistical & math capabilities	yes	wholesale change capability	yes

Support:

application consulting	yes	maintenance and updates	yes
time share available	yes	user training	yes

Recommended for:

Corporate & govt libraries	no	Media center management	no
Public libraries	no	Records & files management	no
School libraries	no	University libraries	yes

Installations:

Initial installation date	1981	Total number of installed sites	no info

Sampling of current clients: Washington University School of Medicine Library; Mercer University School of Medicine Library, Macon, GA.

Price: Software $24,000

Supplier's comments: The BACS bibliographic database is built from OCLC MARC records loaded by tape or from a microcomputer interface at the OCLC printer port. The database is full-text searchable at the MARC level and is optionally full-text searchable at the catalog card level. Wholesale change capabilities are limited to the line level, not the word level. BACS/SEARCH software allows commercially available databases, such as MedLine and Current Contents, to be loaded and searched on an in-house computer which supports MUMPS.

BASISPLUS DOCUMENT DATABASE MANAGEMENT SYSTEM

Information Dimensions, Inc. (a subsidiary of Battelle Memorial Institute)
5080 Tuttle Crossing Blvd.
Dublin, Ohio 43017
(800) DATA MGT   (614) 761-8083
Contact: Tim Corley

Hardware: IBM VM, MVS; DEC VMS, ULTRIX, RISC; HP/UX 9000, SUN, USISYS, SIEMENS, CDC BULL/DPX.

System Requirements: CPU-dependent; .8 - 1.5 MG memory; DOS, VMS, or UNIX for servers

Programming Language: ANSI FORTRAN and Assembler

Components & Applications:

acquisitions	available as TECHLIB	catalog (batch)	available as TECHLIB
catalog (online)	available as TECHLIB	cataloging	available as TECHLIB
CD-ROM interface	no	circulation	available as TECHLIB
formatting bibliographies	no	index of keywords	yes
inter-library loan	no	interface for MARC records	yes
media booking	no	reserve room	no
serials	available as TECHLIB	thesaurus	yes

Updating Modes:

batch update	yes	dynamic update	yes

Features:

Boolean logic searchable	yes	full text searchable	yes
record fields	no limit	record size	no limit
statistical & math capabilities	yes	wholesale change capability	yes

Support:

application consulting	yes	maintenance and updates	yes
time share available	yes	user training	yes

Recommended for:

Corporate & govt libraries	yes	Media center management	yes
Public libraries	yes	Records & files management	yes
School libraries	yes	University libraries	yes

Installations:

Initial installation date	1989	Total number of installed sites	2,500

Sampling of current clients: 2,500 installations worldwide; over 10,000 applications, 120,000 users.

Price: $5,000 - $179,000 range

Supplier's comments: BASISplus is targeted at document management applications where quick and flexible retrieval is important along with the accuracy of the information retrieved. BASISplus is designed for scalable implementations where multi-user access is essential as well as providing unlimited capacity for the number of users, the size of a document and the number of documents being managed.

BASISplus combines RDBMS technology with client-server architecture, imaging and compound document support with high-speed performance. Through this strong foundation, BASISplus is typically installed in large departmental applications or utilized by MIS as core enabling technology for enterprise-wide document management.

With this architecture, BASISplus is used for document retrieval as well as more sophisticated document management applications which require check-in, check-out control, versions control, immediate update, routing and revision history. Many customers have implemented complete document management workflow applications through BASISplus' ability to manage documents and traditional RDBMS information in one integrated environment.

BATAPHONE

Baker & Taylor
652 E. Main Street
P.O. Box 6920
Bridgewater, NJ 08807-0920
(800) 526-3811   (201) 722-8000

Hardware: Hand-held data terminal provided with system

System Requirements: included with system

Programming Language: no info

Components & Applications:

acquisitions	yes	catalog (batch)	no
catalog (online)	no	cataloging	no
CD-ROM interface	no	circulation	no
formatting bibliographies	no	index of keywords	no
inter-library loan	no	interface for MARC records	yes
media booking	no	reserve room	no
serials	no	thesaurus	no

Updating Modes:

batch update	no	dynamic update	yes

Features:

Boolean logic searchable	no	full text searchable	no
record fields	no info	record size	no info
statistical & math capabilities	yes	wholesale change capability	no

Support:

application consulting	yes	maintenance and updates	yes
time share available	no	user training	yes

Recommended for:

Corporate & govt libraries	yes	Media center management	yes
Public libraries	yes	Records & files management	no
School libraries	yes	University libraries	yes

Installations:

Initial installation date	1987	Total number of installed sites	no info
Sampling of current clients:	no info		

Price: $325 per year: includes printed acknowledgement of orders; individual order confirmation slips; and lease of portable data terminal

$275 per year: includes printed acknowledgement of orders; and lease of portable data terminal

Supplier's comments: The BaTaPHONE offers the book ordering convenience of a hand-held terminal which allows libraries to initiate book orders by simply keying in the ISBN and the quantity desired. Orders are then transmitted to Baker & Taylor toll-free over a regular telephone line. The day following the order transmission, a printed confirmation verifying titles as well as inventory status is mailed to the library. This information includes: library name, quantity, title, ISBN, publisher, author, list price, and validation comments.

The BaTaPHONE is a portable data terminal with a movable button keyboard. The terminal is battery-powered and provides approximately sixty-four hours of keying time before battery replacement is necessary. Title are entered by ISBN, with a capacity of 500 titles per order.

Each terminal incorporates an acoustic coupler which can be attached to a standard telephone mouthpiece. The coupler need be attached only during transmission, allowing the user to enter orders from any location in or outside the library.

Varying degrees of interfaces have been established with most key vendors, including OCLC, CLSI, Dynix, and VTLS. These interfaces can allow for system information transfers of data for acquisitions, on-order, cataloging, circulation, and holdings files, depending on the interfacing process established with the individual vendor. The interface service also provides timely updates to the local databases. And information from Baker & Taylor can be down-loaded into the library's system eliminating redundant keying and maintaining up-to-date records. All this allows the library to maintain a fully automated workflow through out its various operations. The benefit is more time to sped giving personalized library service, in addition to a reduction in overhead and operating expenses.

BIB/RITE

Robert E. Litke, Ph.D.
432 Cottage Ave.
Vermillion, SD 57069-2120
(605) 624-2948
Contact: Robert Litke

Hardware: IBM PC and compatibles, Apple II series

System Requirements: PC or MS-DOS 3.0+, OS/2.1+, ProDOS; minimum of 32K user available RAM for Apple II; 256K for DOS.

Programming Language: BASIC; PC is compiled

Components & Applications:

acquisitions	no	catalog (batch)	no
catalog (online)	no	cataloging	no
CD-ROM interface	no	circulation	no
formatting bibliographies	yes	index of keywords	no
inter-library loan	no	interface for MARC records	no
media booking	no	reserve room	no
serials	no	thesaurus	no

Updating Modes:

batch update	no	dynamic update	yes

Features:

Boolean logic searchable	no	full text searchable	yes
record fields	uses sequential records	record size	max. 235 bytes for Apple;32K bytes for PC
statistical & math capabilities	no	wholesale change capability	no

Support:

application consulting	yes	maintenance and updates	yes
time share available	no	user training	yes, if needed

Recommended for:

Corporate & govt libraries	yes	Media center management	no
Public libraries	yes	Records & files management	no
School libraries	yes	University libraries	yes

Installations:

Initial installation date 1983, updated 1992	Total number of installed sites	400

Sampling of current clients: Titusville (FL) High School; Eastern Montana College; Kent State Univ; National Research Council (Canada); Univ. of Kansas; Union Oil Co.; Western Michigan Univ.; School District of Menomonie (WI) Area; St. Thomas Aquinas (FL) High School; Bloomsburg (PA) Univ.; Michigan State University - Library; Alverno College (Milwaukee) - Library; South Texas Library System; University of Akron, School of Communication Disorders; many individuals.

Published reviews & articles:
Andrews, L., "Bib/Rite Gets "B" in Bibliography." *Computer Shopper, v.57,* (October 1984), p.94-95.
Andrews, I., "This Teacher's Pets." *Computer Shopper,* v.7 (10),(October 1987), p.368, 370.
Smith, K.R., "Software Reviews: Bib/Rite." *Asha,* v. 27 (5), (May 1985), p.73-74.
Clymer, E.W., "Software: BIB/RITE." *Asha,* 33(8), (August 1991), p.70-71.

Price:
Individual user	$ 45.95 + $2.50 handling	
Multiple users	$ 150.00 + $2.50 handling	
Class adoptions	5- 9 copies $29.95	
	10-29 copies $27.95	
	30+ copies $24.95	

Free desk copy for 10 or more copies.

Supplier's comments: BIB/RITE can be used to prepare and maintain bibliographies and to learn, and teach standard bibliographic styles. It is, first, a program for formatting reference lists in standard American Psychological Association (APA), Modern Language Association (MLA), or American Medical Association (AMA) styles, and, secondly, a limited data base. It was designed to prepare reference lists for papers prepared for professional journals, student's reference papers, and theses and dissertations. It is also useful for preparing and maintaining reading lists for classes or reading lists on special topics. Daisy wheel, dot-matrix or laser printers are supported.

BIBBASE

Library Technologies, Inc.
1142 E. Bradfield Road
Abington, PA 19001
(215) 576-6983
Contact: Dr. James G. Schoenung, President

Hardware: IBM PC & compatibles

System Requirements: Minimum 10MB fixed disk drive; PC DOS version 3.0 or above; 640Kb RAM

Programming Language: Microsoft Pascal & C

Components & Applications:

acquisitions	yes	catalog(batch)	yes
catalog (online)	yes	cataloging	yes
CD-ROM interface	no	circulation	no
formatting bibliographies	no	index of keywords	no
inter-library loan	no	interface for MARC records	yes
media booking	no	reserve room	no
serials	no	thesaurus	no

Updating Modes:

batch update	yes	dynamic update	yes

Features:

Boolean logic searchable	no	full text searchable	no
record fields	max 50; variable length	record size	100 lines
statistical & math capabilities	yes	wholesale change capability	no

Support:

application consulting	yes	maintenance and updates	yes
time share available	no	user training	yes

Recommended for:

Corporate & govt libraries	yes	Media center management	yes
Public libraries	yes	Records & files management	no
School libraries	yes	University libraries	yes

Installations:

Initial installation date	1984	Total number of installed sites	330
Sampling of current clients:	no info		

Published reviews & articles:
Information Technology and Libraries, June 1989, p. 222-232.

Costs:

Bib-Base Module	Full Program	Demo & Manual	Manual Alone
core	$795	$25	$20
/Acq	$595	$20	$15
/Cat	$595	$20	$15
/Public	$795	$20	$15
/Marc	$595	$20	$15
/Multiuser	$995	$20	$15
/Bisac	$395	$20	$15

Supplier's comments: Bib-Base offers an affordable solution to your library's automation needs. It features flexible record creation, superior error handling capabilities, library-oriented file structures and indexes, modular design, clear documentation, and strong customer support.

BIBL

GMUtant Software
Route 1, Box 296
Hamilton, Virginia 22068
703-993-2219
Contact: Clyde W. Grotophorst

Hardware: IBM compatibles

System Requirements: DOS; BIBL/NET requires a NOVELL (2.x or 3.x) network. 50 simultaneous users are supported.

Programming Language:

Components & Applications:

acquisitions	no	catalog (batch)	no
catalog (online)	yes	cataloging	yes
CD-ROM interface	yes	circulation	no
formatting bibliographies	yes	index of keywords	yes
inter-library loan	no	interface for MARC records	no
media booking	no	reserve room	no
serials	no	thesaurus	no

Updating Modes:

batch update	yes	dynamic update	yes

Features:

Boolean logic searchable	yes	full text searchable	no
record fields	no info	record size	no info
statistical & math capabilities	no	wholesale change capability	no

Support:

application consulting	yes	maintenance and updates	yes
time share available	no	user training	no

Recommended for:

Corporate & govt libraries	yes	Media center management	yes
Public libraries	yes	Records & files management	yes
School libraries	yes	University libraries	yes

Installations:

Initial installation date	1990	Total number of installed sites	130+

Sampling of current clients: National Public Radio, Washington D.C.; AP Newswire Library, New York, NY; Greenpeace, Vancouver Canada; George Mason University, Fairfax, VA; Illinois Community Action Association, multiple copies; Santa Barbara County Law Library, Santa Barbara, CA

Published reviews & articles: BIBL recently received a trophy rating (best program of its type) from Public Brand Software (the nation's leading SHAREWARE vendor)

Price: $39 single user
$150 network (per server).
BIBL is available via SHAREWARE. A copy of the SHAREWARE version of BIBL may be obtained from the GMUtant BBS or CompuServe (IBM Apps forum). Registered version adds additional features.

Supplier's comments: BIBL is a full-featured package for managing your personal and/or corporate library. Features include: multiple databases, mouse support, full-text retrieval, Boolean and/or/not searching supported, keyword validation, 13+ reports, ASCII import-export, and more. Utility programs support import from various CD-ROM sources: ERIC, PsychInfo, Medline, ABI/Inform, and AGRICOLA. BIBL is available via SHAREWARE.
Network version (BIBL/NET) adds security levels to control who may add/edit/delete data in shared databases, intelligent locking, and support for private databases maintained on the server.

BIBLIO-LINKS

Personal Bibliographic Software
P.O. Box 4250
Ann Arbor, MI 48106
(313) 996-1580
Contact: Dan Houdek

Hardware: IBM PC and compatibles; Macintosh

System Requirements: PCDOS or MSDOS; Pro-Cite for the IBM PC, DOS 2.0 256K RAM minimum, DOS 3.0 320K RAM, hard disk or two DS disk drives

Programming Language: PASCAL

Support:

application consulting	no	maintenance and updates	yes
time share available	no	user training	yes

Recommended for:

Corporate & govt libraries	yes	Media center management	yes
Public libraries	yes	Records & files management	yes
School libraries	yes	University libraries	yes

Installations:

Initial installation date	1984	Total number of installed sites	no info
Sampling of current clients: no info			

Price: IBM Biblio-Links - $195 each
Online Biblio-Links - $295
Macintosh Biblio-Links - $295

Suppliers Comments. Biblio-Links are companion programs to Pro-Cite. Each program transfers records downloaded records from online services, CD-ROM and automated library systems, and disk-based data products directly into Pro-Cite. The various bibliographic data elements, such as author, title, and publication date, are automatically transferred into the appropriate fields. Records can then be merged with existing databases or stored in a separate Pro-Cite database.   Once in Pro-Cite, references can be searched, sorted, indexed, and formatted into bibliographies according to any bibliograhic style.
  IBM Biblio-Links: BRS, DIALOG, MEDLARS, SilverPlatter, OCLC, STN, NOTIS, USMARC, DGIS, DROLS, DOBIS, MUMS, and SCORPIO.
  Online Biblio-Links Package for the IBM PC allows the user access to the world's most popular scientific and information databases including BRS, DIALOG, MEDLARS, SilverPlatter, and STN.
  Biblio-Link Package for the Macintosh : BRS, DIALOG, and MEDLARS.

Editor's note: This is a special software package used to transfer downloaded files into Pro-Cite databases; therefore, it does not include the usual list of components and applications.

BIBLIOCENTRE

BIBLIOCENTRE
80 Cowdray Court
Scarborough, Ontario, CANADA M1S 4N1
(416) 754-6600   FAX (416) 299-0902

Hardware: IBM mainframe

System Requirements: MVS/CICS

Programming Language: PL/1 and Assembler

Components & Applications:

acquisitions	yes	catalog (batch)	yes
catalog (online)	yes	cataloging	yes
CD-ROM interface	yes	circulation	yes
formatting bibliographies	yes	index of keywords	no
inter-library loan	some	interface for MARC records	yes
media booking	no	reserve room	no
serials	no	thesaurus	yes

Updating Modes:

batch update	yes	dynamic update	yes

Features:

Boolean logic searchable	yes	full text searchable	no
record fields	no info	record size	variable
statistical & math capabilities	no	wholesale change capability	yes

Support:

application consulting	yes	maintenance and updates	yes
time share available	yes	user training	yes

Recommended for:

Corporate & govt libraries	yes	Media center management	no
Public libraries	yes	Records & files management	no
School libraries	yes	University libraries	yes

Installations:

Initial installation date	no info	Total number of installed sites	no info

Sampling of current clients: Boeing Computer Systems; Transport Canada; 100 campuses of Ontario Community Colleges

Supplier's comments: An integrated system for acquisitions (book & non-book material), cataloging, public access catalog, electronic mail, and circulation control. Supports English & French and can support other languages.

System has also been tailored to support online registration of students in specific courses offered in various disciplines.

BIBLIOFILE "TLC" (TOTAL LIBRARY COMPUTING) SYSTEM

The Library Corporation
Research Park
Inwood, WV 25428
304-229-0100 or 800-624-0559
Fax 304-229- 0295
Contact: Peggy Rulton

Hardware: IBM PC, 640 K memory, Hitachi CD-ROM drive, hard disk drive, and floppy disk drive

System Requirements: MS-DOS

Programming Language: C

Components & Applications:

acquisitions	yes	catalog (batch)	yes
catalog (online)	yes	cataloging	yes
CD-ROM interface	yes	circulation	yes
formatting bibliographies	yes	index of keywords	yes
inter-library loan	yes	interface for MARC records	yes
media booking	planned	reserve room	yes
serials	planned	thesaurus	yes

Updating Modes:

batch update	yes	dynamic update	yes

Features:

Boolean logic searchable	yes	full text searchable	yes
record fields	MARC	record size	MARC
statistical & math capabilities	yes	wholesale change capability	yes

Support:

application consulting	yes	maintenance and updates	yes
time share available	no	user training	yes

Recommended for:

Corporate & govt libraries	yes	Media center management	yes
Public libraries	yes	Records & files management	yes
School libraries	yes	University libraries	yes

Installations:

Initial installation date	1990	Total number of installed sites	7,000
Sampling of current clients:	no info		

Recent Published Articles & Reviews

The American Library Association's *Library Technology Reports* ranked automation products by performance, features, ease of use, customer support, data storage and documentation in the recently released twin issues for March-April and May-June, 1990. On a 1 to 10 scale, TLC's *BiblioFile* family of products received an "Excellent" 9 or 10 in every category. TLC's composite score of 9.5 outranked all 28 other suppliers.

The Library Corporation was listed in the May 1992 issue of *LAN* magazine's LAN 100. TLC was among the top 100 PC-based network integrators in North America; and was the only library automation vendor on the list.

Price: Call for custom quotation

Supplier's comments: Each application module is available separately:
    BiblioFile Cataloging
    BiblioFile Public Access Catalogs
    BiblioFile Circulation
    BiblioFile Acquisitions

BIBLIOGRAPHY MAKER

Right On Programs
755-F New York Avenue
Huntington, NY 11743
(516) 424-7777   FAX (516) 424-7207

Hardware: IBM & compatibles

System Requirements: MS-DOS

Programming Language: Turbo Pascal

Components & Applications:

acquisitions	no	catalog (batch)	no
catalog (online)	no	cataloging	no
CD-ROM interface	no	circulation	no
formatting bibliographies	yes	index of keywords	no
inter-lilrary loan	no	interface for MARC records	no
media booking	no	reserve room	no
serials	no	thesaurus	no

Updating Modes:

batch update	no	dynamic update	yes

Features:

Boolean logic searchabl	no	full text searchable	no
record fields	no info	record size	no info
statistical & math capabilities	yes	wholesale change capability	no

Support:

application consulting	yes	maintenance and updates	yes
time share available	no	user training	no

Recommended for:

Corporate & govt libraries	yes	Media center management	yes
Public libraries	yes	Records & files management	yes
School libraries	yes	University libraries	yes

Installations:

Initial installation date	1989	Total number of installed sites	1700
Sampling of current clients: no info			

Price: $99

Supplier's comments: Whether you are preparing a bibliography for a term paper, a Masters' thesis or a reading list for a student, patient or employee, this new program from Right On Programs makes the job easy and efficient, pleasant and correct.

The program runs from a main menu which tells you the whole story on one screen. Choose the function you want, press the appropriate letter, follow the on-screen prompts and that's all there is to it. Once you've entered the data, the computer will sort it, format it and print it, however and whenever you want it.

You no longer have to worry and wonder about correct form. Using the guide from the Modern Language Association, one author form or any other form of authorship will be formatted correctly.

BIBLIOTECH® SOFTWARE SYSTEMS

Comstow Information Services
P.O. Box 277
Harvard, MA 01451-0277
(508) 772-2001
Contact: Ms. Lynda Moulton

Hardware: DEC VAX and DEC microVAX with VAX/VMS operating system native mode; DEC, SUN, Hewlett-Packard with UNIX

System Requirements: 75 MB or greater disk; 1MB main memory/user; tape drive.

Programming Language: DRS - a DBMS/4GL language which is written in C

Components & Applications:

acquisitions	yes	catalog (batch)	yes
catalog (online)	yes	cataloging	yes
CD-ROM interface	yes	circulation	yes
formatting bibliographies	yes	index of keywords	yes
inter-library loan	yes	interface for MARC records	yes
media booking	no	reserve room	custom
serials	yes	thesaurus	yes

Updating Modes:

batch update	yes	dynamic update	yes

Features:

Boolean logic searchable	yes	full text searchable	yes
record fields	over 900	record size	8000 bytes - bib record; unlimited # item records
statistical & math capabilities	yes	wholesale change capability	yes

Support:

application consulting	yes	maintenance and updates	yes
time share available	no	user training	yes

Recommended for:

Corporate & govt libraries	yes	Media center management	no
Public libraries	no	Records & files management	yes
School libraries	yes	University libraries	no

Installations:

Initial installation date	1981	Total number of installed sites	56

Sampling of current clients: 56 installations including industrial research library; corporate management library; government library; engineering reports management; & public school library; law library.

Published reviews & articles:

American Library Association. *Library Technology Reports* volume 23, no. 5, September/October 1987. New York, American Library Association, 1987, vp.

Howell, Betty. "BiblioTech Software." *Automatome*, 10:6-7; no.3/4, Summer/Fall, 1991.

Lucchetti, Stephen C. "BiblioTech at Ford Motor Company: a Worldwide Information Network." *Blite*, 7:7-11; February, 1990.

Maxant, Vicary. "Implementation of the BiblioTech Library Software System at Raytheon Company." *Journal of Library and Information Science*, 16:48, April 1990.

Moulton, Lynda. "Experience with BiblioTech, the Data Base Management System Based Library Software." In *Proceedings of the 45th ASIS Annual Meeting*, v.19, American Society for Information Science.

Pillsbury, Madison and Sutro. "Choosing an Integrated Library System—the Pillsbury Experience." *San Francisco Bay Regional Chapter of the Special Libraries Association Bulletin*, November/December 1991.

Smith, Caroline L. "Interfacing an IOLS with Data on Optical Disk: Current Reality and Vision for the Future at Ford Motor Company Technical Information Center"; in: *IOLS '90; Proceedings of the Fifth Integrated Online Library Systems Meeting*, held in New York, May 2-3, 1990. Medford, NJ, Learned Information, 1990, pp. 203-208.

Trimble, Kathleen. "BiblioTech's Authority Control and Thesaurus at U.S. News & World Report;" paper presented at PALINET meeting, December 10, 1991. Washington, DC, 12/10/91.

Walton, Robert A. "Automated System Marketplace 1988: Focused on Fulfilling Commitments." *Library Journal*, 41-52, April 1, 1989.

BIBLIOTECH® SOFTWARE SYSTEMS continued

Price: Modular and User-based Pricing. Prices range from $15K - $80K depending on number of modules and number of concurrent users. Contact vendor for specific quotation.

Supplier's comments: Every BiblioTech Module has unique functionality in three areas: data entry screen forms, specialized processing or computation, and powerful report writer for ad hoc reporting to meet retrieving and reporting requirements. Most functions of BiblioTech are handled through screen forms and in a menu-driven environment. Data are validated at entry for correct format and content, and records are easily modified at the time of original entry or at a later session. Multiple users may enter data at the same time in the multi-user version. This version also offers database utilities for roll-back and roll-forward recoveries. Updating a BiblioTech data base is done in real-time. Fields are variable length. All inverted indexes are automatically updated at the time of data entry. For large applications with heavy activity in circulation and periodicals check-in, an optical scanning device can be used.

Current product includes image retrieval, full text displays, interfaces to full text retrieval and word processing packages from the OPAC, and OPAC link with electronic mail. Hotkey functions from citations to full-text and images, and hotkeys to CD-ROMs are available.

A UNIX version of the software is available for Hewlett-Packard and SUN hardware.

Software is designed for corporate information resource and text content management or for government agency libraries.

BOOKENDS

Sensible Software
335 E. Big Beaver   Suite 207
Troy, MI 48083
(313) 528-1950
Contact: Marian Tuttleman, Sales Manager

Hardware: Apple II, II+, IIe, IIc with 64K memory, one disk drive, 40 column monitor; and Apple IIc, IIgs, IIe with Apple extended
80 column card for BOOKENDS EXTENDED

System Requirements: ProDos

Programming Language: Assembly

Components & Applications:

acquisitions	no	catalog (batch)	no
catalog (online)	no	cataloging	no
CD-ROM interface	no	circulation	no
formatting bibliographies	no	index of keywords	yes
inter-library loan	no	interface for MARC records	no
media booking	no	reserve room	no
serials	no	thesaurus	no

Updating Modes:

batch update	no	dynamic update	yes

Features:

Boolean logic searchable	yes	full text searchable	yes
record fields	12	record size	760 characters
statistical & math capabilities	no	wholesale change capability	no

Support:

application consulting	no	maintenance and updates	no
time share available	no	user training	no

Recommended for:

Corporate & govt libraries	no	Media center management	no
Public libraries	no	Records & files management	no
School libraries	yes	University libraries	no

Installations:

Initial installation date	1989	Total number of installed sites	no info
Sampling of current clients:	no info		

Price: no info

Supplier's comments: BOOKENDS - A special-purpose database program that helps you easily enter and print information about your magazines, scientific journals, newspapers, and books into an "electronic" card catalog.

Allows data to be printed in fully customized bibliographic and footnote formats. BOOKENDS EXTENDED works on 80 column equipment.

BOOKPATH

Alpine Data, Inc.
737 So. Townsend Ave.
Montrose, CO 81401
(303) 249-1400
Contact: Jesse Tarshis

Hardware: IBM PC, XT, AT

System Requirements: 10MB hard disk, MS-DOS, 640K RAM

Programming Language: dbXL/Quicksilver

Components & Applications:

acquisitions	no	catalog (batch)	no
catalog (online)	no	cataloging	no
CD-ROM interface	no	circulation	yes
formatting bibliographies	no	index of keywords	yes
inter-library loan	yes	interface for MARC records	no
media booking	no	reserve room	no
serials	no	thesaurus	no

Updating Modes:

batch update	no	dynamic update	yes

Features:

Boolean logic searchable	yes	full text searchable	yes
record fields	fixed	record size	572/ILL request;312/library
statistical & math capabilities	yes	wholesale change capability	yes

Support:

application consulting	yes	maintenance and updates	yes
time share available	no	user training	yes

Recommended for:

Corporate & govt libraries	yes	Media center management	yes
Public libraries	yes	Records & files management	no
School libraries	yes	University libraries	yes

Installations:

Initial installation date	1984	Total number of installed sites	50

Sampling of current clients: Pathfinder Library District, Grand Junction, CO; Three Rivers Library System, Glenwood Springs, CO; Pikes Peak Library System, Colorado Springs, CO.

Price: Purchase for single library stand alone use - $595

Purchase for entire state/district for interactive use: Site License Agreement - $5000 plus $125 per site.

Supplier's comments: BOOKPATH is a system to control interlibrary loans of books, periodicals and newspapers. It prints standard ILL forms. BOOKPATH contains databases to manage libraries, patrons and book requests. Book requests may be accessed, scanned or reported by date, library, author, title, subject, etc.

BOOKTRAK

Richmond Software Corporation
500 Aston Hall Way
Alpharetta, GA 30202
(800) 222-6063
Contact: Bob Stevens

Hardware: Apple

System Requirements: IIe, IIgs

Programming Language: Assembly

Components & Applications:

acquisitions	no	catalog (batch)	no
catalog (online)	no	cataloging	no
CD-ROM interface	no	circulation	yes
formatting bibliographies	no	index of keywords	no
inter-library loan	no	interface for MARC records	no
media booking	no	reserve room	no
serials	no	thesaurus	no

Updating Modes:

batch update	no	dynamic update	yes

Features:

Boolean logic searchable	no	full text searchable	no
record fields	no info	record size	no info
statistical & math capabilities	yes	wholesale change capability	yes

Support:

application consulting	no	maintenance and updates	yes
time share available	no	user training	no

Recommended for:

Corporate & govt libraries	no	Media center management	no
Public libraries	no	Records & files management	no
School libraries	yes	University libraries	no

Installations:

Initial installation date	1986	Total number of installed sites	1000
Sampling of current clients: no info			

Price: $850

Published articles and reviews:
    "Book Trak I." *Library Technology Reports,* January-February 1986, p. 37.

BRS/PDS

Maxwell Online, Inc.
8000 Westpark Drive
McLean, VA 22102
(800) 289-4277   (703) 442-0900
Contact: Bobbi Davis

Hardware: not applicable; this is a time-share service

System Requirements: not applicable

Programming Language: not applicable

Components & Applications:

acquisitions	no	catalog (batch)	no
catalog (online)	yes	cataloging	yes
CD-ROM interface	no	circulation	no
formatting bibliographies	no	index of keywords	yes
inter-library loan	no	interface for MARC records	no
media booking	no	reserve room	no
serials	no	thesaurus	no

Updating Modes:

batch update	yes	dynamic update	no

Features:

Boolean logic searchable	yes	full text searchable	yes
record fields	no limit	record size	no limit
statistical & math capabilities	yes	wholesale change capability	yes

Support:

application consulting	yes	maintenance and updates	yes
time share available	yes	user training	yes

Recommended for:

Corporate & govt libraries	yes	Media center management	no
Public libraries	no	Records & files management	no
School libraries	no	University libraries	no

Installations:

Initial installation date	1977	Total number of installed sites	no info

Sampling of current clients: Time-share clients include: National Institute of Education; U.S. Department of Energy.

Price:

	Creation of ODCS Library	$ 175
	Database Design	5,500
	Database Load Programs	5,500
	Initial File Load	3,500

Online storage of database:
  $28.75 per million characters per month up to 9.9 million characters.
  $23.00 per million characters per month for 10-49.9 million characters.
  $17.25 per million characters per month for 50-199 million characters.
  $11.50 per million characters per month after 200 million characters.
Database updating/editing: $0.23 per record with minimum of $230.
Online searching of file: $18 per connect hour plus telecommunications.

Supplier's comments: BRS is a time-share service. In addition the software is available for in-house installation. This is the same software the BRS Search Service uses. Cross database searching is possible. Boolean logic search arguments available include AND, OR, NOT. Truncation is possible at the end, beginning, or middle of a word. The statistical and mathematical capabilities are limited to addition and subtraction.

BRS/SEARCH ® C VERSION

BRS Software Products
8000 Westpark Drive
McLean, VA 22102
(703) 442-3870

Hardware: IBM PC, AT (XENIX or MS-DOS); CCI POWER 6; DEC VAX (VMS and UNIX); NCR Tower; Pyramid, Sperry, Cray, Unisys, Data General, WANG, Hewlett Packard, Sun, ARIX, NBI

System Requirements: UNIX, Novell, VMS, MS-DOS, VM/CMS, AOS/VS, VS, Ultrix, BSD 4.3

Programming Language: "C" Language

Components & Applications:

acquisitions	yes	catalog (batch)	yes
catalog (online)	yes	cataloging	yes
CD-ROM interface	yes	circulation	yes
formatting bibliographies	no	index of keywords	yes
inter-library loan	no	interface for MARC records	yes
media booking	no	reserve room	no
serials	yes	thesaurus	yes

Updating Modes:

batch update	yes	dynamic update	yes

Features:

Boolean logic searchable	yes	full text searchable	yes
record fields	65,000	record size	4,225,000,000
statistical & math capabilities	yes	wholesale change capability	yes

Support:

application consulting	yes	maintenance and updates	yes
time share available	no	user training	yes

Recommended for:

Corporate & govt libraries	yes	Media center management	no
Public libraries	no	Records & files management	yes
School libraries	no	University libraries	yes

Installations:

Initial installation date	1982	Total number of installed sites	1,000

Sampling of current clients: Dartmouth College Library, AT&T, 3M, Library of Congress.

Price: Software $2,500 - $200,000
Maintenance 15% of license

Supplier's comments: A comprehensive full-text retrieval package, BRS/SEARCH (tm) is ideal for organizing critical information that requires fast, multi-user access. A powerful, word-level index gives users instant access to any document through a word, phrase, or concept. Any search takes only seconds. Users can search complete documents, or just specific fields, paragraphs, or sentences. Now at Release 6.0, BRS/SEARCH offers hypertext links, which allow users to retrieve text and images together.

Standard features include a range of search operators, such as proximity, Boolean logic, and wild cards, and a selection of user interfaces. A fully integrated thesaurus is available. Toolkits are available for integrating BRS/SEARCH into RDBMS, imaging solutions, or other applications software. Also, BRS/SEARCH is completely portable across PCs, networks, minicomputers, and mainframes. Applications include litigation support, campus information systems, government regulations, research and development files, technical documentation, policies and procedures manuals, personnel files, and state-wide networks.

BRS/SEARCH ® MAINFRAME VERSION

BRS Software Products
8000 Westpark Drive
McLean, VA 22102
(703) 442-3870

Hardware: IBM Mainframe or Plug Compatible

System Requirements: MVS/CICS, VM/CMS

Programming Language: Assembler or C

Components & Applications:

acquisitions	no	catalog (batch)	no
catalog (online)	yes	cataloging	yes
CD-ROM interface	no	circulation	no
formatting bibliographies	no	index of keywords	yes
inter-library loan	no	interface for MARC records	no
media booking	no	reserve room	no
serials	no	thesaurus	yes

Updating Modes:

batch update	yes	dynamic update	yes

Features:

Boolean logic searchable	yes	full text searchable	yes
record fields	65,535	record size	2,147,450,880
statistical & math capabilities	yes	wholesale change capability	yes

Support:

application consulting	yes	maintenance and updates	yes
time share available	yes	user training	yes

Recommended for:

Corporate & govt libraries	yes	Media center management	no
Public libraries	no	Records & files management	no
School libraries	no	University libraries	yes

Installations:

Initial installation date	1982	Total number of installed sites	10

Sampling of current clients: R. R. Bowker; Rhom & Haas; University of South Carolina; G-CAM; Litton; Information Handling Services; Air Products; Data Centrallen; G.I.O.

Published reviews and articles:
Datamation, special AIIM section, 3/1/92
Government Computer News, 3/16/92, p.47.
Information Week, special Delphi Consulting Group white paper, 9/92

Price: Software $180,000
Maintenance 15% of license

Supplier's Comments: A comprehensive full-text retrieval package, BRS/SEARCH® is ideal for organizing critical information that requires fast, multi-user access. A powerful, word-level index gives users instant access to any document through a word, phrase, or concept. Any search takes only seconds. Users can search complete documents, or just specific fields, paragraphs or sentences. Now at Release 6.0, BRS/SEARCH offers hypertext links, which allows users to retrieve text and images together.

Standard features include a range of search operators, such as proximity, Boolean logic, and wild cards, and a selection of user interfaces. A fully integrated thesaurus is available. Toolkits are available for integrating BRS/SEARCH into RDBMS, imaging solutions, or other applications software. Also, BRS/SEARCH is completely portable across PCs, networks, minicomputers, and mainframes. Applications include litigation support, campus information systems, government regulations, research and development files, technical documentation, policies and procedures manuals, personnel files, and state-wide networks.

BT LINK

Baker & Taylor
652 E. Main Street
P.O. Box 6920
Bridgewater, NJ 08807-0920
(800) 526-3811   (201) 722-8000

Hardware: IBM PC or compatible computer

System Requirements: Hayes compatible modem

Programming Language: n/a

Components & Applications:

acquisitions	yes	catalog (batch)	no
catalog (online)	no	cataloging	no
CD-ROM interface	no	circulation	no
formatting bibliographies	no	index of keywords	no
inter-library loan	no	interface for MARC records	yes
media booking	no	reserve room	no
serials	no	thesaurus	no

Updating Modes:

batch update	no	dynamic update	yes

Features:

Boolean logic searchable	no	full text searchable	no
record fields	no info	record size	no info
statistical & math capabilities	yes	wholesale change capability	no

Support:

application consulting	yes	maintenance and updates	yes
time share available	no	user training	yes

Recommended for:

Corporate & govt libraries	yes	Media center management	yes
Public libraries	yes	Records & files management	no
School libraries	yes	University libraries	yes

Installations:

Initial installation date	1987	Total number of installed sites	no info
Sampling of current clients:	no info		

Price: Module I: Ordering - free
Module II   Database - $695 annual subscription (updated monthly)
Module III Inventory - $300 annually

Supplier's comments: Placing book, video and audio orders through your personal computer is easier than ever,thanks to Baker & Taylor Books. BT Link : Ordering provides electronic ordering software. You can check orders for duplicates, personalize special orders, and stay within your purchase order limits — all of which makes BT Link: Ordering about as user friendly as a program can get. To place an order, all you need is an IBM or compatible computer and a Hayes compatible modem. Then, key in the ISBN or title/author and quantity, and transmit the order to Baker & Taylor Books via the toll-free phone line.

BT Link: Database on CD-ROM is a break-through product which has raised the standard of database accuracy in the industry. The scope of the 1.2 million title database of books, audio, and video provides excellent information and ordering service of the highest quality. The ordering link is intertwined with the research process (Module II). The result is a search and purchase system which will change the way you do business.

BT LINK: Database on CD-ROM gives you all the information you need to identify and order the right materials. You'll be able to find everything from multiple bindings and alternate ISBNs to the latest price and publication status.

To provide you with maximum speed and efficiency, BTLink: Inventory was designed to work in tandem with BT Link: Database.

BUCAT

TKM Software Limited
P.O. Box 1525
839-18th Street
Brandon, Manitoba CANADA R7A 6N3
(204) 727-3872 or 800-565-6272
Contact: Ross Eastley

Hardware: DEC VAX

System Requirements: VMS

Programming Language: no info

Components & Applications:

acquisitions	in development	catalog (batch)	yes
catalog (online)	yes	cataloging	yes
CD-ROM interface	no	circulation	yes
formatting bibliographies	yes	index of keywords	yes
inter-library loan	in development	interface for MARC records	yes
media booking	in development	reserve room	no
serials	in development	thesaurus	no

Updating Modes:

batch update	no	dynamic update	yes

Features:

Boolean logic searchable	yes	full text searchable	with EDICS
record fields	MARC record	record size	32K max
statistical & math capabilities	no	wholesale change capability	yes

Support:

application consulting	yes	maintenance and updates	yes
time share available	no	user training	yes

Recommended for:

Corporate & govt libraries	yes	Media center management	no
Public libraries	yes	Records & files management	no
School libraries	yes	University libraries	yes

Installations:

Initial installation date	1983	Total number of installed sites	15

Sampling of current clients: Athabasca University; Brandon School Division, Brandon, Manitoba; Brandon University; Camosun College; Cariboo College; College of New Caledonia; East Kootenay community College; Fraser Valley Community College; Kwantlen College; Malaspina College; Northwest Community College; Okanagan College; Prince George School District; Selkirk College; University of Saskatchewan; Westman Regional Library

Price: Pricing is based on the number of records in the library.

Supplier's comments: BuCAT is on online catalogue. All other functions are peripheral: the cataloguing module maintains the shelflist; the circulation module feeds loan-status information to the catalogue; the acquisition module feeds on-order information to the catalogue.

SEARCH capabilities are completely flexible with BuCAT: you choose the fields to be indexed; you can search on any word or phrase in any field; you can combine search terms using both Boolean and relational operators.

DISPLAY capabilities are completely flexible with BuCAT; you can specify which fields will be displayed by the SCAN (Short), LIST (full), or CIRCULATION (status) commands; you can specify any number of different LIST formats, any of which can be chosen at any time; you can FILE records into your personal account; you can PRINT records on any printer you designate.

CALM (CARD AND LABEL MANAGER)

Speak Softly, Inc.
303 Calvert Avenue
Clinton, SC 29325
(803) 833-5407
Contact: Bill Yarborough

Hardware: Apple IIe; IBM PC or AT

System Requirements: DOS 1.1 or later; 1 or 2 disk drives, 64K; Apple - 80 column card

Programming Language: Compiled BASIC and Assembly Language

Components & Applications:

acquisitions	no	catalog (batch)	yes
catalog (online)	no	cataloging	yes
CD-ROM interface	no	circulation	no
formatting bibliographies	no	index of keywords	no
inter-library loan	no	interface for MARC records	no
media booking	no	reserve room	no
serials	no	thesaurus	no

Updating Modes:

batch update	yes	dynamic update	no

Features:

Boolean logic searchable	no	full text searchable	no
record fields	no limit	record size	up to 7 continuation cards
statistical & math capabilities	no	wholesale change capability	no

Support:

application consulting	yes	maintenance and updates	yes
time share available	no	user training	no

Recommended for:

Corporate & govt libraries	yes	Media center management	no
Public libraries	yes	Records & files management	no
School libraries	yes	University libraries	yes

Installations:

Initial installation date	1983	Total number of installed sites	1500
Sampling of current clients:	no info		

Price: $169

Supplier's comments: CARD AND LABEL MANAGER - 4.0 - ISBN 0-918161-01-0

Card and Label Manager (CALM) is a flexible and easy-to-use program for production of catalog cards and card, pocket, and spine labels. The program is menu-driven with on-screen prompts, and has full text-editing capabilities. All call number conventions are supported, and CALM can be used for all types of materials, including books, audio-visuals, and software. Major enhancements of the newest version include unlimited subject and title tracings, up to seven continuation cards automatically formatted, choice of three print sizes with most dot matrix printers, full support of letter quality printers, choice of three different label formats, and the option to have the 'Contents' automatically removed from the shelf list card. Files produced on diskette can be searched by author, title, call number, ISBN, or accession number for update, etc.

Volume discounts are available for district purchases. All versions are available for a 30-day preview without obligation.

CAMPUS MEDIA MANAGER™

VIS Consultants, Inc.
2000 Century Plaza, Suite 400
Columbia, MD 21044
(800) 847-2243 or (410) 997-1116
Contact: Philip E. Sticha

Hardware: Hewlett-Packard 3000 family (Micro-3000 through HP 9XX series)

System Requirements: Depending upon collection size, INTEL 386/486 (running UNIX) with 60-300 mb, 4-8 mb RAM, up to 8 user multiport card.

Programming Language: INFORMIX 4GL RDBMS

Components & Applications:

acquisitions	no	catalog (batch)	yes
catalog (online)	yes	cataloging	yes
CD-ROM interface	no	circulation	yes
formatting bibliographies	no	index of keywords	yes
inter-library loan	yes	interface for MARC records	yes
media booking	yes	reserve room	no
serials	no	thesaurus	partial

Updating Modes:

batch update	yes, w/consulting	dynamic update	yes

Features:

Boolean logic searchable	partial	full text searchable	yes
record fields	can be changed	record size	unlimited
statistical & math capabilities	yes	wholesale change capability	yes

Support:

application consulting	yes	maintenance and updates	yes
time share available	yes	user training	yes

Recommended for:

Corporate & govt libraries	yes	Media center management	yes
Public libraries	yes	Records & files management	no
School libraries	yes	University libraries	yes

Installations:

Initial installation date	1991	Total number of installed sites	3

Sampling of current clients: California Stataue University - Northridge (CA); Shoreline PUblic Schools (WA).

Published reviews & articles:

Price:

Supplier's comments: Resource Scheduler, the keystone of the *Campus Media Manager*™ family of comprehensive, integrated programs, schedules media, equipment, rooms, software, staff, and any other resource that requires scheduling, down to the minute. Media managers in universities, colleges, and corporate training environments can also take advantage of several additional modules. VIS offers a complete turnkey solution, ready to plug in and go. The *Campus Media Manager*™ system provides flexible connectivity options, and VIS offers in-depth customer support through our toll free (800) numbers. Optional on-site training and installation are also available.

CARDMASTER PLUS MS-DOS

Follett Software Company
809 North Front Street
McHenry, IL 60050-5589
(815) 344-8700 or (800) 323-3397
FAX (815) 344-8774
Contact: Michael Hollobow

Hardware: IBM PC or compatible; 20mb hard disk drive

System Requirements: 640K RAM; MS-DOS 3.3 or higher, Microsoft Extensions 2.2 or higher

Programming Language: C

Components & Applications:

acquisitions	no	catalog (batch)	yes
catalog (online)	no	cataloging	no
CD-ROM interface	yes	circulation	no
formatting bibliographies	no	index of keywords	no
inter-library loan	no	interface for MARC records	yes
media booking	no	reserve room	no
serials	no	thesaurus	no

Updating Modes:

batch update	yes	dynamic update	yes

Features:

Boolean logic searchable	no	full text searchable	no
record fields	no info	record size	no info
statistical & math capabilities	no	wholesale change capability	no

Support:

application consulting	no	maintenance and updates	yes
time share available	no	user training	no

Recommended for:

Corporate & govt libraries	no	Media center management	no
Public libraries	no	Records & files management	no
School libraries	yes	University libraries	no

Installations:

Initial installation date	1991	Total number of installed sites	450

Sampling of current clients: References available.

Published reviews & articles:

Price: $295 - introductory price

Supplier's comments: CardMaster Plus is a MARC-based program which provides catalog card and label production, as well as database development capabilities. It is designed with file-card style menus for ease of use and offers two user interface levels, novice and advanced. CardMaster Plus also provides an option to access Follett's Alliance Plus MARC database CD-ROM. This seamless interface provides quality data, greatly reduces original cataloging time, and aids the development of an electronic database.

CARL SYSTEMS

CARL Systems, Inc.
3801 E. Florida Avenue
Bldg D, Suite 300
Denver, CO 80210
303-758-3030 Fax 303-758-0606
Contact: Martha Whittaker

Hardware: Tandem

System Requirements: Tandem GUARDIAN XF

Programming Language: TAL

Components & Applications:

acquisitions	yes	catalog (batch)	no
catalog (online)	yes	cataloging	yes
CD-ROM interface	yes	circulation	yes
formatting bibliographies	interface to PROCITE	index of keywords	no
inter-library loan	no	interface for MARC records	yes
media booking	no	reserve room	yes
serials	yes	thesaurus	no

Updating Modes:

batch update	yes	dynamic update	yes

Features:

Boolean logic searchable	yes	full text searchable	no
record fields	MARC format	record size	MARC format
statistical & math capabilities	yes	wholesale change capability	yes

Support:

application consulting	yes	maintenance and updates	yes
time share available	yes	user training	yes

Recommended for:

Corporate & govt libraries	no	Media center management	no
Public libraries	yes	Records & files management	no
School libraries	yes	University libraries	yes

Installations:

Initial installation date	1981	Total number of installed sites	25

Sampling of current clients:

Published reviews & articles:

Price: Depends on size of system. Call for custom quote.

Supplier's comments: The CARL System provides a powerful and reliable information access and delivery network:
- an Online Public Access Catalog which is the industry standard for combining simplicity with power;
- integrated support for all library needs, including circulation, acquisitions and serials control;
- rapid response time, averaging less than a second, even across a network of 1000 terminals.

Multi-Institutional Support: The CARL System was designed to serve the needs of library consortia and multi-institutional systems. Individual libraries are supported by customized profiles and parameters. The user sees a rich resource representing the collections of many institutions.

An Information Delivery Platform: The CARL System provides libraries with a vision of the future.
- Gives access to information, wherever the information resides;
- serves as the platform for more than 50 different community and commercial information indexes;   -
- supports the local creation of information databases;
- offers a variety of information formats, including full text and optical images; and
- gateways to networks of national and international scope.

The strength of Tandem Computers: The CARL System employs the power and flexibility of Tandem Computers. Known industry-wide for parallel processing and nonstop fault tolerance. Operates with virtually no downtime. Combines with CARL Systems unique application software to make economical use of computing resources.

CARLYLE SYSTEMS

Carlyle Systems, Inc.
2000 Alameda de las Pulgas
San Mateo, CA 94403
(415) 345-2500
Contact: C. Patrick Franklin

Hardware: Sun Microsystems SPARCStations

System Requirements: X-terminals

Programming Language: C, SQL

Components & Applications:

acquisitions	in development	catalog (batch)	yes
catalog (online)	yes	cataloging	yes
CD-ROM interface	in development	circulation	yes
formatting bibs	in development	index of keywords	yes
inter-library loan	in development	interface for MARC records	yes
media booking	in development	reserve room	yes
serials	in development	thesaurus	in development

Updating Modes:

batch update	yes	dynamic update	yes

Features:

Boolean logic searchable	yes	full text searchable	no
record fields	unlimited	record size	unlimited
statistical & math capabilities	no	wholesale change capability	yes

Support:

application consulting	yes	maintenance and updates	yes
time share available	yes	user training	yes

Recommended for:

Corporate & govt libraries	yes	Media center management	no
Public libraries	yes	Records & files management	no
School libraries	yes	University libraries	yes

Installations:

Initial installation date	1992	Total number of installed sites	2

Sampling of current clients: New York Public Library; State University of New York

Price: Call for information

Supplier's comments: Carlyle has designed the Voyager Series — a fully integrated library automation package. The series includes a state-of-the-art OPAC and comprehensive cataloging, circulation, acquisitions, and serials modules. Voyager utilizes an open systems industry standards philosophy that adheres to national and international standards. The Voyager supports ANSI and NISO standards that include but are not limited to all U.S. MARC Formats and the Common Command Language.

The Voyager Series operates in Unix — industry's most widely-supported open systems platform. Complex queries are performed through the INGRES relational database management system. Voyager communicates via local and wide area networks and supports Open Systems Interconnection protocols. Networked either by Ethernet, TCP/IP, or RS232, multiple users may access bibliographic records simultaneously.

The Voyager Series runs on Sun Microsystems' platforms. Using client-server technology, Sun SPARCStations support a full range of distributed-computing hardware configurations and networks. Voyager will allow you to expand your system, as needed.

User features such as Open Windows and Open Look supply each user with the capability to display multiple windows simultaneously. Voyager also offers a choice of user interfaces; an X-Windows graphical user interface (GUI) that moves the novice and casual user effortlessly through multiple windows and functions, and a command-driven ASCII interface.

CAT ME PLUS

OCLC Online Computer Library Center, Inc.
6565 Frantz Road
Dublin, OH 43017-3395
(614) 764-6000
Contact: Marketing

Hardware: IBM compatibles

System Requirements: DOS

Programming Language:

Components & Applications:

acquisitions	no	catalog (batch)	no
catalog (online)	no	cataloging	yes
CD-ROM interface	no	circulation	no
formatting bibliographies	no	index of keywords	no
inter-library loan	no	interface for MARC records	no
media booking	no	reserve room	no
serials	no	thesaurus	no

Updating Modes:

batch update	yes	dynamic update	no

Features:

Boolean logic searchable	yes	full text searchable	no
record fields	MARC format	record size	MARC format
statistical & math capabilities	no	wholesale change capability	no

Support:

application consulting	no	maintenance and updates	yes
time share available	no	user training	yes

Recommended for:

Corporate & govt libraries	yes	Media center management	no
Public libraries	yes	Records & files management	no
School libraries	yes	University libraries	yes

Installations:

Initial installation date	no info	Total number of installed sites	no info
Sampling of current clients:			

Published reviews & articles:

Price:

Supplier's comments: The microcomputer-based, batch-processing capabilities of the Cataloging Micro Enhancer Plus (CAT ME Plus) will give your library:

Cost savings by letting you produce or update records in batch mode after hours to take advantage of OCLC's nonprime time charges. Dial-access users can reduce telecommunications charges by cataloging and editing records offline).

Increased productivity through batch online searching and processing to reduce staff and workstation time for routine cataloging

NEW - Not previously available in the Cataloging MicroEnhancer package - an easy method of transferring records to local systems, in OCLC-MARC format, via the export function.

Flexibility and convenience by letting you edit bibliographic information offline.

Compatibility with the PRISM service (replaces the Cataloging Micro Enhancer package), including the ability to search records interactively using PASSPORT Software and transfer them to CAT ME Plus for editing and online processing.

Training and ongoing support from your Regional Network and OCLC.

CAT ME Plus dials up and logs on to the PRISM service automatically. It retrieves records from the PRISM service and downloads them to your microcomputer hard disk automatically.

CATALOG CARD AND LABEL WRITER

K-12 MicroMedia Publishing, Inc.
6 Arrow Road
Ramsey, NJ 07446
(201) 825-8888 or (800) 922-0401
Contact: Barbara Goldsmith

Hardware: IBM PC & compatibles; Apple IIc, IIGS, enhanced IIe

System Requirements: MS-DOS; Apple-DOS; single disk drive; 128K or better

Programming Language: no info

Components & Applications:

acquisitions	yes	catalog (batch)	yes
catalog (online)	no	cataloging	yes
CD-ROM interface	no	circulation	no
formatting bibliographies	no	index of keywords	no
inter-library loan	no	interface for MARC records	no
media booking	no	reserve room	no
serials	no	thesaurus	no

Updating Modes:

batch update	no	dynamic update	yes

Features:

Boolean logic searchable	no	full text searchable	no
record fields	no info	record size	no info
statistical & math capabilities	no	wholesale change capability	no

Support:

application consulting	no	maintenance and updates	yes
time share available	no	user training	no

Recommended for:

Corporate & govt libraries	yes	Media center management	no
Public libraries	yes	Records & files management	no
School libraries	yes	University libraries	no

Installations:

Initial installation date	1985	Total number of installed sites	25
Sampling of current clients:	no info		

Price: $169.00 for software and documentation

Supplier's comments: Now you can effortlessly produce catalog cards and labels, and you can save this information to an AppleWorks data disk for later use. Catalog Card & Label Writer Version 6.0 for the Apple is an exciting update to this popular program. Among its many new features, this ProDOS version can be installed on a hard disk, has word processor-like editing, and allows you to see what the card will look like before you print it. The IBM version contains all the features of the 6.0 for the Apple.

Catalog Card and Label Writer reduces the time spent on this meticulous yet tedious chore. You input the information when prompted, just once, and your micro becomes a specialized word processor that automatically formats and prints catalog cards and book pocket and spine labels, as many copies as you need. It also works well with audiovisual materials and software.

You can retrieve the information and print at your convenience — one card, all, or a selected group. You can use it with most common word processors to produce accession lists. You have the option of formatting for your individualized punctuation. So, if you wish to follow AACR2, you can.

CATALOG CARD MAKER

Winnebago Software Company
310 West Main St.
Caledonia MN 55921
(507) 724-5411
Contact: Telesales

Hardware: Apple IIe, IIgs, IIc

System Requirements: Apple DOS

Programming Language: Basic

Components & Applications:

acquisitions	no	catalog (batch)	no
catalog (online)	no	cataloging	yes
CD-ROM interface	no	circulation	no
formatting bibliographies	no	index of keywords	no
inter-library loan	no	interface for MARC records	no
media booking	no	reserve room	no
serials	no	thesaurus	no

Updating Modes:

batch update	no	dynamic update	yes

Features:

Boolean logic searchable	no	full text searchable	no
record fields	no info	record size	no info
statistical & math capabilities	no	wholesale change capability	no

Support:

application consulting	no	maintenance and updates	yes
time share available	no	user training	no

Recommended for:

Corporate & govt libraries	yes	Media center management	yes
Public libraries	yes	Records & files management	yes
School libraries	yes	University libraries	yes

Installations:

Initial installation date	1983	Total number of installed sites	no info
Sampling of current clients: no info			

Published reviews & articles:
"Catalog Card Maker III." *School Library Journal* (February 1986), p. 36.
"Catalog Card Maker III." *Media Evaluation Services* (August 1985), p. 14-15.
"Catalog Card Maker III." *Media Evaluation Services* (Dec 1985), p.2.
"Catalog Card Maker" *CMC News* (Spring 1984), pp. 7-8.
"Catalog Card Maker" *CMC News* (Fall 1984) p. 13.

Supplier's comments: Creates library catalog cards.

CATALOG CARDER V.2

Right On Programs
755-F New York Avenue
Huntington, NY 11743
(516) 424-7777 FAX (516) 424-7207

Hardware: IBM & compatibles; Apple; Macintosh

System Requirements: no info

Programming Language: Turbo Pascal

Components & Applications:

acquisitions	no	catalog (batch)	yes
catalog (online)	no	cataloging	yes
CD-ROM interface	no	circulation	no
formatting bibliographies	no	index of keywords	no
inter-library loan	no	interface for MARC records	no
media booking	no	reserve room	no
serials	no	thesaurus	no

Updating Modes:

batch update	no	dynamic update	yes

Features:

Boolean logic searchable	no	full text searchable	no
record fields	no info	record size	no info
statistical & math capabilities	yes	wholesale change capability	no

Support:

application consulting	yes	maintenance and updates	yes
time share available	no	user training	no

Recommended for:

Corporate & govt libraries	yes	Media center management	yes
Public libraries	yes	Records & files management	yes
School libraries	yes	University libraries	no

Installations:

Initial installation date	1991	Total number of installed sites	9000+
Sampling of current clients: no info			

Price: $129

Supplier's comments: This simply wonderful and wonderfully simple program for creating catalog cards has been specifically produced to make using it as easy as possible. It is a wonderful program for making catalog cards, but it is not a data base and is not designed to be one. It is designed to make catalog cards and does that job quickly, easily and economically. It will not save the entries to be maintained on a database. Once the cards are printed, they are deleted from memory.

CATALOG PLUS MULTIUSER (NETWORKED)

Follett Software Company
809 North Front Street
McHenry, IL 60050-5589
(815) 344-8700 or (800) 323-3397
FAX (815) 344-8774
Contact: Karin Kretschmer

Hardware: IBM PC or compatible

System Requirements: 640K RAM

Programming Language: C

Components & Applications:

acquisitions	no	catalog (batch)	no
catalog (online)	yes	cataloging	no
CD-ROM interface	no	circulation	no
formatting bibliographies	no	index of keywords	yes
inter-library loan	no	interface for MARC records	yes
media booking	no	reserve room	no
serials	no	thesaurus	no

Updating Modes:

batch update	yes	dynamic update	no

Features:

Boolean logic searchable	yes	full text searchable	no
record fields	no info	record size	5600 bytes
statistical & math capabilities	no	wholesale change capability	no

Support:

application consulting	no	maintenance and updates	yes
time share available	no	user training	yes

Recommended for:

Corporate & govt libraries	no	Media center management	no
Public libraries	no	Records & files management	no
School libraries	yes	University libraries	no

Installations:

Initial installation date	1985	Total number of installed sites	3600+

Sampling of current clients: References available.

Published reviews & articles:

Price: $3,190

Supplier's comments: A circulation management system and on-line public access catalog which is fully integrated and MARC based. With Circulation and Catalog Plus combined you have a complete automated circulation system along with all the benefits of an on-line catalog.

CATALOG PLUS SINGLE USER (NON-NETWORKED)

Follett Software Company
809 North Front Street
McHenry, IL 60050-5589
(815) 344-8700 or (800) 323-3397
FAX (815) 344-8774
Contact: Karin Kretschmer

Hardware: IBM PC or compatible

System Requirements: 640K RAM

Programming Language: C

Components & Applications:

acquisitions	no	catalog (batch)	no
catalog (online)	yes	cataloging	no
CD-ROM interface	no	circulation	no
formatting bibliographies	no	index of keywords	yes
inter-library loan	no	interface for MARC records	yes
media booking	no	reserve room	no
serials	no	thesaurus	no

Updating Modes:

batch update	yes	dynamic update	yes

Features:

Boolean logic searchable	yes	full text searchable	no
record fields	no info	record size	56 bytes
statistical & math capabilities	no	wholesale change capability	no

Support:

application consulting	no	maintenance and updates	yes
time share available	no	user training	yes

Recommended for:

Corporate & govt libraries	no	Media center management	no
Public libraries	no	Records & files management	no
School libraries	yes	University libraries	no

Installations:

Initial installation date	1985	Total number of installed sites	300+

Sampling of current clients: References available.

Published reviews & articles:

Price: $2,190

Supplier's comments: A circulation management system and on-line public access catalog which is fully integrated and MARC based. With Circulation and Catalog Plus combined you have a complete automated circulation system along with all the benefits of an on-line catalog.

CD-CAT

Library Systems and Services, Inc.
200 Orchard Ridge Drive
Gaithersburg, MD 20878
301-975-9800 or 800-638-8725
Attn: Marketing

Hardware: IBM compatibles; dual floppy drives (or one hard drive & one floppy drive); 640K memory, & CD-ROM drive.

System Requirements: DOS

Programming Language: Microsoft "C"

Components & Applications:

acquisitions	no	catalog (batch)	no
catalog (online)	yes	cataloging	no
CD-ROM interface	yes	circulation	no
formatting bibliographies	no	index of keywords	yes
inter-library loan	no	interface for MARC records	yes
media booking	no	reserve room	no
serials	no	thesaurus	no

Updating Modes:

batch update	yes	dynamic update	no

Features:

Boolean logic searchable	yes	full text searchable	no
record fields	MARC format	record size	MARC format
statistical & math capabilities	no	wholesale change capability	no

Support:

application consulting	yes	maintenance and updates	yes
time share available	yes	user training	no

Recommended for:

Corporate & govt libraries	yes	Media center management	yes
Public libraries	yes	Records & files management	no
School libraries	yes	University libraries	yes

Installations:

Initial installation date	1992	Total number of installed sites	new
Sampling of current clients:			

Published reviews & articles:

Price: $395; $100/year annual maintenance fee

Supplier's comments: CD-CAT is a CD-ROM based catalog that is ideal as a cost effective alternative to a microfiche catalog or as a back-up to an integrated online system. CD-CAT can be run on a dedicated PC and CD-ROM player, or it can share time with other software on existing hardware as needed.

CIRCULATION CONTROL V.2

Right On Programs
755-F New York Avenue
Huntington, NY 11743
(516) 424-7777   FAX (516) 424-7207

Hardware: IBM & compatibles

System Requirements: Hard disk suggested

Programming Language: no info

Components & Applications:

acquisitions	no	catalog (batch)	no
catalog (online)	no	cataloging	no
CD-ROM interface	no	circulation	yes
formatting bibliographies	no	index of keywords	no
inter-library loan	no	interface for MARC records	no
media booking	no	reserve room	no
serials	no	thesaurus	no

Updating Modes:

batch update	no	dynamic update	yes

Features:

Boolean logic searchable	no	full text searchable	no
record fields	no info	record size	no info
statistical & math capabilities	yes	wholesale change capability	no

Support:

application consulting	yes	maintenance and updates	yes
time share available	no	user training	no

Recommended for:

Corporate & govt libraries	yes	Media center management	yes
Public libraries	yes	Records & files management	yes
School libraries	yes	University libraries	yes (small)

Installations:

Initial installation date	1991	Total number of installed sites	2400
Sampling of current clients: no info			

Costs: $349

Supplier's comments: Here, finally, is an easy to use, efficient, economical circulation program from RIGHT ON. This program makes it not only feasible, but sensible, for every library to have an on-line automated circulation program.
Network version also available.

CIRCULATION MANAGER

Professional Software
21 Forest Avenue
Glen Ridge, NJ 07028
(201) 748-7658

Hardware: IBM PC, XT, AT

System Requirements: 256K RAM; DOS

Programming Language: no info

Components & Applications:

acquisitions	see ACQUISITION MANAGER	catalog (batch)	no
catalog (online)	see ONLINE CATALOG	cataloging	no
CD-ROM interface	no	circulation	yes
formatting bibliographies	no	index of keywords	no
inter-library loan	no	interface for MARC records	no
media booking	no	reserve room	no
serials	see SERIAL CONTROL SYSTEM	thesaurus	no

Updating Modes:

batch update	no	dynamic update	yes

Features:

Boolean logic searchable	no	full text searchable	no
record fields	no info	record size	no info
statistical & math capabilities	yes	wholesale change capability	no

Support:

application consulting	no	maintenance and updates	yes
time share available	no	user training	no

Recommended for:

Corporate & govt libraries	yes	Media center management	no
Public libraries	no	Records & files management	no
School libraries	no	University libraries	no

Installations:

Initial installation date	1985	Total number of installed sites	no info
Sampling of current clients:	no info		

Priice: $ 395   software and documentation
$ 50   demo package

Supplier's comments: If you have from 100 to 400 items in circulation at any one time, and if your active patron list numbers up to about 700 patrons, then the "Circulation Manager" is for you. A single floppy diskette is suficient to accommodate this level of activity.

CIRCULATION PLUS APPLE

Follett Software Company
809 North Front Street
McHenry, IL 60050-5589
(815) 344-8700 or (800) 323-3397
FAX (815) 344-8774
Contact: Karin Kretschmer

Hardware: Apple IIe, IIGS; Macintosh LC

System Requirements: 128K RAM; 10 MB hard disk drive and floppy drive

Programming Language: Pascal

Components & Applications:

acquisitions	no	catalog (batch)	no
catalog (online)	no	cataloging	no
CD-ROM interface	no	circulation	yes
formatting bibliographies	no	index of keywords	no
inter-library loan	no	interface for MARC records	no
media booking	no	reserve room	no
serials	no	thesaurus	no

Updating Modes:

batch update	yes	dynamic update	yes

Features:

Boolean logic searchable	no	full text searchable	no
record fields	no info	record size	no info
statistical & math capabilities	no	wholesale change capability	no

Support:

application consulting	no	maintenance and updates	yes
time share available	no	user training	yes

Recommended for:

Corporate & govt libraries	no	Media center management	no
Public libraries	no	Records & files management	no
School libraries	yes	University libraries	no

Installations:

Initial installation date	1983	Total number of installed sites	4800+

Sampling of current clients: References available.

Published reviews & articles:

Price: $895

Supplier's comments: Circulation Plus is a complete library management system which utilizes barcode labels and a barcode scanner for fast, accurate circulations, as well as overdues, statistical reports, complete inventory, etc. The quick, menu-driven system operates using a hard disk drive. Features CircWorks, a data migration utility, that can place Circulation Plus statistics and records into AppleWorks for manipulation.

CIRCULATION PLUS MULTIUSER (NETWORKED)

Follett Software Company
809 North Front Street
McHenry, IL 60050-5589
(815) 344-8700 or (800) 323-3397
FAX (815) 344-8774
Contact: Karin Kretschmer

Hardware: IBM PC or compatible

System Requirements: 640K RAM

Programming Language: C

Components & Applications:

acquisitions	no	catalog (batch)	no
catalog (online)	no	cataloging	no
CD-ROM interface	no	circulation	yes
formatting bibliographies	no	index of keywords	yes
inter-library loan	no	interface for MARC records	yes
media booking	no	reserve room	yes
serials	no	thesaurus	no

Updating Modes:

batch update	yes	dynamic update	yes

Features:

Boolean logic searchable	yes	full text searchable	no
record fields	no info	record size	56 bytes
statistical & math capabilities	no	wholesale change capability	no

Support:

application consulting	no	maintenance and updates	yes
time share available	no	user training	yes

Recommended for:

Corporate & govt libraries	no	Media center management	no
Public libraries	no	Records & files management	no
School libraries	yes	University libraries	no

Installations:

Initial installation date	1983	Total number of installed sites	275

Sampling of current clients: References available.

Published reviews & articles:

Price: $1,895

Supplier's comments: Circulation Plus for MS-DOS is a complete MARC library management system for circulations, as well as overdues, statistical reports, complete inventory, etc. It utilizes barcode labels and a barcode scanner for fast, accurate circulations. The quick, menu-driven system operates using a hard disk drive.

CIRCULATION PLUS SINGLE USER (NON-NETWORKED)

Follett Software Company
809 North Front Street
McHenry, IL 60050-5589
(815) 344-8700 or (800) 323-3397
FAX (815) 344-8774
Contact: Karin Kretschmer

Hardware: IBM PC or compatible

System Requirements: 640K RAM

Programming Language: C

Components & Applications:

acquisitions	no	catalog (batch)	no
catalog (online)	no	cataloging	no
CD-ROM interface	no	circulation	yes
formatting bibliographies	no	index of keywords	yes
inter-library loan	no	interface for MARC records	yes
media booking	no	reserve room	yes
serials	no	thesaurus	no

Updating Modes:

batch update	yes	dynamic update	yes

Features:

Boolean logic searchable	yes	full text searchable	no
record fields	no info	record size	56 bytes
statistical & math capabilities	no	wholesale change capability	no

Support:

application consulting	no	maintenance and updates	yes
time share available	no	user training	yes

Recommended for:

Corporate & govt libraries	no	Media center management	no
Public libraries	no	Records & files management	no
School libraries	yes	University libraries	no

Installations:

Initial installation date	1983	Total number of installed sites	7000+

Sampling of current clients: References available.

Published reviews & articles:

Price: $895

Supplier's comments: Circulation Plus for MS-DOS is a complete MARC library management system for circulations, as well as overdues, statistical reports, complete inventory, etc. It utilizes barcode labels and a barcode scanner for fast, accurate circulations. The quick, menu-driven system operates using a hard disk drive.

COLUMBIA LIBRARY SYSTEM

CTB Macmillan / McGraw-Hill
2500 Garden Road
Monterey, CA 93940
(800) 663-0544
Contact: Michael Ham, Product Manager

Hardware: 80286 PC with DOS

System Requirements: MS-DOS 3.3 or later

Programming Language: C

Components & Applications:

acquisitions	yes	catalog (batch)	yes
catalog (online)	yes	cataloging	yes
CD-ROM interface	yes	circulation	yes
formatting bibliographies	no	index of keywords	yes
inter-library loan	no	interface for MARC records	yes
media booking	no	reserve room	yes
serials	yes	thesaurus	no

Updating Modes:

batch update	yes	dynamic update	yes

Features:

Boolean logic searchable	yes	full text searchable	yes
record fields	no info	record size	variable (MARC format)
statistical & math capabilities	yes	wholesale change capability	yes

Support:

application consulting	yes	maintenance and updates	yes
time share available	no	user training	yes

Recommended for:

Corporate & govt libraries	yes	Media center management	no
Public libraries	yes	Records & files management	no
School libraries	yes	University libraries	no

Installations:

Initial installation date	1980	Total number of installed sites	1500

Sampling of current clients: 80% schools, 20% public libraries, colleges, corporations.

Price: Acquisitions $1,395 maintenance $175 manual $95
Catalog and MARC $1695 maintenance $275
Catalog, Circulation, and MARC $2695 maintenance $470
Catalog/OPAC $1,395 maintenance $195 manual $95
Circulation and MARC $1495 maintenance $305
Circulation $1,195 maintenance $165 manual $95
MARC Interface $595 maintenance $110 manual $95
Serials $745 maintenance $100 manual $95
Multi-Update on request

Supplier's comments: This library management software fully answers the needs of librarians, administrators, and patrons in providing a complete, integrated system. Modules include Circulation, Catalog, Acquisitions, Serials, and MARC Record Interface. Handles up to 300,000 catalog records. Support includes new releases, 800-number hotline, 800-number BBS.

COMMERCIAL RECORDS MANAGEMENT SOFTWARE

Automated Records Management
23011 Moulton Parkway, Suite J-10
Laguna Hills, CA 92653
(714) 855-8780   FAX (714) 855-9078

Hardware: IBM/PC, XT, AT, PS/2 and most IBM compatibles

System Requirements: MS DOS

Programming Language: dBase III Plus and compiled using Foxbase

Components & Applications:

acquisitions	no	catalog (batch)	no
catalog (online)	yes	cataloging	no
CD-ROM interface	no	circulation	no
formatting bibliographies	no	index of keywords	no
inter-library loan	no	interface for MARC records	no
media booking	no	reserve room	no
serials	no	thesaurus	no

Updating Modes:

batch update	no	dynamic update	yes

Features:

Boolean logic searchable	no	full text searchable	no
record fields	no info	record size	no info
statistical & math capabilities	no	wholesale change capability	no

Support:

application consulting	yes	maintenance and updates	yes
time share available	no	user training	yes

Recommended for:

Corporate & govt libraries	no	Media center management	no
Public libraries	no	Records & files management	yes
School libraries	no	University libraries	no

Installations:

Initial installation date	1989	Total number of installed sites	40
Sampling of current clients:	no info		

Price: $5,995

Supplier's comments: Commercial Records Management Software was designed by individuals operating commercial records centers throughout North America. Automatically assigns incoming boxes a unique and permanent box number and location and space number. Provides for entering box Information and up to 999 files for each and every box. Prepares labels for boxes and files, extensive parameter driven reports including inventory, retrieval history tracking, destruction notification, and certificates of destruction. Complete invoicing to include automatic calculation of client's occupied space (or number of boxes stored) with separate rates for each client. Bar Coding provides for printing bar codes on box and file labels for quick OUT and IN. Works in conjunction with ARMS supplied Bar Reader.

COMPLETE INVENTORY CONTROL V.2.2

Right On Programs
755-F New York Avenue
Huntington, NY 11743
(516) 424-7777   Fax (516) 424-7207

Hardware: IBM & compatibles

System Requirements: MS-DOS

Programming Language: Turbo Pascal

Components & Applications:

acquisitions	no	catalog (batch)	yes
catalog (online)	yes	cataloging	yes
CD-ROM interface	no	circulation	no
formatting bibliographies	no	index of keywords	no
inter-library loan	no	interface for MARC records	no
media booking	no	reserve room	no
serials	no	thesaurus	no

Updating Modes:

batch update	no	dynamic update	yes

Features:

Boolean logic searchable	no	full text searchable	no
record fields	no info	record size	no info
statistical & math capabilities	yes	wholesale change capability	no

Support:

application consulting	yes	maintenance and updates	yes
time share available	no	user training	no

Recommended for:

Corporate & govt libraries	yes	Media center management	yes
Public libraries	yes	Records & files management	yes
School libraries	yes	University libraries	yes

Installations:

Initial installation date	1991	Total number of installed sites	340
Sampling of current clients: no info			

Price: $219

Supplier's comments: Combines EQUIPMENT INVENTORY CONTROL and SUPPLIES INVENTORY CONTROL. Network version also available.

COMPUSERVE INFORMATION MANAGER

CompuServe Incorporated
5000 Arlington Centre Blvd.
Columbus, OH 43220
(800) 848-8199   (614) 457-8600

Hardware: 286 PC with DOS; Macintosh

System Requirements: 640K RAM and a hard disk

Programming Language: not applicable

Components & Applications:

acquisitions	no	catalog (batch)	yes
catalog (online)	yes	cataloging	yes
CD-ROM interface	no	circulation	no
formatting bibliographies	no	index of keywords	yes
inter-library loan	no	interface for MARC records	no
media booking	no	reserve room	no
serials	no	thesaurus	no

Updating Modes:

batch update	yes	dynamic update	yes

Features:

Boolean logic searchable	yes	full text searchable	no
record fields	no limit	record size	no limit
statistical & math capabilities	no	wholesale change capability	yes

Support:

application consulting	yes	maintenance and updates	not applicable
time share available	yes	user training	yes

Recommended for:

Corporate & govt libraries	yes	Media center management	no
Public libraries	no	Records & files management	no
School libraries	no	University libraries	no

Installations:

Initial installation date	1970s	Total number of installed sites	time share only
Sampling of current clients:	no info		

Price: Suggested retail cost is $49.95 for a membership kit, which includes the software and a $25 usage credit.

Supplier's comments: CompuServe provides the world's largest information service to modem-equipped personal computer users. The CompuServe Information Manager (CIM), the software used to acccess CompuServe, incorporates pull-down menus, dialog boxes, and several other features that allow members to access, sort, and utilize information more effectively.

COMPUTER CAT

Winnebago Software Company
310 West Main Street
P.O. Box 430
Caledonia, MN 55921
(507) 724-5411 or (800) 533-5430
Contact: Telesales

Hardware: Apple IIe or IIGS

System Requirements: Corvus OmniDrive hard disk or Sider hard disk drive; 2 floppy disk drives

Programming Language: BASIC

Components & Applications:

acquisitions	no	catalog (batch)	no
catalog (online)	yes	cataloging	yes
CD-ROM interface	no	circulation	no
formatting bibliographies	no	index of keywords	no
inter-library loan	no	interface for MARC records	no
media booking	no	reserve room	no
serials	no	thesaurus	no

Updating Modes:

batch update	no	dynamic update	no

Features:

Boolean logic searchable	no	full text searchable	yes
record fields	18	record size	255 char
statistical & math capabilities	no	wholesale change capability	no

Support:

application consulting	yes	maintenance and updates	yes
time share available	no	user training	yes

Recommended for:

Corporate & govt libraries	yes	Media center management	no
Public libraries	yes	Records & files management	yes
School libraries	yes	University libraries	yes

Installations:

Initial installation date	1983	Total number of installed sites	no info
Sampling of current clients:	no info		

Published reviews & articles:
"Kaukauna's Electa Quinney Elementary Library Users Experience Online Card Catalog." *WEMA Dispatch* (March 1989), p. 7.
"Online Card Catalog - The Cat's Meow." *Media Spectrum* (1988), pp. 13-15.
"Computer Technology Has Been Integrated in Blue Earth." *Minnesota Media* (Summer 1987), pp. 10-11.
"One Byte at a Time." *Wisconsin Ideas in Media* (1987), pp. 9-11.
"Electronic Card Catalog x Students/Hr.)Traditional Card Catalog x Students/Hr." *Minnesota Media* (Winter 1987), p.20.
"Computer Cat is a Hit." *School Library Journal* (January 1986), p.4.
"Computer Cat vs. the Card Catalog." *CMC News* (Winter 1986), p.8.
"School Library Technology." *Wilson Library Bulletin* (January 1985), pp. 336-337.

Price: $995

Supplier's comments: Computer Cat is an on-line, computerized replacement for the card catalog which allows patrons to search by subject, author, or title with a response in less than two seconds. It also has several reporting and editing features for the librarian. Handles up to 54,000 titles.

CONCEPT FINDER

MMIMS Inc.
566A S. York Road
Elmhurst IL 60126
(312) 941-0090
Contact: Lorraine Cislak

Hardware: Operates on the IBM PC, XT, AT, PS/2, UNIX and compatibles. Minicomputer and mainframe computer versions also available

System Requirements: Minimum required: 10M Hard disk, 640K RAM, DOS 2.2 or higher

Programming Language: MUMPS

Components & Applications:

acquisitions	no	catalog (batch)	no
catalog (online)	yes	cataloging	yes
CD-ROM interface	no	circulation	no
formatting bibliographies	no	index of keywords	yes
inter-library loan	no	interface for MARC records	no
media booking	no	reserve room	no
serials	no	thesaurus (user-defined)	yes

Updating Modes:

batch update	yes	dynamic update	yes

Features:

Boolean logic searchable	yes	full text searchable	yes
record fields	no limit	record size	no limit
statistical & math capabilities	no	wholesale change capability	no

Support:

application consulting	yes	maintenance and updates	yes
time share available	no	user training	yes

Recommended for:

Corporate & govt libraries	yes	Media center management	yes
Public libraries	no	Records & files management	yes
School libraries	no	University libraries	no

Installations:

Initial installation date	1986	Total number of installed sites	no info

Sampling of current clients: Ethyl Corporation; American Medical Association; Chicago Historical Society

Published reviews & articles:
Arthur W. Hafner, Ph.D., "Putting AMA's Policy Online: Problems and Solutions," *Medical Executive* (Winter 1988): p. 26-27.
John J. Hughes, "Product Reviews: Text Retrieval Programs," *Bits and Bytes Review* (July 1987), p. 5-9.
Elizabeth Wood, "Concept Finder: Search Capabilities Across Multiple Files," *Information Today* (September, 1988) p. 4, 14.
Arthur W. Hafner, Ph.D. and William P. Whitely, "Software Reviews," *Library Software Review* (January/February, 1989) p. 36-39.
Christopher Locke, *Text Based Management—James Martin Productivity Series*, High-Productivity Software, Inc., Marblehead, MA, 1989.

Price: Call vendor for quotes. PC demonstration diskette available for $25.00

Supplier's comments: An advanced text retrieval system. Operates on IBM PC/XT/AT/PS2. Minicomputer and mainframe computer versions are also available. Allows Boolean, proximity, and precedence searching. Loading from disk files, OCR, or modem.
Concept Finder includes index browsing, pattern match searches, full screen data input, batch registration, and an electronic mail feature.

THE DATA MAGICIAN

Folland Software Services
P.O. Box 1571
Guelph, Ontario N1H 6J6 Canada
(519) 836-3453; FAX (519) 763-4344

Hardware: IBM PC compatibles

System Requirements: 512K RAM internal memory; MS-DOS 2.0 or higher

Programming Language: Turbo Basic

Components & Applications:

acquisitions	no	catalog (batch)	no
catalog (online)	no	cataloging	no
circulation	no	data conversion software	yes
formatting bibliographies	no	index of keywords	no
inter-library loan	no	interface for MARC records	yes
media booking	no	reserve room	no
serials	no	thesaurus	no

Updating Modes:

batch update	yes	dynamic update	yes

Features:

Boolean logic searchable	no	full text searchable	no
record fields	200	record size	5000 char
statistical & math capabilities	no	wholesale change capability	yes

Support:

application consulting	yes	maintenance and updates	yes
time share available	no	user training	no

Recommended for:

Corporate & govt libraries	yes	Media center management	yes
Public libraries	yes	Records & files management	no
School libraries	no	University libraries	yes

Installations:

Initial installation date	1989	Total number of installed sites	150

Sampling of current clients: CanTox (Ontario); Computerized Litigation Support (GA); Crew-Noble Associates (CA); Grace Hospital (Alberta); Ministry of Education (Ontario); National Defense Headquarters; National Library of Canada; North Island College (BC); Nova Scotia Research Foundation Corp (NS); Smithsonian Institute (DC); University of Michigan (MI)

Price: $250.00 (U.S.) for software and documentation
$ 25.00 (U.S.) for demo system

Supplier's comments: The purpose of The Data Magician is to take information from one database system and convert it to a format useable by another database system. The Data Magician provides the flexibility to accept data in a variety of formats such as; ASCII "delimited" (used by PC-based databases), "tagged" files (from on-line searches), dBase III files (including Memo fields), INMAGIC files, or MARC Communications files (from most bibliographic sources). You may then move the data out into any of three output formats: ASCII delimited, INMAGIC, or MARC Communications format. In the process, you may map any field to any other field, break data apart, put it together, or perform any of a wide variety of transformations.

DATA RESEARCH SYSTEM

Data Research Associates, Inc.
1276 North Warson Road
P.O. Box 8495
St. Louis, MO. 63132-1806
(314) 432-1100 - Missouri; (800) 325-0888 - U.S.; (800) 314-3515 - Canada
Contact: Mr. Carl Grant, V.P. Marketing

Hardware: DEC VAX

System Requirements: VMS operating system.

Programming Language: C; VAX BASIC; MACRO.

Components & Applications:

acquisitions	yes	catalog (batch)	yes
catalog (online)	yes	cataloging	yes
CD-ROM interface	yes	circulation	yes
formatting bibliographies	yes	index of keywords	yes
inter-library loan	yes	interface for MARC records	yes
media booking	yes	reserve room	yes
serials	yes	thesaurus	yes

Updating Modes:

batch update	yes	dynamic update	yes

Features:

Boolean logic searchable	yes	full text searchable	yes
record fields	MARC format	record size	MARC format
statistical & math capabilities	yes	wholesale change capability	yes

Support:

application consulting	yes	maintenance and updates	yes
time share available	no	user training	yes

Recommended for:

Corporate & govt libraries	yes	Media center management	yes
Public libraries	yes	Records & files management	no
School libraries	yes	University libraries	yes

Installations:

Initial installation date	1976	Total number of installed sites	130

Sampling of current clients: public, academic, and state libraries. Also regional libraries for the blind and physically handicapped. Academic libraries include: Augusta College; Brookings Institution; Genesee Community College; Hope College; Maharishi International University; Maricopa County Community College District; Pan American University; Texas Christian University; University of Texas of the Permian Basin. Consortia include: Bergen County Cooperative Library System; Fenway Libraries; Southeastern Libraries Cooperating; Southern Adirondack Library System. State Libraries include: Arizona State Library for the Blind; California State Library for the Blind; Missouri State Library for the Blind; Vermont Department of Libraries. Public libraries include: Anaheim Public Library System; Boston Public Library; California State Library; Cleveland Public Library; Johnson County Library; Kansas City Public Library; Los Angeles County Public Library; Riverside City and County Library; Scottsdale Public Library. Special libraries include: 3M Corporation. School Libraries include: Country Day School; Grossmont Union High School District; Libraries for the Blind and Physically Handicapped include: Braille Institute of America; Canadian National Institute for the Blind. Overseas libraries include: Canterbury Public Library, Christchurch New Zealand; Manuakau Public Library, Manukau City, New Zealand; Northshore Consortium, New Zealand; Institute of Education, Singapore; Hong Kong University; Hong Kong Polytechnic; Nanyang Technological, Singapore.

Price: Prices will vary depending upon the size of the system. Discounts are available for package configurations.

Supplier's comments: MARC records can be input directly from MARC and OCLC tapes or from the OCLC screen. Any field in a record may be designated to be a key field. System support is offered 24 hours a day. Additional components are newspaper index, union list of serials, and material booking.

DATA-STAR TEACH YOURSELF DISKETTE

Data-Star Teach Yourself
485 Devon Park Drive
Suite 110
Wayne, PA 19087
800-221-7754 Fax: 215- 687-0984
Contact: USA Help-Desk

Hardware: IBM-compatible PC

System Requirements: DOS, 31/2" disk drive

Support:

application consulting	no	maintenance and updates	no
time share available	no	user training	yes

Recommended for:

Corporate & govt libraries	yes	Media center management	no
Public libraries	yes	Records & files management	no
School libraries	yes	University libraries	yes

Installations:

Initial installation date	n/a	Total number of installed sites	n/a

Sampling of current clients: n/a

Published reviews & articles:

Price: $27

Supplier's comments: Online search training aid which demonstrates Data-Star's online search systems.

 The Data-Star Teach Yourself Diskette simulates online searching, and helps you to learn basic commands without having to connect to the system and the telecommunications network. You just insert the diskette into your PC and follow the menu-driven instructions.

 You can order the diskette in either of two versions: business or biomedical. The business TYD teaches the Data-Star command language in the context of business information; the biomedical TYD applies to biomedical information.

 The Teach Yourself Diskette is intended for beginners with no previous experience with online searching. Its menu program allows you to go from one section to another, or to repeat certain parts, as you wish. Upon completion, you will be able to perform real searches on all Data-Star databases.

Editor's note: This is special application software used to teach how to search DATA STAR databases. Therefore, it does not include the usual list of components and applications.

DATALIB

Centel Federal Services Corp.
11400 Commerce Park Drive
Reston VA 22091
(800) 843-4850 or (703) 758-7012
Contact: Greg Sapp

Hardware: Data General MV Series; DEC VAX & MicroVax II

System Requirements: Data General AOS/VS; DEC VAX/VMS; 2MB of main memory; 1 tape drive; disk drives dependent on data base size

Programming Language: FORTRAN 77

Components & Applications:

acquisitions	yes	catalog (batch)	yes
catalog (online)	yes	cataloging	yes
CD-ROM interface	no	circulation	yes
formatting bibliographies	no	index of keywords	yes
inter-library loan	no	interface for MARC records	yes
media booking	no	reserve room	no
serials	yes	thesaurus	yes

Updating Modes:

batch update	yes	dynamic update	yes

Features:

Boolean logic searchable	yes	full text searchable	yes
record fields	no limit	record size	64KB per record
statistical & math capabilities	yes	wholesale change capability	yes

Support:

application consulting	yes	maintenance and updates	yes
time share available	yes	user training	yes

Recommended for:

Corporate & govt libraries	yes	Media center management	no
Public libraries	no	Records & files management	yes
School libraries	no	University libraries	no

Installations:

Initial installation date	1984	Total number of installed sites	24

Sampling of current clients: Several time-sharing users. Other installations include U.S. Dept. of Justice; Kerr-McGee; Schlumberger; General Motors; Martin Marietta; Merck Sharp and Dohme; RCA; Air Products & Chemicals; Dow Chemical; Marion Merrel Dow Pharmaceuticals.

Price:

Full Integrated System	$ 29,500
Profiling & Training	6,000
Maintenance & Support	7,650
TOTAL	$ 43,150

Note: Fully Integrated System modules if purchased separately:

Base & Catalog & Retrieval	$ 18,000
Acquisitions & Accounting (Add-On)	6,000
Circulation (Add-On)	4,500
Serials Management (Add-On)	4,500

Lease (1 year)

Full Integrated System	$ 30,000
Profiling & Training	6,000
TOTAL	$ 36,000

DATALIB continued

Note: Full Integrated System if leased separately:

Base & Catalog & Retrieval	$18,000/yr.
Acquisitions & Accounting (Add-On)	6,000/yr.
Circulation (Add-On)	4,500/yr.
Serials Management (Add-On)	4,500/yr.

Supplier's comments: DataLib is a fully integrated library system designed for functionality and flexibility by Special Librarians with experience in automation. While record types and structures, field descriptions, prompts, reports and help messages, even display formats can be tailored to the user; DataLib also fully supports the MARC stuctures. Each database's functionality and formatting can be tailored to the customer's environment. Conversions of existing databases, including OCLC records, are fully supported as are interfaces with outside databases such as ISI.

The online catalog features the newest innovation from DataLib, PatronSEARCH! A Graphical User Interface combining the power and flexibility of a VAX application with the universal access and user-friendliness of a PC-Windows-like environment. Patron Search! provides a transparent link from each office PC to the library, allowing even first time users to develop sophisticated search strategies, view information in customizable display formats, point and shoot Boolean connectors, and access all request and reserve functions via mouse or "Hot Key" commands. The OPAC also features a super high performance retrieval capability. Any element or term or combination, including proximity searches for text, may be searched. Retrieval usually is a second or less for even complicated search strategies regardless of the number of records. Restriction of functions to the verb level and data to the element level provides an extremely flexible security environment.

The acquisitions and accounting module provides a uniquely comprehensive set of capabilities, unique to DataLib. Multi-item and consignee purchase orders, renewals, receipting, prepaid and approval accounts, multi-level budgets, contract and deposit accounts, automatic budget reserves, overdue notices, serials check-in, routing, claiming, binding, holdings summaries are all supported. Serials and circulation fully integrated with the OPAC and updated in real time.

DATAROUTE

Feld Technologies
155 Federal Street, 16th Floor
Boston, MA 02110
(617) 451-0055
Contact: Bradley Feld

Hardware: IBM PC, XT, AT, PS/2 and compatibles

System Requirements: MS-DOS; hard disk drive recommended

Programming Language: Clipper

Components & Applications:

acquisitions	no	catalog (batch)	no
catalog (online)	no	cataloging	no
CD-ROM interface	no	circulation	no
formatting bibliographies	no	index of keywords	no
inter-library loan	no	interface for MARC records	no
media booking	no	reserve room	no
serials	yes	thesaurus	no

Updating Modes:

batch update	no	dynamic update	yes

Features:

Boolean logic searchable	no	full text searchable	no
record fields	9	record size	no info
statistical & math capabilities	no	wholesale change capability	no

Support:

application consulting	yes	maintenance and updates	yes
time share available	no	user training	yes

Recommended for:

Corporate & govt libraries	yes	Media center management	yes
Public libraries	no	Records & files management	no
School libraries	yes	University libraries	yes

Installations:

Initial installation date	1984	Total number of installed sites	25+

Sampling of current clients: Milbank, Tweed, Hadley & McCloy; Federal Reserve Bank of New York; Microsoft; Cravath, Swaine & Moore

Supplier's comments: A database manager for routing of periodicals. Produces routing lists and generates reports. The fields include:

Periodical name, publisher, subject, frequency
Reader name (short or long), department, rank, location

DIAGNOSTIC TEST OF LIBRARY SKILLS

Learnco Inc.
Box L
Exeter, NH 03833
800-542-0026
Contact: J.H. Smith

Hardware: Apple II, Macintosh, IBM

System Requirements: 128 K, one disk drive (Apple), 1 MB Mac and IBM

Programming Language: Assembly (Apple), Structured BASIC (Mac and IBM)

Support:

application consulting	no	maintenance and updates	yes
time share available	no	user training	no

Recommended for:

Corporate & govt libraries	no	Media center management	no
Public libraries	yes	Records & files management	no
School libraries	yes	University libraries	no

Installations:

Initial installation date	Jun 1991	Total number of installed sites	100
Sampling of current clients:			

Published reviews & articles:

Price: $39.95

Supplier's comments: The Diagnostic Test of Library Skills includes test scoring for individual students and item analysis for groups of students. Without the burden of scoring tests or analyzing results, the teacher/librarian can concentrate on remedial work for student groups. Group analysis and test results can be shown on the computer screen or printed out for a permanent record. There are two test forms, which can be used for pre- and post-testing. Students taking the test can do so by completing all the questions (there are 50 questions for each test "form") in one session or can take the test in two or more sessions. They can skip questions and can come back to them later. When a student answers a question he or she is given feedback as to whether the answer is right or wrong and why. These comments are designed to teach when a wrong answer is given. There is also a set of tutorial exercises designed specifically to teach Alphanumeric skills. This unit can be assigned according to need.

Editor's note: This is a special package for teaching library skills. Therefore, it does not include the usual list of components and applications.

DIAGNOSTIC TEST OF LIBRARY SKILLS ADVANCED

Learnco Inc.
Box L
Exeter, NH 03833
800-542-0026
Contact: J.H. Smith

Hardware: Apple II, Macintosh, IBM

System Requirements: 128 K, one disk drive (Apple), 1 MB Mac and IBM

Programming Language: Assembly (Apple), Structured BASIC (Mac and IBM)

Support:

application consulting	no	maintenance and updates	yes
time share available	no	user training	no

Recommended for:

Corporate & govt libraries	no	Media center management	no
Public libraries	yes	Records & files management	no
School libraries	yes	University libraries	no

Installations:

Initial installation date	Dec 1992	Total number of installed sites	new
Sampling of current clients:			

Published reviews & articles:

Price: $39.95

Supplier's comments: This is for high schools. Librarians and teachers tell us that they need to find out what students know, but how? The Diagnostic Test of Library Skills Advanced is meant to find out.

Editor's Note: This is a special package for teaching library skills. Therefore, it does not include the usual list of components and applications.

DIALOGLINK®

Dialog Information Services, Inc.
3460 Hillview Avenue
Palo Alto, CA 94304
(415) 858-3785

Hardware: IBM PC or compatible with 256K RAM memory

System Requirements: DOS

Programming Language: no info

Components & Applications:

acquisitions	no	catalog (batch)	no
catalog (online)	no	cataloging	no
CD-ROM interface	no	circulation	no
formatting bibliographies	no	index of keywords	no
inter-library loan	no	interface for MARC records	no
media booking	no	reserve room	no
serials	no	thesaurus	no

Updating Modes:

batch update	no	dynamic update	yes

Features:

Boolean logic searchable	no	full text searchable	no
record fields	n/a	record size	n/a
statistical & math capabilities	yes	wholesale change capability	no

Support:

application consulting	yes	maintenance and updates	yes
time share available	no	user training	yes

Recommended for:

Corporate & govt libraries	yes	Media center management	no
Public libraries	yes	Records & files management	no
School libraries	yes	University libraries	yes

Installations:

Initial installation date	1985	Total number of installed sites	no info
Sampling of current clients:			

Price: $99.00 for software and documentation
$15.00 for evaluation disk

Supplier's comments: DIALOGLINK - communications and account management software for IBM PCs and compatibles.

DIX (DOCUMENT INDEX)

JES Library Automation Consulting Services, Inc.
#104-221 Blue Mountain Street
Coquitlam, BC, V3K 4H3 Canada
604-939-6775; fax 604-939-9970
Contact: Peter Smode

Hardware: DEC VAX

System Requirements: VAX/VMS

Programming Language: VAX BASIC

Components & Applications:

acquisitions	n/a	catalog (batch)	yes
catalog (online)	yes	cataloging	yes
CD-ROM interface	yes	circulation	n/a
formatting bibliographies	no	index of keywords	yes
inter-library loan	n/a	interface for MARC records	yes
media booking	n/a	reserve room	n/a
serials	n/a	thesaurus	yes

Updating Modes:

batch update	yes	dynamic update	yes

Features:

Boolean logic searchable	yes	full text searchable	no
record fields	variable	record size	variable
statistical & math capabilities	yes	wholesale change capability	yes

Support:

application consulting	yes	maintenance and updates	yes
time share available	no	user training	yes

Recommended for:

Corporate & govt libraries	yes	Media center management	yes
Public libraries	yes	Records & files management	yes
School libraries	yes	University libraries	yes

Installations:

Initial installation date	1987	Total number of installed sites	5

Sampling of current clients: Burnaby Public Library (BC); Hawaii State Public Library System (HI).

Published reviews & articles:

Price:

Supplier's comments: DIX started as a multi-user system to index and record the location of articles from newspapers and journals found in the library. From this beginning, it has been enhanced to support the indexing and locating of any type of material (files, memos, document data files, graphic images, letters, microfilm, reports, brochures, etc.)

Users create document summaries, which may be accessed by any computer or terminal connected to the site's information network.

An individual document summary will show the document type, location in newspaper or where filed, date, any attached note or abstract, and all subject headings associated with the entry. Note also that the notes and abstracts are fully keyword searchable.

Master listings of document titles, arranged by subject, many be output in printed or COM form. These listings may be generated for all documents in the database, or for selected types of documents.

An optional public access sub-system may be used to give members of the public access to the index.

DYNIX

DYNIX, Inc.
151 East 1700 South
Provo, Utah 84606
(801) 375-2770
Contact: KeithWilson

Hardware: HP, Wyse, IBM, Unisys, Sequoia, Sequent, Data General

System Requirements: Pick Operating System, UNIX/Univers

Programming Language: DATA BASIC

Components & Applications:

acquisitions	yes	catalog (batch)	yes
catalog (online)	yes	cataloging	yes
CD-ROM interface	yes	circulation	yes
formatting bibliographies	in development	index of keywords	yes
inter-library loan	within Dynix Agency Network	interface for MARC records	yes
media booking	yes	reserve room	yes
serials	yes	thesaurus	in development

Updating Modes:

batch update	yes	dynamic update	yes

Features:

Boolean logic searchable	yes	full text searchable	yes
record fields	no limit	record size	MARC format
statistical & math capabilities	yes	wholesale change capability	yes

Support:

application consulting	yes	maintenance and updates	yes
time share available	no	user training	yes

Recommended for:

Corporate & govt libraries	yes	Media center management	yes
Public libraries	yes	Records & files management	no
School libraries	yes	University libraries	yes

Installations:

Initial installation date	1983	Total number of installed sites	950 systems in 1,184 libraries

Sampling of current clients: National Libraries: National Library of Australia (AUS), National Library of Ireland (IRE), National Library of New Zealand (NZ), National Library of Thailand (ASIA), San Joaquin Valley Library System; Art Center College of Design; Federal Libraries: Combined Arms Research Library, H.M. Treasury & Cabinet Office (UK), Saskatchewan Provincial Library (CAN), United States Coast Guard Academy Library.

Price: Depends on hardware configuration.

Supplier's comments: DYNIX is a totally integrated system. The DYNIX system provides a stand-alone turnkey computer system with hardware and software capable of accessing on-line files. DYNIX is also responsible for installation and training and for reformatting bibliographic data from current machine-readable forms. One of the most significant features of DYNIX's system is its user-friendly nature. The online file is effeciently organized to allow for future expansion while providing rapid access to individual records. Procedures for online additions, modifications, and deletions are logical and easy to learn. The system is capable of creating and maintaining a bibliographic database in full MARC II format.

DYNIX MARQUIS

DYNIX, Inc.
151 East 1700 South
Provo, Utah 84606
(801) 226-5508
Contact: Rick Wilson

Hardware: VAX, IBM RS/6000, HP, Sun, other Unix machines, or 486 for server: IBM 386 or 486 or clone, or Macintosh for clients

System Requirements: UNIX, VMS, OS/2, or Netware for server; OS/2, Windows 3.X, or Macintosh OS for clients

Programming Language: MODULSA 2, C.

Components & Applications:

acquisitions	yes	catalog (batch)	no
catalog (online)	yes	cataloging	yes
CD-ROM interface	yes	circulation	yes
formatting bibliographies	yes	index of keywords	yes
inter-library loan	no	interface for MARC records	yes
media booking	no	reserve room	no
serials	yes	thesaurus	no

Updating Modes:

batch update	yes	dynamic update	yes

Features:

Boolean logic searchable	yes	full text searchable	yes
record fields	no limit	record size	MARC format
statistical & math capabilities	yes	wholesale change capability	yes

Support:

application consulting	yes	maintenance and updates	yes
time share available	no	user training	yes

Recommended for:

Corporate & govt libraries	yes	Media center management	no
Public libraries	no	Records & files management	no
School libraries	no	University libraries	yes

Installations:

Initial installation date	1991	Total number of installed sites	5

Sampling of current clients: Microsoft; Gibson, Dunn & Crutcher

Price: Depends on hardware configuration.

Supplier's comments: Marquis introduces a new fully integrated library system designed for operating in a distributed processing/local area network environment with a graphical user interface. The workstations and networks are set up to work with other communications and computing in your institution. Marquis does not just "run beside" other software. It runs with it. If you've started hearing some of these computing terms - client-server computing, SQL Databases, Graphical User Interfaces - and want to know what they have to do with library automation, please come by for a look.

DYNIX SCHOLAR

DYNIX, Inc.
1455 West 820 North
Provo, Utah 84601
(801) 375-2770
Contact: Jim Wilson

Hardware: 386 Pick, 486 UNIX, (all DYNIX platforms)

System Requirements: Pick Operating System, UNIX

Programming Language: DATA BASIC

Components & Applications:

acquisitions	yes	catalog (batch)	no
catalog (online)	yes	cataloging	yes
CD-ROM interface	yes	circulation	yes
formatting bibliographies	yes	index of keywords	yes
inter-library loan	yes	interface for MARC records	yes
media booking	yes	reserve room	yes
serials	yes	thesaurus	no

Updating Modes:

batch update	yes	dynamic update	yes

Features:

Boolean logic searchable	yes	full text searchable	yes
record fields	no limit	record size	MARC format
statistical & math capabilities	yes	wholesale change capability	yes

Support:

application consulting	yes	maintenance and updates	yes
time share available	no	user training	yes

Recommended for:

Corporate & govt libraries	no	Media center management	no
Public libraries	no	Records & files management	no
School libraries	yes	University libraries	no

Installations:

Initial installation date	1991	Total number of installed sites	300

Sampling of current clients: Adlai Stevenson High School; Washington Elementary; Smith Middle School; New Trier Township High School; Jordan Middle School.

Published articles and reviews:

Price: Depends on hardware configuration. Call for a custom quote.

Supplier's comments: Dynix Scholar provides Dynix's full-featured integrated library system to the K-12 school marketplace. While we offer the same powerful software used in public, academic and special libraries worldwide, we have profiled the system for schools and focused on school library concerns. Running on either PC or minicomputer based hardware, the Union Catalog offers exciting options to those multi-school district environments preferring separate smaller systems in local schools, yet with access to a complete index of the District's collection. Dynix Scholar works with Novell networks, installs automatically on an ICLAS (IBM Classroom LAN Administration System) menu system as courseware, or a variety of other environments. Schools may use PC, or Macintosh microcomputer workstations or terminals to access the Scholar System. In addition to local library holdings, access to shared CD-ROM databases of the library's choice can be provided through a network.

E Z LEDGER II V.2.0

Right On Programs
755-F New York Avenue
Huntington, NY 11743
(516) 424-7777   FAX (516) 424-7207

Hardware: IBM & compatibles

System Requirements: MS-DOS

Programming Language: Turbo Pascal

Components & Applications:

acquisitions	yes	catalog (batch)	no
catalog (online)	no	cataloging	no
CD-ROM interface	no	circulation	no
formatting bibliographies	no	index of keywords	no
inter-library loan	no	interface for MARC records	no
media booking	no	reserve room	no
serials	no	thesaurus	no

Updating Modes:

batch update	no	dynamic update	yes

Features:

Boolean logic searchable	no	full text searchable	no
record fields	no info	record size	no info
statistical & math capabilities	yes	wholesale change capability	no

Support:

application consulting	yes	maintenance and updates	yes
time share available	no	user training	no

Recommended for:

Corporate & govt libraries	yes	Media center management	yes
Public libraries	yes	Records & files management	yes
School libraries	yes	University libraries	yes

Installations:

Initial installation date	1991	Total number of installed sites	350
Sampling of current clients: no info			

Price: $149

Supplier's comments: This EZ LEDGER II program allows the user to keep track of all budgeted items. Budget codes are entered with the total amount encumbered in that budget code. As each order is placed, the total for that order is automatically deducted from the appropriate code and the remaining balance is displayed. The budget and budget balance may be displayed to the screen or printer.

EDIBASE

INFORM II - MICROFOR
801 Sherbrooke Street East
Montreal, Quebec, Canada H2L 1K7
(514) 484-5951
Contact: Marc-Andre Ledoux

Hardware: IBM PC or compatibles

System Requirements: 10MB hard disk, 640K, MS-DOS

Programming Language: C

Components & Applications:

acquisitions	no	catalog (batch)	yes
catalog (online)	yes	cataloging	yes
CD-ROM interface	yes	circulation	no
formatting bibliographies	yes	index of keywords	yes
inter-library loan	no	interface for MARC records	no
media booking	no	reserve room	no
serials	no	thesaurus	yes

Updating Modes:

batch update	yes	dynamic update	yes

Features:

Boolean logic searchable	yes	full text searchable	yes
record fields	variable, max 256	record size	unlimited
statistical & math capabilities	no	wholesale change capability	yes

Support:

application consulting	yes	maintenance and updates	yes
time share available	no	user training	yes

Recommended for:

Corporate & govt libraries	yes	Media center management	no
Public libraries	no	Records & files management	yes
School libraries	no	University libraries	no

Installations:

Initial installation date	1985	Total number of installed sites	650

Sampling of current clients: Alcan; Bank of Canada; Bell Canada; Finance Canada; Quebec Government; Royal Bank; Via Rail

Price: Purchase price $1,999.00 (U.S.)
       Maintenance $ 249.00 (U.S.)

Supplier's comments: EDIBASE allows you to retrieve in your databases any record from any word. Whether it is bibliographic citations, information cards, or even full text documents (articles, memos, notes, etc) you can retrieve in a few seconds your information, and this with the greatest easiness there is: you only have to ask your questions in natural language, with the words occurring to you spontaneously. Documents retrieved are ranked by relevance. Phrase, date, and number indexes can be defined and displayed. Users browse the indexes and select and combine terms.

   With the help of a powerful word processor and the validation module, you write every one of your texts and enter your data bases' records. You can also supply your data-bases by interrogating external databases, downloading citations, and then reformatting the newly input records.

   With its report generator, EDIBASE is the ideal tool for documentation centres, information services, and for any organization that has to produce different directories or catalogs. Professionals having to deal with large quantities of written information (teachers, researchers, lawyers, journalists, etc.) will find in EDIBASE a tool for increasing productivity.

   EDIBASE also has a thesaurus management module.

   The software is available for CD-ROM applications.

ELEMENTARY LIBRARY MEDIA SKILLS

Ruth Sather and Associates
2120 Moonlight Bay Drive
Altoona, WI 54720
715-835-5020 or 800-289-0132
Contact: Ruth Sather

Hardware: Apple

System Requirements: Apple DOS

Support:

application consulting	no	maintenance and updates	yes
time share available	no	user training	no

Recommended for:

Corporate & govt libraries	no	Media center management	no
Public libraries	no	Records & files management	no
School libraries	yes	University libraries	no

Installations:

Initial installation date		Total number of installed sites	n/a
Sampling of current clients: n/a			

Published reviews & articles: Booklist, Electronic Learning School Library Media Quarterly

Price: $125 per module
          $350 for all modules

Supplier's comments: Elementary Library Media Skills is a comprehensive computer-based curriculum which provides individualized self-paced learning of the skills needed to use library and media facilties. The program provides highly interactive computer-based lessons comprised of text, graphics, and learning activities, which include effective learning games, tutorials, simulations, and drill and practice.

It has 24 computer based lessons grouped by topic within units. The units are further grouped into four modules:
1 - Discovering Available Resources
2 - Organization of Resources
3 - Locating Resources
4 - Research and Study Skills

Editor's note: This is a software package to teach skills in using the library. Therefore, it does not include the usual list of components and applications.

THE ELOQUENT LIBRARIAN

Eloquent Systems Inc
25 - 1501 Lonsdale Avenue
North Vancouver, British Columbia Canada V7M 2J2
(800) 663-8172
Fax (604) 980-9537
Contact: Marketing

Hardware: IBM AT, PS/2 (80286 12MHz) or compatible

System Requirements: MS-DOS & LANs; 640K RAM, one hard disk, one floppy disk

Programming Language: Revelation

Components & Applications:

acquisitions	yes	catalog (batch)	yes
catalog (online)	yes	cataloging	yes
CD-ROM interface	yes	circulation	yes
formatting bibliographies	yes	index of keywords	yes
inter-library loan	yes	interface for MARC records	yes
media booking	yes	reserve room	no
serials	yes	thesaurus	yes

Updating Modes:

batch update	yes	dynamic update	yes

Features:

Boolean logic searchable	yes	full text searchable	yes
record fields	unlimited	record size	64,000 bytes
statistical & math capabilities	limited	wholesale change capability	limited

Support:

application consulting	yes	maintenance and updates	yes
time share available	no	user training	yes

Recommended for:

Corporate & govt libraries	yes	Media center management	yes
Public libraries	yes	Records & files management	no
School libraries	yes	University libraries	no

Installations:

Initial installation date	1986	Total number of installed sites	350

Sampling of current clients: Winton School District (CA); Will Sinclair High School (AB); Cominco Ltd. (BC); Justice Institute Library (BC); MacMillan Bloedel Research (BC); British Columbia Ministry of Health (BC); Air BC (BC); British Columbia Medical Library Services (BC); Insurance Corporation of British Columbia (BC); Cancer Control Agency of British Columbia (BC)

Price:	Base System	$ 1,200 - $2,900 (based on number of titles)
	Research-only System	$ 950
	MARC Import Module	$ 950
	MARC Export Module	$ 650
	Circulation Module	$ 1,150
	Media Management Module	$ 1,900
	Acquisitions Module	$ 950
	Serials Module	$ 1,900
	Free demo disk	

Supplier's comments: THE ELOQUENT LIBRARIAN catalogs bibliographic data, prints spine and pocket labels, produces catalogs, and provides online public access. The Circulation Module prints barcodes, provides checkout and check-in, places reserves, sends overdue notices, and calculates fines. Acquisitions and Serials modules are available. In education, the Union Catalog permits school districts to enter titles only once, no matter how many schools have copies.

THE ELOQUENT MEDIA MANAGER

Eloquent Systems Inc
25 - 1501 Lonsdale Avenue
North Vancouver, British Columbia Canada V7M 2J2
(800) 663-8172
Fax (604) 980-9537

Hardware: IBM AT, PS/2 (80286 12MHz) or compatible

System Requirements: MS-DOS & LANs; 640K RAM, one hard disk, one floppy disk

Programming Language: Revelation

Components & Applications:

acquisitions	yes	catalog (batch)	yes
catalog (online)	yes	cataloging	yes
CD-ROM interface	no	circulation	yes
formatting bibliographies	no	index of keywords	yes
inter-library loan	no	interface for MARC records	yes
media booking	yes	reserve room	no
serials	no	thesaurus	no

Updating Modes:

batch update	yes	dynamic update	yes

Features:

Boolean logic searchable	yes	full text searchable	yes
record fields	unlimited	record size	64,000 bytes
statistical & math capabilities	limited	wholesale change capability	limited

Support:

application consulting	yes	maintenance and updates	yes
time share available	no	user training	yes

Recommended for:

Corporate & govt libraries	yes	Media center management	yes
Public libraries	yes	Records & files management	yes
School libraries	yes	University libraries	no

Installations:

Initial installation date	1986	Total number of installed sites	35

Sampling of current clients: British Columbia Ministry of Health (BC); Vernon School District No. 22(BC); Penticton School District No. 15 (BC); Cowichan Resource Center School District NO. 65 (BC); Insurance Corporation of British Columbia (BC); Nicholas Mancini Centre Hamilton-Wentworth Roman Catholic Separate School Board (ON)

Price: $3,100 - $5,000
            Free demo disk

Supplier's comments: The ELOQUENT MEDIA MANAGER catalogs films, videos, media-related equipment, etc., and effortlessly monitors all aspects of the booking process, including initial inquiries, reservations, confirmations, shipments and returns. Statistical generation informs users which items were used most, which were never used, and which were not available on the date requested. Therefore, future purchases are based on accurately-calculated demand. Printed catalogs, shipping lists and labels, packing slips, routing lists, etc., are easily produced. MARC Import and Remote Booking are also available.

ENDLINK

Niles and Associates Inc.
2000 Hearst Street
Berkeley, CA 94709
(510) 649-8176
Fax (510) 649-8179
Contact: Sales Dept.

Hardware: IBM PC/Macintosh

System Requirements: DOS

Support:

application consulting	no	maintenance and updates	yes
time share available	no	user training	no

Recommended for:

Corporate & govt libraries	yes	Media center management	no
Public libraries	yes	Records & files management	yes
School libraries	no	University libraries	yes

Installations:

Initial installation date	?	Total number of installed sites	?

Sampling of current clients:

Published reviews & articles:

Price: $99.00

Supplier's comments: EndLink adds to ENDNOTE or ENDNOTE PLUS the capability to translate bibliographic references from online services and other sources of information into EndNote database records. You can add them to your EndNote personal library of references. EndLink works with MEDLINE, BIOSIS, Chem Abstracts, and other databases available through online vendors. Once in your EndNote library, you'll be able to include them in your bibliographies automatically. You'll never have to type a bibliographic reference again!

> EndLink works with these databases:
>
> MEDLINE (through Dialog, BRS, Medlars (NLM), PaperChase, Silver
>   Platter, DataStar, Knowledge Finder, Grateful Med, MediSearch).
> CAS Online (through Dialog and STN)
> Toxline
> BIOSIS
> CANCERLIT
> DIMDI
> Computer Database (through Dialog or CompuServe)
> ABI/INFORM
> BRS databases
> Inspec
> Psyc Info
>
> If you don't find your favorite database in this list, please call us at (415) 649-8176.

ENDNOTE

Niles and Associates Inc.
2000 Hearst Street
Berkeley, CA 94709
(510) 649-8176   Fax (510) 649-8179
Contact: Emanuel Rosen

Hardware: IBM PC or compatible; Apple Macintosh

System Requirements: DOS 3.0 or Mac

Programming Language: C

Components & Applications:

acquisitions	no	catalog (batch)	yes
catalog (online)	yes	cataloging	yes
CD-ROM interface	yes*	circulation	no
formatting bibliographies	yes	index of keywords	yes
inter-library loan	no	interface for MARC records	no
media booking	no	reserve room	no
serials	no	thesaurus	no

Updating Modes:

batch update	no	dynamic update	yes

Features:

Boolean logic searchable	yes	full text searchable	no
record fields	no info	record size	64,000 char.
statistical & math capabilities	no	wholesale change capability	no

Support:

application consulting	no	maintenance and updates	yes
time share available	no	user training	no

Recommended for:

Corporate & govt libraries	yes	Media center management	no
Public libraries	yes	Records & files management	yes
School libraries	no	University libraries	yes

Installations:

Initial installation date	1987	Total number of installed sites	10,000+

Sampling of current clients:

Published reviews & articles:

L.E. Becker Jr., "EndNote Plus Speeds Research Tasks," *MacWEEK*, 5, April 16, 1991. p. 78.
E. Brower, "EndLink Grabs On-line Info," *MacWEEK*, 3, March 7, 1989. p. 19.
S.D. Cohen, "EndNote Plus: Reference Formatter and Compiler," *Information Today*, March 1991. p. 35.
S. Guttman, "EndNote: Useful Tool For Researchers," *MicroTimes*, April 17, 1989. p. 126.
J. Horswill, "EndNote Plus Ends Bibliographical Headaches," *Computer Buyer's Resource*, February 1991. p. 12.
T. Landau, "EndNote Plus, Bookends Mac, and Publish or Perish," *MacUser*, 7, September 1991. p. 62.
R.E. Mandsager, "Endnotes as Bibliography," (letter) *PC WORLD*, 9, June 1991. p. 38.
F. Tessler, "The Medical Desktop," *MacWorld*, 7, March 1990. p. 138.
S. Vandershaf, "Bibliographic Databases," *MacUser*, 7, February 1990. p. 111.
S. Willhite, "EndNote and EndLink," *Library Workstation Report*, April 1990. p. 12.

Price: $249.

Supplier's comments: Whether you are writing an article for *Science* magazine or a term paper for your history class, you face two formidable tasks: keeping track of your references, and typing them into your bibliography. EndNote is a software package that automates these tasks. First, EndNote is a database manager - specialized in storing, managing, and searching for bibliographic references in your private reference library. Second, EndNote is a bibliography maker - it builds lists of cited works automatically. EndNote will scan your document for in-text citations, and compile a bibliography using the information in your database. Finally, it will produce a copy of your document, reformatting the in-text citations and placing the bibliography at the end. Your select the style to use and EndNote does the rest.

    *A CD-Rom interface is available through Endlink which works with certain databases.

ENDNOTE PLUS

Niles and Associates Inc.
2000 Hearst Street
Berkeley, CA 94709
(510) 649-8176   Fax (510) 649-8179
Contact: Emanuel Rosen

Hardware: IBM PC or compatible; Apple Macintosh

System Requirements: DOS 3.0 or Mac

Programming Language: C

Components & Applications:

acquisitions	no	catalog (batch)	yes
catalog (online)	yes	cataloging	yes
CD-ROM interface	yes*	circulation	no
formatting bibliographies	yes	index of keywords	yes
inter-library loan	no	interface for MARC records	no
media booking	no	reserve room	no
serials	no	thesaurus	no

Updating Modes:

batch update	no	dynamic update	yes

Features:

Boolean logic searchable	yes	full text searchable	no
record fields	no info	record size	no info
statistical & math capabilities	no	wholesale change capability	no

Support:

application consulting	no	maintenance and updates	yes
time share available	no	user training	no

Recommended for:

Corporate & govt libraries	yes	Media center management	no
Public libraries	yes	Records & files management	yes
School libraries	no	University libraries	yes

Installations:

Initial installation date	1987	Total number of installed sites	10,000+
Sampling of current clients:			

Published reviews & articles:
L.E. Becker Jr., "EndNote Plus Speeds Research Tasks," *MacWEEK*, 5, April 16, 1991. p. 78.
E. Brower, "EndLink Grabs On-line Info," *MacWEEK*, 3, March 7, 1989. p. 19.
S.D. Cohen, "EndNote Plus: Reference Formatter and Compiler," *Information Today*, March 1991. p. 35.
S. Guttman, "EndNote: Useful Tool For Researchers," *MicroTimes*, April 17, 1989. p. 126.
J. Horswill, "EndNote Plus Ends Bibliographical Headaches," *Computer Buyer's Resource*, February 1991. p. 12.
T. Landau, "EndNote Plus, Bookends Mac, and Publish or Perish," *MacUser*, 7, September 1991. p. 62.
R.E. Mandsager, "Endnotes as Bibliography," (letter) *PC WORLD*, 9, June 1991. p. 38.
F. Tessler, "The Medical Desktop," *MacWorld*, 7, March 1990. p. 138.
S. Vandershaf, "Bibliographic Databases," *MacUser*, 7, February 1990. p. 111.
S. Willhite, "EndNote and EndLink," *Library Workstation Report*, April 1990. p. 12.

Price: $249.

Supplier's comments: If you need a more powerful database management system for your bibliographies, you might want to consider EndNote Plus. In addition to all of EndNote's features, EndNote Plus has more powerful search capabilities. It supports sorting, searching for duplicate records, and more.

Sorting: In EndNote Plus, you can sort a database on up to five fields, and set each to ascending or descending order. This feature can facilitate the process of building a bibliography sorted by subject. In addition, there is an option to define a sorting order as part of a bibliographic style. So, for example, you can define a style in which articles are sorted by year in descending order, a common requirement in Curriculum Vitae.

*A CD-Rom interface is available through Endlink which works with certain databases.

EQUIPMENT INVENTORY CONTROL

Right On Programs
755-F New York Avenue
Huntington, NY 11743
(516) 424-7777   FAX (516) 424-7207

Hardware: IBM & compatibles

System Requirements: MS-DOS

Programming Language: Turbo Pascal

Components & Applications:

acquisitions	no	catalog (batch)	yes
catalog (online)	yes	cataloging	yes
CD-ROM interface	no	circulation	no
formatting bibliographies	no	index of keywords	no
inter-library loan	no	interface for MARC records	no
media booking	no	reserve room	no
serials	no	thesaurus	no

Updating Modes:

batch update	no	dynamic update	yes

Features:

Boolean logic searchable	no	full text searchable	no
record fields	no info	record size	no info
statistical & math capabilities	yes	wholesale change capability	no

Support:

application consulting	yes	maintenance and updates	yes
time share available	no	user training	no

Recommended for:

Corporate & govt libraries	yes	Media center management	yes
Public libraries	yes	Records & files management	yes
School libraries	yes	University libraries	yes

Installations:

Initial installation date	1991	Total number of installed sites	1100
Sampling of current clients: no info			

Price: $139

Supplier's comments: Enter equipment, analyze, and search by many fields. Keeps up-to-date inventory on all equipment, who has it, condition, price, when bought, etc. Generates several reports. Allows user to list all equipment in single location, list all in same condition, same type, etc.

EQUIPMENT SCHEDULER

Right On Programs
755-F New York Avenue
Huntington, NY 11743
(516) 424-7777   FAX (516) 424-7207

Hardware: IBM & compatibles

System Requirements: MS-DOS

Programming Language: Clipper

Updating Modes:

batch update	no	dynamic update	yes

Features:

Boolean logic searchable	no	full text searchable	no
record fields	n/a	record size	n/a
statistical & math capabilities	no	wholesale change capability	no

Support:

application consulting	yes	maintenance and updates	yes
time share available	no	user training	no

Recommended for:

Corporate & govt libraries	yes	Media center management	yes
Public libraries	yes	Records & files management	yes
School libraries	yes	University libraries	yes

Installations:

Initial installation date	1992	Total number of installed sites	150
Sampling of current clients: no info			

Price: $189

Supplier's comments: Keeps accurate records of all equipment, when, where and by whom it is needed. Helps schedule equipment so speakers are not left without what they need. Print out schedules by the day or by the week. Search and print out by many different subject areas.

FILM BOOKING AND LOAN CONTROL

Right On Programs
755-F New York Avenue
Huntington, NY 11743
(516) 424-7777   FAX (516) 424-7207

Hardware: IBM & compatibles

System Requirements: MS-DOS

Programming Language: Clipper

Components & Applications:

acquisitions	no	catalog (batch)	no
catalog (online)	no	cataloging	no
CD-ROM interface	no	circulation	no
formatting bibliographies	no	index of keywords	no
inter-library loan	no	interface for MARC records	no
media booking	yes	reserve room	no
serials	no	thesaurus	no

Updating Modes:

batch update	no	dynamic update	yes

Features:

Boolean logic searchable	no	full text searchable	no
record fields	no info	record size	no info
statistical & math capabilities	yes	wholesale change capability	no

Support:

application consulting	yes	maintenance and updates	yes
time share available	no	user training	no

Recommended for:

Corporate & govt libraries	yes	Media center management	yes
Public libraries	yes	Records & files management	no
School libraries	yes	University libraries	yes

Installations:

Initial installation date	1990	Total number of installed sites	1700
Sampling of current clients: no info			

Price: $149

Supplier's comments: The description of FILM BOOKING AND LOAN CONTROL sounds simple and it is. Titles (and other information) are entered. Requests and reserves are entered and stored. When a film request is received, the request date is automatically checked against current reserves. If the date is already reserved, a warning flashes and double booking is avoided. As each reserve comes due, the computer types out the required information: Name of borrower, title of film, cost, length of loan, when due back and more. A list may be typed to screen or printer and all that's left is pulling and shipping the films.

FILMPATH

Alpine Data, Inc.
737 So. Townsend Ave.
Montrose, CO 81401
(303) 249-1400
Contact: Jesse Tarshis

Hardware: IBM PC-XT/AT or compatible

System Requirements: 20MB hard disk, MS-DOS, 640K RAM

Programming Language: dbXL/Quicksilver

Components & Applications:

acquisitions	yes	catalog (batch)	yes
catalog (online)	yes	cataloging	yes
CD-ROM interface	no	circulation	yes
formatting bibliographies	no	index of keywords	yes
inter-library loan	no	interface for MARC records	no
media booking	yes	reserve room	yes
serials	no	thesaurus	no

Updating Modes:

batch update	no	dynamic update	yes

Features:

Boolean logic searchable	yes	full text searchable	yes
record fields	fixed	record size 660 bytes - film db; 432 bytes - account db	
statistical & math capabilities	yes	wholesale change capability	yes

Support:

application consulting	yes	maintenance and updates	yes
time share available	no	user training	yes

Recommended for:

Corporate & govt libraries	yes	Media center management	yes
Public libraries	yes	Records & files management	no
School libraries	yes	University libraries	yes

Installations:

Initial installation date	1985	Total number of installed sites	25

Sampling of current clients: District 51 Schools, Grand Junction, CO; Denver Public Library, CO

Published reviews & articles:

Kranch, Doug. "Automated Scheduling Systems: A Comparison." *T-H-E Journal*, September 1989, p. 8.

Price: $695 - $995 Purchase for single entity in-house use
$5,000 plus $500 per site Purchase for entire state/county/school system as multiple site license agreement One contact for support per site

Supplier's comments: FILMPATH is an audio-visual cataloging and scheduling system. It contains databases of films, film producers, patrons, equipment, facilities, and accounts. Film/tapes are scheduled automatically for a specific date or first available date. Catalogs of films may be printed by title or subject. Databases may be sorted, scanned or printed in various report formats.

FINDER: THE RETRIEVAL SOFTWARE

Finder Information Tools, Inc.
1430 W. Peachtree Street NW, Suite 312
Atlanta, GA 30309
(404) 872-3488
Contact: Raymond Brown

Hardware: IBM-PCs and compatibles

System Requirements: minimum 256K memory, hard disk required

Programming Language: Compiled BASIC

Components & Applications:

acquisitions	yes	catalog (batch)	no
catalog (online)	yes	cataloging	yes
CD-ROM interface	no	circulation	not recommended
formatting bibliographies	no	index of keywords	yes
inter-library loan	no	interface for MARC records	no
media booking	no	reserve room	no
serials	not recommended	thesaurus	no

Updating Modes:

batch update	no	dynamic update	yes

Features:

Boolean logic searchable	yes	full text searchable	yes
record fields	50	record size	17,000,000 char free text
statistical & math capabilities	yes	wholesale change capability	in development

Support:

application consulting	yes	maintenance and updates	yes
time share available	no	user training	yes

Recommended for:

Corporate & govt libraries	yes	Media center management	no
Public libraries	no	Records & files management	no
School libraries	no	University libraries	no

Installations:

Initial installation date	1984	Total number of installed sites	no info
Sampling of current clients:	no info		

Published Reviews and Articles:

Price: Software - $1,500; no other costs required
Other applicable software: FINDERlink - $300

Supplier's comments: FINDER is very easy to use and would be appropriate for the development of in-house databases in the corporate environment that can be searched by people other than the librarian. FINDER uses a very stable data structure so it is easy to add and update data, and FINDER will not crash. FINDER can also be adapted to LAN and other multi-user environments that use MS-DOS.

FINDER: The Retrieval Software is an information storage and retrieval system of special interest to libraries and other information collections. FINDER uses inverted indexing to combine sophisticated retrieval with the ability to handle thousands of records.

FINDER is also easy to use, both for the searcher and the database administrator, runs on inexpensive and commonly available microcomputers, and is very reliable.

FINDER comes with its own data-entry and database design sections and allows for flexible output to screen, printer, or disk. You may also load data into FINDER from other electronic files using FINDERlink, available separately.

FINDERLINK

Finder Information Tools, Inc.
1430 W. Peachtree Street NW, Suite 312
Atlanta, GA 30309
(404) 872-3488
Contact: Raymond Brown

Hardware: IBM PCs and compatibles

System Requirements: DOS

Programming Language: no info

Components & Applications:

acquisitions	no	catalog (batch)	no
catalog (online)	no	cataloging	no
CD-ROM interface	no	circulation	no
formatting bibliographies	no	index of keywords	no
inter-library loan	no	interface for MARC records	yes
media booking	no	reserve room	no
serials	no	thesaurus	no

Updating Modes:

batch update	yes	dynamic update	no

Features:

Boolean logic searchable	no	full text searchable	no
record fields	n/a	record size	n/a
statistical & math capabilities	no	wholesale change capability	no

Support:

application consulting	no	maintenance and updates	yes
time share available	no	user training	no

Recommended for:

Corporate & govt libraries	yes	Media center management	no
Public libraries	no	Records & files management	no
School libraries	no	University libraries	no

Installations:

Initial installation date	1984	Total number of installed sites	no info
Sampling of current clients:	no info		

Published Reviews and Articles:

Price: no info

Supplier's Comments:

Editor's note: See Finder

GALAXY®

Gaylord Information Systems
Box 4901
Syracuse, NY 13221
(315) 457-5070 or (800) 962-9580

Hardware: DEC VAX

System Requirements: VMS

Programming Language: Assembler and C

Components & Applications:

acquisitions	yes	catalog (batch)	no
catalog (online)	yes	cataloging	yes
CD-ROM interface	yes	circulation	yes
formatting bibliographies	no	index of keywords	yes
inter-library loan	yes	interface for MARC records	yes
media booking	no	reserve room	yes
serials	yes	thesaurus	no

Updating Modes:

batch update	no	dynamic update	yes

Features:

Boolean logic searchable	yes	full text searchable	no
record fields	MARC	record size	MARC
statistical & math capabilities	no	wholesale change capability	no

Support:

application consulting	yes	maintenance and updates	yes
time share available	yes	user training	yes

Recommended for:

Corporate & govt libraries	yes	Media center management	no
Public libraries	yes	Records & files management	no
School libraries	yes	University libraries	yes

Installations:

Initial installation date	1989	Total number of installed sites	78

Sampling of current clients: Appomattox Regional Library, Hopewell, VA

Price: Quoted on request.
        Free demo disks are available

Supplier's comments: GALAXY's state-of-the-art software includes complete modules for networking, individual access, acquisitions, serials control, cataloging, circulation control, online public access catalog, including authority control and reserve book room capabilities, report generation and electronic mail.

Plus, the Gaylord Guarantee Program combines this new generation of automation design with the complete consulting, conversion service, and comprehensive support programs that you would expect from Gaylord. In short, we guarantee the success of your library's automation program.

GENCAT

Eloquent Systems Inc
25 - 1501 Lonsdale Avenue
North Vancouver, British Columbia   Canada   V7M 2J2
(800) 663-8172
Fax: (604) 980-9537

Hardware: IBM AT, PS/2 (80286) or compatible

System Requirements: MS-DOS & LANs; 640K RAM, one hard disk, one floppy disk

Programming Language: Revelation

Components & Applications:

acquisitions	no	catalog (batch)	yes
catalog (online)	yes	cataloging	yes
CD-ROM interface	no	circulation	no
formatting bibliographies	no	index of keywords	yes
inter-library loan	no	interface for MARC records	yes
media booking	no	reserve room	no
serials	no	thesaurus	no

Updating Modes:

batch update	yes	dynamic update	yes

Features:

Boolean logic searchable	yes	full text searchable	yes
record fields	unlimited	record size	64,000 bytes
statistical & math capabilities	limited	wholesale change capability	limited

Support:

application consulting	yes	maintenance and updates	yes
time share available	no	user training	yes

Recommended for:

Corporate & govt libraries	yes	Media center management	no
Public libraries	yes	Records & files management	yes
School libraries	yes	University libraries	no

Installations:

Initial installation date	1986	Total number of installed sites	100

Sampling of current clients: California Academy of Sciences (CA); Pardee Home Foundation (CA); Hayward Area Historical Society (CA); Washington State Archives (WA); University of Washington School of Medicine (WA); Perkins & Coie (WA); Bekins Northwest (WA); University of Connecticut (CT); Museums Association of Saskatchewan (SK); Law Society of Upper Canada (ON); British Columbia Hydro Legal Services (BC)

Published reviews & articles:

Price: $450 - $9,000
            Free demo disk

Supplier's comments: GENCAT Relational Cataloging Software offers librarians, archivists, and record managers user-defined screens for data entry and research; variable-length fields to prevent truncation; synonyms to prevent incomplete searches by cross-referencing similar names and terms; authority files for user-authorized names and terms to maintain consistent data entry; hierarchical structures for classifying data into any number of levels; security levels to protect information with need-to-know access; custom-built import/export utilities for data exchange.

GENIFER 3.01

Bytel Corporation
1029 Solano Avenue
Albany, CA 94706
800-777-0126 Fax 510-527-6957

Hardware: IBM PC

System Requirements: DOS

Programming Language: need info

Support:

application consulting	no	maintenance and updates	yes
time share available	no	user training	no

Recommended for:

Corporate & govt libraries	yes	Media center management	no
Public libraries	no	Records & files management	yes
School libraries	no	University libraries	yes

Installations:

Initial installation date	1986	Total number of installed sites	25,000

Sampling of current clients:

Published reviews & articles:
 Lovegrove, T. and Michels, F. "Genifer III: Another Generation." *Library Hi Tech News*, June 1987, pp. 28-29.

Price: $395

Supplier's comments: An application generator which permits the user to design database applications using a screen editor and responses to softweare generated queries. The program then writes the source code for the application. Able to create relational database applications. Supports: dBASE, FoxPro, Clipper, Arago, dBXL.

Editor's Note: This is a DBMS software package used to generate relational database applications; therefore, it does not include the usual list of components and applications.

GEORGETOWN UNIVERSITY
LIBRARY INFORMATION SYSTEM (LIS)

Dahlgren Memorial Library
Georgetown University Medical Center
3900 Reservoir Road, N.W.
Washington, D.C. 20007
(202) 687-1176
Contact: Naomi Broering

Hardware: DEC PDP-11 series with at least 512KB of main memory or the DEC VAX series with 1-3 MB under M/SQL-MO operating system. Various micros running under standard MUMPS operating system.

System Requirements: M11+ or M/SQL-MO operating system.

Programming Language: ANSI standard MUMPS (Datatree MUMPS for LISNet)

Components & Applications:

acquisitions	yes	catalog (batch)	yes
catalog (online)	yes	cataloging	yes
CD-ROM interface	yes	circulation	yes
formatting bibliographies	no	index of keywords	yes
inter-library loan	yes	interface for MARC records	yes
media booking	no	reserve room	yes
serials	yes	thesaurus	yes

Updating Modes:

batch update	yes	dynamic update	yes

Features:

Boolean logic searchable	yes	full text searchable	no (planned)
record fields	no limit	record size	no max size
statistical & math capabilities	no	wholesale change capability	yes

Support:

application consulting	yes	maintenance and updates	yes
time share available	no	user training	yes

Recommended for:

Corporate & govt libraries	yes	Media center management	no
Public libraries	no	Records & files management	no
School libraries	no	University libraries	yes

Installations:

Initial installation date	1981	Total number of installed sites	38
Sampling of current clients:	no info		

Price:

LIS Software, Support & Training	$68,750
miniMEDLINE System	$ 9,500
LIS and miniMEDLINE System	$78,280
ALERTS/ Current contents	$ 9,500
Reserves Info	$ 2,500
Document Delivery System	$ 2,500
LIS and all options:	$92,750

Supplier's comments: The Georgetown University™ Library Information System (LIS) is an integrated library information system designed to meet the needs of health science and special libraries. The system is available on the DEC PDP 11 or VAX/VMS series of minicomputers. The thesaurus is on-line MeSH (National Library of Medicine's Medical Subject Headings) and author/series authority file. The basic software includes the Online Catalog, MARC Utilities, Circulation, Serials Control, Acquisitions, and Word Processing. Two optional modules, Reserves Information and the Document Delivery System (DDS), can be added. Two modules which may be acquired in conjunction with LIS or independently are available: The miniMEDLINE SYSTEM™, a subset of the National Library of Medicine's MEDLINE file, and ALERTS™/Current Contents SEARCH SYSTEM, a subset of the Institute for Scientific Information's (ISI) Current Contents database.

GET-A-REF

Dataid
P.O. Box 8865
Madison, WI 53708-8865
(608) 241-9521
Contact: Brian Rust

Hardware: IBM PC, XT, AT, 386/PS and compatibles

System Requirements: no info

Programming Language: no info

Components & Applications:

acquisitions	no	catalog (batch)	yes
catalog (online)	yes	cataloging	yes
CD-ROM interface	no	circulation	no
formatting bibliographies	no	index of keywords	no
inter-library loan	no	interface for MARC records	no
media booking	no	reserve room	no
serials	no	thesaurus	no

Updating Modes:

batch update	no	dynamic update	yes

Features:

Boolean logic searchable	no	full text searchable	yes
record fields	32,000 records	record size	16,000 char.
statistical & math capabilities	no	wholesale change capability	no

Support:

application consulting	yes	maintenance and updates	yes
time share available	no	user training	no

Recommended for:

Corporate & govt libraries	yes	Media center management	no
Public libraries	yes-limited	Records & files management	yes
School libraries	yes	University libraries	yes

Installations:

Initial installation date	1986	Total number of installed sites	500

Sampling of current clients: Researchers, doctors, scientists, graduate students.

Published reviews & articles:
The Scientist, 10/3/89. (Review in reference management article)
Bioscience, 9/89. (Product article)
Science, 4/28/89. ((Product article)
Personal Computing, 8/89. (Product article)
Wilson Library Bulletin, 5/89. (Product article)
Wilson Library Bulletin, 11/89 (Review)
Library Journal, 4/1/89. (Product article)
Library High Tech News, 4/89. (Product article)

Price: $250 and discounts are available for multiple copies;
$100 is the price for graduate students

Supplier's comments: Get-A-Ref is a RAM-resident reference handling software program for PCs and compatibles. It stores, manages, formats, searches, and inserts all kinds of reference data for use in a variety of word processing programs. Stores 32,000 reference files-each with up to 16,000 characters of text. Searches on words or phrases at 100,000 characters per second. Includes conversion utility for database screen dumps.

GOPAC™

Data Trek, Inc.
5838 Edison Place
Carlsbad CA 92008
619-431-8400 or 800-876-5484;   FAX 619-431-8448
Contact: Kimberly Gates

Hardware: 386SX or Compatibles 2MB (4MB recommended), VGA & Windows

System Requirements: MS/DOS; 640K minimum

Programming Language: C

Components & Applications:

acquisitions	no	catalog (batch)	no
catalog (online)	yes	cataloging	no
CD-ROM interface	no	circulation	yes
formatting bibliographies	yes	index of keywords	yes
inter-library loan	no	interface for MARC records	yes
media booking	no	reserve room	no
serials	no	thesaurus	no

Updating Modes:

batch update	yes	dynamic update	yes

Features:

Boolean logic searchable	yes	full text searchable	yes
record fields	user defined	record size	unlimited
statistical & math capabilities	yes	wholesale change capability	no

Support:

application consulting	yes	maintenance and updates	yes
time share available	no	user training	yes

Recommended for:

Corporate & govt libraries	yes	Media center management	no
Public libraries	yes	Records & files management	yes
School libraries	yes	University libraries	yes

Installations:

Initial installation date	1992	Total number of installed sites	new

Sampling of current clients: As a courtesy to our clients, a list is available after serious interest is shown.

Costs: Based on the number of concurrent users

Supplier's comments: GoPAC™ (Graphical Online Public Access Catalog) is the newest addition to Data Trek's line of library automation software products. It provides a Microsoft Windows(tm) graphical interface for the online public access catalog. Searching capabilities include Boolean, keyword, field specific, nested and more at every skill level. It has straight-forward screens, point-and click searching and "Start Over" functions. GoPAC™ supports a variety of patron access options including remote modem and standard multi-user access like that provided by local area networks. GoPAC also handles locally-defined setups, image support, and hypersearch.

GROM HAYES LIBRARY SYSTEM

Hartford State Technical College
401 Flatbush Avenue
Hartford, CT 06106
(203) 527-4111
Contact: Dr. Larry Yother

Hardware: DEC VAX

System Requirements: VAX/VMS/RMS operating system, 3 blocks (1536 bytes) per record plus temporary 0.8 block storage required

Programming Language: VAX BASIC

Components & Applications:

acquisitions	no	catalog (batch)	yes
catalog (online)	yes	cataloging	yes
CD-ROM interface	no	circulation	yes
formatting bibliographies	no	index of keywords	yes
inter-library loan	no	interface for MARC records	no
media booking	no	reserve room	yes
serials	yes	thesaurus	no

Updating Modes:

batch update	no	dynamic update	yes

Features:

Boolean logic searchable	yes	full text searchable	yes
record fields	max 34 fields	record size	1024 bytes
statistical & math capabilities	limited	wholesale change capability	yes

Support:

application consulting	yes	maintenance and updates	yes
time share available	no	user training	yes

Recommended for:

Corporate & govt libraries	yes	Media center management	yes
Public libraries	yes	Records & files management	no
School libraries	yes	University libraries	yes

Installations:

Initial installation date	1985	Total number of installed sites	no info

Sampling of current clients: Kauai Community College, Hawaii; STS Consultants, Illinois; Materials Sciences Corp., Pennsylvania; Galson Technical Services, New York; and others.

Price: no info

Supplier's comments: Systems include cataloging, circulation, reporting, periodicals control, and inventory. Anything in the circulation file may be searched, items may be flagged for reserve, and overdues are generated automatically. Both online searching and card printing are available. Two-key searching is available, a printed copy of a record can be made, the system can search the circulation record to see if a given title has been checked out, and can search any word in any record. Printed backups (book catalogs) may be created. Recent acquisitions may be listed for cataloging elsewhere. A list of titles and accession numbers is maintained. Books, pamphlets, AV software, periodicals, AV equipment, and library equipment may be printed in order of storage for check-off. Periodicals may be checked-in and searched online. An inventory of back issues is maintained.

HOOVER™

SandPoint Corporation
124 Mount Auburn Street
Cambridge, MA 02138
Contact: Ellen P. Slaby, Manager of Marketing Services
(617) 868-444; Fax (617) 868-5562

Hardware: IBM-PC or compatible

System requirement: 386 PC, OS/2 1.3 or higher, 12 MB RAM, 100 MB disk storage

Programming Language: C

Components & Applications:

acquisitions	no	catalog (batch)	yes
catalog (online)	yes	cataloging	no
CD-ROM interface	yes	circulation	no
formatting bibliographies	no	index of keywords	yes
inter-library loan	no	interface for MARC records	no
media booking	no	reserve room	no
serials	no	thesaurus	no

Updating Modes:

batch update	yes	dynamic update	yes

Features:

Boolean logic searchable	yes	full text searchable	yes
record fields	yes	record size	yes
statistical & math capabilities	no	wholesale change capability	yes

Support:

application consulting	yes	maintenance and update	yes
time share available	no	user training	yes

Recommended for:

Corporate & govt libraries	yes	Media center management	yes
Public libraries	no	Records & files management	yes
School libraries	no	University libraries	yes

Initial installation date	5/91	Total number of installed sites	20+

Sampling of current clients: Price Waterhouse, AT&T, Pacific Gas & Electric

Published reviews & articles:
PC Week Magazine, September 9, 1991

Price: available upon request.

Supplier's comments: Providing a single user interface, Hoover is an active information agent that searches, retrieves, and integrates information from multiple external sources. Hoover then automatically organizes that information according to the context of the end user's need or function. Designed for groups of users, Hoover works together with Lotus Notes, the first client/server software that gives people the tools to assemble, organize, distribute, view and share information across a network, regardless of their location.

IMAGECATCHER™

Dialog Information Services, Inc.
3460 Hillview Avenue
Palo Alto, CA 94304
(415) 858-2700

Hardware: MACINTOSH

System Requirements: MAC

Programming Language: no info

Components & Applications:

acquisitions	no	catalog (batch)	no
catalog (online)	no	cataloging	no
CD-ROM interface	no	circulation	no
formatting bibliographies	no	index of keywords	no
inter-library loan	no	interface for MARC records	no
media booking	no	reserve room	no
serials	no	thesaurus	no

Updating Modes:

batch update	no	dynamic update	yes

Features:

Boolean logic searchable	no	full text searchable	no
record fields	n/a	record size	n/a
statistical & math capabilities	yes	wholesale change capability	no

Support:

application consulting	yes	maintenance and updates	yes
time share available	no	user training	yes

Recommended for:

Corporate & govt libraries	yes	Media center management	no
Public libraries	yes	Records & files management	no
School libraries	yes	University libraries	yes

Installations:

Initial installation date	1985	Total number of installed sites	no info
Sampling of current clients:			

Price: $99.00 for software and documentation
$15.00 for evaluation disk

Supplier's comments: IMAGECATCHER™ - Macintosh desk accessory for displaying, printing, and saving images retrieved on DIALOG.

IMPACT™ CD-ROM PUBLIC ACCESS CATALOG SYSTEM

Auto-Graphics, Inc.
3201 Temple Avenue
Pomona CA 91768
(714)595-7204; (800)776-6939; FAX (714)595-3506
Contact: Sales/Marketing Dept.

Hardware: IBM/PC and compatibles

System Requirements: 1 MB RAM, DOS 3.2 or higher, MS-DOS extensions; hard disk for some modules. Hitachi, Amdek, Sony, Philips, or any other CD-ROM drive using MS-DOS extensions

Programming Language: C, Vitamin C

Components & Applications:

acquisitions	no	catalog (batch)	yes
catalog (online)	yes	cataloging	yes
CD-ROM interface	yes	circulation	no
formatting bibliographies	no	index of keywords	yes
inter-library loan	yes	interface for MARC records	yes
media booking	no	reserve room	no
serials	no	thesaurus	no

Updating Modes:

batch update	yes	dynamic update	yes

Features:

Boolean logic searchable	yes	full text searchable	n/a
record fields	MARC	record size	MARC
statistical & math capabilities	no	wholesale change capability	no

Support:

application consulting	yes	maintenance and updates	yes
time share available	n/a	user training	yes

Recommended for:

Corporate & govt libraries	yes	Media center management	yes
Public libraries	yes	Records & files management	no
School libraries	yes	University libraries	yes

Installations:

Initial installation date	1987
Total number of installed sites	4000 workstations in North America

Sampling of current clients: Baltimore County Public Library; Memorial University of Newfoundland; Independent School Library Exchange; Mountain Valley Library System; Connecticut State Library; Dade County (FL) Public Schools; S.E. Florida Library and Information Network.

Published reviews & articles:

Morrow, Blaine. "Optical Product Review: IMPACT Public Access Catalog." *CD-ROM Librarian*, v.4, n.1, Jan. 1989, pp. 22-26.
Lee, Joel M. "IMPACT" in Crawford, Walt. *The Online Catalog Book* (New York: G.K.Hall, 1992). Appears in different form in Crawford, Walt, ed. The Catalog Collection (Distributed by Library and Information Technology Association; 1992).

Supplier's comments: A CD-ROM public access catalog system which operates with the IBM/PC and compatibles. Cost is dependent on size of collection and frequency of update and remastering. Especially well suited to union database applications for multi-branch libraries and multi-library consortia, state and regional networks, etc. The IMPACT CD-ROM based public access catalog system provides sophisticated indexing techniques, simple screen designs, access levels ranging from browsing, to simple searching, to more complex searching. Special features include update capability through the cataloging module, locations handling for multi-branch systems and consortia, profile flexibility, and access to local files such as Information and Referral. The electronic interlibrary loan module is file server based, and features automatic dial-up and store-and-forward functions.

IMPACT SMALL LIBRARY MANAGEMENT SYSTEM (IMPACT/SLIMS™)

Auto-Graphics, Inc.
3201 Temple Avenue
Pomona CA 91768
(714) 595-7204; (800) 776-6939; FAX (714) 595-3506
Contact: Sales/Marketing Dept.

Hardware: IBM PCs and compatibles

System Requirements: 1 MB RAM, DOS 5.0 or higher; hard disk; color monitor; optional bar code scanner.

Programming Language: C, Btrieve

Components & Applications:

acquisitions	no	catalog (batch)	yes
catalog (online)	yes	cataloging	yes
CD-ROM interface	yes	circulation	yes
formatting bibliographies	no	index of keywords	yes
inter-library loan	no	interface for MARC records	yes
media booking	no	reserve room	no
serials	no	thesaurus	no

Updating Modes:

batch update	yes	dynamic update	yes

Features:

Boolean logic searchable	no	full text searchable	n/a
record fields	MARC	record size	MARC
statistical & math capabilities	no	wholesale change capability	no

Support:

application consulting	yes	maintenance and updates	yes
time share available	n/a	user training	yes

Recommended for:

Corporate & govt libraries	yes	Media center management	yes
Public libraries	yes	Records & files management	no
School libraries	yes	University libraries	yes

Installations:

Initial installation date	1987
Total number of installed sites	2500 workstations in North America

Sampling of current clients: Baltimore County Public Library; Memorial University of Newfoundland; Independent School Library Exchange; Mountain Valley Library System; Maine State Library.

Published reviews & articles:
Morrow, Blaine. "Optical Product Review: IMPACT Public Access Catalog." *CD-ROM Librarian*, v.4, no.1, January 1989, pp. 22-26.

Supplier's comments: The IMPACT Small Library Management System is designed for smaller libraries with less than 40,000 volumes. It supports a variety of operations: Online Catalog, Circulation, Catalog Maintenance, Reporting, System Administration.

Each function is performed within a separate software module, but all modules are integrated to form a total system.

The Online Catalog lets users search by browsing or keyword access methods. Copy data and circulation status can be displayed when a record is selected.

The Circulation system automates check-out and check-in, patron records, overdues, fines, and reserves. It accommodates varying policies on patron and item types, loan, renewal, and "grace" periods, fine categories, and more. Bar codes and optional scanners are available.

Original MARC records can be created manually, or imported from diskettes.

In the System Administration module, staff define categories of users and materials for loan terms and fine accumulation, control password access to other modules, and customize patron displays and reports.

INDEX TO PERIODICALS

Ruth Sather and Associates
2120 Moonlight Bay Drive
Altoona, WI 54720
715-835-5020 or 800-289-0132
Contact: Ruth Sather

Hardware: Apple

System Requirements: Apple DOS

Support:

application consulting	no	maintenance and updates	yes
time share available	no	user training	no

Recommended for:

Corporate & govt libraries	no	Media center management	no
Public libraries	no	Records & files management	no
School libraries	yes	University libraries	no

Installations:

Initial installation date	1985	Total number of installed sites	installed internationally
Sampling of current clients:			

Published reviews & articles: *Booklist*, May 1, 1985

Price: $50

Supplier's comments: This comprehensive computer-based program provides individualized, self-paced instruction on how to retrieve information from periodicals. Five lessons cover how to use Readers Guide to Periodical Literature.

Editor's comments: This software provides training in library skills. Therefore, it does not include the usual list of components and applications.

INDEXAID 2

Santa Barbara Software Products, Inc.
1400 Dover Rd.
Santa Barbara CA 93103
(805) 963-4886
Contact: Robert Eisberg

Hardware: IBM-PC and compatible

System Requirements: 2 disk drives, 256K RAM

Programming Language: PASCAL

Components & Applications:

acquisitions	no	catalog (batch)	no
catalog (online)	no	cataloging	no
CD-ROM interface	no	circulation	no
formatting bibliographies	no	index of keywords	yes
inter-library loan	no	interface for MARC records	no
media booking	no	reserve room	no
serials	no	thesaurus	no

Updating Modes:

batch update	no	dynamic update	yes

Features:

Boolean logic searchable	no	full text searchable	yes
record fields	n/a	record size	n/a
statistical & math capabilities	no	wholesale change capability	no

Support:

application consulting	no	maintenance and updates	yes
time share available	no	user training	no

Recommended for:

Corporate & govt libraries	no	Media center management	no
Public libraries	no	Records & files management	yes
School libraries	no	University libraries	no

Installations:

Initial installation date	1986	Total number of installed sites	120

Sampling of current clients: M.I.T.; Burroughs Wellcome; Univ. Pittsburg; Univ. Minnesota; Brown Univ.; Univ. Maryland; Arizona State Univ.; Univ. Michigan; Univ. Indiana; Univ. North Carolina; and many other university presses. Also, Upjohn; Ashton-Tate; Maryland State Archives; Howard Sams & Co.

Published quotes from vendor literature:

"It knows what an index should look like and how to produce it. The authors of this program have done their homework well. IndexAid may be the software utility you've been waiting for." *IEEE Software*, v.4, n.1

"The strongest feature of IndexAid is its ability to handle the myriad (and confusing!) rules of ordering an index correctly. The program is worth it's modest price for this sophisticated sorting function alone." *The Jeffries Report*, v.5, n.1

"Menus, function-key operations, and instant availability of on screen help text assure that novice computer users will not feel intimidated by this package. Performance was flawless." *The Electronic Library*, v.4, n.5

"IndexAid is an inexpensive and more than adequate indexing software package. It is easy to learn. Santa Barbara Software Products has made a significant contribution." *Library Software Review*, v.5, n.4

"Perhaps the major strength of IndexAid is the ability to create exactly the style of index wanted in camera-ready form. The finished product will require little or no further editing. For these purposes, it is the best of several packages this reviewer has seen." *Information Today*, v.4, issue 4

"IndexAid 2 keeps the entire index in memory as you work and consequently runs very quickly. It is particularly good for the occasional indexer since it asks for all the information it needs." *A Guide to Indexing Software*, 2d ed. (American Society of Indexers)

"IndexAid eases your indexing chores. And it produces a professional index that follows the rules of indexing." *PC Magazine* v.6, n.18

INDEXAID 2 continued

Price: $99.95 + $5.00 shipping.   Demo disk: $5.00

Supplier's comments: IndexAid 2 has been developed with input from three senior members of the American Society of Indexers, as well as many other users of the first version. It can produce a fully professional index to a book, instruction manual, report, or similar document — yet is easy for a novice to operate. Some of its properties are:

There can be independence from all other software or, if desired, a list of phrases from almost any word processor can be imported for the editor to convert to index entries.

The editor is optimized for writing index entries and includes many special functions such as automatic production of transposed or "see also" versions of a basic entry.

There is a style checker that can find typing and other mistakes.

The program can handle the single-number pagination of books, the double- or triple-number pagination of manuals and reports, and also independent appendix and insert pagination.

There is automatic separation into name and subject indexes.

The sorter knows all the complicated exceptions to alphabetical order in the rules of indexing, eliminating the burden (and possible errors) of manual sorting. It accommodates the letter-by-letter ordering used in the humanities, including the special ordering of certain history books, as well as the word-by-word ordering used in technical fields.

The formatter completely eliminates the laborious retyping usually needed at the final stage of preparing an index. It allows the run-in style typical of the humanities and three variations of the indented style employed in technical fields.

The formatted index can be printed on paper or written to an ASCII file for a typesetter or word processor. Typesetter codes or word processor control characters can be embedded in the file.

INFOLOGICS/ERS II

Infologics, Inc.
77 North Oak Knoll Avenue
Pasadena, CA 91101-1812
(818) 795-5167
Contact: Lowrie W. McIntosh, President

Hardware: IBM PC, XT, AT, and compatibles; WANG VS; VAX; and IBM Mainframes. Available for all machines using FOCUS.

System Requirements: for PC's, DOS 2.2 (or higher); 640 KB with minimum 5 MB disk storage

Programming Language: PC FOCUS, FOCUS

Components & Applications:

acquisitions	no	catalog (batch)	yes
catalog (online)	yes	cataloging	yes
CD-ROM interface	no	circulation	no
formatting bibliographies	no	index of keywords	yes
inter-library loan	no	interface for MARC records	no
media booking	no	reserve room	no
serials	no	thesaurus	yes

Updating Modes:

batch update	yes	dynamic update	yes

Features:

Boolean logic searchable	yes	full text searchable	yes
record fields	depends on version	record size	depends on version
statistical & math capabilities	yes	wholesale change capability	yes

Support:

application consulting	yes	maintenance and updates	yes
time share available	no	user training	yes

Recommended for:

Corporate & govt libraries	yes	Media center management	no
Public libraries	no	Records & files management	yes
School libraries	no	University libraries	no

Installations:

Initial installation date	1982	Total number of installed sites	24

Sampling of current clients: American Honda; Pennzoil; Merck; International Monetary Fund; Ciba-Geigy; Metromedia; Allianz Insurance; and many others

Price: ERS II PC/FOCUS (single applications) Purchase: starts @ $ 6,500

ERS III includes user available help screens, uses windows, faster response, etc. Purchase starts @ $9,500

PC/FOCUS NETWORK Purchase 1-4 units starts @ $15,995 Lease: $750/month

VAX, WANG VS: Purchase: starts @ $ 18,000 Lease: (depends on version)

IBM MAINFRAME: Purchase: starts @ $ 35,000 Lease: (depends on version)

Supplier's comments: Primary applications installed to manage active (office) and inactive (records centers) records, including data processing documentation libraries, central and distributed library collections, policy and procedures manuals and maintenance, and inventories of various kinds.

Completely menu driven, with 80 screens and menus, ERS II is a powerful software product with all the capabilities characteristic of a state-of-the-art 4th generation language (FOCUS). Exceptional for litigation support and CAR systems applications. Co-mingles all types of inventories through the use of a unique and comprehensive classification system. Contains legal and administrative references for records retention and automatically applies retentions. Functions with FOCUS VISION. Includes an optical disk version with up to 1.6 gigabytes of storage per PC.

INFORMATION NAVIGATOR

IME Systems, Inc.
990 Washington St.
Dedham, MA 02026-6790
617-320-0303
Contact: Jim Hiltz

Hardware: IBM Compatible PC or UNIX

System Requirements: MS-DOS & UNIX

Programming Language: need info

Components & Applications:

acquisitions	yes	catalog (batch)	yes
catalog (online)	yes	cataloging	yes
CD-ROM interface	no	circulation	yes
formatting bibliographies	yes	index of keywords	yes
inter-library loan	yes	interface for MARC records	yes
media booking	no	reserve room	no
serials	yes	thesaurus	yes

Updating Modes:

batch update	no	dynamic update	yes

Features:

Boolean logic searchable	yes	full text searchable	yes
record fields	yes	record size	unlimited
statistical & math capabilities	yes	wholesale change capability	yes

Support:

application consulting	yes	maintenance and updates	yes
time share available	no	user training	yes

Recommended for:

Corporate & govt libraries	yes	Media center management	yes
Public libraries	yes	Records & files management	no
School libraries	no	University libraries	yes

Installations:

Initial installation date	1986	Total number of installed sites	1,500
Sampling of current clients:	no info		

Published reviews & articles: "Automated System Marketplace." *Library Journal*, April 1, 1992.

Price: Information available upon request

Supplier's comments: The INFORMATION NAVIGATOR from IME Systems, Inc., is a comprehensive fully integrated library automation system. Its open-system architecture permits flexible, networked configurations in MS-DOS and UNIX operating environments. Modules for cataloging, public access, circulation, serial and acquisitions feature INTELLIGENT WINDOWS for authority control, order status, checking verification of patron records, etc. The INFORMATION NAVIGATOR can be installed in a PC-Based system and expanded to a larger unix-based system as a library's needs increase.

INLEX

INLEX, Inc.
P.O. Box 1349
Monterey CA 93942
800-553-1202;   FAX (408) 646-0651
Contact: Marketing Dept.

Hardware: HP 3000, all models including the 900 series

System Requirements: Minimum 2 MB of main memory; MPE V or MPE XL

Programming Language: PASCAL and C

Components & Applications:

acquisitions	yes	catalog (batch)	yes
catalog (online)	yes	cataloging	yes
CD-ROM interface	no	circulation	yes
formatting bibliographies	yes	index of keywords	yes
inter-library loan	yes	interface for MARC records	yes
media booking	in development	reserve room	in development
serials	in development	thesaurus	no

Updating Modes:

batch update	yes	dynamic update	yes

Features:

Boolean logic searchable	yes	full text searchable	yes
record fields	no limit	record size	MARC format
statistical & math capabilities	yes	wholesale change capability	in development

Support:

application consulting	yes	maintenance and updates	yes
time share available	no	user training	yes

Recommended for:

Corporate & govt libraries	no	Media center management	no
Public libraries	yes	Records & files management	no
School libraries	yes	University libraries	yes

Installations:

Initial installation date	1984	Total number of installed sites	100+

Sampling of current clients: Adams County School District, CO; Amateur Athletic Foundation, CA; Arcadia Public Library, CA; Ashland Public Library, OH; Bellevue Community College, WA; Bellevue School District, WA; Biola University, CA; Carlsbad City Library, CA; Chabot College Learning Res. Center, CA; Chesapeake Public Library, VA; Clackamas County Library Network, OR; Corona Public Library, CA; Edmonds; WA; Elk Grove Unified School District, CA; El Paso Library System, TX; Fairfax County Public Library, VA;

Published reviews & articles:
Alley, Brian. "INLEX: A Vendor Profile." *Technicalities*, v.7, no. 4, April 1987.
"INLEX on the Move in California - Really!" (column) Michael Rogers. *Library Journal,* June 1, 1990 v115 n10 p48 (1).
Pringle, Howard "INLEX Online Catalog" in *The Online Public Catalog*, Walt Crawford, ed., G. K. Hall 1992.
Waller, Earl and Melvin Pearce. "Performance Issues of Automated Library Systems: Enhancing INLEX—A Case Study." *Library Hi Tech News*, May 1988.

Price: $30,000 to $200,000 depending upon size of installation. Training, installation, and documentation included. Monthly/annual support and update available.

Supplier's comments: Base module enhancements available as options on upcoming releases include: Patron Placed Holds, Fund Accounting.
Other modules currently available: Inventory Control; Community Information & Referral; Journal Citation Databases; Gateway to External Hosts; Portable Circulation; Reporter (Ad Hoc Reports); Authority Control; Retrospective Conversion and Smart Barcode Processing.

INMAGIC PLUS

Inmagic, Inc.
2067 Massachusetts Avenue
Cambridge, MA 02140
(617) 661-8124
Contact: Judy Smith, Marketing & Sales

Hardware: DEC VAX, MicroVAX, IBM PC/XT/AT (and compatible)

System Requirements: VMS; DOS 3.0 or greater. Memory requirements - 512K for the micro version; 64K for the mini version.

Programming Language: C

Components & Applications:

acquisitions	yes	catalog (batch)	yes
catalog (online)	yes	cataloging	yes
CD-ROM interface	no	circulation	yes
formatting bibliographies	no	index of keywords	yes
inter-library loan	yes	interface for MARC records	yes
media booking	possible, not pre-written	reserve room	possible, not pre-written
serials	yes	thesaurus	yes

Updating Modes:

batch update	yes	dynamic update	yes

Features:

Boolean logic searchable	yes	full text searchable	yes
record fields	75 fields; unlimited # of repeating fields	record size	no limit
statistical & math capabilities	yes	wholesale change capability	yes

Support:

application consulting	yes	maintenance and updates	yes
time share available	no	user training	yes

Recommended for:

Corporate & govt libraries	yes	Media center management	yes
Public libraries	yes, special collections	Records & files management	yes
School libraries	yes	University libraries	yes

Installations:

Initial installation date	1980	Total number of installed sites	6000

Sampling of current clients: Air Products & Chemicals; Alberta Energy; American Health Foundation; American Soybean Association; Atlantic Richfield; Best Foods; Biogen Research Corp.; Boys Town Hall of History; Center for Governmental Research; Crown Life Insurance Company; General Foods; Genesco; Hewlett Packard Company; Johns Hopkins University; Lawrence Livermore National Laboratory; Los Angeles Public Library; National Library of Canada; Northern Telecom; Price Waterhouse; Rutan & Tucker; Uniroyal Chemical; U.S. Attorney's Office; University of Vermont; Westinghouse Electric Corporation.

Published reviews & articles:

"Enabling Blind and Visually Impaired Library Users: INMAGIC and Adaptive Technologies," by Leslie Rosen. *Library Hi Tech*, Issue 35, vol. 9, no.3, pp.45-61.

"INMAGIC," by Robert E. Riger. *Automatome*, Vol 10, No. 3/4, Summer/Fall 1991, pp. 11-12.

"Integrated Library Systems in Canadian Public, Academic and Special Libraries," by Bobbie Merilees. *Canadian Library Journal*, June 1991, pp. 171-179.

"Making the Most of INMAGIC Software," by Peggy Ho. *Database*, October 1991, pp. 86-87.

"Moving Information—A Conversion Project Toolbox," by Elizabeth B. Eddison. *Database*, June 1991, pp. 15-22.

"Records Control in Local Government Using INMAGIC and SearchMAGIC Software," by Thomas F. Lee. *Records Management Quarterly*, January 1992, pp. 22-24, 57.

"The Reference Expert: A Computerized Database Utilizing INMAGIC and A WORM Drive," by Nancy J. Butkovich, Marilyn M. Browning and Kathryn L. Taylor. *Database*, December 1991, pp. 35-38.

"The Magic of INMAGIC." *Information Retrieval and Library Automation*, February 1988, v.23, n.9, pp. 1-4.

Jones-Randall, Kate. "Micros at Work: Developing a Microcomputer-Based Index to a Local Newspaper." *Computers in Libraries*, June 1989, pp..20-23.

INMAGIC PLUS continued

Price: INMAGIC Plus Micro - $1400 (includes Library GUIDE, formerly BIBLIO GUIDE)
           VAX/MicroVAX - Starting at $4,000
           Guide - $225 (included with INMAGIC Plus for Libraries)

Supplier's comments: INMAGIC currently has over 12,000 installations in more than 55 countries. Used most widely by libraries and information centers, the software is also popular with law firms, universities, government agencies and other businesses.

INMAGIC is text management software used for online catalogs, serials, loans, acquisitions and more. The software is noted as a flexible and easy to use package. There is no limit on the size of a field, or the number of records in a database. INMAGIC can perform rapid searches for any word or word stem in a given field, and supports Boolean operators (and, or, not) to narrow or broaden a search to meet specific criteria. The software's report generator allows users to create any number of formats for printing search results. Included in *INMAGIC for Libraries* are pre-designed database and report models, helping libraries get started quickly without training.

INMAGIC Plus includes enhancements such as fill-in-the-blank searching, data validation and authority lists, proximity searching, and the ability to manage the full text of documents.

INNOPAC

Innovative Interfaces, Inc.
2344 Sixth Street
Berkeley, CA 94710
(510) 644-3600
Contact: Tom Jacobson, Manager of Sales Services

Hardware: UNIX computers such as Mips, DEC, Convergent, Hewlett-Packard, Sun, and IBM.

System Requirements: Hardware and software are configured for the library depending on the number of terminals required (up to 300) and the number of records to be stored (up to 3,000,000)

Programming Language: C written under the UNIX operating system

Components & Applications:

acquisitions	yes	catalog (batch)	yes
catalog (online)	yes	cataloging	yes
CD-ROM interface	no	circulation	yes
formatting bibliographies	yes	index of keywords	yes
inter-library loan	yes	interface for MARC records	yes
media booking	yes	reserve room	yes
serials	yes	thesaurus	no

Updating Modes:

batch update	yes	dynamic update	yes

Features:

Boolean logic searchable	yes	full text searchable	no
record fields	variable length repeatable fields	record size	10,000 char
statistical & math capabilities	yes	wholesale change capability	yes

Support:

application consulting	yes	maintenance and updates	yes
time share available	no	user training	yes

Recommended for:

Corporate & govt libraries	yes	Media center management	yes
Public libraries	yes	Records & files management	yes
School libraries	yes	University libraries	yes

Installations:

Initial installation date	1981	Total number of installed sites	275

Sampling of current clients: University of California; University of Maine; Columbia Law School; Wellesley College; Federal Reserve Board; Beverly Hills Public Library.

Published reviews and articles:

Cibbarelli, Pamela. "Modern Times: User-Ratings of INNOVACQ & INNOPAC Software." *OASIS: Observations of the American Society for Information Science, Los Angeles Chapter,* 1992.

Price: $50,000 and up

Supplier's comments: The INNOPAC On-Line Public Access Catalog and Circulation system (with Acquisitions and Serials Control) is suitable for both small libraries as well as large libraries with hundreds of terminals and a large database. The INNOPAC will support a database of MARC records in all formats. The database may be created using archive tapes from a bibliographic utility, by downloading records online from a utility, or by keying directly into the system.

The Public Access Catalog is very easy to use. Once the patron has begun a search, the system will always offer a positive response and retain the original search terms. If the search results in a unique match, the entire record is displayed. If the search does not result in a unique match, the patron may browse through citations which are close to the search keyed. To facilitate the identification of the desired record, different elements of the records may be displayed. For example, if the patron has begun a search by author, he or she may display the browse screen records with author, title or call number in a two line display, thereby increasing the probability that the desired item is correctly identified. Keyword searching is also supported.

In addition to the flexible display options, the patron may opt to "see items nearby on shelf." This converts an author or title search into a call number search without having to re-key search arguments. Similarly, "see other" items with the same subjects,

INNOPAC continued

"see" and "see also" subject headings may be used to convert an author or title search into a subject search. The patron can always return to the original search term without starting over.

An authority control module currently supports "see" and "see also" references and the ability to search and replace headings globally.

The Circulation module of the INNOPAC supports both Code 39 and Codabar barcoding schemes. If your library has item records in machine readable form, smart barcodes can be generated and/or existing barcodes can be retained. Barcodes are input via hand held wands or laser scanners. Circulation supports checkout and checkin, overdues, holds, and fines. The system supports a complete Reserve Book Room module. All circulation data is immediately reflected in the Public Catalog.

The INNOPAC is integrated for Acquisitions and Serials Control. Records for new orders are automatically displayed in the public catalog, as is information about recent receipts, claims and binding information for serials holdings as each issue is checked in.

The full function Acquisitions system supports ordering, claiming, receiving, fund accounting, invoicing and management reporting for all types of orders and payments. Complete audit trails are supported for funds. Statistics and performance analysis can be maintained on vendors. The Serials Control module includes all ordering and payment activities in addition to check-in, claiming, routing, label production, and binding of continuation materials.

Links with OCLC, RLIN, and UTLAS are available, as well as interfaces with automated circulation and on-line catalog systems. Interfaces with vendors are also supported on the Acquisitions module. Currently operational are approval plan links with Blackwell North American, Baker & Taylor, Coutts, and Midwest Library Service.

Interfaces with Faxon & EBSCO serials vendors are available which permit the system to accept serials invoice data on tape.

INNOVATION PLUS

Scribe Software, Inc.
4435 N. Saddlebag Trail, Suite 1
Scottsdale, AZ 85251
(800) 443-7890
Contact: Marketing/Sales

Hardware: IBM PC-XT/AT and compatibles

System Requirements: MS-DOS 3.1 or greater, hard disk (approx. 2MB/1,000 items), 256K minimum

Programming Language: Micro Adapt (compiled C-BASIC)

Components & Applications:

acquisitions	yes	catalog (batch)	yes
catalog (online)	yes	cataloging	yes
CD-ROM interface	no	circulation	yes
formatting bibliographies	yes	index of keywords	yes
inter-library loan	yes	interface for MARC records	yes
media booking	no	reserve room	yes
serials	no	thesaurus	no

Updating Modes:

batch update	yes	dynamic update	yes

Features:

Boolean logic searchable	yes	full text searchable	no
record fields	item - 38; patron - 21	record size	item - 680 char; patron - 212 char
statistical & math capabilities	yes	wholesale change	only author authority

Support:

application consulting	yes	maintenance and updates	yes
time share available	no	user training	yes

Recommended for:

Corporate & govt libraries	no	Media center management	yes
Public libraries	yes	Records & files management	no
School libraries	yes	University libraries	no

Installations:

Initial installation date	1984	Total number of installed sites	65
Sampling of current clients:	no info		

Price: Purchase - $3,195 plus $195 per year for phone and modum support and updates.

Supplier's comments: INNOVATION PLUS is a fully integrated library management system designed for school libraries. Acquisition, circulation, on-line catalog, patron access, statistics and inventory. Book and patron information is typed only one time. It is then used throughout - from book acquisition to circulation, from inventory control to usage statistics. Library management, analysis, planning, and development are aided by monitoring reading profiles, school-wide and by grade level, and inventory and collection usage reports. Many upgrades to the 250 plus programs are scheduled for release by the time of this publication.

INQUIRE/TEXT CLIENT SERVER

Infodata Systems, Inc.
5205 Leesburg Pike
Falls Church, VA 22041
(703) 578-3430
Contact: Jim Desper

Hardware: IBM 370; 30xx; 4300; or compatible

System Requirements: MVS, VM. Supports TSO and CICS or CMS.

Programming Language: PL/1 and Assembler

Components & Applications:

acquisitions	yes	catalog (batch)	yes
catalog (online)	yes	cataloging	yes
CD-ROM interface	no	circulation	yes
formatting bibliographies	no	index of keywords	yes
inter-library loan	no	interface for MARC records	no
media booking	no	reserve room	no
serials	yes	thesaurus	yes

Updating Modes:

batch update	yes	dynamic update	yes

Features:

Boolean logic searchable	yes	full text searchable	yes
record fields	1,000	record size	no logical limit
statistical & math capabilities	yes	wholesale change capability	yes

Support:

application consulting	yes	maintenance and updates	yes
time share available	yes	user training	yes

Recommended for:

Corporate & govt libraries	yes	Media center management	no
Public libraries	no	Records & files management	yes
School libraries	no	University libraries	no

Installations:

Initial installation date	1969	Total number of installed sites	300

Sampling of current clients: Shell Oil, National Library of Medicine, Burroughs Wellcome, Mobil, U.S. Air Force, AMOCO, Sandia National Labs.

Price:
INQUIRE/Text ClIENT-SERVER	$194,000
Optional AVOCON Thesaurus	$ 20,000

Supplier's comments: INQUIRE/Text includes online definition and creation of text databases, full-text proximity and fixed-field keyword retrieval and reporting using The Text Searching Facility (TSF) - a CUA standard interface. Advanced applications development is provided by the User Language and Procedural Language Interface. Maintenance is online, full-screen, and indexing is done automatically. Databases can be accessed concurrently by multiple users for maintenance and retrieval.

Under the Field Service Agreement, users are provided new releases of the product and problem-solving support through a "hot-line" service. A full range of subscription and on-site training courses are offered. Consulting services are available. An active user group holds regular regional, national, and international meetings.

INSTANT AUTHORITY VERSION 2.0

Crystal Software (Canada) Inc.
157 Sunpoint Crescent
Waterloo, Ontario Canada N2V 1T9
(519) 746-2754
Contact: Chris W. Bruner

Hardware: IBM compatibles

System Requirements: DOS

Programming Language:

Components & Applications:

acquisitions	no	catalog (batch)	no
catalog (online)	no	cataloging	no
CD-ROM interface	no	circulation	no
formatting bibliographies	no	index of keywords	yes
inter-library loan	no	interface for MARC records	no
media booking	no	reserve room	no
serials	no	thesaurus	yes

Updating Modes:

batch update	yes	dynamic update	yes

Features:

Boolean logic searchable	no	full text searchable	yes
record fields	no info	record size 400 char main entry; 1000 char sub-entries	
statistical & math capabilities	no	wholesale change capability	no

Support:

application consulting	yes	maintenance and updates	no
time share available	no	user training	no

Recommended for:

Corporate & govt libraries	yes	Media center management	yes
Public libraries	yes	Records & files management	yes
School libraries	yes	University libraries	yes

Installations:

Initial installation date	1992	Total number of installed sites	200

Sampling of current clients: Revenue Canada; Defense Dept. of Canada; Roman Catholic Separate School Board; Vancouver Aquarium; New Brunswick Museum; Banff National Park; many law firms.

Published reviews & articles: "We highly recommend this program to anyone who enters repetitive data, such as address lists and controlled language lists." *DATABASE CANADA*, Oct. 1991.

Price: $175

Supplier's comments: A Pop up program (TSR) that can be used to hold lists of terms. This means that you use it with your existing application. Each term can have extra information under it (including See, See Also, Definitions...). The terms are looked up as you type, when you push the ENTER key the complete term is typed out for you. It is useful as a List of Authorities manager, as a thesaurus or dictionary, or as a client tracker.

A big advantage in using Instant Authority is that it allows you to use your list of terms across many different applications (i.e., word processors, databases). It is a good general purpose tool that is especially useful in the library environment. Works with Bibliofiles, Inmagic, DBASE, WordPerfect, Bar-code readers.

INTEGRATED LIBRARY SYSTEMS (ILS)

National Technical Information Service
Office of Data Base Services
5285 Port Royal Rd.
Springfield, VA 22161
(703) 487-4660

Hardware: IBM Series 1; DEC PDP-11/XX; Data General ECLIPSE

System Requirements: UNIX

Programming Language:

Components & Applications:

acquisitions	no	catalog (batch)	yes
catalog (online)	yes	cataloging	yes
CD-ROM interface	no	circulation	yes
formatting bibliographies	no	index of keywords	yes
inter-library loan	no	interface for MARC records	yes
media booking	no	reserve room	no
serials	yes	thesaurus	yes

Updating Modes:

batch update	yes	dynamic update	yes

Features:

Boolean logic searchable	yes	full text searchable	yes
record fields	MARC format	record size	MARC format
statistical & math capabilities	yes	wholesale change capability	yes

Support:

application consulting	yes	maintenance and updates	yes
time share available	yes	user training	yes

Recommended for:

Corporate & govt libraries	yes	Media center management	no
Public libraries	no	Records & files management	yes
School libraries	no	University libraries	yes

Installations:

Initial installation date	1980	Total number of installed sites	no info

Sampling of current clients: Army Library, Pentagon; University of Maryland Health Sciences Library; Naval Research Laboratory Welch Library, Johns Hopkins University; Carnegie Mellon University Library

Price: Purchase - $5,700

Editor's comments: ILS is another software package developed with U.S. government funds; and, therefore, is in the public domain. The software is sold as a mag tape (ASCII, 9 track, 1/2" tape). The index of keywords does provide a frequency display. The thesaurus is not hierarchical but does permit SEE and SEE ALSO references. The option of an OCLC interface is available. Order from NTIS as PB 85243285.

MUMPS version no longer supported.

INTERACTIVE ACCESS SYSTEM ™

Brodart Automation (a division of Brodart Co.)
500 Arch Street
Williamsport, PA 17705
(800) 233-8467 ext. 522
Contact: Tom Sumpter, National Sales Manager

Hardware: IBM or Telex 078 display terminal

System Requirements: Time share environment

Programming Language: COBOL

Components & Applications:

acquisitions	no	catalog (batch)	no
catalog (online)	yes	cataloging	yes
CD-ROM interface	no	circulation	no
formatting bibliographies	no	index of keywords	yes
inter-library loan	yes	interface for MARC records	yes
media booking	no	reserve room	no
serials	no	thesaurus	no

Updating Modes:

batch update	no	dynamic update	yes

Features:

Boolean logic searchable	yes	full text searchable	no
record fields MARC format; variable length		record size MARC format; variable length	
statistical & math capabilities	no	wholesale change capability	yes

Support:

application consulting	yes	maintenance and updates	yes
time share available	no	user training	yes

Recommended for:

Corporate & govt libraries	yes	Media center management	no
Public libraries	yes	Records & files management	no
School libraries	yes	University libraries	yes

Installations:

Initial installation date	1983	Total number of installed sites	40
Sampling of current clients:	no info		

Price: Call for quote

Supplier's comments: The Interactive Access System™ (IAS) is an easy, efficient way to catalog and maintain a bibliographic database. Over 12 million records are available as a cataloging resource database. The cataloging module can interface with the public access and interlibrary loan modules to provide continuous, up-to-date information. Even though IAS operates in a time-share environment, each library's database is maintained as a separate and unique file.

INTERLEND

TKM Software Limited
P.O. Box 1525
Brandon, Manitoba R7A 6N3 Canada
204-727-3873 or 800-565-6272
Contact: Ross Eastley

Hardware: IBM compatibles

System Requirements: DOS, Novell

Programming Language: "C"

Components & Applications:

acquisitions	no	catalog (batch)	no
catalog (online)	no	cataloging	no
CD-ROM interface	no	circulation	no
formatting bibliographies	no	index of keywords	no
inter-library loan	yes	interface for MARC records	no
media booking	no	reserve room	no
serials	no	thesaurus	no

Updating Modes:

batch update	no	dynamic update	yes

Features:

Boolean logic searchable	no	full text searchable	no
record fields	no info	record size	no info
statistical & math capabilities	no	wholesale change capability	no

Support:

application consulting	no	maintenance and updates	yes
time share available	no	user training	no

Recommended for:

Corporate & govt libraries	yes	Media center management	no
Public libraries	yes	Records & files management	no
School libraries	yes	University libraries	yes

Installations:

Initial installation date	1992	Total number of installed sites	new
Sampling of current clients:			

Published reviews & articles:

Price: $500

Supplier's comments: InterLEND is an inter library loan management software program which complies with the internationally approved Inter Library Loan (ILL) Protocol.

An inter library loan protocol has been developed to facilitate resource sharing in a computerized library environment. The protocol defines a standard which permits the exchange of ILL messages between bibliographic institutions that use different computer systems and communication services.

The use of the ILL protocol enables an operator to record in a consistent and structured manner the various stages of an ILL transaction. The protocol does not introduce new processes but merely formalizes activities that were previously handled by manual means.

The fundamental benefit of a protocol-based service is the ability of ILL systems to exchange messages regardless of the design of the ILL software, the configuration of the hardware used to run the system, or the communication services selected to transmit the ILL protocol messages.

Because it standardizes the messages to be exchanged and the format of these messages, the protocol also provides a framework for the development of sophisticated ILL systems which can automatically process both transmitted and received messages. These systems will support improved ILL transaction control and management and provide all the advantages inherent in automating ILL, such as offline preparation and storage of protocol messages and the elimination of such clerical activities as filing, searching, sorting and counting.

INTERLIBRARY LOAN CONTROL

Right On Programs
755-F New York Avenue
Huntington, NY 11743
(516) 424-7777   FAX (516) 424-7207

Hardware: IBM & compatibles

System Requirements: MS-DOS

Programming Language: Turbo Pascal

Components & Applications:

acquisitions	no	catalog (batch)	no
catalog (online)	no	cataloging	no
CD-ROM interface	no	circulation	no
formatting bibliographies	no	index of keywords	no
inter-library loan	yes	interface for MARC records	no
media booking	no	reserve room	no
serials	no	thesaurus	no

Updating Modes:

batch update	no	dynamic update	yes

Features:

Boolean logic searchable	no	full text searchable	no
record fields	no info	record size	no info
statistical & math capabilities	yes	wholesale change capability	no

Support:

application consulting	yes	maintenance and updates	no
time share available	no	user training	no

Recommended for:

Corporate & govt libraries	yes	Media center management	yes
Public libraries	yes	Records & files management	yes
School libraries	yes	University libraries	yes

Installations:

Initial installation date	1990	Total number of installed sites	1200
Sampling of current clients: no info			

Costs: $169

Supplier's comments: INTERLIBRARY LOAN CONTROL is another easy to learn, easy to use program from RIGHT ON PRO-GRAMS. It generates its own forms based on the standard ALA forms so entering data simply means following the on-screen prompts.

INTERLIBRARY LOAN CONTROL also takes the statistics out of your hands and head. It totals number of requests per month and year, number of times per month and year requests are sent to a particular library; stores names, addresses and titles so a wild card may be used to recall the information.

INTERLIBRARY LOAN RECORD KEEPING SYSTEM (ILLRKS)

Arnold Library Systems
1400 Grand Avenue
Laramie, WY 82070
(307) 745-3505
Contact: Mark Arnold

Hardware: no info

System Requirements: no info

Programming Language: no info

Components & Applications:

acquisitions	no	catalog (batch)	no
catalog (online)	no	cataloging	no
CD-ROM interface	no	circulation	no
formatting bibliographies	no	index of keywords	no
inter-library loan	yes	interface for MARC records	no
media booking	no	reserve room	no
serials	no	thesaurus	no

Updating Modes:

batch update	no	dynamic update	yes

Features:

Boolean logic searchable	yes	full text searchable	no
record fields	no info	record size	no info
statistical & math capabilities	yes	wholesale change capability	no

Support:

application consulting	no	maintenance and updates	no
time share available	no	user training	no

Recommended for:

Corporate & govt libraries	yes	Media center management	no
Public libraries	yes	Records & files management	no
School libraries	no	University libraries	yes

Installations:

Initial installation date	1986	Total number of installed sites	30

Sampling of current clients: University of Utah; John Hopkins; California State University, Northridge; Penn State University; Notre Dame; Colorado State University

Published reviews & articles:
OCLC Micro, v.2, n.6, Aug 1986, p.10.

Price: $500 - ILLRKS
$250 - OCLANG

Supplier's comments: The Interlibrary Loan Record Keeping System (ILLRKS) increases productivity for the borrowing side of Interlibrary Loan. ILLRKS can track active requests through receipt, renewal, return and completion with greater ease and accuracy.

There is an optional module for the loaning side of interlibrary loan. With this module, ILLRKS can track photocopy and loan requests you receive from other libraries through all phases of processing.

INTERMEDIATE LIBRARY MEDIA SKILLS

Ruth Sather and Associates
2120 Moonlight Bay Drive
Altoona, WI 54720
715-835-5020 or 800-289-0132
Contact: Ruth Sather

Hardware: Apple II plus, IIe, IIc

System Requirements: Apple DOS

Support:

application consulting	no	maintenance and updates	yes
time share available	no	user training	no

Recommended for:

Corporate & govt libraries	no	Media center management	no
Public libraries	no	Records & files management	no
School libraries	yes	University libraries	no

Installations:

Initial installation date	1986	Total number of installed sites	n/a
Sampling of current clients: n/a			

Published reviews & articles:
Booklist, October 1, 1986.
School Library Media Quarterly, Fall 1986.

Price: $125 per module
           $350 for all modules

Supplier's comments: Intermediate Library Media Skills is a comprehensive computer-based curriculum which provides individualized self-paced learning of the skills needed to use library and media facilties. The program provides highly interactive computer-based lessons comprised of text, graphics, and learning activites, which include effective learning games, tutorials, simulations, and drill and practice.
　　　　It has 24 computer based lessons grouped by topic within units. The units are further grouped into four modules:
　　　　　　　　1 - Discovering Available Resources
　　　　　　　　2 - Organization of Resources
　　　　　　　　3 - Locating Resources
　　　　　　　　4 - Resource and Study Skills

Editor's comments: This is a software package to teach skills in using the library. Therefore, it does not include the usual list of components and applications.

KAWARE2

Knowledge Access International
1685 Marine Way, Suite 1305
Mountain View, CA 94043
415-969-0606 FAX 415-964-2027
Contact: William J. Paisley

Hardware: IBM compatibles

System Requirements: DOS, CD or disk drive, 640K RAM

Programming Language: C, Assembly

Components & Applications:

acquisitions	no	catalog (batch)	yes
catalog (online)	yes	cataloging	yes
CD-ROM interface	yes	circulation	no
formatting bibliographies	no	index of keywords	in development
inter-library loan	no	interface for MARC records	no
media booking	no	reserve room	no
serials	no	thesaurus	no

Updating Modes:

batch update	yes	dynamic update	no

Features:

Boolean logic searchable	yes	full text searchable	yes
record fields	999/record	record size	8K per field
statistical & math capabilities	no	wholesale change capability	no

Support:

application consulting	yes	maintenance and updates	yes
time share available	no	user training	yes

Recommended for:

Corporate & govt libraries	yes	Media center management	no
Public libraries	yes	Records & files management	yes
School libraries	yes	University libraries	yes

Installations:

Initial installation date	1987	Total number of installed sites	400+

Sampling of current clients:

Published reviews & articles:

Han, Isaac and Paul Travis Nicholls. "Evaluation of KAware Disk Publisher and KAware2 Retrieval System." *CD-ROM Professional,* May 1990, p. 45-50.

Hogan, Thomas, *Information Today,* May 1991, p.1.

"KAware Disk Publisher/Full Text and KAware2 Retrieval System" (review). *Online Libraries and Microcomputers,* November, 1989, p. 7-9.

Price: $995 for KAware Disk Publisher/Text
$995 for KAware Disk Publisher/Fielded
$495 for add-on Image Module
KAware2 Retrieval Systems priced by volume. Range is $5 - $30.

Supplier's comments: The KAware Disk Publisher is a powerful indexing software product that makes it easy to create both full-text and fielded library applications. TIF and PCX images can easily be added. The KAware2 Retrieval System makes it easy to access the information. It features pull-down menus, hypertext search, word, phrase, proximity, wildcard, and Boolean searches.

Two new products:

- P.I. Kaware lets you manage downloaded, local, and personal databases—just index and search. Price: $99.

- Publish on Disk! The Knowledge Access Guide to Desktop Disk Publishing. CD-ROM workbook, based on a series of highly successful seminars, is an illustrated 200-page treasury containing tips and examples for using KAware Disk Publisher and KAware2 Retrieval System. Price: $30.

KEYSTONE LIBRARY AUTOMATION SYSTEM (KLAS)

Keystone Systems, Inc.
4513 Creedmoor Rd. Suite 301
Raleigh,NC 27612
(919) 782-1142 or (800) 222-9711
FAX (919) 782-6835
Contact: Kay M. Holloman or Kevin M. Klimczyk

Hardware: compatible with over 300 hardware platforms which use versions of the UNIX or AIX operating system including the IBM RS/6000, HP9000, and NCR 3000.

System Requirements: UNIX or AIX Operating Systems. The amount of memory required by the system is 1 MB for the first user and an additional 1/2 MB for each additional user.

Programming Language: Progress 4th Generation Relational Database Language

Components & Applications:

acquisitions	yes	catalog (batch)	yes
catalog (online)	yes	cataloging	yes
CD-ROM interface	yes	circulation	yes
formatting bibliographies	no	index of keywords	yes
inter-library loan	yes	interface for MARC records	yes
media booking	yes	reserve room	yes
serials	yes	thesaurus	no

Updating Modes:

batch update	yes	dynamic update	yes

Features:

Boolean logic searchable	yes	full text searchable	yes
record fields	variable length	record size	variable length
statistical & math capabilities	yes	wholesale change capability	yes

Support:

application consulting	yes	maintenance and updates	yes
time share available	no	user training	yes

Recommended for:

Corporate & govt libraries	yes	Media center management	yes
Public libraries	yes	Records & files management	yes
School libraries	yes	University libraries	yes

Installations:

Initial installation date	1983	Total number of installed sites	3

Sampling of current clients: Perkins School for the Blind; N.C. Audio-Visual Library

Published reviews & articles:

Price:

Module:	Number of Concurrent Users			
	1 - 2	3 - 8	9 - 16	17 - 32
Holdings Management (Required)	$5,000	$7,500	$10,000	$12,500
Catalogue Management	$5,000	$7,500	$10,000	$12,500
Circulation Control	$5,000	$7,500	$10,000	$12,500
Patron Services	$5,000	$3,750	$10,000	$12,500
Serials Control	$2,500	$3,750	$ 5,000	$ 6,250
Branch/Bookmobile	$2,500	$3,750	$ 5,000	$ 6,250
Public Access/Control	$1,000	$1,500	$ 2,000	$ 2,500
Equipment Service	$2,500	$3,750	$ 5,000	$ 6,250
Materials Booking/Audio-Visual	$5,000	$7,500	$10,000	$12,500
Technical Services	$2,500	$3,750	$ 5,000	$ 6,250
Acquisitions	$2,500	$3,750	$ 5,000	$ 6,250
All Modules	$38,500	$57,750	$77,000	$96,250

KEYSTONE LIBRARY AUTOMATION SYSTEM (KLAS) continued

Recommended 3 weeks training/consultation services: $15,000 plus expenses

Supplier's comments: The Keystone Library Automation System is a computerized data storage and retrieval system designed for maximum flexibility and expandability. It is used by medium and large libraries to manage catalogues, collections, and borrower activity. It uses the powerful relational database manager Progress and operates with the AIX/Unix operating system. The system uses bar-code technology for a quick check-in/check-out procedure, tighter inventory control of materials, and accurate records of borrowers. However, the system can function with or without bar code readers/printers. It is designed and implemented in a modular approach for use by smaller libraries, museums, and repositories which can benefit from the inventory, local authority cataloguing, and circulation control functions. The menu system is customized and grouped by functions for each library and user.

Currently the modules which are available are: Holdings Management, Catalogue Management, Public Access, Patron Services, Circulation, Serial Control, Media Booking/Audio-Visual, Acquisitions, Branch Library/Bookmobile, and Equipment Service. Because of the modular design of this system, a library may choose to install either the full system or only the modules that are required to meet its needs. In either case, KLAS provides a very powerful and flexible solution of a library's needs.

Additional features available in KLAS are:
- Extensive report writing facility
- Adaptable for the physically challenged
- Library defined fields
- Library defined defaults
- Library modifiable menus
- Multi-volume/media tracking capability
- Extensive on-line context sensitive "Help"
- Pull down Menus
- Unlimited "Note Taking"
- Parameter driven with table look-ups
- Extensive Reader Services facility
- "Quick Key Access" to other modules

KWIK-FILE

The Software Connection
7000 E. Belleview Ave. Suite 217
Englewood, CO 80111
(800) 345-1463

Hardware: Wang VS

System Requirements: 256K memory

Programming Language: COBOL 74

Components & Applications:

acquisitions	no	catalog (batch)	no
catalog (online)	yes	cataloging	yes
CD-ROM interface	no	circulation	no
formatting bibliographies	no	index of keywords	yes
inter-library loan	no	interface for MARC records	no
media booking	no	reserve room	no
serials	no	thesaurus	no

Updating Modes:

batch update	yes	dynamic update	yes

Features:

Boolean logic searchable	yes	full text searchable	yes
record fields	n/a	record size	n/a
statistical & math capabilities	no	wholesale change capability	n/a

Support:

application consulting	yes	maintenance and updates	yes
time share available	no	user training	yes

Recommended for:

Corporate & govt libraries	yes	Media center management	no
Public libraries	no	Records & files management	no
School libraries	no	University libraries	no

Installations:

Initial installation date	1984	Total number of installed sites	60
Sampling of current clients:	no info		

Price: $8,000 approximately

Supplier's comments: Kwik-File is document management software which combines full text retrieval and database management technologies to produce an easy-to-use, on-line information retrieval system. The system "files" documents by creating a textual database of the words contained within user-chosen fields of the document summary page, and/or the text within the body of the document, and/or user-created filing categories.

KWIK-SEARCH

The Software Connection
7000 E. Belleview Avenue, Suite 217
Englewood, CO 80111
(800) 345-1463

Hardware: Wang VS

System Requirements: 256KB minimum memory

Programming Language: COBOL 74

Components & Applications:

acquisitions	no	catalog (batch)	no
catalog (online)	no	cataloging	no
CD-ROM interface	no	circulation	no
formatting bibliographies	no	index of keywords	yes
inter-library loan	no	interface for MARC records	no
media booking	no	reserve room	no
serials	no	thesaurus	no

Updating Modes:

batch update	no	dynamic update	no

Features:

Boolean logic searchable	yes	full text searchable	yes
record fields	n/a	record size	n/a
statistical & math capabilities	no	wholesale change capability	no

Support:

application consulting	yes	maintenance and updates	yes
time share available	no	user training	yes

Recommended for:

Corporate & govt libraries	yes	Media center management	no
Public libraries	no	Records & files management	no
School libraries	no	University libraries	no

Installations:

Initial installation date	1983	Total number of installed sites	no info
Sampling of current clients:	no info		

Price:	Purchase price	$3,000
	Annual Maintenance Fee	$ 500

Supplier's comments: Kwik-Search provides a keyword indexing system for Wang Word Processing documents.

LABEL MAKER III

Winnebago Software Company
310 West Main Street
Caledonia, MN 55921
(800) 533-5430; (507) 724-5411
Contact: Telesales

Hardware: Apple

System Requirements: Apple DOS

Programming Language: Apple BASIC and Assembler

Components & Applications:

acquisitions	no	catalog (batch)	no
catalog (online)	no	cataloging	yes
CD-ROM interface	no	circulation	no
formatting bibliographies	no	index of keywords	no
inter-library loan	no	interface for MARC records	no
media booking	no	reserve room	no
serials	no	thesaurus	no

Updating Modes:

batch update	no	dynamic update	yes

Features:

Boolean logic searchable	no	full text searchable	no
record fields	no info	record size	no info
statistical & math capabilities	no	wholesale change capability	no

Support:

application consulting	no	maintenance and updates	no
time share available	no	user training	no

Recommended for:

Corporate & govt libraries	yes	Media center management	yes
Public libraries	yes	Records & files management	yes
School libraries	yes	University libraries	yes

Installations:

Initial installation date	1985	Total number of installed sites	no info
Sampling of current clients: no info			

Costs: $29.95

Supplier's comments: Software written specifically for library labels.

LAMP

Winnebago Software Company
310 West Main Street
Caledonia, MN 55921
(800) 533-5430; (507) 724-5411
Contact: Telesales

Hardware: IBM or compatible hardware

System Requirements: Internal or external hard disk drive, bar wand

Programming Language: Clipper

Components & Applications:

acquisitions	yes	catalog (batch)	no
catalog (online)	no	cataloging	yes
CD-ROM interface	no	circulation	no
formatting bibliographies	no	index of keywords	no
inter-library loan	no	interface for MARC records	yes
media booking	no	reserve room	no
serials	no	thesaurus	no

Updating Modes:

batch update	yes	dynamic update	yes

Features:

Boolean logic searchable	no	full text searchable	no
record fields	MARC	record size	MARC
statistical & math capabilities	yes	wholesale change capability	no

Support:

application consulting	yes	maintenance and updates	yes
time share available	no	user training	yes

Recommended for:

Corporate & govt libraries	yes	Media center management	no
Public libraries	yes	Records & files management	yes
School libraries	yes	University libraries	yes

Installations:

Initial installation date	1991	Total number of installed sites	no info
Sampling of current clients: no info			

Published reviews & articles:

Price: $695

Supplier's comments: Winnebago's Library Acquisitions Management Program (LAMP) leads you out of the dark ages of ordering library materials. One of the most trying of library functions is deciding what materials to order, ordering them, and keeping track of the order as well as the funds that are paying for the materials. Winnebago LAMP makes ordering as easy as one, two, three. First, you make a wish-list of all possible materials to order. Second, you select the materials from that list which you will order. Third, you send in your order. You can print your order for mailing or send your order to the book jobber via a modem. Winnebago LAMP provides you with complete fund accounting and lets you keep track of your order, from it being a pending order, an active order, a closed order, and then a reconciled order.

LASERBRIDGE

WLN
P.O. Box 3888
Lacey, Washington 98503-0888
(206) 459-6518 or (800) DIAL-WLN   FAX (206) 459-6341
Contact: Rushton Brandis

Hardware: WLN PC or IBM compatible

System Requirements: 192K RAM, 2 floppy drives

Programming Language: no info

Components & Applications:

acquisitions	no	catalog (batch)	no
catalog (online)	no	cataloging	yes
CD-ROM interface	yes	circulation	no
formatting bibliographies	no	index of keywords	no
inter-library loan	no	interface for MARC records	yes
media booking	no	reserve room	no
serials	no	thesaurus	no

Updating Modes:

batch update	yes	dynamic update	no

Features:

Boolean logic searchable	no	full text searchable	no
record fields	MARC	record size	MARC
statistical & math capabilities	no	wholesale change capability	no

Support:

application consulting	yes	maintenance and updates	yes
time share available	no	user training	yes

Recommended for:

Corporate & govt libraries	yes	Media center management	no
Public libraries	yes	Records & files management	no
School libraries	yes	University libraries	yes

Installations:

Initial installation date	1988	Total number of installed sites	no info
Sampling of current clients:	no info		

Price: $200

Supplier's comments: WLN's software program LaserBridge allows libraries to convert records downloaded from LaserCat into a form which can be used by many database programs including Lotus 1-2-3, dBase II, dBase III, PC-File III.

LaserBridge will also process MARC records from other sources including records downloaded from the database using WLN's Download Facility.

LaserBridge and a library's downloaded records can be used to create booklists, bibliographies, indexes, local resource files, documents or serials controls, local circulation systems.

LASERCAT

WLN
P.O. Box 3888
Lacey, Washington 98503-0888
(206) 459-6518; (800) DIAL-WLN; FAX (206) 459-6341
Contact: Rushton Brandis

Hardware: IBM PC, XT, AT, PS/2 model 30, 286, 386 or selected compatibles

System Requirements: 640K RAM; 2 floppy drives or 1 hard disk and one floppy; two Hitachi CD-ROM drives or two Sony; DOS
3.1 or higher; Meridian Device Driver software (available from WLN)

Programming Language: no info

Components & Applications:

acquisitions	no	catalog (batch)	yes
catalog (online)	yes	cataloging	yes
CD-ROM interface	yes	circulation	no
formatting bibliographies	yes	index of keywords	yes
inter-library loan	yes	interface for MARC records	yes
media booking	no	reserve room	no
serials	no	thesaurus	yes

Updating Modes:

batch update	yes	dynamic update	yes

Features:

Boolean logic searchable	yes	full text searchable	no
record fields	MARC	record size	MARC
statistical & math capabilities	no	wholesale change capability	no

Support:

application consulting	yes	maintenance and updates	yes
time share available	yes	user training	yes

Recommended for:

Corporate & govt libraries	yes	Media center management	no
Public libraries	yes	Records & files management	no
School libraries	yes	University libraries	yes

Installations:

Initial installation date	1986	Total number of installed sites	no info
Sampling of current clients: no info			

Published reviews & articles:

Beiser, Karl. "Microcomputing: WLN Previews CD-ROM Product." *Wilson Library Bulletin*, Nov. 1986, p. 41.

Burger, Robert H. "Artificial Intelligence and Authority Control." *Library Resources and Technical Services*, v. 28 (1984), p. 337-45.

Coyne, Fumiko H. "Automatic Authorities Maintenance at the Western Library Network." *Technical Services Quarterly 5*, no. 1, 1987, p. 33-47.

Fink, Teri. "LaserCat goes to High School." *Wilson Library Bulletin,* March 1988, p. 55-56, 109.

Funabiki, Ruth P. "Use of the WLN Authority Control System by an ARL Library." *Library Resources and Technical Services*, v. 27, 1983, p. 391-4.

Griffin, David. "WLN Users and Staff: A Two-Pronged Approach to Quality Control." A paper presented before the RTSD CCS Heads of Cataloging Discussion Group, American Library Association, Dallas, June 25, 1989.

Harvey, Suzanne. WLN Extends Its Boundaries with LaserCat. *Trends in Law Library Management and Technolgy*, Dec-Jan 1988-89.

Hoffman, Jake. "Strengthening Small Library Service with WLN's LaserCat CD-ROM." *Optical Publishing and Storage Proceedings* (1987), p.57-75.

Price: $1300

LASERCAT continued

Supplier's comments: LaserCAT is the Western Library Network on CD-ROM. LaserCat includes 3 discs updated each quarter during the year's subscription. Name and Subject cross-references under full authority control are available at no extra charge.

With LaserCat, your library can find records on the disk, attach a tag to a copy of that record on a floppy diskette, and send the diskette to WLN. This process would begin to build your library inventory on the WLN mainframe so you could receive any of several products back from WLN.

      1) a custom LaserCat CD-ROM disk for your organization.

      2) WLN also can produce a LaserCat for you when magnetic computer tapes of your records are sent to us

      3) inclusion of the library's inventory on the next quarterly issue of the CD-ROM.

Powerful searching capabilities: LaserCat features a variety of powerful, easy-to-use searching capabilities: author, title, subject, or standard book numbers by exact, keyword, or browsing search strategies. Searches may be limited by library, groups of libraries, material type, language, publication date, government publications, large print items, and juvenile materials. LaserCat also supports Boolean searching. Limiting LaserCat searches by library or group of libraries allows the CD-ROM database to be used as a local catalog or a union catalog for a particular region or special type of library.

At the Reference Desk: LaserCat is the perfect tool, allowing searches by author, title, or subject using keyword, exact or browse approaches. LaserCat also prints bibliographies. Reference librarians say LaserCat is one of their most valuable reader advisory tools.

Cataloging: LaserCat is ideal for cataloging. The Ultracard Marc program which is included in each subscription allows LaserCat to print catalog cards and a wide variety of spine and pocket labels. Conformity to MARC and AACR2 standards in the LaserCat database means consistent quality data for your library.

Downloading Records: LaserCat comes equipped to download complete bibliographic records to floppy or hard disk in USMARC communications format. The procedure is as simple as pressing a single key.

LASERGUIDE

General Research Corporation, Library Systems
5383 Hollister Avenue
Santa Barbara, CA 93111
(800) 933-5383 or (805) 964-7724
FAX (805) 967-7094
Contact: Darcy Cook

Hardware: IBM PC-XT/AT/PS/2 and CD-ROM drive

System Requirements: PC or MS-DOS, 640K memory

Programming Language: FORTRAN

Components & Applications:

acquisitions	no	catalog (batch)	no
catalog (online)	yes	cataloging	no
CD-ROM interface	yes	circulation	no
formatting bibliographies	no	index of keywords	yes
inter-library loan	yes	interface for MARC records	yes
media booking	no	reserve room	no
serials	yes	thesaurus	yes

Updating Modes:

batch update	yes	dynamic update	no

Features:

Boolean logic searchable	yes	full text searchable	yes
record fields	MARC	record size	variable
statistical & math capabilities	in development	wholesale change capability	yes

Support:

application consulting	yes	maintenance and updates	yes
time share available	no	user training	yes

Recommended for:

Corporate & govt libraries	yes	Media center management	yes
Public libraries	yes	Records & files management	no
School libraries	yes	University libraries	yes

Installations:

Initial installation date	1987	Total number of installed sites	hundreds

Sampling of current clients: (References provided upon request)

Published reviews & articles:
Information Retrieval & Library Automation, v.24, n.5, (October 1988) p. 1-4.

Price: Quoted upon request.

Supplier's comments: LaserGuide is a CD-ROM Patron Access Catalog for libraries. The library's own data is stored on CD-ROM discs. LaserGuide meets all of the usual requirements of searching and accessing cataloging information, using authors, titles, and subjects. Both Keyword and Boolean searching are available. LaserGuide provides simple and attractive screens for search requests, and suggests additional topics to be searched. Subjects and authors are extracted from the results of previous searches. These new items also can be quickly searched. Optionally, cross-references from the Library of Congress files, supplemented with local records, can be added to a LaserGuide catalog to provide even more suggestions for searching. A shelf list browse is also included and floor plans may be incorporated to locate books. LaserGuide can be updated in the library using LaserMerge and the LaserQuest CD-ROM Cataloging system.

LASERQUEST

General Research Corporation, Library Systems
5383 Hollister Avenue
Santa Barbara, CA 93111
(800) 933-5383 or (805) 964-7724
FAX (805) 967-7094
Contact: Darcy Cook

Hardware: IBM PC-XT/AT/PS/2 and CD-ROM

System Requirements: PC or MS-DOS, 512K memory

Programming Language: FORTRAN

Components & Applications:

acquisitions	no	catalog (batch)	no
catalog (online)	yes	cataloging	yes
CD-ROM interface	yes	circulation	no
formatting bibliographies	no	index of keywords	no
inter-library loan	no	interface for MARC records	yes
media booking	no	reserve room	no
serials	yes	thesaurus	no

Updating Modes:

batch update	yes	dynamic update	no

Features:

Boolean logic searchable	no	full text searchable	yes
record fields	MARC	record size	variable
statistical & math capabilities	yes, limited	wholesale change capability	no

Support:

application consulting	yes	maintenance and updates	yes
time share available	no	user training	yes

Recommended for:

Corporate & govt libraries	yes	Media center management	yes
Public libraries	yes	Records & files management	no
School libraries	yes	University libraries	yes

Installations:

Initial installation date	1986	Total number of installed sites	hundreds

Sampling of current clients: (References provided upon request)

Published reviews & articles:
Information Retrieval & Library Automation, v. 24, no. 5 (Oct 1988), p. 1-4.

Price: $4300 first year; $2600 second and subsequent years

Supplier's comments: LaserQuest is the world's largest CD-ROM cataloging workstation for libraries for retrospective conversion and for on-going cataloging. The GRC Resource Database of over 7 million MARC records is recorded on six CD-ROM laser discs. Records for books, serials, computer files, music, visual materials, maps and manuscripts are included. Access is numeric and by title.

Title searches provide full MARC records which can be optionally modified. The record is then saved to diskette. These diskettes then can be: 1) sent to an "on-line" system via an RS232C port; 2) used to produce catalog cards; 3) sent to GRC for creation and maintenance of the library's database; or 4) instantly uploaded to LaserGuide, CD-ROM PAC. Network licenses available.

LE PAC®

Brodart Automation (a division of Brodart Co.)
500 Arch Street
Williamsport, PA 17705
(800) 233-8467 ext. 522
Contact: Tom Sumpter, National Sales Manager

Hardware: MS DOS compatible; 640K available memory; CD-ROM drive

System Requirements: MS-DOS release 3.2 or higher

Programming Language: C

Components & Applications:

acquisitions	no	catalog (batch)	yes
catalog (online)	no	cataloging	no
CD-ROM interface	yes	circulation	no
formatting bibliographies	yes	index of keywords	yes
inter-library loan	yes	interface for MARC records	yes
media booking	no	reserve room	no
serials	no	thesaurus	no

Updating Modes:

batch update	yes	dynamic update	no

Features:

Boolean logic searchable	yes	full text searchable	no
record fields	MARC format; variable length	record size	MARC format; variable length
statistical & math capabilities	no	wholesale change capability	no

Support:

application consulting	yes	maintenance and updates	yes
time share available	no	user training	yes

Recommended for:

Corporate & govt libraries	yes	Media center management	no
Public libraries	yes	Records & files management	no
School libraries	yes	University libraries	yes

Installations:

Initial installation date	1986	Total number of installed sites	4000
Sampling of current clients:	no info		

Published reviews & articles:
Information Retrieval and Library Automation, Sept 1988.
Library Hi Tech, Fall 1987.

Price: Call for quote. Free demo diskette.

Supplier's comments: Le Pac® is a microcomputer/CD-ROM-based public access catalog. Each client library's catalog is recorded on one (or more) compact discs. Searches access the data via author, title, and subject fields. Additional parts of the record may be indexed and used as access points in the ANYWORD field. Further options include the ability to combine catalogs and do interlibrary loan.

LEXICO INFORMATION MANAGEMENT SYSTEM

Project Management, Inc.
6317 Poe Rd.
Bethesda, MD 20817
Contact: Ms. E. E. Neil, President
(301) 469-9001

Hardware: DEC/VAX or 386s

System Requirements: VMS or OS/2

Programming Language: FORTRAN, C++ and C

Components & Applications:

acquisitions	no	catalog (batch)	yes
catalog (online)	yes	cataloging	yes
CD-ROM interface	no	circulation	no
formatting bibliographies	no	index of keywords	yes
inter-library loan	no	interface for MARC records	no
media booking	no	reserve room	no
serials	no	thesaurus	yes

Updating Modes:

batch update	yes	dynamic update	yes

Features:

Boolean logic searchable	n/a	full text searchable	n/a
record fields	unlimited	record size	unlimited
statistical & math capabilities	yes	wholesale change capability	yes

Support:

application consulting	yes	maintenance and updates	yes
time share available	no	user training	yes

Recommended for:

Corporate & govt libraries	yes	Media center management	yes
Public libraries	no	Records & files management	yes
School libraries	no	University libraries	no

Installations:

Initial installation date	1981	Total number of installed sites	no info

Sampling of current clients: U.S. General Accounting Office, Washington, D.C.; U.S. Library of Congress, Washington, D.C.; General Electric Co., Gaithersburg, MD.; Farm Credit Administration, McLean, VA.

Price: Purchase Price - $7,500 to $25,000 depending on specific options and features desired.
Includes installation, training and customization.

Supplier's comments: LEXICO Information Management System is a thesaurus build-and-maintenance system operating in a completely interactive mode. Features include: unlimited record/field length and occurrences of a field; automatic insertion of new entries into correct alphabetic sequence; automatic cross-posting of relationships; full validation of relationships; multi-level password protection of any function; candidate/approved term concept on all outputs. Output can be to CRT, typesetter or line printer in various formats: contents of a record; alphabetic or hierarchical display; micro-thesaurus in alphabetic or hierarchical format; KWIC or KWOC listings. Full ANSI FORTRAN; update/dump/dictionary maintenance tools; programming language interface. A query command language processor and an interactive report writer allow all major information management functions to be performed.

LEXIS PRIVATE DATABASE SERVICES

Mead Data Central
9393 Springboro Pike
P.O. Box 933
Dayton OH 45401
(800) 227-9597 x7897
Contact: Bill Cummins, Branch Manger

Hardware: Terminals provided by LEXIS or customer provided PC's utilizing the LEXIS Session Manager Software

System Requirements: not applicable

Programming Language: Proprietary LEXIS Software

Components & Applications:

acquisitions	no	catalog (batch)	yes
catalog (online)	yes	cataloging	yes
CD-ROM interface	no	circulation	no
formatting bibliographies	no	index of keywords	yes
inter-library loan	no	interface for MARC records	no
media booking	no	reserve room	no
serials	no	thesaurus	no

Updating Modes:

batch update	yes	dynamic update	no

Features:

Boolean logic searchable	yes	full text searchable	yes
record fields	no limit	record size	no limit
statistical & math capabilities	no	wholesale change capability	no

Support:

application consulting	yes	maintenance and updates	yes
time share available	yes	user training	yes

Recommended for:

Corporate & govt libraries	yes	Media center management	yes
Public libraries	yes	Records & files management	yes
School libraries	yes	University libraries	yes

Installations:

Initial installation date	1975	Total number of installed sites	100+
Sampling of current clients:	no info provided		

Published reviews and articles: n/a

Price: n/a

Supplier's comments: A major vendor of online services for the legal profession. The private library service uses the same software and hardware as the LEXIS system to automate internal documents. In addition to legal applications, LEXIS Private Database Services is utilized to catalog library and media collections, corporate meeting minutes, and press releases.

LH ONLINE

Scarecrow Press
52 Liberty Street
Metuchen, NJ 08840
Contact: Al Daub
(908) 548-8600 or (800) 537-7107

Hardware: IBM 286/386

System Requirements: 1 MB memory; 16 MHz or faster

Programming Language: C

Components & Applications:

acquisitions	no	catalog (batch)	yes
catalog (online)	yes	cataloging	yes
CD-ROM interface	no	circulation	no
formatting bibliographies	no	index of keywords	yes
inter-library loan	no	interface for MARC records	yes
media booking	no	reserve room	no
serials	no	thesaurus	no

Updating Modes:

batch update	no	dynamic update	yes

Features:

Boolean logic searchable	yes	full text searchable	no
record fields	78 fields	record size	1.2 MB of disk space/1000 records
statistical & math capabilities	no	wholesale change capability	no

Support:

application consulting	yes	maintenance and updates	yes
time share available	no	user training	no

Recommended for:

Corporate & govt libraries	yes	Media center management	yes
Public libraries	yes	Records & files management	yes
School libraries	no	University libraries	no

Installations:

Initial installation date	1991	Total # of installed sites	19

Sampling of current clients: Ontario Science Centre; U.S. Dept. of Labor; Lauren Rogers Museum of Art (Laurel MS); American Council for the Arts (NY,NY); St. John & West Shore Hospital (Westlake, OH).

Published reviews & articles:

Price:

Single user	$ 600
Network, 1-5 terminals	$ 900
Unlimited terminals	$1200

Supplier's comments: LH Online is a stand-alone catalog for a small library or a special collection in a larger library. It displays cards in AACR2 format and is very user-friendly. Reports may be made and sorted by author, title, publisher or call number. Author and Subject authority reports may be made as well.

THE LIBRARIAN

K-12 MicroMedia Publishing
6 Arrow Road
Ramsey, NJ 07446
(201) 825-8888
Contact: Barbara Goldsmith

Hardware: Apple with 48K RAM memory

System Requirements: Apple DOS

Programming Language: no info

Components & Applications:

acquisitions	no	catalog (batch)	no
catalog (online)	yes	cataloging	yes
CD-ROM interface	no	circulation	no
formatting bibliographies	no	index of keywords	no
inter-library loan	no	interface for MARC records	no
media booking	no	reserve room	no
serials	no	thesaurus	no

Updating Modes:

batch update	no	dynamic update	yes

Features:

Boolean logic searchable	no	full text searchable	yes
record fields	no info	record size	no info
statistical & math capabilities	no	wholesale change capability	no

Support:

application consulting	no	maintenance and updates	no
time share available	no	user training	no

Recommended for:

Corporate & govt libraries	yes	Media center management	yes
Public libraries	no	Records & files management	yes
School libraries	no	University libraries	no

Installations:

Initial installation date	1985	Total number of installed sites	450
Sampling of current clients:	no info		

Price: $49

Supplier's comments: The Librarian economically allows you to store and retrieve bibliographic abstracts of magazine articles, chapters of books, songs, videotape recording, computer programs, recipes, or any other indexable item when an abstract is desirable. Up to 500 items may be stored per disk and you may continue storing on other disks.

When entering items into the data base, you may specify up to 8 retrieval categories and an abstract of up to 252 characters. When searching a disk, you may specify by both categories and key works.

LIBRARIAN'S HELPER

Scarecrow Press
52 Liberty Street
Metuchen, NJ 08840
Contact: Al Daub
(908) 548-8600 or (800) 537-7107

Hardware: IBM PC-XT/AT; Apple with CP/M card

System Requirements: Dual floppy disks or floppy plus hard disk; For PC-DOS or MS-DOS, 256K RAM. For CP/M (including Apple with CP/M card) 64K RAM and two disk drives.

Programming Language: CB86

Components & Applications:

acquisitions	no	catalog (batch)	yes
catalog (online)	no	cataloging	yes
CD-ROM interface	no	circulation	no
formatting bibliographies	no	index of keywords	no
inter-library loan	no	interface for MARC records	no
media booking	no	reserve room	no
serials	no	thesaurus	no

Updating Modes:

batch update	no	dynamic update	yes

Features:

Boolean logic searchable	no	full text searchable	no
record fields	78 fields	record size	3000 bytes
statistical & math capabilities	no	wholesale change capability	no

Support:

application consulting	yes	maintenance and updates	yes
time share available	no	user training	no

Recommended for:

Corporate & govt libraries	yes	Media center management	no
Public libraries	yes	Records & files management	yes
School libraries	yes	University libraries	no

Installations:

Initial installation date	1985	Total number of installed sites	3500

Sampling of current clients: Kelloggs; Motorola; New Mexico State Library; Los Angeles Public Health; Naval Post Graduate School, Monterey; Indiana Univ.; Hawaii Institute of Geophysics; National Academy of Sciences; Fiji School of Medicine; Pontifiero Instituto Biblio, Rome.

Published reviews & articles: (Quotes from vendor's brochure)
"For the small library..., The Librarian's Helper is possibly the best software available at a reasonable price..." Candy Schwartz, *LRTS*
"...Prints a balanced, legible card, complete with proper AACR2 punctuation, without requiring substantial expertise on the part of the user...A good choice..." *Public Libraries*
"This is a superb, professional quality program in which nothing seems to have been left out." Patrick Dewey, *Wilson Library Bulletin*
" An extremely competent piece of work." *Library Journal*
" An easy to use, inexpensive timesaver...produces a professional-looking product." Mary C. Hall, *RTSD Newsletter*
"...Powerful yet easy-to-use..." *Booklist*
"...An excellent package....Highly recommended." *Information Today*

Price:
IBM	$250	
Apple CP/M	$350	
Updates	$ 30	

Free demo disk (IBM version only)

Supplier's comments: The Librarian's Helper is an easy-to-use stand-alone, menu-driven computer program designed to produce catalog cards and labels for spine, book pocket, and circulation cards in conformity to AACR2 standards. Cards and labels may be created for books, maps, documents, audiovisuals, or any other material that needs cataloging. The program assumes no knowledge of computers and minimal knowledge of cataloging. Even part-time volunteers can prepare high-quality cards and labels.

LIBRARY CARD PROGRAMS

Learnco Inc.
Box L
Exeter, NH 03833
800-542-0026
Contact: J.H. Smith

Hardware: Macintosh, IBM

System Requirements: I MB

Programming Language: Structured BASIC

Support:

application consulting	no	maintenance and updates	yes
time share available	no	user training	no

Recommended for:

Corporate & govt libraries	no	Media center management	no
Public libraries	yes	Records & files management	no
School libraries	yes	University libraries	no

Installations:

Initial installation date	Dec 92	Total number of installed sites	new
Sampling of current clients:			

Published reviews & articles:

Price: $19.95

Supplier's comments: This is a series of three Library Card games: Library Card Concentration, Library Card Pyramid, The Great Library Card Sort. They are designed to teach a wide range of alphanumeric skills and to teach students what information is on a library catalog card. Included is an exercise book. All-in-all, this is a terrific value!

Editor's comments: This is a special package for teaching library skills. Therefore, it does not include the usual list of components and applications.

LIBRARY CIRCULATION MANAGER

K-12 MicroMedia Publishing, Inc.
6 Arrow Road
Ramsey, NJ 07446
(201) 825-8888
Contact: Barbara Goldsmith

Hardware: Apple; TRS-80

System Requirements: DOS

Programming Language: no info

Components & Applications:

acquisitions	no	catalog (batch)	no
catalog (online)	no	cataloging	no
CD-ROM interface	no	circulation	yes
formatting bibliographies	no	index of keywords	no
inter-library loan	no	interface for MARC records	no
media booking	no	reserve room	no
serials	no	thesaurus	no

Updating Modes:

batch update	no	dynamic update	yes

Features:

Boolean logic searchable	no	full text searchable	no
record fields	no info	record size	no info
statistical & math capabilities	no	wholesale change capability	no

Support:

application consulting	no	maintenance and updates	no
time share available	no	user training	no

Recommended for:

Corporate & govt libraries	no	Media center management	no
Public libraries	no	Records & files management	no
School libraries	yes	University libraries	no

Installations:

Initial installation date	1985	Total number of installed sites	no info
Sampling of current clients: no info			

Price: $199 software and documentation
          $ 25 demo disk

Supplier's comments: Library Circulation Manager was specifically developed for small school libraries. Up to 2200 students can borrow up to six items each (up to 3600 if you're using 3 1/2" drives). Student names, numbers, addresses, and homeroom numbers remain on file until they graduate and can be easily updated as necessary.

Library Circulation Manager records: items taken out; items renewed; fine due; fine paid.

LIBRARY CIRCULATION SYSTEM II

Winnebago Software Company
310 West Main Street
Caledonia, MN 55921
(800) 533-5430; (507) 724-5411
Contact: Telesales

Hardware: Apple IIe or II+ with 64K

System Requirements: 2 floppy disk drives; bar wand

Programming Language: BASIC

Components & Applications:

acquisitions	no	catalog (batch)	no
catalog (online)	no	cataloging	no
CD-ROM interface	no	circulation	yes
formatting bibliographies	no	index of keywords	no
inter-library loan	no	interface for MARC records	no
media booking	no	reserve room	no
serials	no	thesaurus	no

Updating Modes:

batch update	no	dynamic update	yes

Features:

Boolean logic searchable	no	full text searchable	no
record fields	5 material fields; 4 patron fields	record size	65 characters - mat'ls; 32 characters - patrons
statistical & math capabilities	yes	wholesale change capability	no

Support:

application consulting	yes	maintenance and updates	yes
time share available	no	user training	yes

Recommended for:

Corporate & govt libraries	yes	Media center management	no
Public libraries	yes	Records & files management	no
School libraries	yes	University libraries	no

Installations:

Initial installation date	1984	Total number of installed sites	no info
Sampling of current clients:	no info		

Published reviews & articles:
"Software for Library Management: Selection & Evaluation." *Library Computing* (November 1987), pp. 58-62.
"Microcomputer Circulation Review." *Library Technology Report* (January/February 1986).
"Library Circulation System II Software Review." *CMC News* (Winter 1984), pp. 8-9.

Price: $895.00

Supplier's comments: Library Circulation System II is a full circulation program designed for the multi-media library. The program is a floppy disk program requiring 2 disk drives. Thirty-two different user defined material categories are recognized by the computer, and a different loan period and renewal specification can be entered for each. Five different user-defined material headings and 4 different user-defined patron headings are also recognized by the computer. Circulation is accomplished through the use of bar codes and a bar wand. The system also includes an inventory routine. Handles a collection up to 60,000 materials and 3,500 patrons.

LIBRARY CIRCULATION SYSTEM III

Winnebago Software Company
310 West Main Street
Caledonia, MN 55921
(800) 533-5430; (507) 724-5411
Contact: Telesales

Hardware: Apple IIe or II+ with 64K

System Requirements: 2 floppy disk drives; bar wand

Programming Language: BASIC

Components & Applications:

acquisitions	no	catalog (batch)	no
catalog (online)	no	cataloging	no
CD-ROM interface	no	circulation	yes
formatting bibliographies	no	index of keywords	no
inter-library loan	no	interface for MARC records	no
media booking	no	reserve room	no
serials	no	thesaurus	no

Updating Modes:

batch update	no	dynamic update	yes

Features:

Boolean logic searchable	no	full text searchable	no
record fields	5 material fields; 4 patron fields	record size	65 characters - mat'ls; 32 characters - patrons
statistical & math capabilities	yes	wholesale change capability	no

Support:

application consulting	yes	maintenance and updates	yes
time share available	no	user training	yes

Recommended for:

Corporate & govt libraries	yes	Media center management	no
Public libraries	yes	Records & files management	no
School libraries	yes	University libraries	no

Installations:

Initial installation date	1984	Total number of installed sites	no info
Sampling of current clients:	no info		

Published reviews & articles:
"Software for Library Management: Selection & Evaluation." *Library Computing* (November 1987), pp. 58-62.
"Getting the Most Out of Your Computer Circulation System." *The Book Report* (Sep/Oct 1989), pp. 13-14.
"The Computer, School Libraries, and Staff." *Virginia Librarian* (January/March 1988), pp.4.

Price: $995.00

Supplier's comments: Library Circulation System III is a full circulation program designed for the multi-media library. All data are stored on a Corvus OmniDrive hard disk, thus eliminating all disk manipulation. Thirty-two different user defined material categories are recognized by the computer, and a different loan period and renewal specification can be entered for each. Five different user defined material headings and 4 different user defined patron headings are also recognized by the computer. Circulation is accomplished through the use of bar codes and a bar wand. The system also includes an inventory routine. Handles a collection up to 60,000 items and 5,000 patrons. See also WINNEBAGO CIRC.

LIBRARY PROCESSES SYSTEM

Library Process System
919 W. Canadian St.
Vinita, OK 74301
(918) 256-8598
Contact: Fran Grant

Hardware: IBM PC and compatibles; Apple II family; Radio Shack Model III/IV

System Requirements: 2 disk, 80 column text, printer suitable for cards, IBM - 256K, Apple - 128K, Radio Shack - 64K

Programming Language: GW-BASIC interpreted

Components & Applications:

acquisitions	no	catalog (batch)	yes
catalog (online)	no	cataloging	no
CD-ROM interface	no	circulation	no
formatting bibliographies	no	index of keywords	yes
inter-library loan	no	interface for MARC records	no
media booking	no	reserve room	no
serials	no	thesaurus	no

Updating Modes:

batch update	no	dynamic update	no

Features:

Boolean logic searchable	yes	full text searchable	yes
record fields	12	record size	256K bytes
statistical & math capabilities	no	wholesale change capability	no

Support:

application consulting	no	maintenance and updates	yes
time share available	no	user training	phone support

Recommended for:

Corporate & govt libraries	yes	Media center management	no
Public libraries	yes	Records & files management	no
School libraries	yes	University libraries	no

Installations:

Initial installation date	1981	Total number of installed sites	625
Sampling of current clients: no info			

Price:

Full System (Catalog Card w/labels)	$250.00
Audio Visual	$225.00
Apple (Catalog Cards only)	$200.00

Supplier's comments: Library Processes System CATALOG CARD PROGRAM allows AACR II rules - first level description; prints full or partial sets of catalog cards, book lists, inventory lists, and does subject search and bibliographies. Features include: add or delete entries; sort numerically by call number and/or alphabetically by author; allows Dewey, LC, or local cataloging.

The companion software, SPINE/ POCKET/CARD LABELS PROGRAM makes labels from data already entered and stored in the CATALOG CARD PROGRAM. Requires 6-hole tractor-feed catalog cards. Fully documented. Free updates for 1 year; minimal revision charges.

The AUDIO VISUAL CARD/DIRECTORY PROGRAM permanently stores entries on disk to allow several processes, including printing individual (up to 5) or full sets of catalog cards; AV lists, inventories, subject searches, as well as directories of AV software. Allows Dewey, LC or local cataloging; designates "type" (Kit, FS, etc.); adds and/or deletes entries. Fully documented. Free "generic" labels program included, with examples for use.

THE LIBRARY SYSTEM

Bar Code Applications, Inc
810 Peace Portal Way #113
Blaine, WA 98230
(604) 682-5497; FAX (604) 683-6725
Contact: M.A. Endelman

Hardware: IBM PC with 512K RAM memory

System Requirements: MS-DOS

Programming Language: no info

Components & Applications:

acquisitions	no	catalog (batch)	no
catalog (online)	yes	cataloging	yes
CD-ROM interface	no	circulation	yes
formatting bibliographies	no	index of keywords	no
inter-library loan	no	interface for MARC records	no
media booking	no	reserve room	no
serials	no	thesaurus	no

Updating Modes:

batch update	no	dynamic update	yes

Features:

Boolean logic searchable	no	full text searchable	no
record fields	no info	record size	no info
statistical & math capabilities	no	wholesale change capability	no

Support:

application consulting	no	maintenance and updates	yes
time share available	no	user training	yes

Recommended for:

Corporate & govt libraries	yes	Media center management	no
Public libraries	yes	Records & files management	no
School libraries	yes	University libraries	no

Installations:

Initial installation date	1985	Total number of installed sites	no info
Sampling of current clients: no info			

Price: $2495

Supplier's comments: The Library System features charge/discharge using bar code scanning, quick bibliographic searching by author, title, call number, or subject. Handles multiple loan periods and multiple borrower types.

LIBRARYWORKS™, LIBRARYBROWSER™, and LIBRARYDISC™

CASPR, Inc.
20111 Stevens Creek Blvd., Suite 270
Cupertino, CA 95014
(408) 446-3075 or (800) 852-2777

Hardware: Macintosh Plus (or better)

System Requirements: 2Mb memory for System 6; 4Mb memory for System 7

Programming Language: C

Components & Applications:

acquisitions	yes	catalog (batch)	yes
catalog (online)	yes	cataloging	yes
CD-ROM interface	yes	circulation	yes
formatting bibliographies	yes	index of keywords	yes
inter-library loan	yes	interface for MARC records	yes
media booking	no	reserve room	yes
serials	yes	thesaurus	no

Updating Modes:

batch update	yes	dynamic update	yes

Features:

Boolean logic searchable	yes	full text searchable	yes
record fields	variable	record size	variable
statistical & math capabilities	yes	wholesale change capability	yes

Support:

application consulting	yes	maintenance and updates	yes
time share available	no	user training	yes

Recommended for:

Corporate & govt libraries	yes	Media center management	yes
Public libraries	yes	Records & files management	yes
School libraries	yes	University libraries	yes

Installations:

Initial installation date	1988	Total number of installed sites	600

Sampling of current clients: Apple Computer, Hughes Aircraft, British Petroleum, Northern Telecom, University of Chicago, University of Georgia, Temple Emanu El, Mill Creek School District, Carleton School District, San Jose Unified School District.

Published articles and reviews:
Cibbarelli, Pamela R. "Modern Times: User-Ratings of the Mac Library System Software." *OASIS: Observations of the American Society for Information Science, Los Angeles Chapter*. March 1991, p. 10.
Information Today, August 1992.
Jones, A. James. "Media Technologies: The Macintoshed Library - LibraryWorks - A Review." *Learning & Media*, Winter 1992.
Nelson, Nancy Melin. "Newsline...the Latest in Automation Products, Systems and Services." *Computers in Libraries*, March 1992.
"New Products." *MacWorld*, June 1992.

Price:	LibraryWorks	LibraryBrowser
	$ 1,295 - single station	$195
	$ 4,995 - multi-station site; maximum $25,000/organization (worldwide)	$1,995/$15,000
	$ 70 - demo disk	
	$ 750 - training per day (plus travel expenses)	
	$ 295 - bar code wand (3 other scanners available)	
	$ 25 - manual	

LIBRARYWORKS™, LIBRARYBROWSER™, and LIBRARYDISC™ continued

Supplier's comments: LibraryWorks is a fully integrated library automation system providing a full solution for information management. Functions included are acquisitions, cataloging, circulation and serials control. LibraryBrowser is the companion software for
patron access, which provides powerful searching capabilities through an easy to use interface. These two programs together provide
all the functions and power of much more expensive systems, in a client-server environment that can be configured to suit libraries of
all types, from very small to quite large. Combined with LibraryDisc™ CD-ROM databases connected to the file server, with the
option of connecting on a network to other libraries using LibraryWorks, a user can be given access to a broad range of types and
sources of information through the same user interface provided by LibraryBrowser.

LibraryWorks and LibraryBrowser currently run on Apple Macintosh computers. LibraryBrowser for MS-DOS computers
is scheduled for release in September 1992. LibraryBrowser for the Apple IIe and IIgs is scheduled for release in October 1992.
Retrospective conversion, training, user group support, maintenance and technical support are related services provided by CASPR.

LIBRARYDISC™

LibraryDisc is a new product from CASPR which incorporates the LibraryBrowser user friendly interface to provide a new
dimension of access to libraries and patrons by delivering high-quality published information via CD-ROM discs. CD-ROM
databases become an extension to your library's own collection. Typical database applications include access to serials collections
with published abstracts and indexes to the individual articles, and MARC records to support retrospective conversion.

LibraryDisc is the first CD-ROM collection to be fully integrated with a personal computer based library automation system.
LibraryDisc takes full advantage of the library's existing investment in personal computers and local area network. LibraryDisc
eliminates the need to install dedicated workstations, and support multiple user interfaces. This represents a substantial savings in
both capital expenditures and support costs, and leads to optimal use of the installed hardware. The only additional hardware needed
is an Apple compatible CD-ROM drive.

Installing Library Disc collections in your library allows patrons throughout your organization to expand their information
base without buying new hardware or learning new commands.

Library Disc Titles are:

MARC School Edition™	Machine readable records from Catalog Card Company, with Dewey classification and Sears subject indexing.
ERIC Journals™	The CIJE section of the ERIC database, providing indexing and abstracting of journal articles related to education.
Magazine Article Summaries™	Indexes and abstracts to magazine articles from EBSCO Publishing.

LIBS 100PLUS

CLSI, Inc.
320 Nevada Street
Newtonville, MA 02160
(617) 965-6310
Contact: Richard Porter, Director, Marketing Services

Hardware: Sequent computers; Symmetry model S2000/S250,S2000/S450, S2000/S750; Altos computers #3862000; IBM RS/6000 platforms

System Requirements: UNIX operating system

Programming Language: C

Components & Applications:

acquisitions	yes	catalog (batch)	no
catalog (online)	yes	cataloging	yes
CD-ROM interface	yes	circulation	yes
formatting bibliographies	no	index of keywords	yes
inter-library loan	no	interface for MARC records	yes
media booking	no	reserve room	yes
serials	yes	thesaurus	no

Updating Modes:

batch update	yes	dynamic update	yes

Features:

Boolean logic searchable	yes	full text searchable	yes
record fields	MARC	record size	MARC
statistical & math capabilities	yes	wholesale change capability	yes

Support:

application consulting	yes	maintenance and updates	yes
time share available	no	user training	yes

Recommended for:

Corporate & govt libraries	yes	Media center management	yes
Public libraries	yes	Records & files management	yes
School libraries	yes	University libraries	yes

Installations:

Initial installation date	1991	Total number of installed sites	330+

Sampling of current clients: Over 330 installations with 2,000 individual libraries in the U.S., Canada, Australia, and Western Europe.

Published reviews & articles:

Robinson, Gene, "Technologies to Facilitate Access." *Library Journal*, February 1, 1989.

Shekhel, Alex and Mike O'Brien. "Selecting a Relational Database Management System for Library Automation Systems," *Library Hi Tech*, Consecutive Issue 26, Volume 7, No. 2, 1989.

Shekhel, Alex and Freemen, Eva. "Parallel Processing Creates a Low-Cost Growth Path." *Library Hi Tech*, Consecutive Issue 18; Volume 5, No. 2, Summer 1987.

Price: Prices begin at $50,000

Supplier's comments: CLSI provides Unix-based integrated systems, with modules for the automation of all major library operations including acquisitions, cataloging, circulation control, online public access catalog and serials management. There are also modules for community information and journal citations. Each turnkey system includes software, hardware, training, documentation, customer service and support, and is regularly enhanced because of CLSI's ongoing product development program.

LION

Computer Assisted Library Instruction Co., Inc. (CALICO)
P.O. Box 15916
St.Louis, MO 63114
(314) 863-8028

Hardware: IBM compatible with 640K RAM memory

System Requirements: DOS 3.1 or higher

Programming Language: .EXE files

Components & Applications:

acquisitions	no	catalog (batch)	no
catalog (online)	yes	cataloging	yes
CD-ROM interface	no	circulation	yes
formatting bibliographies	no	index of keywords	yes
inter-library loan	no	interface for MARC records	yes
media booking	no	reserve room	yes
serials	no	thesaurus	yes

Updating Modes:

batch update	yes	dynamic update	yes

Features:

Boolean logic searchable	"and" & "not"	full text searchable	no
record fields	300 bytes each	record size	60,000 bytes
statistical & math capabilities	no	wholesale change capability	yes

Support:

application consulting	yes	maintenance and updates	yes
time share available	no	user training	yes

Recommended for:

Corporate & govt libraries	yes	Media center management	no
Public libraries	yes	Records & files management	yes
School libraries	yes	University libraries	yes

Installations:

Initial installation date	1985	Total number of installed sites	no info
Sampling of current clients:	no info		

Published reviews and articles:

Price: $750 - $1500

Supplier's comments:

LIU-PALMER THESAURUS CONSTRUCTION SYSTEM: PROFESSIONAL EDITION

Liu-Palmer
11666 Gateway Boulevard, Suite 195
Los Angeles, CA 90064
(310) 390-4884; FAX (310) 390-9270

Hardware: IBM PC XT, AT, PS/2 or compatible

System Requirements: 640 KB of RAM and DOS 3.3 or higher, and any size fixed disk

Programming Language: Clipper

Components & Applications:

acquisitions	no	catalog (batch)	no
catalog (online)	no	cataloging	no
CD-ROM interface	no	circulation	no
formatting bibliographies	no	index of keywords	no
inter-library loan	no	interface for MARC records	no
media booking	no	reserve room	no
serials	no	thesaurus	yes

Updating Modes:

batch update	no	dynamic update	yes

Features:

Boolean logic searchable	no	full text searchable	no
record fields	no info	record size	no info
statistical & math capabilities	yes	wholesale change capability	no

Support:

application consulting	yes	maintenance and updates	yes
time share available	no	user training	yes

Recommended for:

Corporate & govt libraries	yes	Media center management	yes
Public libraries	yes	Records & files management	yes
School libraries	yes	University libraries	yes

Installations:

Initial installation date	1991	Total number of installed sites	150

Sampling of current clients: User group information available from producer.

Published reviews & articles:
Bearman, David, The Liu-Palmer Thesaurus Construction System: Professional Edition. *Archives and Museum Informatics* Spring 1991, v.5 n.1.

Price: $450 for software and documentation

Supplier's comments: TCS facilitates the design and building of controlled vocabularies. It does the clerical work of maintaining term relationships and displaying terms in the ways thesaurus developers and users require.

Users of the system may create one or more hierarchies with narrower terms at multiple levels and links among hierarchies and to synonyms and guide terms. Control key combinations permit editing terms, adding synonyms, related terms, guide terms, and new hierarchies. Terms may be deleted and whole sections of terms can be moved with a single keystroke. Polyhierarchical relationships are supported. Extensive search and report capabilities are included. All reports can be sent either to printer or to file for further processing.

LOANET

Library Systems and Services, Inc.
200 Orchard Ridge Drive
Gaithersburg, MD 20878
301-975-9800 or 800-638-8725
Attn: Marketing

Hardware: IBM compatibles; dual floppy drives (or one hard drive & one floppy drive); 640K memory, & CD-ROM drive; Hayes modem or compatible.

System Requirements: DOS version 2.1 or later

Programming Language: Microsoft "C"

Components & Applications:

acquisitions	no	catalog (batch)	yes
catalog (online)	yes	cataloging	no
CD-ROM interface	yes	circulation	no
formatting bibliographies	no	index of keywords	no
inter-library loan	yes	interface for MARC records	yes
media booking	no	reserve room	no
serials	yes	thesaurus	no

Updating Modes:

batch update	yes	dynamic update	no

Features:

Boolean logic searchable	yes	full text searchable	no
record fields	MARC format	record size	MARC format
statistical & math capabilities	yes	wholesale change capability	no

Support:

application consulting	yes	maintenance and updates	yes
time share available	no	user training	yes

Recommended for:

Corporate & govt libraries	yes	Media center management	yes
Public libraries	yes	Records & files management	no
School libraries	yes	University libraries	yes

Installations:

Initial installation date	1986	Total number of installed sites	120+
Sampling of current clients:			

Published reviews & articles:

Price: $200; $100/year annual maintenance fee

Supplier's comments: LOANet is a CD-ROM based Interlibrary Loan System designed to operate easily and inexpensively. LOANet accesses a MARC-based union catalog and supports lookups, input, communication, and maintenance on interlibrary loan requests and responses.

=M=C=D=2 AND =M=C=D=8

FYI, Inc.
130 Woodland Trail
Leander, TX 78641
(512) 259-2839
Contact: Steve James, President

Hardware: IBM PC, AT, 386, PS/2

System Requirements: Hard disk; Hayes (or clone) modem

Programming Language: Proprietary (FORTH-like)

Components & Applications:

acquisitions	no	catalog (batch)	yes
catalog (online)	yes	cataloging	yes
CD-ROM interface	no	circulation	no
formatting bibliographies	no	index of keywords	yes
inter-library loan	no	interface for MARC records	no
media booking	no	reserve room	no
serials	no	thesaurus	no

Updating Modes:

batch update	yes	dynamic update	no

Features:

Boolean logic searchable	yes	full text searchable	yes
record fields	max 8 million entries/db	record size	max 65,000 char/entry
statistical & math capabilities	no	wholesale change capability	no

Support:

application consulting	yes	maintenance and updates	yes
time share available	no	user training	yes

Recommended for:

Corporate & govt libraries	yes	Media center management	no
Public libraries	yes	Records & files management	yes
School libraries	yes	University libraries	yes

Installations:

Initial installation date	1988	Total number of installed sites	20

Sampling of current clients: Advanced Micro Devices; Houston Light & Power Company; Austin Area Legal Record; Central America Resource Center; University of Texas School of Engineering; TVA National Fertilizer Development Center; Buffalo Museum of Science.

Price: =M=C=D=2 $ 595.00
        =M=C=D=8 $ 1,995.00

Supplier's comments: =M=C=D= gives your patrons dial-in access to your library's vast information resources. You can conduct realtime on-line conferences with 9 participants. You and your patrons can send private E-mail messages and stop playing phone tag. You can host long-term conferences and turn them into on-line databases.

=M=C=D= is a multiline BBS with full text indexed data base searching online 2 thru 8 lines (modems or terminals) at up to 9600 baud. 32,000 users possible. Includes Chat, E-mail, Conferences, X-modem file transfers, General File Area, and much more.

To see =M=C=D= in action, please call (512) 794-8511 at 300/1200/2400 baud 8bits, no parity, 1 stop bit.

M/SERIES 10

Utlas International
3300 Bloor St., West
16th Floor, West Tower
Etobicoke, Ontario, Canada M8X 2X2
(416) 236-7171   FAX (416) 236-7489

Hardware: IBM PC and compatibles

System Requirements: MS-DOS

Programming Language: no info

Components & Applications:

acquisitions	no	catalog (batch)	no
catalog (online)	yes	cataloging	no*
CD-ROM interface	no	circulation	yes
formatting bibliographies	no	index of keywords	yes (Title and subject only)
inter-library loan	no	interface for MARC records	no
media booking	no	reserve room	no
serials	no	thesaurus	no

Updating Modes:

batch update	no	dynamic update	yes

Features:

Boolean logic searchable	yes	full text searchable	no
record fields	no info	record size	no info
statistical & math capabilities	yes	wholesale change capability	no

Support:

application consulting	no	maintenance and updates	yes
time share available	no	user training	yes

Recommended for:

Corporate & govt libraries	no	Media center management	no
Public libraries	no	Records & files management	no
School libraries	yes	University libraries	no

Installations:

Initial installation date	1985	Total number of installed sites	over 750
Sampling of current clients: no info			

Published articles and reviews: "Test Report, M/Series 10" *Library Technology Reports*, May-June 1991, p.347-352

Price: Single library
                   OPAC $415
                   CIRC $335
         License to School Boards for multiple installations:
                   OPAC $3725
                   CIRC $3000
         Record transfer $ .14 per record and $3.35 - $7.00 per diskette
         Annual software maintenance
                   OPAC $100
                   CIRC $100
Demo package $50 including manual

M/SERIES 10 continued

Supplier's comments: M/Series 10 is a microcomputer-based local library system designed specifically for school libraries. The product consists of two modules:

- OPAC which carries full functionality of an online catalogue including searching by author, subject and title, as well as Boolean and keyword searching. A major feature of the OPAC is the presence of cross-references with automatic display of "see" and "see also" references and automatic directing to the entries under the referred term without rekeying the search. The OPAC module also generates statistics of patron usage.

- CIRC which has strong functionality including check-out, check-in, holds, notice-generation, patron file maintenance, item file maintenance, statistics-generation, support of bar codes and bar code wanding, as well as an interface with school registration records for the generation of a patron file. In addition, the CIRC module has an inventory utility.

For customers purchasing M/Series 10, the OPAC module is mandatory while the CIRC module is optional.

Cataloguing for the M/Series 20 is carried out in the Utlas online cataloguing system, CATSS. CATSS provides a MARC database of some 55 million records and offers full interactive authority control. Cataloguing completed in CATSS may be downloaded to M/Series 10 via the bibliographic and authority record transfer on diskettes.

*Cataloging is done on the Utlas online cataloging facility, CATSS. Records are downloaded to M/Series 10 via diskette.

MAC THE LIBRARIAN

Richmond Software Corporation
500 Aston Hall Way
Alpharetta, GA 30202
(800) 222-6063
Contact: Bob Stevens

Hardware: Apple

System Requirements: IIe, IIgs

Programming Language: Assembly

Components & Applications:

acquisitions	yes	catalog (batch)	yes
catalog (online)	yes	cataloging	yes
CD-ROM interface	no	circulation	yes
formatting bibliographies	no	index of keywords	yes
inter-library loan	no	interface for MARC records	no
media booking	no	reserve room	no
serials	yes	thesaurus	no

Updating Modes:

batch update	no	dynamic update	yes

Features:

Boolean logic searchable	no	full text searchable	no
record fields	no info	record size	no info
statistical & math capabilities	yes	wholesale change capability	yes

Support:

application consulting	no	maintenance and updates	yes
time share available	no	user training	no

Recommended for:

Corporate & govt libraries	no	Media center management	no
Public libraries	no	Records & files management	no
School libraries	yes	University libraries	no

Installations:

Initial installation date	1991	Total number of installed sites	n/a
Sampling of current clients: no info			

Price: $2495   Public access
$ 250   Circulation
$ 250   Acquisitions
$ 250   Serials
$ 250   Card Printing

Published articles and reviews:

Supplier's comments:

MACCARDS™

CASPR, Inc.
20111 Stevens Creek Blvd., Suite 270
Cupertino, CA 95014
(408) 446-3075 or (800) 852-2777

Hardware: Macintosh.

System Requirements: 1 Mb memory; ImageWriter 2

Programming Language: C

Components & Applications:

acquisitions	no	catalog (batch)	yes
catalog (online)	no	cataloging	yes
CD-ROM interface	no	circulation	no
formatting bibliographies	no	index of keywords	no
inter-library loan	no	interface for MARC records	no
media booking	no	reserve room	no
serials	no	thesaurus	no

Updating Modes:

batch update	no	dynamic update	yes

Features:

Boolean logic searchable	no	full text searchable	no
record fields	variable length	record size	512 max
statistical & math capabilities	no	wholesale change capability	no

Support:

application consulting	no	maintenance and updates	yes
time share available	no	user training	no

Recommended for:

Corporate & govt libraries	yes	Media center management	no
Public libraries	no	Records & files management	yes
School libraries	yes	University libraries	no

Installations:

Initial installation date	1986	Total number of installed sites	1,200
Sampling of current clients:			

Published articles and reviews:

Price: $269.00

Supplier's comments: Library card and label production system for the Apple Macintosh computer.

MAGAZINE ARTICLE FILER

Right On Programs
755-F New York Avenue
Huntington, NY 11743
(516) 424-7777 FAX (516) 424-7207

Hardware: IBM & compatibles; Apple Series

System Requirements: MS-DOS

Programming Language: no info

Components & Applications:

acquisitions	no	catalog (batch)	no
catalog (online)	yes	cataloging	yes
CD-ROM interface	no	circulation	no
formatting bibliographies	no	index of keywords	yes
inter-library loan	no	interface for MARC records	no
media booking	no	reserve room	no
serials	no	thesaurus	no

Updating Modes:

batch update	no	dynamic update	yes

Features:

Boolean logic searchable	no	full text searchable	no
record fields	no info	record size	no info
statistical & math capabilities	yes	wholesale change capability	no

Support:

application consulting	yes	maintenance and updates	yes
time share available	no	user training	no

Recommended for:

Corporate & govt libraries	yes	Media center management	yes
Public libraries	yes	Records & files management	yes
School libraries	yes	University libraries	yes

Installations:

Initial installation date	1991	Total number of installed sites	1250
Sampling of current clients:	no info		

Price: $129

Supplier's comments: Allows you ten subject headings (plus six other searchable fields) so the patron may search for materials in ten places and so has a much better chance to find what is needed.

The librarian or cataloger assigns the next consecutive reference number to the next piece of materials, names two appropriate subject headings and places the material right into the program. As you get them, number them and place them directly in back of the last piece inserted.

Then, all the patron has to do is type in the desired subject heading, copy the appropriate titles and numbers and quickly pick them out of the file. Information may be called to the screen or to the printer.

MANAGER SERIES

Data Trek, Inc.
5838 Edison Place
Carlsbad, CA 92008
(619) 431-8400 or 1-800-876-5484
FAX #619-431-8448
Contact: Kimberly Gates

Hardware: Apple; IBM PC, XT, AT & IBM Compatibles; DEC VAX/VMS

System Requirements: MS/DOS 640K minimum; Novell for networks

Programming Language: dBASE III and C

Components & Applications:

acquisitions	yes	catalog (batch)	yes
catalog (online)	yes	cataloging	yes
CD-ROM interface	no	circulation	yes
formatting bibliographies	no	index of keywords	yes
inter-library loan	no	interface for MARC records	yes
media booking	no	reserve room	no
serials	yes	thesaurus	no

Updating Modes:

batch update	no	dynamic update	yes

Features:

Boolean logic searchable	yes	full text searchable	yes
record fields	predefined	record size	unlimited
statistical & math capabilities	yes	wholesale change capability	yes

Support:

application consulting	yes	maintenance and updates	yes
time share available	no	user training	yes

Recommended for:

Corporate & govt libraries	yes	Media center management	no
Public libraries	yes	Records & files management	no
School libraries	yes	University libraries	yes

Installations:

Initial installation date	1982	Total number of installed sites	1900

Sampling of current clients: As a courtesy to our clients, a list is available after serious interest is shown.

Price: Discounts available for multiple purchases as well as for school and government installations.

Supplier's comments: Manager Series is a user-friendly, microcomputer-based automation software package which encompasses modules for Cataloging, Acquisitions, Circulation, Serials,.Databridge, OPAC and Report Generator. The Cataloging module features a flexible database management system which generates new book lists, shelf lists, catalog cards and reports by author, title and subject headings.The Acquisitions Module provides an accounting system for the fund accounts, invoice tracking and processing and collection maintenance.The Circulation Module supervises the library's book transactions by providing check-in, check-out, overdue and hold notice printing, and patron usage reports. The Serials Module is a complete system for journal and serials control— including check-in, claiming and tracking, subscription history, budget and revenue reporting. It also interfaces with major subscription services. The Databridge Module is designed to import bibliographic data stored in MARC sources to the other Manager series Modules. It also exports the data into the standard MARC format used world-wide by libraries. The OPAC (Online Public Access Catalog) Module is a powerful searching tool which searches for any term or combination of terms in any desired field. The Report Generator Module is designed for greater control over the information contained in the Cataloging, Circulation, Serials and Acquisitions standard reports. Full-screen editing enables the user to remove, re-position and add fields and thereby customize reports as needed. It also has multi-user benefits allowing for networking capabilities.

MANDARIN

Media Flex, Inc.
P.O. Box 1107
Champlain, NY 12919
(518) 298-2970   FAX (514) 336-8217

Hardware: IBM PC with 640K RAM memory, Hard Disk

System Requirements: DOS, or LAN software

Programming Language: Microsoft "C"

Components & Applications:

acquisitions	no	catalog (batch)	yes
catalog (online)	yes	cataloging	yes
CD-ROM interface	in development	circulation	yes
formatting bibliographies	yes	index of keywords	yes
inter-library loan	yes	interface for MARC records	yes
media booking	yes	reserve room	no
serials	no	thesaurus	yes

Updating Modes:

batch update	yes	dynamic update	yes

Features:

Boolean logic searchable	yes	full text searchable	yes
record fields	any field	record size	unlimited
statistical & math capabilities	yes	wholesale change capability	yes

Support:

application consulting	yes	maintenance and updates	yes
time share available	no	user training	yes

Recommended for:

Corporate & govt libraries	yes	Media center management	yes
Public libraries	yes	Records & files management	yes
School libraries	yes	University libraries	yes

Installations:

Initial installation date	1985	Total number of installed sites	621

Sampling of current clients: Nassau County School Library System, NY; Gwinnett County Public Schools, Lawrenceville, GA; University of Hawaii - Tourism Industry Library, Honolulu, HI; Whyte Museum & Archives of the Canadian Rockies, Banff, Alberta; Canadian International Development Agency, Ottawa, Canada (Field sites: ex. Costa Rica); GO (Government of Ontario) Transit (Regional Transit Authority), Toronto, Canada; Victor Public Library, Victor, NY

Price: $2500 to $5000

Supplier's Comments: The Mandarin system was introduced in 1987 as one of the first truly integrated, microcomputer-based library management systems. Mandarin programmers departed from previous system design strategies and focused on developing a powerful, but flexible catalog as the heart of the modular system. This approach enabled the evolution of an integrated system in which modules such as public access catalog, data entry, circulation, statistics, inventory and report generator could take advantage of data stored in a centralized data base.

The developers have used MICROSOFT "C" programming language to ensure system portability as well as text storage and manipulation capabilities.

Modules includes: catalog, catalog maintenance, report generation, circulation, networks.

MARCIVE

Marcive Inc.
P.O. Box 47508
San Antonio TX 78265-7508

Hardware: n/a

System Requirements: n/a

Programming Language: n/a

Components & Applications:

acquisitions	no	catalog (batch)	yes
catalog (online)	no	cataloging	yes
CD-ROM interface	no	circulation	no
formatting bibliographies	no	index of keywords	no
inter-library loan	no	interface for MARC records	yes
media booking	no	reserve room	no
serials	no	thesaurus	no

Updating Modes:

batch update	yes	dynamic update	no

Features:

Boolean logic searchable	no	full text searchable	no
record fields	MARC	record size	MARC
statistical & math capabilities	no	wholesale change capability	no

Support:

application consulting	yes	maintenance and updates	yes
time share available	yes	user training	yes

Recommended for:

Corporate & govt libraries	yes	Media center management	no
Public libraries	yes	Records & files management	no
School libraries	yes	University libraries	yes

Installations:

Initial installation date	1975	Total number of installed sites	no info
Sampling of current clients: no info			

Price: time share service

Supplier's comments: A fully automatic cataloging service by which a library can create catalog cards and labels; generate book and COM catalogs; and perform retrospective conversions.

MATSS

Midwest Library Service
11443 St. Charles Rock Road
Bridgeton, MO 63044
(800) 325-8833
Contact: Corey R. Hudson, Director of Library Systems

Hardware: IBM, 80286, Compaq, or true compatible microcomputer.
SINGLE: 640Kb min RAM (IMB expanded RAM preferred);
MULTI: (File Server) 3.5-4.5 MB

System Requirements: SINGLE: DOS 3.0 or higher.
MULTI: Novel 2.0 or higher, Ethernet, Token Ring, or ARCNET

Programming Language: n/a

Components & Applications:

acquisitions	yes	catalog (batch)	no
catalog (online)	no	cataloging	no
CD-ROM interface	yes	circulation	no
formatting bibliographies	no	index of keywords	yes
inter-library loan	no	interface for MARC records	yes
media booking	no	reserve room	no
serials	no	thesaurus	no

Updating Modes:

batch update	yes	dynamic update	yes

Features:

Boolean logic searchable	no	full text searchable	no
record fields	yes	record size	variable
statistical & math capabilities	yes	wholesale change capability	no

Support:

application consulting	no	maintenance and updates	yes
time share available	no	user training	yes

Recommended for:

Corporate & govt libraries	yes	Media center management	no
Public libraries	yes	Records & files management	no
School libraries	yes	University libraries	yes

Installations:

Initial installation date	1986	Total number of installed sites	80

Sampling of current clients: Arapahoe Library District (CO); Barton College (NC); Delaware College (DE); Dickinson College (PA); New Mexico Inst. of Tech (NM); Oregon State Library (OR); St. Louis University (MO); Whittier College (CA); Idaho State University (ID); University of Massachusetts at Dartmouth (MA); Western Connecticut University (CT); Monsanto Corporation (MO).

Published reviews & articles:
Library Software Review, Meckler Corporation, 1988.

Price: Single: $6995   Multi: $10,495

Supplier's comments: MATSS is a PC-based software package designed to automate various technical services, including vendor and fund accounting, ordering, acquisitions, claims/cancellations, and receiving. MATSS offers multi-terminal capabilities that will run on a local area network as well as single-terminal capabilities. Supervisory functions are on a separate menu from the production menu. Online help text is provided throughout the system along with 2 user manuals.

MATSS programs include: 1) Vendor file containing information such as name, address, telephone numbers, ordering format, and claim/cancellation policy. Vendor reports and labels included in this program. 2) Fund Accounting creates, maintains, reports, and automatically expends/encumbers funds during ordering, cancelling, and receiving processes. 3) Ordering includes the creation of orders and their placement in the database. MATSS can create BISAC files for electronic order transmission. Utilizing its Communication Interface, MATSS will use MARC records from bibliographic utilities and modify them for the production of orders.

MEDIA MANAGER™

VIS Consultants, Inc.
2000 Century Plaza, Suite 400
Columbia, MD 21044
(800) 847-2243 or (410) 997-1116
Contact: Philip E. Sticha

Hardware: Hewlett-Packard 3000 family (Micro-3000 through HP 9XX series)

System Requirements: Depending upon collection size, 81MB - 304MB disc and 1-6 ports plus LaserJet printer

Programming Language: Compiled BASIC (HP/3000)

Components & Applications:

acquisitions	partial	catalog (batch)	yes
catalog (online)	yes	cataloging	yes
CD-ROM interface	no	circulation	yes
formatting bibliographies	no	index of keywords	yes
inter-library loan	no	interface for MARC records	yes
media booking	yes	reserve room	no
serials	another product	thesaurus	yes

Updating Modes:

batch update	yes, w/consulting	dynamic update	yes

Features:

Boolean logic searchable	yes	full text searchable	yes
record fields	variable	record size	variable
statistical & math capabilities	yes	wholesale change capability	yes

Support:

application consulting	yes	maintenance and updates	yes
time share available	yes	user training	yes

Recommended for:

Corporate & govt libraries	yes	Media center management	yes
Public libraries	yes	Records & files management	no
School libraries	yes	University libraries	yes

Installations:

Initial installation date	1976	Total number of installed sites	39

Sampling of current clients: Prince George's County Public Schools (MD); King County Library System (WA); Region 10 ESC (TX); Mid-Hudson Regional Library System (NY); Irving Independent School District (TX); Enoch Pratt Free Library (MD).

Published reviews & articles:

Miller, Michael D. "NYSCAT, New York's Automated Union Catalog of Film and Video." *SIGHTLINES*, Spring 1984, p. 25.

Price: Starts at $3,995.
A package including scheduling, online catalog, catalog production plus hardware - $24,500.
System maintenance - $2,500 - 5,500/year depending upon modules covered and level of service chosen.

Supplier's comments: Media Manager™ is an automated booking and catalog system consisting of a group of integrated modules. The two main modules are: a complete materials management system and an on-line catalog system with true Boolean searching capabilities. Although either of these systems may be used independently, they are much more powerful when used together. Designed for a multi-user, multi-tasking environment, Media Manager™ and its add-on modules offer outstanding functionality and flexibility. For example: 1. Scheduling and distribution modules offer extensive configuration capabilities to respond to the unique requirements of individual media centers while maintaining program uniformity for all users; 2. Remote access capabilities allow media center patrons to perform on-line catalog searches and/or interactive booking while the system maintains appropriate security controls; 3. Catalog production software produces superior camera-ready laser typesetting of the entire media collection or any part of the collection.

MEDIANET

MediaNet, Inc.
P.O. Box 449
Astoria, OR 97103
(503) 325-4800
FAX (503)325-3648
Contact: Dave Roberts

Hardware: IBM AS/400

System Requirements: OS/400 Version 2 Release 1.0

Programming Language: Cobol

Components & Applications:

acquisitions	yes	catalog (batch)	yes
catalog (online)	yes	cataloging	yes
CD-ROM interface	no	circulation	yes
formatting bibliographies	no	index of keywords	no
inter-library loan	yes	interface for MARC records	yes
media booking	yes	reserve room	no
serials	no	thesaurus	no

Updating Modes:

batch update	yes	dynamic update	yes

Features:

Boolean logic searchable	yes	full text searchable	yes
record fields	163	record size	5430
statistical & math capabilities	yes	wholesale change capability	yes

Support:

application consulting	yes	maintenance and updates	yes
time share available	no	user training	yes

Recommended for:

Corporate & govt libraries	yes	Media center management	yes
Public libraries	yes	Records & files management	no
School libraries	yes	University libraries	no

Installations:

Initial installation date	1976	Total number of installed sites	11

Sampling of current clients: City of Kelso, WA, Public Library; Hillsboro, OR, Elementary School District

Published reviews & articles:

Price: Call for pricing

Supplier's comments:

MEDIATRACK

Dalton Computer Services, Inc.
P.O. Box 2469
Dalton, GA 30722
(706) 259-3327
Contact: David Merritt

Hardware: IBM PC or compatibles

System Requirements: MS-DOS or PC-DOS

Programming Language: "Z" from Zortec, Inc., Nashville, TN

Components & Applications:

acquisitions	no	catalog (batch)	no
catalog (online)	yes	cataloging	no
CD-ROM interface	yes	circulation	yes
formatting bibliographies	no	index of keywords	yes
inter-library loan	no	interface for MARC records	yes
media booking	yes	reserve room	no
serials	no	thesaurus	no

Updating Modes:

batch update	no	dynamic update	yes

Features:

Boolean logic searchable	optional	full text searchable	yes, with Boolean
record fields	no info	record size	no info
statistical & math capabilities	yes, circ stats	wholesale change capability	no

Support:

application consulting	no	maintenance and updates	yes
time share available	no	user training	yes

Recommended for:

Corporate & govt libraries	no	Media center management	yes
Public libraries	no	Records & files management	no
School libraries	yes	University libraries	yes

Installations:

Initial installation date	1982	Total number of installed sites	250

Sampling of current clients: M.I.M.S.C., Sarasota, FL; Richardson I.S.D. Materials Center, Richardson, TX; Evans High School, Evans, GA; Lakeview High School, Garland, TX; Whitfield County School Board, Dalton, GA; Seminole County Schools, Sanford, FL; Henry County High School, McDonough, GA.

Price: Software is $1700 to $3286 depending on options.

Supplier's comments: MediaTrack was designed for rapid access of data and to automate some of the more tedious functions of library management.

MediaTrack has circulation using bar codes, overdue reports, physical inventory, fund usage statistics, and extensive item information.

MediaTrack permits rapid catalog searches by author, title, subject, or call number.

MICRO-VTLS

VTLS, Inc.
1800 Kraft Drive
Blacksburg, VA 24060
(703) 231-3605
Contact: Deveron Milne

Hardware: MULTIPLE USER SYSTEM: DOS or MS-DOS compatible 386 or 486 with at least 2 Mb memory, floppy drive, hard drive large enough to accommodate records for file server, LAN software, networking boards for each microcomputer, hubs, cables & connectors.

SINGLE USER SYSTEM: DOS or MS-DOS compatible 286, 386, or 486 with at least 640K memory.

To calculate the hard disk storage required for the system, allow at least one megabyte for each 1,000 titles (MARC bibliographic records).

Programming Language: Compiled dBASEIII Plus

Components & Applications:

acquisitions	yes	catalog (batch)	yes
catalog (online)	yes	cataloging	yes
CD-ROM interface	yes	circulation	yes
formatting bibliographies	no	index of keywords	yes
inter-library loan	no	interface for MARC records	yes
media booking	yes	reserve room	no
serials	release date Jan 93	thesaurus	no

Updating Modes:

batch update	yes	dynamic update	yes

Features:

Boolean logic searchable	yes	full text searchable	yes
record fields	variable length records	record size	any length
statistical & math capabilities	yes	wholesale change capability	no

Support:

application consulting	yes	maintenance and updates	yes
time share available	no	user training	yes

Recommended for:

Corporate & govt libraries	yes	Media center management	no
Public libraries	yes	Records & files management	no
School libraries	yes	University libraries	yes

Installations:

Initial installation date	1986	Total number of installed sites	75
Sampling of current clients:	Proprietary information.		

Price:

License	$ 4,975
Maintenance	$ 1,145
Training (on-site)	$ 2,000
Total	$ 8,120

VTLS provides a two-day training course at the VTLS headquarters as a part of the Maintenance Contract. Two-day on-site training is an available option.

Supplier's comments: With the redesign of the Micro-VTLS product, VTLS Inc. can now offer small to medium size libraries a complete library automation solution at a reasonable price. Micro-VTLS integrates OPAC, cataloging/data management reporting and system management. Micro-VTLS features that are essential to providing a friendly and free environment for both patrons and library staff include: full integration, special search features, multimedia record support, display language options, effortless user-ID management, online help, online documentation, MARC and Non-MARC support and multiple character set support. Micro-VTLS is designed to be user installed. It comes with a self-training guide and with remote dial-in support and service package. For an additional fee, VTLS Inc. provides on-site installation and training to customers. A demonstration version is available.

MICROCAT

TKM Software Limited
P.O. Box 1525
839-18th Street
Brandon, Manitoba CANADA R7A 6N3
(204) 727-3872 or 800-565-6272
Contact: Ross Eastley

Hardware: IBM PC or compatible

System Requirements: Xenix; MS-DOS; Novell

Programming Language: "C"

Components & Applications:

acquisitions	in development	catalog (batch)	yes
catalog (online)	yes	cataloging	yes
CD-ROM interface	yes	circulation	yes
formatting bibliographies	yes	index of keywords	yes
inter-library loan	see INTERLEND	interface for MARC records	yes
media booking	no	reserve room	no
serials	no	thesaurus	no

Updating Modes:

batch update	yes	dynamic update	yes

Features:

Boolean logic searchable	yes	full text searchable	with EDICS
record fields	MARC	record size	32K
statistical & math capabilities	no	wholesale change capability	yes

Support:

application consulting	yes	maintenance and updates	yes
time share available	no	user training	yes

Recommended for:

Corporate & govt libraries	yes	Media center management	no
Public libraries	yes	Records & files management	no
School libraries	yes	University libraries	yes

Installations:

Initial installation date	1984	Total number of installed sites	no info

Sampling of current clients: Athol Murray College of Notre Dame; British Columbians for the Handicapped; Hopkins High School; Manitoba Association of School Trustees; Saskatchewan Dept. of Education; Seven Oaks School Division; Swift Current School Division; Winnipeg Bible College.

Price: $399 - single user version
$849 - multi user version
$ 59 - teaching version

Supplier's comments: MicroCAT is a version of BuCAT which operates on an IBM PC or compatible microcomputer. MicroCAT is available as a single-user system running under MS-DOS or as a multi-user system running under Xenix.

Editor's note: MicroCAT also available in the U.S. from the Highsmith Company

MILS (MICRO-INTEGRATED LIBRARY SYSTEM)

Loma Linda University Medical Center
PO Box 2000
Loma Linda, CA 92354
714-824-0800
Contact: Paul Kittle

Hardware: IBM PC

System Requirements: DOS, 128K RAM

Programming Language: Clipper

Components & Applications:

acquisitions	yes	catalog (batch)	no
catalog (online)	yes	cataloging	yes
CD-ROM interface	no	circulation	yes
formatting bibliographies	no	index of keywords	no
inter-library loan	yes	interface for MARC records	no
media booking	yes	reserve room	no
serials	yes	thesaurus	no

Updating Modes:

batch update	no	dynamic update	yes

Features:

Boolean logic searchable	no	full text searchable	no
record fields	no info	record size	no info
statistical & math capabilities	no	wholesale change capability	no

Support:

application consulting	no	maintenance and updates	yes
time share available	no	user training	no

Recommended for:

Corporate & govt libraries	no	Media center management	no
Public libraries	no	Records & files management	no
School libraries	no	University libraries	no
Medical libraries	yes		

Installations:

Initial installation date	1987	Total number of installed sites	50

Sampling of current clients: no info

Published reviews & articles:
Way, S. "An Integrated System for a Microcomputer" *Database*, 11(2), April 1988, p. 117-122.

Price: $395

Supplier's comments:

MINISIS

International Development Research Centre
P.O. Box 8500
Ottawa, ON K1G 3H9 CANADA
(613) 236-6163; FAX (613) 238-7230
Contact: Richard Palmer

Hardware: Any standard Hewlett-Packard 3000 configuration

System Requirements: minimum configuration

Programming Language: SPL

Components & Applications:

acquisitions	yes	catalog (batch)	yes
catalog (online)	yes	cataloging	yes
CD-ROM interface	no	circulation	yes
formatting bibliographies	yes	index of keywords	yes
inter-library loan	no	interface for MARC records	yes
media booking	no	reserve room	no
serials	yes	thesaurus	yes

Updating Modes:

batch update	yes	dynamic update	yes

Features:

Boolean logic searchable	yes	full text searchable	yes
record fields	up to 256 unique fields, repeatable 800 times		
record size	65,536 characters max		
statistical & math capabilities	limited	wholesale change capability	yes

Support:

application consulting	yes	maintenance and updates	yes
time share available	no	user training	yes

Recommended for:

Corporate & govt libraries	yes	Media center management	no
Public libraries	yes	Records & files management	yes
School libraries	yes	University libraries	yes

Installations:

Initial installation date	1978	Total number of installed sites	350+

Sampling of current clients: In the United States-Connecticut Historical Society, Cranbrook Educational Community, United Nations, Historic Orleans Collection, International Monetary Fund, National Conference of State Legislatures, US Navy, Recording for the Blind, the Asian Art Museum of San Francisco, The Brooklyn Museum, The J. Paul Getty Museum, United States Agency for International Development, United States Army, Wadsworth Atheneum, Westreco Inc., and the World Bank. In other countries - The National Library of Canada, The National Library of Malaysia, The Agricultural University of the Netherlands, and the French Senate. There are installations in over 60 countries world-wide.

Costs: Software $12,500-56,500; Maintenance $1,920-5,440; Total $14,420-60,940.

Supplier's comments: MINISIS is a generalized system which can be tailored, without programming, to fit a wide range of applications. Its primary orientation has been the management of text intensive collections. The system can handle multiple character sets, even within a single field. Character sets in use include: Roman-based languages such as English, French, and Spanish, and character based languages such as Chinese and Thai. Documentation is included in the cost of the software and is updated regularly. MINISIS has a simple menu driven approach to data entry and searching.

MITINET/MARC

Information Transform, Inc.
502 Leonard St.
Madison WI 53711
(608) 255-4800 or 800-TAG-MARC
FAX: (608) 255-4800
Contact: Hank Epstein

Hardware: Apple IIe, IIc, IIGS; IBM-PC, XT, AT, PS/2; Macintosh

System Requirements: PCs 256K RAM with 2 floppy drives or 1 floppy drive & a hard disk and MS DOS 3.1 or higher; Apple II -
128K RAM with 2 floppy drives or 1 floppy drive & a hard disk;
Macintosh - 1MB, system 6.02 or higher, with 2 floppy drives or 1 floppy drive & a hard disk

Programming Language: C

Components & Applications:

acquisitions	no	catalog (batch)	no
catalog (online)	no	cataloging	yes
CD-ROM interface	no	circulation	no
formatting bibliographies	no	index of keywords	no
inter-library loan	no	interface for MARC records	yes
media booking	no	reserve room	no
serials	no	thesaurus	no

Updating Modes:

batch update	no	dynamic update	yes

Features:

Boolean logic searchable	no	full text searchable	no
record fields	unlimited	record size	unlimited
statistical & math capabilities	no	wholesale change capability	no

Support:

application consulting	no	maintenance and updates	yes
time share available	no	user training	no

Recommended for:

Corporate & govt libraries	yes	Media center management	yes
Public libraries	yes	Records & files management	no
School libraries	yes	University libraries	yes

Installations:

Initial installation date	1985	Total number of installed sites	800+

Sampling of current clients: Cass Lake Elementary School (MN); Chagrin Falls High School (OH); Fairfax County Public Schools (VA); Hawaii Department of Education (HI); Monterey Peninsula Unified School District (CA); Queens Borough Public Library (NY); Tampa Bay Library Consortium (FL); Medicine Hat Public Library (Alberta); Florida Power Corporation (FL); Los Alamos National Laboratory (NM); Unisys Corporation (PA); British Library (England); John Rylands University Library (England); National Taiwan University (Taiwan); South Australian Institute of Technology (Australia); Stanford University (CA); University of Essex (England); University of New Brunswick (NB)

Published reviews & articles:
Cibbarelli, Pamela R., "Modern Times: User Ratings of MITITNET/marc Software" in *OASIS: Observations of the American Association for Information Science, Los Angeles Chapter* . (March 1992): 4.
Deacon, Jim, "MITINET/marc Software Review" in *CMC News*, Summer 1991, p. 6.
Epstein, Hank, "Creating Original MARC Records on a Mac - the Easy Way" in *Apple Library Users Group Newsletter* 9:2 (April 1991): 87-89.
Johnson, Susan W., "MITINET/marc: Easy Does It" in *Information Retrieval & Library Automation*, 26:9 (February 1991): 1-3.
Matthews, Joseph, "MITINET/marc (Macintosh Version)" (software review) in *Library Technology Reports*, 27:3 (May/June 1991): 341-346.

MITINET/MARC continued

Matthews, Joseph, "MITINET/marc" (software review) in *Library Technology Reports*, 27:3 (May/June 1991): 335-340.

Epstein, Hank. "Library Automation: Creating MARC Records on a Micro." *Library Software Review*, March-April 1989, p. 80-81.

Moore-Jansen, Cathy. "MITINET/marc: (software review)." Micro Software Evaluations Library Edition, IV, 1988, p. 61-67.

Epstein, Hank. "The First Step in Ohio School Library/Media Automation: A Leadership Challenge." *Ohio Media Spectrum*, v.40, n.1, Spring 1988, p. 14-24.

Badertscher, David A. "Software Reviews: MITINET/marc." *Information Technology and Libraries*, v.7, n.3, September 1988, p. 326-330.

Epstein, Hank. "The First Step in School Library Automation: Converting for the Last Time (Part 1)." *Apple Library Users Group Newsletter*, v.6, n.2, April 1988, p. 55-59.

Epstein, Hank. "The First Step in School Library Automation: Converting for the Last Time (Part 2)." *Apple Library Users Group Newsletter*, v.6, n.3, July 1988, p. 49-52.

Epstein, Hank. "The First Step in Library Automation: Creating MARC Records on a Micro." *SCIL 1988, Third Annual Software/ Computer Database/CD ROM Conference and Exposition*, March 7-9, 1988, p. 27-28.

Anderson, Eric. "The Golden Hits of the Golden Disks." (MITINET/marc was named as the "Best Overall Library Software" of 1987) in *The Wired Librarian's Newsletter*, Dec 1987-Jan 1988, p. 14.

Beiser, Karl. "Micro Computing: MITINET/marc." (Software review). *Wilson Library Bulletin*, v.62, n.1, Sep 1987, P. 61-62, 111.

Epstein, Hank. "An Expert System for Novice MARC Catalogers." *Wilson Library Bulletin*, v.62, Nov 1987, p. 33-36.

O'Connor, James P. "One Happy Hybrid." *American Libraries*, April 1987, p. 290-292.

"Information Transform Offers MITINET/marc Software." *Library Hi Tech News*, Oct 1986, p. 15.

Aveny, Brian and Sally Drew. "Automated Resource Sharing: Wisconsin Spreads its Nets." *Wilson Library Bulletin*, v.57, May 1983, p. 742-746.

Price: $399

> There is also an educational version for library schools.
> Demo disk and instructions - free

Vendor's comments: MITINET/marc enables you to create full MARC records from your original cataloging. A library clerk can learn to use the system to create MARC records in less than two hours. From these records, Mitinet generates MARC printouts, and MARC records for storage on floppy or hard disk. Does not require the knowledge of MARC terminology.

> A free demo disk is available which does everything the main system does except write records to storage device.

MITINET/marc is compatible with the following 60 library automation packages:

AARCS (NSC)	ACQcess (Midwest Library Service)	Advance (GEAC)
Agile II (AutoGraphics)	Alexandria (COMpanion)	Assistant (INLEX)
BiBase (Library Technology Inc.)	BiblioFile (Library Corporation)	CardMaster Plus (Follett)
CARL	Carlyle	Catalog Plus (Follett)
CD CATSS (Utlas)	Circ Plus (Follett)	Columbia
Data Research	Data Trek	Davex Plus (Faxon)
DOBIS	Dynix	Dynix Scholar
Eloquent	EYRING	Galaxy (Gaylord)
GEAC	Georgetown LIS	IMPACT/CD ROM
IMPACT/SLiMS (AutoGraphics)	INLEX	Inmagic
Innopac	Intelligent Catalog (Library Corporation)	Intelligent Catalog
LaserCat (WLN)	LePac (BroDart)	Library Works (Caspr)
LOANet (LSSI)	Mac Library System (Caspr)	Mac the Librarian
MacBook (COMpanion)	MacSchool (Chancery)	Mandarin (Media Flex)
Marcive/PAC	MATSS (Midwest Library Service)	Media Manager (VIS)
Media Minder (Canopy Road)	Molli (Nichols Advanced Technologies)	MultiLIS (Sobeco)
Oscar (Software Technology)	PALS (Unisys)	ProCite (PBS)
Sirsi	SuperCat (Gaylord)	Surpass (Compell)
Sydney (International Library Systems)	TD-Media Booking (Tek Data)	TD-Media Catalog
UltraCard/MARC	VTLS	Winnebago Circ/Cat

MOLLI, MICRO ONLINE LIBRARY INFORMATION

Nichols Advanced Technologies Inc.
3452 Losey Boulevard South
La Crosse, WI 54601
(800) 658-9453   FAX (608) 787-8337

Hardware: IBM XT/AT/PS/2 or compatible

System Requirements: PC or MS-DOS version 3.2 or greater; 640K bytes memory; hard disk; printer; NOVELL or Lantastic network users.

Programming Language: C and compiled dBase

Components & Applications:

acquisitions	limited	catalog (batch)	yes
catalog (online)	yes	cataloging	yes
CD-ROM interface	yes	circulation	yes
formatting bibliographies	yes	index of keywords	yes
inter-library loan	limited	interface for MARC records	yes
media booking	limited	reserve room	no
serials	limited	thesaurus	no

Updating Modes:

batch update	yes	dynamic update	yes

Features:

Boolean logic searchable	yes	full text searchable	yes
record fields	MARC	record size	MARC
statistical & math capabilities	yes	wholesale change capability	no

Support:

application consulting	no	maintenance and updates	yes
time share available	no	user training	yes

Recommended for:

Corporate & govt libraries	yes	Media center management	yes
Public libraries	yes	Records & files management	yes
School libraries	yes	University libraries	yes

Installations:

Initial installation date	1985	Total # of installed sites	1000

   Sampling of current clients: A variety of schools, public libraries, corporations and other organizations throughout the U.S., Canada, and Australia including AT&T, U.S. Dept. of Interior, U.S. Dept. of Immigration & Naturalization, NASA, MCI-Tellicom, International Association of Machinists & Aerospace workers. MOLLI user contacts in your area are available on request.

Published reviews & articles:
Erdmer, Elizabeth. "Library Automation Software: Questions to Ask." *MEDIA & METHODS*, Sept/Oct 1990.
Baldwin, Keith & Schulman, Gail. "Information Age in an Elementary School Setting." *LIBRARY TALK*, Jan/Feb 1992, p.9.

Price: $1,795 Single User; $2,695 Multi User. Technical support free first year; $200 Single User, $250 Multi User annually thereafter.   Free demo disks.

Supplier's comments: MOLLI is an integrated library automation system providing searching, cataloging, circulation and inventory functions on IBM compatible PCs and LANs. MOLLI is easy-to-use yet flexible for use in corporate, school, and public libraries throughout North America and Australia. Multiple collections for books, articles, A/V materials, files, product catalogs, etc. Quick searches require entry of a single search term; Boolean searches and complete bibliography, searching and printing facility may also be used. MOLLI is 100% MARC compatible maintaining full MARC records internally. Technical support is available toll-free. 100% hit rate retrospective conversion service is available.

MSUS/PALS

Mankato State University
Mankato, MN 56001
(507) 389-5062
Contact: Dale Carrison

Hardware: UNISYS 1100 and 2200

System Requirements: TIP, DMS, CMS, OS1100

Programming Language: COBOL on mainframe; PASCAL on staff workstation.

Components & Applications:

acquisitions	yes	catalog (batch)	yes
catalog (online)	yes	cataloging	yes
CD-ROM interface	no	circulation	yes
formatting bibliographies	yes	index of keywords	yes
inter-library loan	yes	interface for MARC records	yes
media booking	no	reserve room	yes
serials	yes	thesaurus	yes

Updating Modes:

batch update	yes	dynamic update	yes

Features:

Boolean logic searchable	yes	full text searchable	yes
record fields	all MARC fields	record size	MARC format
statistical & math capabilities	yes	wholesale change capability	yes

Support:

application consulting	yes	maintenance and updates	yes
time share available	no	user training	yes

Recommended for:

Corporate & govt libraries	yes	Media center management	yes
Public libraries	yes	Records & files management	yes
School libraries	no	University libraries	yes

Installations:

Initial installation date 1980   Total number of installed sites   33

     Sampling of current clients: Minnesota State University System (52 agencies, 1200 terminals); 32 other sites in U.S., Australia, Canada, South Africa, and Spain.

Price: Software $100,000 (cost varies depending on computer hardware configuration)

Supplier's comments: MSUS/PALS catalog module is able to build a database from MARC format tapes. The circulation control, interlibrary loan, acquisitions, and serials systems are fully integrated with the online catalog module.

MULTILIS

Sobeco Group Inc.
Immeuble Sobeco
505 Rene-Levesque Blvd. W.
Montreal, Quebec H2Z 1Y7 Canada
(514) 878-9090

U.S. DISTRIBUTOR:
Immeuble Sobeco
Multicore Library Services
6631 C Commerce Parkway
Dublin, OH 43017-3239
(800) 753-0053
Contact: David Colombo

Hardware: Digital VAX, NCR Tower, and MIPS computers

System Requirements: 4 MB RAM memory minimum; VAX requires VMS; NCR & MIPS require UNIX System V

Programming Language: Pascal and C

Components & Applications:

acquisitions	yes	catalog (batch)	yes
catalog (online)	yes	cataloging	yes
CD-ROM interface	yes	circulation	yes
formatting bibliographies	yes	index of keywords	yes
inter-library loan	no	interface for MARC records	yes
media booking	no	reserve room	yes
serials	yes	thesaurus	yes

Updating Modes:

batch update	yes	dynamic update	yes

Features:

Boolean logic searchable	yes	full text searchable	no
record fields	80	record size	4000 char
statistical & math capabilities	yes	wholesale change capability	no

Support:

application consulting	yes	maintenance and updates	yes
time share available	no	user training	yes

Recommended for:

Corporate & govt libraries	yes	Media center management	yes
Public libraries	yes	Records & files management	no
School libraries	yes	University libraries	yes

Installations:

Initial installation date	1985	Total number of installed sites	69

Sampling of current clients: Barhead Public Library/County Schools (AL); Baylor University Libraries (TX); Bibliotheque Municipale de Boucherville (PQ); Bibliotheque de L'Universite de Sherbrooke (PQ); Brockville Public Library (ON); Energy Mines & Resources Canmet Library (ON); Federation des Cegeps (PQ); Jamestown Community College (NY); King Township Public Library (ON); Lethbridge Community College (AB); Lindsay Public Library (ON);New Castle Public Library (PA); Newcastle Public Library (ON); Red Deer Public Library (AB); Red Deer College Learning Resource Center (AB); The Ontario Institute of Studies in Education (ON); Union Carbide Corporation (NY)

Price: $15,000 - $100,000

Supplier's comments: A turnkey, integrated system which operates on Digital VAX, MIPS, and NCR Tower computers. The current modules include: acquisitions, authority control, cataloging and indexing, collection routing, circulation, reserve room management, online public access, electronic patron interface, management statistics and reports, and a report generator.

MUSIC CATALOGER

Right On Programs
755-F New York Avenue
Huntington, NY 11743
(516) 424-7777   FAX (516) 424-7207

Hardware: IBM & compatibles; Apple series

System Requirements: MS-DOS

Programming Language: no info

Components & Applications:

acquisitions	no	catalog (batch)	yes
catalog (online)	yes	cataloging	yes
CD-ROM interface	no	circulation	no
formatting bibliographies	no	index of keywords	no
inter-library loan	no	interface for MARC records	no
media booking	no	reserve room	no
serials	no	thesaurus	no

Updating Modes:

batch update	no	dynamic update	yes

Features:

Boolean logic searchable	no	full text searchable	no
record fields	no info	record size	no info
statistical & math capabilities	no	wholesale change capability	no

Support:

application consulting	yes	maintenance and updates	yes
time share available	no	user training	no

Recommended for:

Corporate & govt libraries	yes	Media center management	yes
Public libraries	yes	Records & files management	yes
School libraries	yes	University libraries	yes

Installations:

Initial installation date	1987	Total number of installed sites	no info
Sampling of current clients:	no info		

Price: $99

Supplier's comments: This is an excellent program to catalog music and music books. Print complete list to paper or 3 x 5 cards. Follow the on-screen prompts. Type in the author or composer and sheet music (or book) title. That's all and that's enough. Once the information is entered, you can print out a complete list in alphabetical order by author (or composer) or title to screen or printer. Or, if you'd like to keep the information in a card file, print to 3 x 5 cards (which come with the program). Print so either the title or composer appears on the top line.

NONESUCH ACQUISITIONS SYSTEM

Ringgold Management Systems, Inc.
Box 368
Beaverton, OR 97075-0368
(503) 645-3502
Contact: Ralph Shoffner

Hardware: IBM PC; UNISYS; other MS/DOS, PC/DOS, UNIX, and XENIX-based systems

System Requirements: 240KB memory minimum; hard disk

Programming Language: BASIC II

Components & Applications:

acquisitions	yes	catalog (batch)	no
catalog (online)	no	cataloging	no
CD-ROM interface	yes	circulation see NONESUCH CIRCULATION SYSTEM	
formatting bibliographies	no	index of keywords	no
inter-library loan	no	interface for MARC records	yes
media booking	no	reserve room see NONESUCH CIRCULATION SYSTEM	
serials	fund accounting only	thesaurus	no

Updating Modes:

batch update	yes	dynamic update	yes

Features:

Boolean logic searchable	yes (embedded)	full text searchable	no
record fields	no info	record size	512 order/85 expenditure
statistical & math capabilities	23/12	wholesale change capability	limited

Support:

application consulting	yes	maintenance and updates	yes
time share available	no	user training	yes

Recommended for:

Corporate & govt libraries	yes	Media center management	no
Public libraries	yes	Records & files management	no
School libraries	yes	University libraries	yes

Installations:

Initial installation date	1981	Total number of installed sites	30

Sampling of current clients: Yakima Valley Regional Library (WA); Northwestern Regional Library (NC); Chautauqua-Cattaraugus Library System (NY); Whatcom County Library System (WA); Jackson County Library System (OR); University of Detroit Library (MI); Rockford Public Library (IL); NASA Headquarters (DC); Douglas County Library System (OR); Kanawha County Public Library (WV); Western New England College (MA); Northern Illinois University (IL); Elmhurst Public Library (IL).

Price: $2,500 per terminal to a maximum of $15,000. Special quotes available.

Supplier's comments: Acquisitions - Operates on a range of micro & minicomputers. Provides full fund accounting and in-process control, as well as electronic ordering, electronic invoice processing, and automatic claiming. Uses input from other sources, e.g., OCLC and CD-ROM databases. System supplied as software only, or as both hardware and software.

Ringgold quotes separately for optional training; optional annual maintenance is available for $500 per terminal, to a maximum of $3,000. The software is written in BASIC and supports both online and batch operations. The minimum hardware configuration requires 512 KB RAM, on diskette drive, a 10 MB rigid disk unit and a printer.

NONESUCH CIRCULATION SYSTEM

Ringgold Management Systems, Inc.
Box 368
Beaverton, OR 97075-0368
(503) 645-3502
Contact: Ralph Shoffner

Hardware: IBM PC; UNISYS; other MS/DOS, PC/DOS, UNIX, and XENIX-based systems

System Requirements: 512KB memory minimum; hard disk

Programming Language: COBOL

Components & Applications:

acquisitions see NONESUCH ACQUISITION SYSTEM		catalog (batch)	no
catalog (online)	no	cataloging	no
CD-ROM interface	yes	circulation	yes
formatting bibliographies	no	index of keywords	no
inter-library loan	no	interface for MARC records	yes
media booking	no	reserve room	yes
serials	yes	thesaurus	no

Updating Modes:

batch update	yes	dynamic update	yes

Features:

Boolean logic searchable	no	full text searchable	no
record fields	no info	record size	no info
statistical & math capabilities	yes	wholesale change capability	limited

Support:

application consulting	yes	maintenance and updates	yes
time share available	no	user training	yes

Recommended for:

Corporate & govt libraries	no	Media center management	no
Public libraries	yes	Records & files management	no
School libraries	yes	University libraries	yes

Installations:

Initial installation date	1984	Total number of installed sites	8

Sampling of current clients: Yakima Valley Regional Library (WA); McAllen Memorial Library (TX); Klamath County Library (OR); Warner Pacific College Library (OR); University of the West Indies Library (Barbados); Baldwin Wallace College (OH); Curtis Memorial (ME); Guilford Technical Community College (NC).

Price: $2,500 per terminal to a maximum of $15,000. Special quotes available.

Supplier's comments: Circulation - Operates on a range of micro and minicomputers. Provides full control of inventory, both on shelf and charged out, multiple branch capability, reserves, holds, books by mail, overdues, and fines.

Ringgold quotes separately for optional training; optional annual maintenance is available for $500 per terminal, to a maximum of $3,000. The software is written in COBOL and supports both online and batch operations.

NOTEBOOK II

Pro/Tem Software Inc.
814 Tolman Drive
Stanford, CA 94305
Contact: Robert Baker
(415) 947-1024

Hardware: IBM PC-XT/AT

System Requirements: 256K; 2 floppy disk drives or hard disk

Programming Language: C

Components & Applications:

acquisitions	yes	catalog (batch)	no
catalog (online)	yes	cataloging	yes
CD-ROM interface	no	circulation	no
formatting bibliographies	yes	index of keywords	yes
inter-library loan	no	interface for MARC records	yes
media booking	no	reserve room	no
serials	no	thesaurus	no

Updating Modes:

batch update	no	dynamic update	yes

Features:

Boolean logic searchable	yes	full text searchable	yes
record fields	50 fields, up to 50,000char/field, limited only by total record size	record size	50,000 characters
statistical & math capabilities	no	wholesale change capability	no

Support:

application consulting	yes	maintenance and updates	yes
time share available	no	user training	tutorial

Recommended for:

Corporate & govt libraries	yes	Media center management	yes
Public libraries	no	Records & files management	yes
School libraries	yes	University libraries	yes

Installations:

Initial installation date	1982	Total number of installed sites	21,000
Sampling of current clients:	no info		

Published articles and reviews:

Price: $189 plus shipping and handling charge

Supplier's comments: Notebook II is a text database manager specifically designed for entering, retrieving, and printing research notes and bibliographies. Records can have up to 50,000 characters and 50 fields per record; fields expand dynamically as you enter text. Notebook II is menu-driven and has context-sensitive help.

Notebook II includes a full-screen editor with automatic word wrap. You can enter foreign and other special characters. You can also import files from you own word processor and from other databases that produce ASCII text files.

You can browse through the database or quickly find any record. Notebook II's powerful selection function lets you assemble records containing any combination of words of phrases you specify — in the same field or in different fields. You can also sort records on the text beginning any field.

Notebook II requires an IBM PC-XT/AT with at least 256K of RAM. Two accessory programs are available. Bibliography compares citations in a manuscript with entries in a Notebook II database and automatically compiles a bibliography of all works cited. Convert facilitates importing records from four on-line databases (Knowledge Index, BRS, DIALOG, and Medline) into a Notebook II database.

NOTIS

NOTIS Systems, Inc.
1007 Church Street
Evanston IL 60201
(708) 866-0150
Contact: Marketing Department

Hardware: IBM Mainframes, IBM 4300 Series, IBM compatible

System Requirements: MVS or DOS/VSE operating system with CICS/VS monitor and Pl/1 compiler

Programming Language: IBM's BASIC ASSEMBLER plus Pl/1

Components & Applications:

acquisitions	yes	catalog (batch)	yes
catalog (online)	yes	cataloging	yes
CD-ROM interface	no	circulation	yes
formatting bibliographies	no	index of keywords	yes
inter-library loan	no	interface for MARC records	yes
media booking	no	reserve room	yes
serials	yes	thesaurus	yes

Updating Modes:

batch update	yes	dynamic update	yes

Features:

Boolean logic searchable	yes	full text searchable	yes
record fields	unlimited; based on MARC format	record size	variable
statistical & math capabilities	yes	wholesale change capability	yes

Support:

application consulting	yes	maintenance and updates	yes
time share available	no	user training	yes

Recommended for:

Corporate & govt libraries	no	Media center management	no
Records & files management	no	Public libraries	yes
School libraries	no	University libraries	yes

Installations:

Initial installation date	1970	Total number of installed sites	225
Sampling of current clients:	no info		

Published Articles and Reviews:
Not available

Price: 1st year license fee   Library Management System $150,000 - $350,000
Annual maintenance fee 12%

On-site assistance is available at $1,000.00 per day. Ten days are included in package price. Consulting packages available.

Supplier's comments: NOTIS is a fully integrated online library system.

NSC

NSC Inc.
428 W. Ryan Street
Brillion, WI 54110
(800) 624-5720
Contact: Larry Nies

Hardware: Wang VS, IBM S/38, IBM AS400 (mid-range)

System Requirements: Approximately 50 MB

Programming Language: RPG II,RPG III and RPG/400

Components & Applications:

acquisitions	yes	catalog (batch)	yes
catalog (online)	yes	cataloging	yes
CD-ROM interface	yes	circulation	yes
formatting bibliographies	yes	index of keywords	yes
inter-library loan	yes	interface for MARC records	yes
media booking	yes	reserve room	yes
serials	yes	thesaurus	no

Updating Modes:

batch update	yes	dynamic update	yes

Features:

Boolean logic searchable	yes	full text searchable	yes
record fields	full MARC records	record size	full MARC records
statistical & math capabilities	yes	wholesale change capability	yes

Support:

application consulting	yes	maintenance and updates	yes
time share available	no	user training	yes

Recommended for:

Corporate & govt libraries	yes	Media center management	yes
Public libraries	yes	Records & files management	yes
School libraries	yes	University libraries	yes

Installations:

Initial installation date	1984	Total number of installed sites	22

Sampling of current clients: International Paper Co., Dallas, TX; Northwestern Mutual Life, Milwaukee, WI; Brown County Library, Wisconsin; Colonial Williamsburg Foundation, Williamsburg, VA; Brookfield Public Library, Brookfield, WI; Rowan County Public Library, Salisbury, NC; Fond Du Lac Public Library, Fond du Lac, WI.

Price: Please contact vendor

Supplier's comments: NSC's Library System provides a comprehensive, easy-to-use environment for managing the information requirements of today's library. Resident functions enable cataloging, collection management, multi-path inquire, and the sophisticated circulation control needed in the private sector. All updates occur interactively in real time, assuring that any records sought displays its current status. Compact modular design provides inherent flexibility in implementation, while offering a stable base system supportive of library-selected enhancements and future integration of additional modules as the library's system evolves. Functions enable creation update of bibliographic files, cataloging, management reporting, circulation processing, acquisitions, and serials control.

Editor's note: The software also has a community information and referral module.

OCLC CAT CD450 SYSTEM

OCLC Online Computer Library Center, Inc.
6565 Frantz Road
Dublin, OH 43017-3395
(614) 764-6000
Contact: Marketing

Hardware: OCLC workstation or IBM PC compatible

System Requirements: DOS; 640K RAM; Hard disk; MS-DOS extensions; & modem.

Programming Language: no info

Components & Applications:

acquisitions	no	catalog (batch)	no
catalog (online)	no	cataloging	yes
CD-ROM interface	no	circulation	no
formatting bibliographies	no	index of keywords	no
inter-library loan	no	interface for MARC records	no
media booking	no	reserve room	no
serials	no	thesaurus	no

Updating Modes:

batch update	no	dynamic update	yes

Features:

Boolean logic searchable	no	full text searchable	no
record fields	MARC format	record size	MARC format
statistical & math capabilities	no	wholesale change capability	no

Support:

application consulting	no	maintenance and updates	yes
time share available	no	user training	yes

Recommended for:

Corporate & govt libraries	yes	Media center management	yes
Public libraries	yes	Records & files management	no
School libraries	yes	University libraries	yes

Installations:

Initial installation date	no info	Total number of installed sites	no info
Sampling of current clients:	no info		

Published reviews & articles: no info

Price: no info

Supplier's comments: The OCLC CAT CD450 system combines offline cataloging with batch processing to decrease costs and increase cataloging options in your library. As an OCLC member library, you contribute to the growth of an international database by adding records to the OCLC Online Union Catalog (OLUC). The OLUC includes over 23 million bibliographic records, representing items in over 370 languages, and covering a wider range of subjects and formats than is available from any other bibliographic source. Because OCLC membership is a prerequisite for purchase, the CAT CD450 system is the only compact disc cataloging system that gives you access to such a large and diverse database. You also enjoy the many benefits of being part of OCLC's vast resource sharing network, including access to a growing international database and a comprehensive Union Listing Subsystem.

OCLC ILL MICRO ENHANCER VERSION 5.0

OCLC Online Computer Library Center, Inc.
6565 Frantz Road
Dublin, OH 43017-3395
(614) 764-6000
Contact: Marketing

Hardware: IBM compatibles

System Requirements: DOS 3.1 or higher; PASSPORT Software; 256K RAM; modem

Programming Language: no info

Components & Applications:

acquisitions	no	catalog (batch)	no
catalog (online)	no	cataloging	no
CD-ROM interface	no	circulation	no
formatting bibliographies	no	index of keywords	no
inter-library loan	yes	interface for MARC records	no
media booking	no	reserve room	no
serials	no	thesaurus	no

Updating Modes:

batch update	no	dynamic update	yes

Features:

Boolean logic searchable	no	full text searchable	no
record fields	no info	record size	no info
statistical & math capabilities	no	wholesale change capability	no

Support:

application consulting	no	maintenance and updates	yes
time share available	no	user training	yes

Recommended for:

Corporate & govt libraries	yes	Media center management	no
Public libraries	yes	Records & files management	no
School libraries	yes	University libraries	yes

Installations:

Initial installation date	no info	Total number of installed sites	no info
Sampling of current clients:	no info		

Published reviews & articles:

Price: no info

Supplier's comments: How can you improve ILL service without increasing costs? Put the OCLC ILL Micro Enhancer software to work for you. This easy-to-use program turns your workstation into a hard-working assistant for your ILL staff..

Improve productivity. Automatic downloading of your Message Waiting File helps you respond promptly to incoming requests and monitor current ILL transactions. Batch updating lets you complete most steps in the ILL workflow without time-consuming online interaction. Just enter request numbers offline to fill requests for loans or photocopies, confirm that you've shipped or received items, and handle renewals or recalls.

Speed number entry with barcodes. You can print ILL number barcodes on downloaded requests and then scan the barcodes to enter ILL numbers for batch updating. By scanning barcodes instead of typing ILL numbers, you can complete ILL number entry up to 50% faster.

Use workstations effectively. With the ILL Micro enhancer software doing routine online tasks automatically, after hours, you can use your ILL workstation for other activities. Whether you need to create ILL requests, reduce your cataloging backlog, or search online databases, you'll have more equipment to help you get the job done.

Over 1,800 libraries already use this powerful productivity tool. Once you discover its benefits, you'll wonder how you managed the ILL workload without the ILL Micro Enhancer software.

ON-LINE AUDIO ACCESS

Right On Programs
755-F New York Avenue
Huntington, NY 11743
(516) 424-7777   FAX (516) 424-7207

Hardware: IBM & compatibles

System Requirements: MS-DOS; Hard disk suggested

Programming Language: Turbo Pascal

Components & Applications:

acquisitions	no	catalog (batch)	no
catalog (online)	yes	cataloging	no
CD-ROM interface	no	circulation	no
formatting bibliographies	no	index of keywords	no
inter-library loan	no	interface for MARC records	no
media booking	no	reserve room	no
serials	no	thesaurus	no

Updating Modes:

batch update	no	dynamic update	yes

Features:

Boolean logic searchable	no	full text searchable	no
record fields	no info	record size	no info
statistical & math capabilities	yes	wholesale change capability	no

Support:

application consulting	yes	maintenance and updates	yes
time share available	no	user training	no

Recommended for:

Corporate & govt libraries	yes	Media center management	yes
Public libraries	yes	Records & files management	yes
School libraries	yes	University libraries	yes

Installations:

Initial installation date	1989	Total number of installed sites	750
Sampling of current clients:	no info		

Price: $229

Supplier's comments: Based on the same format and functions of ON-LINE CATALOG, ON-LINE AUDIO ACCESS enables you to catalog all records, tapes, CDs and call back information in the most wonderful ways.

Follow the on-screen prompts and type in Call or Reference number, Composer, Title, Artists, Publishing Information, Copyright date, Play Information, up to a 2-line description and up to twenty keywords. That means if your record or tape has as many as 20 songs on it, you can catalog, search for AND FIND any of those titles. You can finally locate your favorite song, etude, sonata, ballet, rag, rap, jazz, dixieland...whatever, by title or part of title.

LC#, ISBN #, Accession #, Location and Price may also be included if desired. Any of those fields may be bypassed if unnecessary. Also, if desired, a shelf list card may be generated.

For all libraries with audio collections, music departments or music libraries, music stores, and certainly "musical" people.

ON-LINE CATALOG

Right On Programs
755-F New York Avenue
Huntington, NY 11743
(516) 424-7777   FAX (516) 424-7207

Hardware: IBM & compatibles; Macintosh

System Requirements: MS-DOS

Programming Language: no info

Components & Applications:

acquisitions	no	catalog (batch)	yes
catalog (online)	yes	cataloging	yes
CD-ROM interface	no	circulation	no
formatting bibliographies	no	index of keywords	no
inter-library loan	no	interface for MARC records	no
media booking	no	reserve room	no
serials	no	thesaurus	no

Updating Modes:

batch update	no	dynamic update	yes

Features:

Boolean logic searchable	no	full text searchable	no
record fields	no info	record size	no info
statistical & math capabilities	no	wholesale change capability	no

Support:

application consulting	yes	maintenance and updates	yes
time share available	no	user training	no

Recommended for:

Corporate & govt libraries	yes	Media center management	no
Public libraries	yes	Records & files management	no
School libraries	yes	University libraries	yes

Installations:

Initial installation date	1985	Total number of installed sites	4000
Sampling of current clients:	no info		

Price: $279

Supplier's comments: A self contained "ON-LINE" CATALOG for the IBM and compatibles (and Macintosh).

For the smaller library or for a specific collection in the largest library, ON-LINE is recommended for medical, law, engineering, college, school, church or synagogue, corporate, etc., libraries. Also for individuals who wish to catalog private, home, or office collections. ON-LINE will hold up to 20,000 titles in memory on a 20Mb hard disk.

ON-LINE CATALOG PLUS V.2

Right On Programs
755-F New York Avenue
Huntington, NY 11743
(516) 424-7777   FAX (516) 424-7207

Hardware: IBM & compatibles

System Requirements: MS-DOS

Programming Language: no info

Components & Applications:

acquisitions	no	catalog (batch)	yes
catalog (online)	yes	cataloging	yes
CD-ROM interface	no	circulation	no
formatting bibliographies	no	index of keywords	no
inter-library loan	no	interface for MARC records	no
media booking	no	reserve room	no
serials	no	thesaurus	no

Updating Modes:

batch update	no	dynamic update	yes

Features:

Boolean logic searchable	no	full text searchable	no
record fields	no info	record size	no info
statistical & math capabilities	no	wholesale change capability	no

Support:

application consulting	yes	maintenance and updates	yes
time share available	no	user training	no

Recommended for:

Corporate & govt libraries	yes	Media center management	yes
Public libraries	yes	Records & files management	yes
School libraries	yes	University libraries	yes

Installations:

Initial installation date	1991	Total number of installed sites	1000
Sampling of current clients:	no info		

Price: $369

Supplier's comments: Combination of ON-LINE CATALOG and CATALOG CARDER. Please see info on them.
Network version also available.

ON-LINE PHOTO CATALOG V.2

Right On Programs
755-F New York Avenue
Huntington, NY 11743
(516) 424-7777   FAX (516) 424-7207

Hardware: IBM & compatibles; Macintosh

System Requirements: MS-DOS

Programming Language: no info

Components & Applications:

acquisitions	no	catalog (batch)	yes
catalog (online)	yes	cataloging	no
CD-ROM interface	no	circulation	no
formatting bibliographies	no	index of keywords	no
inter-library loan	no	interface for MARC records	no
media booking	no	reserve room	no
serials	no	thesaurus	no

Updating Modes:

batch update	no	dynamic update	yes

Features:

Boolean logic searchable	no	full text searchable	no
record fields	no info	record size	no info
statistical & math capabilities	no	wholesale change capability	no

Support:

application consulting	no	maintenance and updates	yes
time share available	no	user training	no

Recommended for:

Corporate & govt libraries	yes	Media center management	no
Public libraries	no	Records & files management	no
School libraries	no	University libraries	no

Installations:

Initial installation date	1991	Total number of installed sites	750
Sampling of current clients:	no info		

Price: $229

Supplier's comments: A self contained ON-LINE PHOTO CATALOG for the IBM and compatibles (and Macintosh).

For the smaller library or for a specific collection in the largest library, ON-LINE PHOTO CATALOG is recommended for medical, law, engineering, college, school, church or synagogue, corporate, etc., libraries. Also for individuals who wish to catalog private, home, or office collections.

ON-LINE PRODUCT INFORMATION CATALOG V.2

Right On Programs
755-F New York Avenue
Huntington, NY 11743
(516) 424-7777   FAX (516) 424-7207

Hardware: IBM & compatibles

System Requirements: MS-DOS

Programming Language: TURBO PASCAL

Components & Applications:

acquisitions	no	catalog (batch)	no
catalog (online)	yes	cataloging	yes
CD-ROM interface	no	circulation	no
formatting bibliographies	no	index of keywords	no
inter-library loan	no	interface for MARC records	no
media booking	no	reserve room	no
serials	no	thesaurus	no

Updating Modes:

batch update	no	dynamic update	yes

Features:

Boolean logic searchable	no	full text searchable	no
record fields	no info	record size	no info
statistical & math capabilities	no	wholesale change capability	no

Support:

application consulting	yes	maintenance and updates	yes
time share available	no	user training	no

Recommended for:

Corporate & govt libraries	yes	Media center management	yes
Public libraries	yes	Records & files management	yes
School libraries	yes	University libraries	yes

Installations:

Initial installation date	1991	Total number of installed sites	125
Sampling of current clients:	no info		

Price: $229

Supplier's comments: On-line catalog for catalogs of products, etc. Based on our on-line catalog.

ON-LINE VIDEO ACCESS

Right On Programs
755-F New York Avenue
Huntington, NY 11743
(516) 424-7777   FAX (516) 424-7207

Hardware: IBM & compatibles

System Requirements: MS-DOS

Programming Language: no info

Components & Applications:

acquisitions	no	catalog (batch)	no
catalog (online)	yes	cataloging	yes
CD-ROM interface	no	circulation	no
formatting bibliographies	no	index of keywords	no
inter-library loan	no	interface for MARC records	no
media booking	no	reserve room	no
serials	no	thesaurus	no

Updating Modes:

batch update	no	dynamic update	yes

Features:

Boolean logic searchable	no	full text searchable	no
record fields	no info	record size	no info
statistical & math capabilities	yes	wholesale change capability	no

Support:

application consulting	yes	maintenance and updates	yes
time share available	no	user training	no

Recommended for:

Corporate & govt libraries	no	Media center management	yes
Public libraries	yes	Records & files management	no
School libraries	yes	University libraries	yes

Installations:

Initial installation date	1989	Total number of installed sites	850
Sampling of current clients:	no info		

Price: $229

Supplier's comments: Similar in format to our very successful ON-LINE CATALOG (for books), ON-LINE VIDEO ACCESS will create the same type of records for all video holdings.

ONLINE CATALOG

Professional Software
21 Forest Avenue
Glen Ridge, NJ 07028
(201) 748-7658

Hardware: IBM PC, XT, AT

System Requirements: 256K RAM; DOS

Programming Language: no info

Components & Applications:

acquisitions see ACQUISITION MANAGER		catalog (batch)	yes
catalog (online)	yes	cataloging	no
CD-ROM interface	no	circulation see CIRCULATION MANAGER	
formatting bibliographies	no	index of keywords	no
inter-library loan	no	interface for MARC records	yes
media booking	no	reserve room	no
serials see SERIAL CONTROL SYSTEM		thesaurus	no

Updating Modes:

batch update	no	dynamic update	yes

Features:

Boolean logic searchable	no	full text searchable	no
record fields	no info	record size	no info
statistical & math capabilities	yes	wholesale change capability	no

Support:

application consulting	no	maintenance and updates	yes
time share available	no	user training	no

Recommended for:

Corporate & govt libraries	yes	Media center management	no
Public libraries	no	Records & files management	no
School libraries	no	University libraries	no

Installations:

Initial installation date	1989	Total number of installed sites	no info
Sampling of current clients:	no info		

Published reviews and articles: no info

Price:

$900	Single-user catalog
$300	Bar-code manager (requires purchase of Circulation Mgr for $395)
$300	Link to Acquisitions (requires purchase of Acquisition Mgr for $495)
$200/terminal	Multi-Terminal option
$450	Remote patron access

Supplier's comments:

ONLINE INFORMATION RETRIEVAL

Ruth Sather and Associates
2120 Moonlight Bay Drive
Altoona,WI 54720
715-835-5020 or 800-289-0132
Contact: Ruth Sather

Hardware: Apple II plus, IIe, IIc

System Requirements: Apple DOS

Support:

application consulting	no	maintenance and updates	yes
time share available	no	user training	no

Recommended for:

Corporate & govt libraries	no	Media center management	no
Public libraries	no	Records & files management	no
School libraries	yes	University libraries	no

Installations:

Initial installation date	n/a	Total number of installed sites	n/a
Sampling of current clients:	n/a		

Published reviews & articles:

Price: $95

Supplier's comments: This is a computer-based tutorial designed to provide individualized instruction on retrieving information from databases.

Editor's note: This is a software package to teach skills in using the library. Therefore, it does not include the usual list of components and applications.

OPTI-WARE

Online Computer Systems, Inc.
20251 Century Boulevard
Germantown MD 20874
(301) 428-3700 or (800) 922-9204
Contact: Steve Carton

Hardware: IBM PC; OS/2; Macintosh

System Requirements: DOS; UNIX.

Programming Language: no info

Components & Applications:

acquisitions	yes	catalog (batch)	yes
catalog (online)	yes	cataloging	yes
CD-ROM interface	yes	circulation	yes
formatting bibliographies	yes	index of keywords	yes
inter-library loan	no	interface for MARC records	yes
media booking	no	reserve room	yes
serials	yes	thesaurus	yes

Updating Modes:

batch update	yes	dynamic update	yes

Features:

Boolean logic searchable	yes	full text searchable	yes
record fields	yes	record size	no limits
statistical & math capabilities	no	wholesale change capability	no

Support:

application consulting	yes	maintenance and updates	yes
time share available	yes	user training	yes

Recommended for:

Corporate & govt libraries	yes	Media center management	no
Public libraries	yes	Records & files management	yes
School libraries	yes	University libraries	yes

Installations:

Initial installation date:	1985	Total number of installed sites	no info

Sampling of current clients: Bowker Electronic Publishing; Library of Congress; National Geographic; National Library of Canada

Price: Varies according to hardware platform

Supplier's comments: Online's Opti-Ware software supports any application for publishing in electronic form including document display, bibliographic & directory systems, full text retrieval, image storage, digital audio, numerical databases, demand printing systems, interactive training & information. It includes database build, indexing, search & retrieval and CD-ROM premastering. Online can provide complete solutions including systems integration, hardware and networking, installation, and maintenance.

Online provides complete turnkey services to clients who wish to publish on optical or magnetic media. Online has developed its Opti-Ware tools so that each customer's product is designed to meet the unique needs of the client's market. Online provides the following services to fulfill this objective: Database Build Services for all data types; Data Conversion to digital format from paper or magnetic source material; Image Processing - scanning, video, graphics production for digital or analog images. Output in any industry standard format; Product Documentation & Packaging; Product Distribution; Custom Engineering - hardware and software solutions; Systems Integration, Installation and Maintenance; and premastering Facility Specification and Design.

ORBIT

Orbit Information Technologies
A Division of Pergamon Orbit Infoline, Inc.
8000 Westpark Drive
McLean, VA 22102
(703) 442-0900, (800) 421-7229
Contact: M. Winiarski

Hardware: IBM or plug compatible

System Requirements: IBM Multiple Virtual Storage; random access disks and associated controllers; tape drives and teleprocessing capability are not required but usually present.

Programming Language: PL/1 and Assembler

Components & Applications:

acquisitions	no	catalog (batch)	yes
catalog (online)	yes	cataloging	no
CD-ROM interface	no	circulation	no
formatting bibliographies	no	index of keywords	yes
inter-library loan	no	interface for MARC records	yes
media booking	no	reserve room	no
serials	no	thesaurus	yes

Updating Modes:

batch update	yes	dynamic update	no

Features:

Boolean logic searchable	yes	full text searchable	yes
record fields	255 unique fields; any field can be repeated	record size	maximum 64,000 char
statistical & math capabilities	SAS interface	wholesale change capability	yes

Support:

application consulting	yes	maintenance and updates	yes
time share available	yes on network	user training	yes

Recommended for:

Corporate & govt libraries	yes	Media center management	no
Public libraries	no	Records & files management	yes
School libraries	no	University libraries	no

Installations:

Initial installation date	1965	Total number of installed sites	no info

Sampling of current clients: U.S. Department of Defense; Department of State; Coca Cola, Atlanta, GA; Bell Canada, Toronto; Exxon

Price: Base price ranges from $80,000 to $350,000, depending upon whether or not the purchaser wants the image retrieval capability and associated teleprocessing and reporting programs for usage management.

Supplier's comments: ORBIT is the same software package as the one which drives the powerful SDC ON-LINE SEARCH SERVICE. It is made available for building private files. Boolean logic search capabilities are fully developed. Various procedures are used at the SDC facility to protect data security.

ORBIT is designed for interactively searching very large text and numeric databases. The user interface is English command driven, and the commands may be modified to the particular language or style of the user. Capabilities include both Boolean and free-style queries, single or multiple file searching, and displaying or printing the results of a search in user specified formats.

ORBIT SEARCHMASTER

Orbit Information Technologies
A Division of Pergamon Orbit Infoline, Inc.
8000 Westpark Drive
McLean, VA 22102
(703) 442-0900, (800) 421-7229
Contact: M. Winiarski

Hardware: IBM PC

System Requirements: MS DOS

Programming Language: no info

Components & Applications:

acquisitions	no	catalog (batch)	no
catalog (online)	no	cataloging	no
CD-ROM interface	no	circulation	no
formatting bibliographies	no	index of keywords	no
inter-library loan	no	interface for MARC records	yes
media booking	no	reserve room	no
serials	no	thesaurus	no

Updating Modes:

batch update	no	dynamic update	yes

Features:

Boolean logic searchable	no	full text searchable	no
record fields	n/a	record size	n/a
statistical & math capabilities	no	wholesale change capability	no

Support:

application consulting	no	maintenance and updates	yes
time share available	no	user training	no

Recommended for:

Corporate & govt libraries	yes	Media center management	no
Public libraries	no	Records & files management	no
School libraries	no	University libraries	yes

Installations:

Initial installation date	1984	Total number of installed sites	600
Sampling of current clients:	no info		

Price: $300

OVERDUE BOOK CONTROL V.2

Right On Programs
755-F New York Avenue
Huntington, NY 11743
(516) 424-7777   FAX (516) 424-7207

Hardware: IBM & compatibles; School version available for the Apple series

System Requirements: MS-DOS

Programming Language: Turbo Pascal

Components & Applications:

acquisitions	no	catalog (batch)	no
catalog (online)	no	cataloging	no
CD-ROM interface	no	circulation	yes
formatting bibliographies	no	index of keywords	no
inter-library loan	no	interface for MARC records	no
media booking	no	reserve room	no
serials	no	thesaurus	no

Updating Modes:

batch update	no	dynamic update	yes

Features:

Boolean logic searchable	no	full text searchable	no
record fields	no info	record size	no info
statistical & math capabilities	yes	wholesale change capability	no

Support:

application consulting	yes	maintenance and updates	yes
time share available	no	user training	no

Recommended for:

Corporate & govt libraries	no	Media center management	no
Public libraries	yes	Records & files management	no
School libraries	yes	University libraries	no

Installations:

Initial installation date	1990	Total number of installed sites	2700
Sampling of current clients:	no info		

Price: $129

Supplier's comments: OVERDUE BOOK CONTROL keeps track of overdue materials. There are three versions:

"ID" - identifies patron by personal identification number and produces a list in numerical order;

"NAME" - enters the patron's name first and list is produced in alphabetical order by name;

"SCHOOL" - has fields that are tailored especially to a school situation - student, teacher, homeroom, etc.

All versions work in the same way. Data are entered according to the on-screen prompts. Information can be printed out on paper or to preprinted, continuous feed multi-copy forms (included with the package).

Simple instruction booklet tells you the options and then lets you get going.

Only the School Version is available for the Apple series computers.

P1 INTEGRATED SYSTEM®

Brodart Automation (a division of Brodart Co.)
500 Arch Street
Williamsport, PA 17705
(800) 233-8467 ext. 640
Contact: Joe Torres, National Sales Manager

Hardware: PC Compatible - configuration will vary according to size of installation

System Requirements: MS DOS 5.0

Programming Language: C

Components & Applications:

acquisitions	in development	catalog (batch)	no
catalog (online)	yes	cataloging	yes
CD-ROM interface	yes	circulation	yes
formatting bibliographies	yes	index of keywords	yes
inter-library loan	yes	interface for MARC records	yes
media booking	in development	reserve room	yes
serials	no	thesaurus	no

Updating Modes:

batch update	yes	dynamic update	yes

Features:

Boolean logic searchable	yes	full text searchable	no
record fields	MARC variable length	record size	MARC variable length
statistical & math capabilities	yes	wholesale change capability	no

Support:

application consulting	yes	maintenance and updates	yes
time share available	no	user training	yes

Recommended for:

Corporate & govt libraries	yes	Media center management	in development
Public libraries	yes	Records & files management	yes
School libraries	yes	University libraries	no

Installations:

Initial installation date	1992	Total number of installed sites	10
Sampling of current clients:	no info		

Price: Call for quote

Supplier's comments: Brodart Automation's microcomputer, CD-ROM-based P1 Integrated System® provides automated management for libraries from the planning of the collection to circulating the material. Designed for operation in a Local Area Network (LAN) environment, the system allows libraries wishing to efficiently share resources, the ability to manage and automate many library functions.

PALS

Unisys
Townshipline & Jolly Rds
Blue Bell,PA 19424-0001
215-986-6583
Contact: Gary Fry

Hardware: Unisys 1100/2200

System Requirements: EXEC, 4MW

Programming Language: COBOL

Components & Applications:

acquisitions	yes	catalog (batch)	yes
catalog (online)	yes	cataloging	yes
CD-ROM interface	no	circulation	yes
formatting bibliographies	yes	index of keywords	yes
inter-library loan	yes	interface for MARC records	yes
media booking	no	reserve room	yes
serials	yes	thesaurus	no

Updating Modes:

batch update	yes	dynamic update	yes

Features:

Boolean logic searchable	yes	full text searchable	yes
record fields	no	record size	no
statistical & math capabilities	no	wholesale change capability	yes

Support:

application consulting	yes	maintenance and updates	yes
time share available	yes	user training	yes

Recommended for:

Corporate & govt libraries	yes	Media center management	yes
Public libraries	yes	Records & files management	yes
School libraries	yes	University libraries	yes

Installations:

Initial installation date	9/80	Total number of installed sites	200+ libraries

Sampling of current clients: Shippensburg University; South Dakota Library Network; Traverse de Sioux; University of Manitoba

Published reviews & articles:

Price: $27,000 - $248,000 (Software)

Supplier's comments: PALS provides a very powerful search capability to your online catalog. Through built-in gateways, these same search commands can be used to search other libraries with PALS installed, or other commercial or local reference databases. Administrative functions for all library departments are facilitated via state-of-the-art PC workstation software.
Consortia and remote branches are supported.

PASSPORT 2.00 SOFTWARE

OCLC Online Computer Library Center, Inc.
6565 Frantz Road
Dublin, OH 43017-3395
(614) 764-6000
Contact: Marketing

Hardware: OCLC workstation or IBM PC compatibles

System Requirements: DOS; 256K RAM; Hercules Graphics adapter, Color Graphics Adapter; Enhanced keyboard; and modem.

Programming Language: no info

Support:

application consulting	no	maintenance and updates	yes
time share available	no	user training	yes

Recommended for:

Corporate & govt libraries	yes	Media center management	yes
Public libraries	yes	Records & files management	no
School libraries	yes	University libraries	yes

Installations:

Initial installation date	no info	Total number of installed sites	no info
Sampling of current clients: no info			

Published reviews & articles: no info

Price: no info

Supplier's comments: PASSPORT Software gives you more options for efficient access to online services. It lets you log on to the
PRISM service
EPIC service (including access to EasyNet)
FirstSearch Catalog
OCLC Online System
Online Journal of Current Clinical Trials
Other non-OCLC online information services

Benefits:
Quick. Perform complex tasks with a few keystrokes.
Easy-to-use. We've designed PASSPORT so that even the new computer user will feel at home with it.
Dependable. PASSPORT has been fully tested with OCLC services.
Well-supported. PASSPORT is backed on on-going OCLC & affiliated Regional Network support & training.
Yours to copy. You can make as many copies of PASSPORT as you want & install it on as many workstations as needed.
PASSPORT 2.00 includes both 5 1/4" and 3 1/2" copies of the software.

PERIODICAL INDEXING MANAGER

Right On Programs
755-F New York Avenue
Huntington, NY 11743
(516) 424-7777   Fax (516) 424-7207

Hardware: IBM & compatibles; Apple series

System Requirements: MS-DOS

Programming Language: no info

Components & Applications:

acquisitions	no	catalog (batch)	no
catalog (online)	no	cataloging	no
CD-ROM interface	no	circulation	no
formatting bibliographies	no	index of keywords	yes
inter-library loan	no	interface for MARC records	no
media booking	no	reserve room	no
serials	no	thesaurus	no

Updating Modes:

batch update	no	dynamic update	yes

Features:

Boolean logic searchable	no	full text searchable	no
record fields	no info	record size	no info
statistical & math capabilities	yes	wholesale change capability	no

Support:

application consulting	yes	maintenance and updates	yes
time share available	no	user training	no

Recommended for:

Corporate & govt libraries	yes	Media center management	yes
Public libraries	yes	Records & files management	yes
School libraries	yes	University libraries	yes

Installations:

Initial installation date	1991	Total number of installed sites	700
Sampling of current clients:	no info		

Published reviews and articles:

Price: $149

Supplier's comments: A program for medical, law, engineering, church, synagogue, corporate and other special libraries, as well as school and private.
   Indexes periodicals quickly and easily, and permits customizing of subject headings.

PERIODICAL MANAGER

Right On Programs
755-F New York Avenue
Huntington, NY 11743
(516) 424-7777   Fax (516) 424-7207

Hardware: IBM & compatibles

System Requirements: MS-DOS

Programming Language: Turbo Pascal

Components & Applications:

acquisitions	no	catalog (batch)	no
catalog (online)	no	cataloging	no
CD-ROM interface	no	circulation	no
formatting bibliographies	no	index of keywords	no
inter-library loan	no	interface for MARC records	no
media booking	no	reserve room	no
serials	yes	thesaurus	no

Updating Modes:

batch update	no	dynamic update	yes

Features:

Boolean logic searchable	no	full text searchable	no
record fields	no info	record size	no info
statistical & math capabilities	no	wholesale change capability	no

Support:

application consulting	yes	maintenance and updates	yes
time share available	no	user training	no

Recommended for:

Corporate & govt libraries	yes	Media center management	yes
Public libraries	yes	Records & files management	yes
School libraries	yes	University libraries	yes

Installations:

Initial installation date	1991	Total number of installed sites	1000
Sampling of current clients:	no info		

Price: $269

Supplier's comments: Periodical Manager combines two programs: Subscription Manager and Routing Manager.
The Subscription Manager features the following:
- Keeps track of all periodical subscriptions in all types of libraries;
- Keeps track of issues received as well as those still to come;
- Keeps track of titles, number ordered, starting date, and expiration date;
- Maintains lists of publishers and suppliers;
- Label printing capability;
- Add or delete magazines in "batches" to make getting started easier;
- Checks in expected or unexpected supplements.

The Routing Manager picks up the data entered in Subscription and, after entering employees, it creates routing slips. The printout may be by assigned priority numbers, alphabetical order, or a combination of both. A starter package of routing paper is included.

Network version also available.

PERSONAL LIBRARIAN

Cucumber Information Systems
5611 Kraft Drive
Rockville, MD 20852
(301) 984-3539
Contact: David J. Harris

Hardware: 16 & 32 bit computers running MS-DOS, UNIX, VMS.
    Includes: IBM PC and compatibles, and VAX; any UNIX system.

System Requirements: 196K; hard disk suggested

Programming Language: C

Components & Applications:

acquisitions	no	catalog (batch)	yes
catalog (online)	yes	cataloging	yes
CD-ROM interface	no	circulation	no
formatting bibliographies	no	index of keywords	yes
inter-library loan	no	interface for MARC records	no
media booking	no	reserve room	no
serials	no	thesaurus	yes

Updating Modes:

batch update	yes	dynamic update	no

Features:

Boolean logic searchable	yes	full text searchable	yes
record fields	256	record size	unlimited
statistical & math capabilities	limited	wholesale change capability	no

Support:

application consulting	yes	maintenance and updates	yes
time share available	no	user training	yes

Recommended for:

Corporate & govt libraries	yes	Media center management	no
Public libraries	no	Records & files management	no
School libraries	yes	University libraries	yes

Installations:

Initial installation date	1984	Total number of installed sites	no info
Sampling of current clients: no info			

Price:

Single user (PC)	$ 995.
Multi-user (UNIX, IBM mainframe, or VAX)	$10,000.
Multi-user PC	$ 4,975.

Supplier's comments: PERSONAL LIBRARIAN is an information retrieval system that offers automatic full-text indexing on up to 256 fields per document, with no limits on the lengths of fields or documents. Queries can be in natural language, and may also utilize full Boolean logic, including parentheses and reusing previous searches, adjacency, numeric ranges, field limiting and partial matches. Words are automatically matched on their roots. Retrieved documents are ranked according to their likely usefulness. Documents may be included in a query to look for similar documents. A word or phrase can be expanded to show related words; this is done automatically by statistical methods, without the user setting up a thesaurus.

   Most searches take only a few seconds, even on large databases. PERSONAL LIBRARIAN also comes with simple database definition and loading utilities.

PERSONNEL SCHEDULER V.1.2

Right On Programs
755-F New York Avenue
Huntington, NY 11743
(516) 424-7777   Fax (516) 424-7207

Hardware: IBM & compatibles

System Requirements: MS-DOS

Programming Language: CLIPPER

Updating Modes:

batch update	no	dynamic update	yes

Features:

Boolean logic searchable	no	full text searchable	no
record fields	no info	record size	no info
statistical & math capabilities	no	wholesale change capability	no

Support:

application consulting	yes	maintenance and updates	yes
time share available	no	user training	no

Recommended for:

Corporate & govt libraries	yes	Media center management	yes
Public libraries	yes	Records & files management	yes
School libraries	yes	University libraries	yes

Installations:

Initial installation date	1992	Total number of installed sites	70
Sampling of current clients:	no info		

Price: $249

Supplier's comments: Program creates a calendar and schedules all personnel. "Takes care of" holidays, vacations, sick time, personal time, etc. Enter the information and the computer will prompt when it is the proper time to schedule. People who leave can be deleted, and removed from schedules. Program maintains records of work schedules, prompts when someone is needed on each shift.

PRECISION ONE®

Brodart Automation (a division of Brodart Co.)
500 Arch Street
Williamsport, PA 17705
(800) 233-8467 ext. 522
Contact: Tom Sumpter, National Sales Manager

Hardware: Basic Configuration - MS-DOS PC Compatible, 640 K available memory, CD-ROM Drive, Hard Disk Drive

System Requirements: MS DOS 3.2 or Higher

Programming Language: C

Components & Applications:

acquisitions	no	catalog (batch)	no
catalog (online)	no	cataloging	yes
CD-ROM interface	yes	circulation	no
formatting bibliographies	no	index of keywords	yes
inter-library loan	no	interface for MARC records	yes
media booking	no	reserve room	no
serials	no	thesaurus	no

Updating Modes:

batch update	no	dynamic update	yes

Features:

Boolean logic searchable	no	full text searchable	no
record fields	MARC, variable	record size	MARC, variable
statistical & math capabilities	no	wholesale change capability	no

Support:

application consulting	yes	maintenance and updates	yes
time share available	no	user training	yes

Recommended for:

Corporate & govt libraries	yes	Media center management	no
Public libraries	yes	Records & files management	no
School libraries	yes	University libraries	yes

Installations:

Initial installation date	1990	Total number of installed sites	over 500
Sampling of current clients: no info			

Price:

OPTION A $650.00

    Precision One Retro & Current Cataloging System
        Includes one Retro CD DISC
        One year subscription to Precision One Current
        Cataloging (Monthly updates)

OPTION B $850.00

    Four CD databases plus Precision One Retro/Current
        The Software Toolworks World & U.S. Atlas
        Toolworks Reference Library
        The Software Toolworks Illustrated Encyclopedia
        Time Almanac

OPTION C $1,450.00

    Hitachi Model 3700 External CD-ROM Drive with
    MS-DOS Extensions, Precision One Retro/
    Current plus four CD databases

OPTION D $2,000

    Two Hitachi Model 3700 External CD-ROM Drives
    with MS-DOS Extensions, Precision One Retro/
    Current plus four CD databases

PRECISION ONE® continued

OPTION E $3,300.00

        One personal computer configured as follows:

                80386 Processor, 20MHZ

                2 MB SIMM RAM

                1.2 OR 1.44 MB Floppy Drive

                14" VGA Color Monitor

                Enhanced 101 Keyboard

                2 CD-ROM External Drives

                MS DOS 5.0, MS DOS Extensions

                1 Year Hardware Repair

                1 40 MB Hard Disk Drive

        Precision One Retro/Current Cataloging System

        Four CD databases

Free Demonstration Disk Available.

Supplier's comments: Precision One is a compact disc-based retrospective conversion/cataloging tool. Brodart Automation developed Precision One to offer school and public libraries an affordable, efficient, and accurate method of converting their records to MARC format.

PRO-CITE 2.0

Personal Bibliographic Software
P.O. Box 4250
Ann Arbor, MI 48106
(313) 996-1580
Contact: Dan Houdek

Hardware: IBM PC or compatibles; or Mac Plus or greater

System requirements: IBM - DOS 2.0 256K RAM minimum; DOS 3.0 320K RAM; hard disk or two floppy disk drives
Macintosh - System 6.0.2 or greater; Hard disk recommended

Programming Language: PASCAL

Components & Applications:

acquisitions	no	catalog (batch)	yes
catalog (online)	yes	cataloging	yes
CD-ROM interface	yes, Biblio-Link	circulation	no
formatting bibliographies	yes	index of keywords	yes
inter-library loan	no	interface for MARC records	yes
media booking	no	reserve room	no
serials	yes	thesaurus	no

Updating Modes:

batch update	yes	dynamic update	yes

Features:

Boolean logic searchable	yes	full text searchable	yes
record fields	no info	record size	16K
statistical & math capabilities	no	wholesale change capability	yes

Support:

application consulting	no	maintenance and updates	yes
time share available	no	user training	yes

Recommended for:

Corporate & govt libraries	yes	Media center management	yes
Public libraries	yes	Records & files management	yes
School libraries	yes	University libraries	yes

Installations:

Initial installation date	1992	Total number of installed sites	Thousands
Sampling of current clients: no info			

Price: $395.00
Upgrade Price: $95

Suppliers Comments. Pro-Cite is a powerful database program that saves you hours of time, energy and frustration by enabling you to manage and format bibliographic and text information automatically. Pro-Cite has become an essential tool for librarians, scientists and researchers to manage their research, create acquisitions or serials lists, produce course reserve lists, and publish bibliographies, among many other applications. Each Pro-Cite database can hold an unlimited number of references from books, journals, dissertations or any other source using any of the 26 pre-defined workforms (record types). Workforms can hold up to approximately 16 pages of text (32,000 characters) and users can also design up to six workforms of their own in each database. Quickly and easily organize information from books, journals, serials, collections or any other source. Records can be entered into Pro-Cite manually, imported from other database programs, or transferred automatically using Biblio-Links programs. Once in Pro-Cite, references can be easily searched, sorted, indexed, and formatted into bibliographies according to any bibliographic style.

PRO-SEARCH

Personal Bibliographic Software
P.O. Box 4250
Ann Arbor, MI 48106
(313) 996-1580
Contact: Julie Wood

Hardware: IBM Personal Computer or compatible with PCDOS or MSDOS; or Mac Plus or greater

System Requirements: PCs - DOS 2.1 or higher 256K RAM minimum, DOS 3.0 320K RAM, hard disk or two DS disk drives; Macintosh System 6.0.2 or higher; one MB memory, two 800K disk drives or hard disk; modem; BRSor DIALOG passwords

Programming Language: PASCAL

Support:

application consulting	no	maintenance and updates	yes
time share available	no	user training	yes

Recommended for:

Corporate & govt libraries	yes	Media center management	yes
Public libraries	yes	Records & files management	yes
School libraries	yes	University libraries	yes

Installations:

Initial installation date	1986	Total number of installed sites	no info
Sampling of current clients:	no info		

Price: IBM Pro-Search 1.08 $495.00, optional subscription service $150.00   Upgrade Price: $45.00
Mac Pro-Search 1.1 $295.00, optional subscription service $150.00

Suppliers Comments. Pro-Search is a specialized front-end software program that simplifies searching of DIALOG databases. Pro-Search's unique, menu-driven interface helps you select the most useful database to search by providing bluesheet data on disk. Search strategies can be constructed and stored offline, reducing online connect time and charges. Pro-Search also tracks online charges through a built-in accounting feature. An optional quarterly subscription service includes free program upgrades and keeps your Bluesheet disk up-to-date with data for new and modified databases.

Editor's note: This is software which serves as a front-end processor for searching online databases.

PROFESSIONAL SERIES

Data Trek, Inc.
5838 Edison Place
Carlsbad, CA 92008
(619) 431-8400 or 1- 800-876-5484; FAX #619-431-8448
Contact: Kimberly Gates

Hardware: IBM AT & IBM Compatibles

System Requirements: MS/DOS; 640K minimum

Programming Language: C, VBASE

Components & Applications:

acquisitions	in development	catalog (batch)	yes
catalog (online)	yes	cataloging	yes
CD-ROM interface	no	circulation	yes
formatting bibliographies	user defined	index of keywords	yes
inter-library loan	yes	interface for MARC records	yes
media booking	no	reserve room	yes
serials	in development	thesaurus	no

Updating Modes:

batch update	yes	dynamic update	yes

Features:

Boolean logic searchable	yes	full text searchable	yes
record fields	user defined	record size	unlimited
statistical & math capabilities	yes	wholesale change capability	no

Support:

application consulting	yes	maintenance and updates	yes
time share available	no	user training	yes

Recommended for:

Corporate & govt libraries	yes	Media center management	no
Public libraries	yes	Records & files management	yes
School libraries	yes	University libraries	yes

Installations:

Initial installation date	1989	Total number of installed sites	80

Sampling of current clients: As a courtesy to our clients, a list is available after serious interest is shown.

Price: Discounts available for multiple purchases as well as for school and government installations.

Supplier's comments: The Professional Series represents a series of evolutionary phases for complete integration of all information management functions and library technology. In addition to unparalleled search speed, the Professional Series offers user-defined control of all fields and full integration of modules. Fields may be of variable length and are repeatable, and records may be simultaneously updated and searched in a multi-user environment. Written in the "C" programming language, the Professional Series is transportable to a wide variety of hardware configurations. Full-screen editing and full MARC compatibility will be of particular interest to librarians sharing lengthy catalog records with other libraries. The ability to download, store, edit and output complete MARC records is now easily accomplished. This Series allows the user to input data in an easy-entry format and the system will create MARC tags and records. Switching between the MARC record and the easy-entry format is enabled with a single keystroke. The system also features variable length fields, the ability to add fields and a powerful internal search utility. It is user-friendly incorporating cascading menus, open and closed pick lists, zooming and scrolling fields, browsing capabilities and extensive online help. Searching capabilities include Boolean, Keyword, field specific, nested and more. Module-to-module transfer from the main menu with complete integration allows the user to move easily within the database and access bibliographic data from any module once it has been keyed into the system.

QUICK CARD APPLE AND MS-DOS

Follett Software Company
809 North Front Street
McHenry, IL 60050-5589
(815) 344-8700 or (800) 323-3397
FAX (815) 344-8774
Contact: Michael Hollobow

Hardware: IBM PC or compatible with hard disk drive and floppy drive; Apple IIe, IIGS with two floppy disk drives

System Requirements: 256K RAM MS-DOS ; 64K RAM Apple

Programming Language: PASCAL

Components & Applications:

acquisitions	no	catalog (batch)	yes
catalog (online)	no	cataloging	no
CD-ROM interface	no	circulation	no
formatting bibliographies	no	index of keywords	no
inter-library loan	no	interface for MARC records	no
media booking	no	reserve room	no
serials	no	thesaurus	no

Updating Modes:

batch update	yes	dynamic update	yes

Features:

Boolean logic searchable	no	full text searchable	no
record fields	no info	record size	no info
statistical & math capabilities	no	wholesale change capability	no

Support:

application consulting	no	maintenance and updates	yes
time share available	no	user training	no

Recommended for:

Corporate & govt libraries	no	Media center management	no
Public libraries	no	Records & files management	no
School libraries	yes	University libraries	no

Installations:

Initial installation date	1985	Total number of installed sites	11,000+

Sampling of current clients: References available.

Published reviews & articles:

Price: $234.95

Supplier's comments: Quick Card is a program for printing catalog cards, spine labels, book card labels, and book pocket labels. The information for the main entry card is typed and the program automatically prints the shelflist card, author card, title card, all subject cards, additional cards as appropriate, and labels. The Apple Quick Card data can be used by Apple Circulation Plus, therefore, rekeying of data is not required.

R LIBRARY CARDS

Rachels
111 Innsbruck Drive
Clayton, NC 27520
919-553-5511 or 800-869-7390

Hardware: Macintosh

System Requirements: Macintosh OS

Programming Language: C

Components & Applications:

acquisitions	no	catalog (batch)	yes
catalog (online)	no	cataloging	yes
CD-ROM interface	no	circulation	no
formatting bibliographies	no	index of keywords	no
inter-library loan	no	interface for MARC records	no
media booking	no	reserve room	no
serials	no	thesaurus	no

Updating Modes:

batch update	no	dynamic update	yes

Features:

Boolean logic searchable	no	full text searchable	no
record fields	no info	record size	no info
statistical & math capabilities	no	wholesale change capability	no

Support:

application consulting	no	maintenance and updates	yes
time share available	no	user training	no

Recommended for:

Corporate & govt libraries	yes	Media center management	yes
Public libraries	yes	Records & files management	yes
School libraries	yes	University libraries	no

Installations:

Initial installation date	1990	Total number of installed sites	30

Sampling of current clients:

Published reviews & articles:
Apple Library Users Group Newsletter, January 1990.
British Library Assoc. Record, January 1990.
Technical Services Quarterly, v.8, n.2.

Price: $144   demo $5

Supplier's comments: Prints catalog cards and spine and pocket labels.

R LIBRARY CARDS II

Rachels
111 Innsbruck Drive
Clayton, NC 27520
919-553-5511 or 800-869-7390

Hardware: Macintosh

System Requirements: Macintosh OS

Programming Language: C

Components & Applications:

acquisitions	no	catalog (batch)	yes
catalog (online)	no	cataloging	yes
CD-ROM interface	no	circulation	no
formatting bibliographies	no	index of keywords	no
inter-library loan	no	interface for MARC records	no
media booking	no	reserve room	no
serials	no	thesaurus	no

Updating Modes:

batch update	no	dynamic update	yes

Features:

Boolean logic searchable	no	full text searchable	no
record fields	no info	record size	no info
statistical & math capabilities	no	wholesale change capability	no

Support:

application consulting	no	maintenance and updates	yes
time share available	no	user training	no

Recommended for:

Corporate & govt libraries	yes	Media center management	yes
Public libraries	yes	Records & files management	yes
School libraries	yes	University libraries	no

Installations:

Initial installation date	1991	Total number of installed sites	5

Sampling of current clients:

Published reviews & articles:

Price: $274   demo $5

Supplier's comments: Supports choice of font and font size. Supports laser printers and network printers. Prints cards and spine and pocket labels. Can print spine labels by themselves.

RACHELS CATALOG CARD PRINTER

Rachels
111 Innsbruck Drive
Clayton, NC 27520
919-553-5511 or 800-869-7390

Hardware: IBM PC with DOS; Apple; Macintosh

System Requirements: DOS

Programming Language: Basic, C

Components & Applications:

acquisitions	no	catalog (batch)	yes
catalog (online)	no	cataloging	yes
CD-ROM interface	no	circulation	no
formatting bibliographies	no	index of keywords	no
inter-library loan	no	interface for MARC records	no
media booking	no	reserve room	no
serials	no	thesaurus	no

Updating Modes:

batch update	no	dynamic update	yes

Features:

Boolean logic searchable	no	full text searchable	no
record fields	no info	record size	no info
statistical & math capabilities	no	wholesale change capability	no

Support:

application consulting	no	maintenance and updates	yes
time share available	no	user training	no

Recommended for:

Corporate & govt libraries	yes	Media center management	yes
Public libraries	yes	Records & files management	yes
School libraries	yes	University libraries	no

Installations:

Initial installation date	1984	Total number of installed sites	1000+

Sampling of current clients:

Published reviews & articles:
Apple Library Users Group Newsletter, April 1989.
CMC News, v.10, n.3, Winter 1990.

Price: $27- Apple   demo $2
$32- IBM   demo $3
$44- Macintosh   demo $5

Supplier's comments: Prints catalog cards and spine and pocket labels.

RECORDS MANAGEMENT CONTROL

Right On Programs
755-F New York Avenue
Huntington, NY 11743
(516) 424-7777   FAX (516) 424-7207

Hardware: IBM & compatibles

System Requirements: MS-DOS

Programming Language: Turbo Pascal

Components & Applications:

acquisitions	no	catalog (batch)	yes
catalog (online)	yes	cataloging	yes
CD-ROM interface	no	circulation	no
formatting bibliographies	no	index of keywords	no
inter-library loan	no	interface for MARC records	no
media booking	no	reserve room	no
serials	no	thesaurus	no

Updating Modes:

batch update	no	dynamic update	yes

Features:

Boolean logic searchable	no	full text searchable	no
record fields	no info	record size	no info
statistical & math capabilities	no	wholesale change capability	no

Support:

application consulting	yes	maintenance and updates	yes
time share available	no	user training	no

Recommended for:

Corporate & govt libraries	no	Media center management	no
Public libraries	no	Records & files management	yes
School libraries	no	University libraries	no

Installations:

Initial installation date	1992	Total number of installed sites	75
Sampling of current clients: no info			

Price: $189

Supplier's comments: Manages all company records whether for tax, historical, archival, legal or whatever reasons. Tells you where they are, who is responsible for them, where the backup copies are, on what medium they are stored, how long they will be kept and when they will be destroyed or moved to an inactive location. File and find by number, by name, by code, by color or whatever you choose. Records may be searched and edited or printed by FOURTEEN fields. There is room for a two-line message and two blank user fields of your choice. All are searchable.

REF-11

DG Systems
322 Prospect Avenue
Hartford, CT 06106
(203) 247-8500
Contact: Robert Parker

Hardware: DEC VAX, PDP-11; IBM PC or MS-DOS machine; CPM/80 machine

System Requirements: VMS, RT-11, RT-11 with TSX-Plus, RSX- 11, PC-DOS, MS-DOS, P/OS, CPM/80

Programming Language: PASCAL+ MACRO

Components & Applications:

acquisitions	no	catalog (batch)	yes
catalog (online)	yes	cataloging	yes
CD-ROM interface	no	circulation	no
formatting bibliographies	yes	index of keywords	yes
inter-library loan	no	interface for MARC records	no
media booking	no	reserve room	no
serials	no	thesaurus	no

Updating Modes:

batch update	no	dynamic update	yes

Features:

Boolean logic searchable	yes	full text searchable	yes
record fields	65		
record size	up to 5000 characters (variable length records)		
statistical & math capabilities	no	wholesale change capability	no

Support:

application consulting	no	maintenance and updates	yes
time share available	no	user training	no

Recommended for:

Corporate & govt libraries	yes	Media center management	no
Public libraries	no	Records & files management	no
School libraries	no	University libraries	no

Installations:

Initial installation date	1983	Total number of installed sites	15,000+
Sampling of current clients: no info			

Price: $195 - $350

Supplier's Comments: REF-11 is a database management system for bibliographic references. A database of references can be created, searched, updated and output in various forms using the REF-11 system. Bibliographies can be produced formatted exactly as you want them. A utility program is available that will read references downloaded from any database including National Library of Medicine (NLM), BRS, and DIALOG and store them in reference volumes (data files). Another utility program can read a paper, insert reference citations in the appropriate places in the paper and produce a bibliography of the references cited.

REFERENCE MANAGER

Research Information Systems, Inc.
Camino Corporate Center
2355 Camino Vida Roble
Carlsbad, CA 92009
(619)438-5526 Main office; (619)438-5547 Customer Support
FAX (619)438-5573
Contact: Earl B. Beutler

Hardware: IBM PC/compatibles; Macintosh, and NEC 9801 series

System Requirements: IBM & NEC: 384K RAM, hard disk; Macintosh: 1Mb RAM

Programming Language: Turbo Pascal

Components & Applications:

acquisitions	no	catalog (batch)	yes
catalog (online)	no	cataloging	yes
CD-ROM interface	no	circulation	no
formatting bibliographies	yes	index of keywords	yes
inter-library loan	no	interface for MARC records	no
media booking	no	reserve room	no
serials	no	thesaurus	no

Updating Modes:

batch update	yes	dynamic update	yes

Features:

Boolean logic searchable	yes	full text searchable	yes
record fields	variable	record size	variable
statistical & math capabilities	no	wholesale change capability	yes

Support:

application consulting	no	maintenance and updates	yes
time share available	no	user training	yes

Recommended for:

Corporate & govt libraries	yes	Media center management	no
Public libraries	no	Records & files management	yes
School libraries	no	University libraries	yes

Installations:

Initial installation date	1984	Total number of installed sites	20,000+
Sampling of current clients:	no info		

Published reviews & articles:

Adelson, Dave. "Reference Manager." *Biotechnology Software,* July-August 1988.

Matus, Nancy and Earl B. Beutler, "Reference Update and Reference Manager: Personal Computer Programs for Locating and Managing References." *BioTechniques,* v.7, n.6, 1989.

Price: $299 - $499
Special Student Edition available for $79.

Supplier's Comments: REFERENCE MANAGER is a microcomputer-based software package designed specifically for publishing scientists. A specialized database management program combined with a text-reformatting module, REFERENCE MANAGER is used to store bibliographic references on a computer system and later incorporate them into a manuscript for publication.

References may be entered into REFERENCE MANAGER at the computer keyboard, or by downloading from an on-line service such as Medline or BRS Colleague (using the optional "Capture" module). You may enter any keywords of your choosing, or select the keywords assigned by the on-line service.

REFERENCE UPDATE

Research Information Systems, Inc.
Camino Corporate Center
2355 Camino Vida Roble
Carlsbad, CA 92009
(619)438-5526 Main office; (619)438-5547 Customer Support
FAX (619)438-5573
Contact: Earl B. Beutler

Hardware: IBM PC/compatibles; Macintosh, and NEC 9801 series

System Requirements: 640K RAM for IBM & NEC; 1Mb RAM for Macintosh

Programming Language: Pascal

Components & Applications:

acquisitions	no	catalog (batch)	yes
catalog (online)	no	cataloging	yes
CD-ROM interface	no	circulation	no
formatting bibliographies	no	index of keywords	yes
inter-library loan	no	interface for MARC records	no
media booking	no	reserve room	no
serials	no	thesaurus	no

Updating Modes:

batch update	yes	dynamic update	yes

Features:

Boolean logic searchable	yes	full text searchable	yes
record fields	variable	record size	variable
statistical & math capabilities	no	wholesale change capability	no

Support:

application consulting	no	maintenance and updates	yes
time share available	no	user training	yes

Recommended for:

Corporate & govt libraries	yes	Media center management	no
Public libraries	yes	Records & files management	yes
School libraries	no	University libraries	yes

Installations:

Initial installation date	1988	Total number of installed sites	10,000+
Sampling of current clients:	no info		

Price:

Basic edition	$330
Deluxe edition	$425
Deluxe Abstract edition	$949

Supplier's Comments: Reference Update is a microcomputer based current awareness service that provides a weekly diskette containing the Table of Contents information for hundreds of scientific journals. The software for searching and reporting information is included with the initial subscription package. Numerous search strategies can be designed and saved for subsequent weekly issues using any combination of authors, journal names, and phrases. The software includes a number of reporting functions such as printing lists of references, printing reporting request cards, exporting selected references directly to Reference Manager and downloading selected references to a disk file.

REMO: AUTOMATED SERIALS MANAGEMENT SYSTEM

Readmore, Inc.
22 Cortlandt Street
New York, NY 10007
(212) 349-5540
Contact: Judy Schott

Hardware: IBM PC or compatible

System Requirements: 15 MB; 1MB

Programming Language: Advanced Revelation

Components & Applications:

acquisitions	no	catalog (batch)	no
catalog (online)	no	cataloging	no
CD-ROM interface	no	circulation	no
formatting bibliographies	yes	index of keywords	no
inter-library loan	no	interface for MARC records	yes
media booking	no	reserve room	no
serials	yes	thesaurus	no

Updating Modes:

batch update	yes	dynamic update	no

Features:

Boolean logic searchable	yes	full text searchable	yes
record fields	variable	record size	2000 bytes
statistical & math capabilities	yes	wholesale change capability	yes

Support:

application consulting	yes	maintenance and updates	yes
time share available	no	user training	yes

Recommended for:

Corporate & govt libraries	yes	Media center management	no
Public libraries	no	Records & files management	yes
School libraries	no	University libraries	yes

Installations:

Initial installation date	1984	Total number of installed sites	300
Sampling of current clients:	no info		

Published reviews & articles:
Serials Librarian, v.16 (1/2) 1985
Serials Review, v.14, #4, 1988

Price:		
	Basic System	$2,995.00
	Standard System with 1 option	$3,295.00
	Complete System	$3,996.00
	Demo disk	free

Supplier's Comments: REMO Serials Control System is a microcomputer based software package that entails all aspects of serials control. Performs library based functions such as serials check-in, claiming, bindery functions, statistical and bibliographic reporting, claiming and purchase order functions. File transfer and telecommunications codes for direct micro-based communication functions are also available. Ability to network using proprietary local area networks is available. Added option is inclusion of BiblioFile MARC database, which contains Library of Congress MARC records for up to three million titles. User can create and edit bibliographic, statistical and fiscal reports by using built-in database management system unique to REMO. User can bypass menu-driven functions and monitor control and presentation of data. User-Inquiry mode allows non-library personnel access to database while blocking unauthorized input.

RESOURCE LIBRARIAN

Accuware Business Solutions Ltd.
Suite 300, 914-15 Avenue South West
Calgary, Alberta, Canada, T2R 0S3
(403) 245-0477
Contact: Deanna Petersson

Hardware: IBM PC or compatible (386 or 486); All models of the Macintosh and Macintosh II series except Mac 512K .

System Requirements: 2MB RAM Macintosh, 2 MB minimum RAM IBM PC or compatibles; Windows 3.0 or greater; Postscript printer; TOPS, Appleshare, 3-Com, or Novell network for multiuser use.

Programming Language: OMNIS, C++; Oracle and C++ for Remote and Public Access Module

Components & Applications:

acquisitions	yes	catalog (batch)	yes
catalog (online)	yes	cataloging	yes
CD-ROM interface	no	circulation	yes
formatting bibliographies	no	index of keywords	yes
inter-library loan	no	interface for MARC records	yes
media booking	yes	reserve room	yes
serials	yes	thesaurus	no

Updating Modes:

batch update	no	dynamic update	yes

Features:

Boolean logic searchable	yes	full text searchable	yes
record fields	variable length, 32K max	record size	variable length
statistical & math capabilities	yes	wholesale change capability	no

Support:

application consulting	yes	maintenance and updates	yes
time share available	no	user training	yes

Recommended for:

Corporate & govt libraries	yes	Media center management	yes
Public libraries	yes	Records & files management	yes
School libraries	yes	University libraries	yes

Installations:

Initial installation date	1990	Total number of installed sites	11

Sampling of current clients: Corporate libraries, Special libraries, Media centers, School libraries including Long Term Inservice Center (Calgary, Alberta) and Cecil County Public Schools (Elkton, MD).

Published reviews & articles: ALUG Newsletter June 1992; The Online Catalog Book by Walt Crawford, 1992; The Catalog Collection by Walt Crawford, 1992; Library Technology Reports review of earlier version called RCM (Resource Center Management) system May-June 1990.

Price: Resource Librarian Package (acquisitions, cataloging, circulation, serials) $1845 U.S.; or modules sold separately as follows: acquisitions module $295, serials module $295, cataloging module $925, circulation module $625 U.S.. Please call us for current pricing on our RPAC (Remote and Public Access) module. Free demos available. Demo with manual $50.

Supplier's Comments: Resource Librarian is an easy to use solution for cataloging and general user browsing of library information at the desktop. It looks, feels, and functions the same on both Apple Macintosh® and IBM PC's® or Compatibles running Windows 3.0 or greater. Users can even have both types of machines on the same network sharing the same data file! There is no re-training necessary to move between platforms. Resource Librarian's unique graphical user interface makes it so easy to use that users will be amazed at the power they can gain with it in a very short period of time. Just ask our users for confirmation! Our security system protects your information from unauthorized users. With our new remote access module, now library users can get access to library information and create electronic requests for resources from anywhere! All of the application modules are fully integrated. Resource Librarian even gives each library the ability to customize certain functional areas of the application to meet the individual needs of the resource center. Call us for a demo today!

RETENTION MANAGEMENT SOFTWARE

Automated Records Management
23011 Moulton Parkway, Suite J-10
Laguna Hills, CA 92653
(714) 855-8780   FAX (714) 855-9078

Hardware: IBM/PC, XT, AT, PS/2 and most IBM compatibles

System Requirements: MS DOS

Programming Language: dBase III Plus and compiled using Foxbase

Components & Applications:

acquisitions	no	catalog (batch)	no
catalog (online)	yes	cataloging	no
CD-ROM interface	no	circulation	no
formatting bibliographies	no	index of keywords	no
inter-library loan	no	interface for MARC records	no
media booking	no	reserve room	no
serials	no	thesaurus	no

Updating Modes:

batch update	no	dynamic update	yes

Features:

Boolean logic searchable	no	full text searchable	no
record fields	no info	record size	no info
statistical & math capabilities	no	wholesale change capability	no

Support:

application consulting	yes	maintenance and updates	yes
time share available	no	user training	yes

Recommended for:

Corporate & govt libraries	no	Media center management	no
Public libraries	no	Records & files management	yes
School libraries	no	University libraries	no

Installations:

Initial installation date	1990	Total number of installed sites	150

Sampling of current clients:

Price: $249

Supplier's Comments: Manages and prints retention schedules.

Working with your departments, internal audit, legal, etc., you collect and identify all records giving them a Record Title Code, establish how long the department should keep the records, how long the company should keep the records, etc.

This information is entered into your computer and from it a variety of reports and retention schedules are printed.

RIM

Records & Information Management Solutions
8547 Edney Ridge Drive
Cordova, TN 38018
(901) 372-7774
Contact: Jean Hiltenbrand

Hardware: IBM PC and compatibles; IBM S34/36/38; IBM AS/400; all IBM mainframes

System Requirements: no info

Programming Language: PC dBase and other compiling languages;
For IBM AS/400 and IBM/S36-RPG

Components & Applications:

acquisitions	no	catalog (batch)	yes
catalog (online)	yes	cataloging	yes
CD-ROM interface	no	circulation	no
formatting bibliographies	no	index of keywords	yes
inter-library loan	no	interface for MARC records	no
media booking	no	reserve room	no
serials	no	thesaurus	no
records centers	yes	active file tracking	yes
records retention	yes		

Updating Modes:

batch update	yes	dynamic update	yes

Features:

Boolean logic searchable	yes	full text searchable	no
record fields	yes	record size	no limit
statistical & math capabilities	yes	wholesale change capability	yes

Support:

application consulting	yes	maintenance and updates	yes
time share available	no	user training	yes

Recommended for:

Corporate & govt libraries	yes	Media center management	yes
Public libraries	no	Records & files management	yes
School libraries	no	University libraries	yes

Installations:

Initial installation date	May 1987	Total number of installed sites	15
Sampling of current clients:	upon request		

Published reviews & articles:
Hiltenbrand, Jean. "Computerized Records Management: Information and Records Management Software System (INFORM)." *The Records & Retrieval Report,* May 1987, p.5.

Price: varies with hardware

Supplier's comments: RIM - Records and Information Management software system manages the total operations of a records storage center. In September 1987, a national research and development company studied 70 software packages. RIM was the only system in the U.S. that met all criteria for automated records management.

There are several modules: Active Records Module, Inactive Records Module, Magnetic Media Module, Financial Module, Bar Code Module.

ROOMER3

Hufnagel Software
501 H Main Street
PO Box 747
Clarion,PA 16214
814-226-5600   FAX 814 226 5551
Contact:

Hardware: IBM PC/XT/AT/PS2/286/386/486

System Requirements: 640KB of memory, DOS 3.0 or later, a hard disk with 3MB of available space, a VGA, EGA, CGA or Hercules graphics board and monitor, a printer or a plotter. A mouse and math coprocessors are supported but are not required.

Support:

application consulting	no	maintenance and updates	yes
time share available	no	user training	no

Recommended for:

Corporate & govt libraries	yes	Media center management	no
Public libraries	yes	Records & files management	no
School libraries	yes	University libraries	yes

Installations:

Initial installation date	1990	Total number of installed sites	1,000

Sampling of current clients: on request

Published reviews & articles:
Phenix,K. "Software for Libraries" *Wilson Library Bulletin*, Nov 1991, pp 77-79

Price: $395 includes free disk of 3D library furniture for those who request it.
      Other modules: Interiors $75 for interior designers
                        Computer Layouts $75 for computer center designers
                        Outside $75 for designing exteriors
                        The ROOMER3 Video is available separately for $10

Supplier's comments: Allows you to quickly and easily create scale floor plans and furniture/fixture arrangements of proposed interior projects. Creates 3D renderings of these which allow you to see what your finished facility will look like before work begins.

Editor's note: This is a special software package for libraries which creates floor plans and room arrangements giving 3D views from various perspectives. Therefore, it does not include the usual list of components and applications.

ROUTING LIST MANAGER

Professional Software
21 Forest Avenue
Glen Ridge, NJ 07028
(201) 748-7658

Hardware: IBM PC, XT, AT

System Requirements: 256K RAM; DOS

Programming Language: no info

Components & Applications:

acquisitions	see ACQUISITION MANAGER	catalog (batch)	no
catalog (online)	see ONLINE CATALOG	cataloging	no
CD-ROM interface	no	circulation	see CIRCULATION MANAGER
formatting bibliographies	no	index of keywords	no
inter-library loan	no	interface for MARC records	no
media booking	no	reserve room	no
serials	see SERIAL CONTROL SYSTEM	thesaurus	no

Updating Modes:

batch update	no	dynamic update	yes

Features:

Boolean logic searchable	no	full text searchable	no
record fields	no info	record size	32,000 Patrons; 11,000 Titles
statistical & math capabilities	yes	wholesale change capability	yes

Support:

application consulting	no	maintenance and updates	yes
time share available	no	user training	no

Recommended for:

Corporate & govt libraries	yes	Media center management	no
Public libraries	no	Records & files management	no
School libraries	no	University libraries	no

Installations:

Initial installation date	1985	Total number of installed sites	no info
Sampling of current clients:	no info		

Price: $ 550 software and documentation

Supplier's comments: You can establish up to 12 routing lists for any one journal. Each routing list can have up to 14 names on it, so you can route any journal to as many as 168 people.
   Integrates with SERIAL CONTROL SYSTEM by Professional Software.

ROUTING MANAGER

Right On Programs
755-F New York Avenue
Huntington, NY 11743
(516) 424-7777   FAX (516) 424-7207

Hardware: IBM & compatibles

System Requirements: MS-DOS

Programming Language: Turbo Pascal

Components & Applications:

acquisitions	no	catalog (batch)	no
catalog (online)	no	cataloging	no
CD-ROM interface	no	circulation	no
formatting bibliographies	no	index of keywords	no
inter-library loan	no	interface for MARC records	no
media booking	no	reserve room	no
serials	yes	thesaurus	no

Updating Modes:

batch update	no	dynamic update	yes

Features:

Boolean logic searchable	no	full text searchable	no
record fields	no info	record size	no info
statistical & math capabilities	yes	wholesale change capability	no

Support:

application consulting	yes	maintenance and updates	yes
time share available	no	user training	no

Recommended for:

Corporate & govt libraries	yes	Media center management	yes
Public libraries	yes	Records & files management	yes
School libraries	yes	University libraries	yes

Installations:

Initial installation date	1991	Total number of installed sites	650
Sampling of current clients: no info			

Price: $139

Supplier's comments: This routing program allows you to list all the magazines you receive and all the people who are receiving copies of each one. You can pull a Master list to the screen or printer and see who is getting what. When a new person arrives in the hospital, school, university, office or whatever, type in the person's name, the name of the magazine(s) that person is to receive and that's it. Similarly, if someone leaves, type in the name and request that it be deleted. All magazines routed to that person will be deleted automatically.

SEARCHEXPRESS DOCUMENT IMAGING SYSTEM

Executive Technologies Inc.
2120 16th Avenue South
Birmingham,AL 35205
205-933-5494
Fax (205) 930-5509
Contact: Marketing

Hardware: IBM PC

System Requirements: DOS, Windows (with our Windows version)

Updating Modes:

batch update	no, search only	dynamic update	no, search only

Features:

Boolean logic searchable	yes	full text searchable	yes
record fields	yes	record size	2.4MB
statistical & math capabilities	no	wholesale change capability	no

Support:

application consulting	yes	maintenance and updates	yes
time share available	no	user training	yes

Recommended for:

Corporate & govt libraries	yes	Media center management	no
Public libraries	yes	Records & files management	yes
School libraries	no	University libraries	yes

Installations:

Initial installation date	1986	Total number of installed sites	1,000

Sampling of current clients: Ontario Hydro, Lockheed, U.S. Navy, Bell South, Rockwell International, various law firms.

Published reviews & articles:

Price:　　$ 5,995 single station - Free demo disk available
　　　　　$10,000 1 - 5 user network
　　　　　(New prices reflect software license fees only - no hardware)

Supplier's comments: The SearchExpress Document Imaging System allows for high-speed scanning of documents and Optical Character Recognition (OCR) of the scanned images. The images are compressed in TIFF Group IV format. The SearchExpress system uses a sophisticated parallel processing system allowing thousands of pages to be scanned and OCRed daily. Features include an OCR proofing editor which displays both the image and OVRed text simultaneously on the screen. Full-text as well as fielded data searches will retrieve documents in seconds. Users can display both the original image (including any signatures, handwritten notations, or photographs) as well as the linked ASCII text. Supports importation of documents from all major word processors. Also supports all major optical storage devices. The system includes a high-speed scanner, OCR processor, optional optical disk storage, and full-text document retrieval software. Supports Boolean Searching, Concept Searching, and Relevancy Ranking.

Editors's note: This is a special package for retrieving images and full text. Therefore, it does not include the usual list of components and applications.

SERIAL CONTROL SYSTEM

Professional Software
21 Forest Avenue
Glen Ridge, NJ 07028
(201) 748-7658

Hardware: IBM PC, XT, AT, PS/2

System Requirements: 256K RAM; DOS

Programming Language: no info

Components & Applications:

acquisitions	see ACQUISITION MANAGER	catalog (batch)	no
catalog (online)	see ONLINE CATALOG	cataloging	no
CD-ROM interface	no	circulation	see CIRCULATION MANAGER
formatting bibliographies	no	index of keywords	no
inter-library loan	no	interface for MARC records	no
media booking	no	reserve room	no
serials	yes	thesaurus	no

Updating Modes:

batch update	no	dynamic update	yes

Features:

Boolean logic searchable	no	full text searchable	no
record fields	no info	record size	no info
statistical & math capabilities	yes	wholesale change capability	no

Support:

application consulting	no	maintenance and updates	yes
time share available	no	user training	no

Recommended for:

Corporate & govt libraries	yes	Media center management	no
Public libraries	no	Records & files management	no
School libraries	no	University libraries	yes

Installations:

Initial installation date	1985	Total number of installed sites	no info
Sampling of current clients:	no info		

Price:

$900	Check in, Claiming, Subscription Management
$400	Holdings-List Module
$300	Bindery/Microfilm Module
$450	Routing-List Module
$ .60/title	Pre-Loaded Journal Data for Hospital Libraries
$ .60/title	Pre-Loaded Journal Data for Small College Libraries
$ 85	Demo Package

Supplier's comments: The Serial Control System starts with a basic system that provides check-in, claiming, and subscription management. To this basic system you can add components used to manage holdings lists, schedule and track bindery operations, and maintain routing lists.
   Integrates with Routing List Manager by Professional Software.

SHAREPAC

OCLC Online Computer Library Center, Inc.
6565 Frantz Road
Dublin, OH 43017-3395
(614) 764-6000
Contact: Marketing

Auto-Graphics, Inc.
3201 Temple Avenue
Pomona, CA 91768-3200
(714) 595-7204 or (800) 776-6939 Fax (714) 595-3506
Contact: Joel M. Lee, Marketing Manager

Hardware: IBM compatibles

System Requirements: DOS 3.2 or higher; 20 MB hard-disk; 640K RAM; CD Drive; modem

Programming Language: no info

Components & Applications:

acquisitions	no	catalog (batch)	no
catalog (online)	no	cataloging	no
CD-ROM interface	no	circulation	no
formatting bibliographies	no	index of keywords	no
inter-library loan	yes	interface for MARC records	no
media booking	no	reserve room	no
serials	no	thesaurus	no

Updating Modes:

batch update	yes	dynamic update	no

Features:

Boolean logic searchable	yes	full text searchable	no
record fields	MARC format	record size	MARC format
statistical & math capabilities	no	wholesale change capability	no

Support:

application consulting	no	maintenance and updates	yes
time share available	no	user training	no

Recommended for:

Corporate & govt libraries	yes	Media center management	no
Public libraries	yes	Records & files management	no
School libraries	yes	University libraries	yes

Installations:

Initial installation date	no info	Total number of installed sites	no info
Sampling of current clients:			

Published reviews & articles:

Price:

Supplier's comments: If you need an easy-to-use, affordable, multipurpose resource sharing system, the SharePAC system from OCLC and Auto-Graphics is the answer.

Built on IMPACT, Auto-Graphics' CD-ROM public access catalog, and enhanced by the addition of a direct link to the OCLC Interlibrary Loan network, the SharePAC system gives you access to the more than 25 million bibliographic records in the OCLC Online Union Catalog (OLUC), and moves you into the realm of a comprehensive, fully automated ILL network. The SharePAC system offers you more than just a friendly public access catalog and expanded resource sharing capability; it facilitates cooperative collection management, reciprocal borrowing, and database maintenance.

SMART

Southern Michigan Automated Retrieval Technologies
1651 Minoka Trail
Okemos, MI 48864
(517) 349-0513   FAX - 517- 372-0341
Contact: Richard Barnes

Hardware: IBM PC, AT, or XT

System Requirements: 1 floppy drive; 20 Mb Hard disk; DOS 3.1 or higher

Programming Language: Nutshell Plus Relational File Manager

Components & Applications:

acquisitions	yes	catalog (batch)	no
catalog (online)	yes	cataloging	yes
CD-ROM interface	no	circulation	yes
formatting bibliographies	no	index of keywords	yes
inter-library loan	yes	interface for MARC records	no
media booking	no	reserve room	no
serials	yes	thesaurus	no

Updating Modes:

batch update	no	dynamic update	yes

Features:

Boolean logic searchable	AND &OR	full text searchable	yes
record fields	unlimited	record size	unlimited
statistical & math capabilities	yes	wholesale change capability	on indexed fields

Support:

application consulting	no	maintenance and updates	yes
time share available	no	user training	no

Recommended for:

Corporate & govt libraries	yes	Media center management	yes
Public libraries	yes	Records & files management	yes
School libraries	yes	University libraries	no

Installations:

Initial installation date	1988	Total number of installed sites	8

Sampling of current clients: Sparrow Hospital (MI); St. Lawrence Hospital (MI); Lansing General Hospital (MI); Hackley Hospital; Sisters of Mercy Hospital

Published reviews & articles:
Barnes, Judith, et al. "Micro-Based Integration System with Nutshell Plus." *Computers in Libraries* , v.9, no. 9, October 1989.

Price: $495 for the full system; $300 for templates only

Supplier's comments: A relational Library Management System that combines flexibility and ease of use with an affordable price. This is a system that you can adjust to meet your library's individual needs.

STAR®

Cuadra Associates, Inc.
11835 W. Olympic Blvd., Suite 855
Los Angeles, CA 90064
(310) 478-0066 or (800) 366-1390 FAX (310) 477-1078
Contact: Judith Wanger, Vice President

Hardware: Runs on over 150 different hardware platforms, under several multi-user operating systems: (1) on 386 and 486 PCs, under either SCO UNIX or AT&T System V UNIX; (2) on all models of Sun-3, SPARC workstations/servers, under SunOS (and Solaris); (3) on all models of Alpha Micro servers, under AMOS or the applicable UNIX operating system; and (4) on IBM RISC/6000 systems, under AIX. Can be used in all popular LANs with PC workstations, using STAR in a window or hot-keying between STAR and local DOS applications.

System Requirements: Varies by type of hardware platform/operating system.

Programming Language: C

Components & Applications:

acquisitions	yes	catalog (batch)	yes
catalog (online)	yes	cataloging	yes
CD-ROM interface	no	circulation	yes
formatting bibliographies	yes	index of keywords	yes
inter-library loan	yes	interface for MARC records	yes
media booking	yes	reserve room	yes
serials	yes	thesaurus	yes

Updating Modes:

batch update	yes	dynamic update	yes

Features:

Boolean logic searchable	yes	full text searchable	yes
record fields	500 max; any can be variable length or repeating		
record size	2 million char		
statistical & math capabilities	yes	wholesale change capability	yes

Support:

application consulting	yes	maintenance and updates	yes
time share available	yes	user training	yes

Recommended for:

Corporate & govt libraries	yes	Media center management	yes
Public libraries	yes	Records & files management	yes
School libraries	yes	University libraries	yes

Installations:

Initial installation date	1982	Total number of installed sites	240

Sampling of current clients: Library of Congress, Federal Research Division and Congressional Research Service; Department of Agriculture and National Agricultural Library; Federal Deposit Insurance Corporation and FDIC Library; FDA Library; National Emergency Training Center; Naval Research Laboratory; League of Minnesota Cities; Los Angeles County Public Library, C.A.L.L.; New York State Department of Education; Thousand Oaks Public Library; Michigan State University; Exxon and Exxon Biomedical Sciences; Gas Research Institute Library; BBC, News Division Library; The Royal Armouries, Tower of London; University of Mexico Library; El Colegio Library (Mexico); Cinematheque Ontario, Film Reference Library (Canada); Community Information Centres (ACICO) of Ontario (Canada).

Published reviews & articles:

"Cuadra Associates is a "STAR" at Allergan, Inc." *EDMS*, volume 2, issue 1, September 1991.

Calvano, Margaret, Director of Library and Information Services, National Multiple Sclerosis Society. "Consumer Health Information and the Not-for-Profit Health Agency," *Bulletin of the Medical Library Association*, volume 79, issue 2, April 1991, pages 189-194.

"Shannon & Wilson Expands Computer Capabilities." *Seattle Daily Journal of Commerce*, February 13, 1991.

Cibbarelli, Pamela. "Cibbarelli's Surveys: Automation in Review. User-Ratings of STAR Software." *Computers in Libraries*, September 1992.

Cibbarelli, Pamela. "User Ratings of STAR Software." *OASIS Newsletter*, February 1990.

Cuadra, Carlos A. "STAR: History, Development, and Use." *Information Services & Use*, 1990, pages 381.390.

STAR® continued

Price: STAR licenses—for one user to over 50 simultaneous users—include a full year of software updates and assistance. Prices vary with the number of simultaneous users to be supported (e.g., 2-user license, $4,500; 6-user license, $11,525).

Pre-defined library and records management applications are available as options. For example, MARCplus, including both import and export programs, is $3,500.

Supplier's comments: STAR® is a multi-user system designed for developing, managing, and using databases of bibliographic and non-bibliographic information. Also provides for "content-based" retrieval of images associated with records in STAR databases that describe or represent items in a collection.

Without programming, users can define databases (or modify pre-defined library and records management applications) to meet their needs: to control and validate input, specify the way that fields are to be indexed and searched, design many different types of report formats, and support ordering, serials check-in and routing, circulation, and other management/service processes.

The latest release provides several major new capabilities, including: an end-user search interface that can be tailored for use with different types of databases and different types of inquiries and user groups; thesaurus support in searching, to provide for automatic "lookup" of search terms in another (e.g., authority-file) database; relational report generation for dynamically integrating data from multiple databases into a single report; generation of statistics directly and dynamically at report generation time; full MARC support; and new output re-formatting capabilities of use with MARC and other record structures with subfields.

STATUS

C P International Inc
210 South Street
New York, NY 10002
(212) 815-8691 ext 8691

Hardware: IBM micros; Wang PC, Fortune PC

System Requirements: DOS or UNIX

Programming Language: no info

Components & Applications:

acquisitions	no	catalog (batch)	yes
catalog (online)	yes	cataloging	no
CD-ROM interface	no	circulation	no
formatting bibliographies	no	index of keywords	yes
inter-library loan	no	interface for MARC records	no
media booking	no	reserve room	no
serials	no	thesaurus	no

Updating Modes:

batch update	yes	dynamic update	yes

Features:

Boolean logic searchable	yes	full text searchable	yes
record fields	no info	record size	no info
statistical & math capabilities	no	wholesale change capability	yes

Support:

application consulting	no	maintenance and updates	yes
time share available	no	user training	yes

Recommended for:

Corporate & govt libraries	yes	Media center management	no
Public libraries	no	Records & files management	yes
School libraries	no	University libraries	no

Installations:

Initial installation date	1980	Total number of installed sites	200
Sampling of current clients:	no info		

Published reviews and articles: no info

Price: $2000.00
Supplier's comments: no info

STILAS

Sirsi Corporation
110 Walker Ave.
Huntsville, AL 35801
(205) 536-5881
Contact: Sales/Marketing Dept.

Hardware: Any computer running UNIX operating systems

System Requirements: UNIX operating system; disk and memory requirements vary with collection size and library requirements

Programming Language: C

Components & Applications:

acquisitions	yes	catalog (batch)	yes
catalog (online)	yes	cataloging	yes
CD-ROM interface	yes	circulation	yes
formatting bibliographies	no	index of keywords	yes
inter-library loan	yes	interface for MARC records	yes
media booking	yes	reserve room	yes
serials	yes	thesaurus	yes

Updating Modes:

batch update	yes	dynamic update	yes

Features:

Boolean logic searchable	yes	full text searchable	yes
record fields	no info	record size	unlimited
statistical & math capabilities	yes	wholesale change capability	yes

Support:

application consulting	yes	maintenance and updates	yes
time share available	no	user training	yes

Recommended for:

Corporate & govt libraries	yes	Media center management	yes
Public libraries	yes	Records & files management	yes
School libraries	yes	University libraries	yes

Installations:

Initial installation date	1982	Total number of installed sites	175
Sampling of current clients:			

Published reviews & articles:

"Introducing the Redstone Scientific Information Center", *DIGEST*, Volume 92, Number 2, April, 1992, p.4;
"Local Company Holds First International Users Group", DIRECTIONS, Volume 2, Issue 12, May, 1992, p.6;
"Companies in the News", *Wilson Library Bulletin*, June, 1992, p.17;
"Insider Report", *Media & Methods*, May/June, 1992, p.36;
"News Briefs", *Academic and Library Computing, Vol 9/No.5, May, 1992, p.8.*

Price: Each software module is priced separately.

Supplier's comments: Sirsi's STILAS is a fully integrated UNIX-based library system which automates all aspects of a library's operation: cataloging (any format), authority control, public access, circulation, academic reserves, acquisitions, reference database manager, serials control, and electronic mail modules. The Retrieval Interface Manager module even connects the user automatically to multiple remote data bases and lets the user search them with STILAS commands. Modules can be configured according to need. All types of libraries can benefit from STILAS. Sirsi's customer base includes public, academic, school, government research, corporate and law libraries.

STILAS's unique, user friendly user interface makes menus obsolete, giving simultaneous access to all system commands. STILAS can be purchased for single or multiple access locations. Cooperating libraries can also network.

A variety of peripherals, including laser, bar code and OCR readers, receipt and screen printers, can be connected optionally to STILAS workstations.

Sirsi is a full-service company, providing conversion services, training and support. Direct interfaces to laser disk, OCLC and other cataloging sources are available to enable the librarian to transfer records from these sources directly to STILAS. STILAS host computers range from 386 PCs to mainframes, making STILAS fit any budget.

STN EXPRESS

STN International
c/o CAS
2540 Olentangy River Road
P.O. Box 3012
Columbus, OH 43210-0012
800-848-6533 or 614-447-3698
Fax 614-447-3713
Contact: Director of Marketing

Hardware: IBM PC; Macintosh

System Requirements: DOS or Macintosh OS; modem.

Features:

Boolean logic searchable	yes	full text searchable	yes
record fields	no info	record size	no info
statistical & math capabilities	yes	wholesale change capability	no

Support:

application consulting	no	maintenance and updates	yes
time share available	no	user training	no

Recommended for:

Corporate & govt libraries	yes	Media center management	no
Public libraries	yes	Records & files management	no
School libraries	yes	University libraries	yes

Installations:

nitial installation date	no info	Total number of installed sites	no info

Sampling of current clients:

Published reviews & articles:

Price: $460

Supplier's comments: STN Express is software that works with your personal computer to provide streamlined searching of databases on STN International, the scientific and technical information network, and other online hosts. STN Express will guide you quickly through efficient online searches of some of the most valuable databases in the areas of life sciences, chemistry, physics and engineering, etc. You'll find the informtaion you need more rapidly and with less effort than ever before.

SUBSCRIPTION MANAGER

Right On Programs
755-F New York Avenue
Huntington, NY 11743
(516) 424-7777   FAX (516) 424-7207

Hardware: IBM & compatibles; Apple Series

System Requirements: MS-DOS

Programming Language: Turbo Pascal

Components & Applications:

acquisitions	no	catalog (batch)	no
catalog (online)	no	cataloging	no
CD-ROM interface	no	circulation	no
formatting bibliographies	no	index of keywords	no
inter-library loan	no	interface for MARC records	no
media booking	no	reserve room	no
serials	yes	thesaurus	no

Updating Modes:

batch update	no	dynamic update	yes

Features:

Boolean logic searchable	no	full text searchable	no
record fields	no info	record size	no info
statistical & math capabilities	yes	wholesale change capability	no

Support:

application consulting	yes	maintenance and updates	yes
time share available	no	user training	no

Recommended for:

Corporate & govt libraries	yes	Media center management	yes
Public libraries	yes	Records & files management	yes
School libraries	yes	University libraries	yes

Installations:

Initial installation date	1991	Total number of installed sites	700
Sampling of current clients: no info			

Price: $139

Supplier's comments: SUBSCRIPTION MANAGER keeps track of all the periodical subscriptions in all libraries. Keeps track of not only the issues you've received but also the ones you haven't received. Keeps track of subscription title, orders placed, number of subscriptions ordered. Prints out a complete list of one or all magazine titles designating every missing issue. Maintains list of suppliers and publishers. Will print address labels to publisher or supplier when correspondence is necessary. Easy to learn and use.

SUPER CIRCULATION CONTROL V.2.1

Right On Programs
755-F New York Avenue
Huntington, NY 11743
(516) 424-7777   FAX (516) 424-7207

Hardware: IBM & compatibles

System Requirements: MS-DOS

Programming Language:

Components & Applications:

acquisitions	no	catalog (batch)	no
catalog (online)	yes	cataloging	yes
CD-ROM interface	no	circulation	yes
formatting bibliographies	no	index of keywords	no
inter-library loan	no	interface for MARC records	no
media booking	no	reserve room	no
serials	no	thesaurus	no

Updating Modes:

batch update	no	dynamic update	yes

Features:

Boolean logic searchable	no	full text searchable	no
record fields	no info	record size	no info
statistical & math capabilities	yes	wholesale change capability	no

Support:

application consulting	yes	maintenance and updates	yes
time share available	no	user training	no

Recommended for:

Corporate & govt libraries	yes	Media center management	yes
Public libraries	yes	Records & files management	yes
School libraries	yes	University libraries	yes

Installations:

Initial installation date	1991	Total number of installed sites	800
Sampling of current clients:	no info		

Price: $479

Supplier's comments: Combines CIRCULATION CONTROL and ON-LINE CATALOG. See them for info. Network version also available.

SUPERCAT ®

Gaylord Information Systems
Box 4901
Syracuse, NY 13221
(315) 457-5070 or (800) 962-9580

Hardware: IBM PC XT or compatible

System Requirements: MS-DOS

Programming Language: Assembler

Components & Applications:

acquisitions	no	catalog (batch)	no
catalog (online)	no	cataloging	yes
CD-ROM interface	yes	circulation	no
formatting bibliographies	no	index of keywords	no
inter-library loan	no	interface for MARC records	no
media booking	no	reserve room	no
serials	no	thesaurus	no

Updating Modes:

batch update	no	dynamic update	yes

Features:

Boolean logic searchable	no	full text searchable	yes
record fields	MARC	record size	MARC
statistical & math capabilities	no	wholesale change capability	no

Support:

application consulting	yes	maintenance and updates	yes
time share available	no	user training	yes

Recommended for:

Corporate & govt libraries	yes	Media center management	yes
Public libraries	yes	Records & files management	no
School libraries	yes	University libraries	yes

Installations:

Initial installation date	1988	Total number of installed sites	224
Sampling of current clients: no info			

Published reviews & articles:
Morrow, Blaine. "SuperCAT Cataloger's Workstation." *CD-ROM Librarian*. Sept 1989, p. 28-35.

Price: $1,500.00. Free demonstration and tutorial disks are available.

Supplier's comments: SuperCAT is a complete cataloging support system for libraries of all types and size. The complete Library of Congress database, of over 4 million bibliographic records, is available on three CD-ROM discs. Additionally, SuperCat accesses the National Library of Medicine's medical bibliographic records, Cassidy Cataloging Services's law and business records, Hennepin County's audio-visual records as well as nearly 100,000 A/V records from Professional Media Services, Inc. The full ALA character set of diacritics and special figures is supported on screen and can be printed. Free demonstration and tutorial disks are available.

Version 6.40 of SuperCAT can be used as the cataloging module on the GALAXY Integrated Library System.

SUPERFILE

Software Marketing Associates
P.O. Box 200115
Austin, TX 78720
(512) 250-9175
Contact: Ken Logsdon

Hardware: IBM-PC and compatibles; most MS-DOS and CP/M formats

System Requirements: 2 disk drives

Programming Language: CONVERS (FORTH)

Components & Applications:

acquisitions	no	catalog (batch)	yes
catalog (online)	yes	cataloging	yes
CD-ROM interface	no	circulation	no
formatting bibliographies	no	index of keywords	yes
inter-library loan	no	interface for MARC records	no
media booking	no	reserve room	no
serials	no	thesaurus	no

Updating Modes:

batch update	no	dynamic update	yes

Features:

Boolean logic searchable	yes	full text searchable	no
record fields	250 keywords/phrases	record size	512K
statistical & math capabilities	no	wholesale change capability	no

Support:

application consulting	telephone support	maintenance and updates	yes
time share available	no	user training	tutorial & manual

Recommended for:

Corporate & govt libraries	yes	Media center management	no
Public libraries	no	Records & files management	no
School libraries	no	University libraries	no

Installations:

Initial installation date	1983	Total number of installed sites	6000

Sampling of current clients:

Price: $195.00 one-time, single user fee

Published articles and reviews:

Supplier's comments: SuperFile is a database program developed specifically for filing and retrieving free-form information. This design offers many benefits over other database programs when handling large amounts of textual information.

SuperFile lets you combine up to 64 key words with AND, OR and NOT to retrieve specific information from your database. Each SuperFile database can manage up to 65,000 entries (free-form information up to 512,000 characters each), on up to 255 floppy disks, or a hard disk. And, at approximately 100 entries per second, it searches even very large databases in seconds. No need to re-key your information into forms or fields, simply take your word processing, or other ASCII format files, and add our special markers at the beginning and end of each entry. Then, you add up to 250 key words or phrases to describe the contents of that entry. Retrieved text can be viewed on the screen, printed, and/or sent to a new disk file. The program is very easy to learn and use. The combination of its plain English menus, and step-by-step instruction manual and tutorial allow immediate productivity with the package.

SUPPLIES INVENTORY CONTROL V. 2.0

Right On Programs
755-F New York Avenue
Huntington, NY 11743
(516) 424-7777   FAX (516) 424-7207

Hardware: IBM & compatibles

System Requirements: MS-DOS

Programming Language: Turbo Pascal

Components & Applications:

acquisitions	no	catalog (batch)	yes
catalog (online)	yes	cataloging	yes
CD-ROM interface	no	circulation	no
formatting bibliographies	no	index of keywords	no
inter-library loan	no	interface for MARC records	no
media booking	no	reserve room	no
serials	no	thesaurus	no

Updating Modes:

batch update	no	dynamic update	yes

Features:

Boolean logic searchable	no	full text searchable	no
record fields	no info	record size	no info
statistical & math capabilities	yes	wholesale change capability	no

Support:

application consulting	yes	maintenance and updates	yes
time share available	no	user training	no

Recommended for:

Corporate & govt libraries	yes	Media center management	yes
Public libraries	yes	Records & files management	yes
School libraries	yes	University libraries	yes

Installations:

Initial installation date	1991	Total number of installed sites	400
Sampling of current clients: no info			

Price: $139

Supplier's comments: Keeps up to the minute check on all kinds of items in supply category. When supplies arrive, enter all items and suppliers. Then, enter all users. When items are requested, enter item and user. Easy to see who uses what, how much, and how often. Generates several reports. Allows for reordering of frequently used items from same vendor. Indicates price paid previous time. Takes the hassle out of supplies and the supply room.

SYDNEYPLUS LIBRARY MANAGEMENT (DEC VAX)

International Library Systems Corp.
320 - 2600 Granville Street
Vancouver, B.C. Canada V6H 3V3
(604) 734-8882
Contact: Leanne Cowie, Marketing Coordinator

Hardware: DEC VAX

System Requirements: VMS

Programming Language: C

Components & Applications:

acquisitions	yes	catalog (batch)	yes
catalog (online)	yes	cataloging	yes
CD-ROM interface	yes	circulation	yes
formatting bibliographies	yes	index of keywords	yes
inter-library loan	planned	interface for MARC records	yes
media booking	yes	reserve room	planned
serials	yes	thesaurus	yes

Updating Modes:

batch update	yes	dynamic update	yes

Features:

Boolean logic searchable	yes	full text searchable	yes
record fields	unlimited	record size	unlimited
statistical & math capabilities	yes	wholesale change capability	yes

Support:

application consulting	yes	maintenance and updates	yes
time share available	possible	user training	yes

Recommended for:

Corporate & govt libraries	yes	Media center management	yes
Public libraries	no	Records & files management	yes
School libraries	yes	University libraries	yes

Installations:

Initial installation date	1986	Total # of installed sites	50

Sampling of current clients: Customers include Fortune 500 companies, professional associations, academic libraries, medical libraries, government and special libraries.

Published reviews and articles: no info

Price:

Cataloging & Queries	$18,000
Customization	$ 5,000
Acquisitions	$ 5,000
Circulation	$ 5,000
Serials Control	$ 5,000
MARC Record Interface	$ 2,500

Supplier's comments: The SydneyPLUS Library System is a fully integrated system specifically designed to meet the needs of special libraries. The system operates on the VAX VMS operating system. Choosing from the available modules, libraries can tailor the system to meet their needs.

SYDNEYPLUS LIBRARY MANAGEMENT (PCS & NETWORKS)

International Library Systems Corp.
320 - 2600 Granville Street
Vancouver, B.C. Canada V6H 3V3
(604) 734-8882
Contact: Leanne Cowie, Marketing Coordinator

Hardware: IBM PC, XT, AT, 386, 486 and 100% compatibles.

System Requirements: minimum 640K memory, MS-DOS 3.0 hard disk (15MB for programs, 2MB per each 1000 titles).

Programming Language: C

Components & Applications:

acquisitions	yes	catalog (batch)	yes
catalog (online)	yes	cataloging	yes
CD-ROM interface	yes	circulation	yes
formatting bibliographies	yes	index of keywords	yes
inter-library loan	no	interface for MARC records	yes
media booking	no	reserve room	no
serials	yes	thesaurus	yes

Updating Modes:

batch update	yes	dynamic update	yes

Features:

Boolean logic searchable	yes	full text searchable	yes
record fields	unlimited	record size	unlimited
statistical & math capabilities	yes	wholesale change capability	yes

Support:

application consulting	yes	maintenance and updates	yes
time share available	no	user training	yes

Recommended for:

Corporate & govt libraries	yes	Media center management	no
Public libraries	no	Records & files management	yes
School libraries	yes	University libraries	yes

Installations:

Initial installation date	1984	Total # of installed sites	450

Sampling of current clients: Customers include Fortune 500 companies, professional associations, educational libraries, medical libraries, government and special libraries.

Published reviews and articles: no info

Price:

Cataloging & Queries (OPAC)	$ 2,500
Customization	$ 3,500
Acquisitions	$ 3,500
Circulation	$ 2,500
Serials Control	$ 3,500
MARC Record Interface	$ 2,500

Supplier's comments: The SydneyPLUS Library Management System is a fully integrated system specifically designed to meet the needs of special libraries. The system operates on MS-DOS PCs and a variety of network operating systems and features an optional Customization module for designing fields and databases which are unique to a particular site and collection specialty.

TD-5 PROFESSIONAL CATALOG SYSTEM

Tek Data Systems Co.
1111 West Park Ave.
Libertyville, IL 60048
708-367-8800
Contact   Frank J. Schmidt, President
          Bert Arnold, V.P. Sales Manager

Hardware: IBM PC compatible

System Requirements: PC-DOS,

Programming Language: PC-DOS, PC MOS

Components & Applications:

acquisitions	yes	catalog (batch)	yes
catalog (online)	yes	cataloging	yes
CD-ROM interface	no	circulation	yes
formatting bibliographies	no	index of keywords	yes
inter-library loan	no	interface for MARC records	see MITINET/marc
media booking	no	reserve room	no
serials	yes	thesaurus	yes

Updating Modes:

batch update	yes	dynamic update	yes

Features:

Boolean logic searchable	yes	full text searchable	yes
record fields	variable	record size	4,000 char.
statistical & math capabilities	yes	wholesale change capability	yes

Support:

application consulting	yes	maintenance and updates	yes
time share available	no	user training	yes

Recommended for:

Corporate & govt libraries	yes	Media center management	yes
Public libraries	yes	Records & files management	yes
School libraries	yes	University libraries	yes

Installations:

Initial installation date	no info	Total number of installed sites	390
Sampling of current clients:	no info		

Price: $2,000 basic
         $3,995 Professional

Supplier's comments: Interfaces to Aldus Page-Maker.

TECHLIBPLUS

Information Dimensions, Inc. (a subsidiary of Battelle Memorial Institute)
5080 Tuttle Crossing Blvd.
Dublin, Ohio 43017
(800) DATA MGT   (614) 761-8083
Contact: Tim Corley

Hardware: IBM VM, MVS; DEC VMS, ULTRIX, RISC; HP/UX 9000, SUN, USISYS, SIEMENS, CDC BULL/DPX.

System Requirements: CPU-dependent; .8 - 1.5 MG memory; DOS, VMS, or UNIX for servers

Programming Language: ANSI FORTRAN and Assembler

Components & Applications:

acquisitions	yes	catalog (batch)	yes
catalog (online)	yes	cataloging	yes
CD-ROM interface	no	circulation	yes
formatting bibliographies	no	index of keywords	yes
inter-library loan	no	interface for MARC records	yes
media booking	no	reserve room	no
serials	yes	thesaurus	yes

Updating Modes:

batch update	yes	dynamic update	yes

Features:

Boolean logic searchable	yes	full text searchable	yes
record fields	no limit	record size	no limit
statistical & math capabilities	yes	wholesale change capability	yes

Support:

application consulting	yes	maintenance and updates	yes
time share available	yes	user training	yes

Recommended for:

Corporate & govt libraries	yes	Media center management	yes
Public libraries	yes	Records & files management	yes
School libraries	yes	University libraries	yes

Installations:

Initial installation date	1989	Total number of installed sites	2,500
Sampling of current clients:			

Price: $5,000 - $179,000 range

Supplier's comments: TECHLIBplus gives the "Plus" you need to excel in the Information Age.

Today's special library is the central resource for valuable corporate information. This information is evolving from simple text to more sophisticated forms. Important knowledge is conveyed through graphics, images, and multi-media. As this material multiplies in size and complexity, it becomes more difficult to manage. Patrons still need quick, easy access to growing library collections while staff need greater control over operations.

TECHLIBplus is the answer. It easily manages your current library collections and has capabilities that keep pace with expanding collections. It flexibly conforms to your library's unique profiling requirements and maintains that tailoring in new releases.

TECHLIBplus streamlines library operations with integrated modules for patron access, catalog maintenance, circulation, serial management, acquisition processing, and MARC cataloging.

Plus, it links to full-text databases with images. For example, users throughout your organization can expand the scope of their research by searching technical documentation stored in a BASISplus database. At the same time, they can display corresponding images that accompany the text.

Based on BASISplus, the foremost document management and text retrieval system, TECHLIBplus provides full-text access to library documents in seconds.

TEK DATA

Tek Data Systems Co.
1111 West Park Ave.
Libertyville, IL 60048
708-367-8800
Contact   Frank J. Schmidt, President
            Bert Arnold, V.P. Sales Manager

Hardware: IBM PC

System Requirements: PC-DOS, poly FORTH Level II, III

Programming Language: PC-DOS, MULTILINK, polyFORTH multi-user

Components & Applications:

acquisitions	yes	catalog (batch)	yes
catalog (online)	yes	cataloging	yes
CD-ROM interface	no	circulation	yes
formatting bibliographies	no	index of keywords	yes
inter-library loan	no	interface for MARC records	see MITINET/Marc
media booking	yes	reserve room	no
serials	yes	thesaurus	yes

Updating Modes:

batch update	yes	dynamic update	yes

Features:

Boolean logic searchable	yes	full text searchable	no
record fields	unlimited	record size	fixed length w/PC-DOS; variable w/polyFORTH
statistical & math capabilities	yes	wholesale change capability	no

Support:

application consulting	yes	maintenance and updates	yes
time share available	no	user training	yes

Recommended for:

Corporate & govt libraries	yes	Media center management	yes
Public libraries	yes	Records & files management	yes
School libraries	yes	University libraries	yes

Installations:

Initial installation date	no info	Total number of installed	87
Sampling of current clients:	no info		

Price:

$10,000   Single user: hardware and software
$16,000   Multi-user: software, booking and cataloging
$ 7,000   Hardware
$50,000   Multi-user 32 Micro up to 15 terminals, booking, cataloging, remote card reader, wand loaded

Supplier's comments: An audio visual media booking system designed for online booking, alternate date displays, confirmations, shipping lists, management reports, and a report generator. On-line catalog, direct dial capability. Also, available through TCP-IP to AS400.

TEXTBOOK PLUS

Follett Software Company
809 North Front Street
McHenry, IL 60050-5589
(815) 344-8700 or (800) 323-3397
FAX (815) 344-8774
Contact: Michael Hollobow

Hardware: IBM PC or compatible; 20mb hard disk drive

System Requirements: 640K RAM; MS-DOS 3.3 or higher, Microsoft Extensions 2.2 or higher

Programming Language: C

Components & Applications:

acquisitions	no	catalog (batch)	no
catalog (online)	no	cataloging	no
CD-ROM interface	no	circulation	yes
formatting bibliographies	no	index of keywords	no
inter-library loan	no	interface for MARC records	yes
media booking	no	reserve room	no
serials	no	thesaurus	no

Updating Modes:

batch update	yes	dynamic update	yes

Features:

Boolean logic searchable	no	full text searchable	no
record fields	no info	record size	no info
statistical & math capabilities	no	wholesale change capability	no

Support:

application consulting	no	maintenance and updates	yes
time share available	no	user training	yes

Recommended for:

Corporate & govt libraries	no	Media center management	no
Public libraries	no	Records & files management	no
School libraries	yes	University libraries	no

Installations:

Initial installation date	1987	Total number of installed sites	300

Sampling of current clients: References available.

Published reviews & articles:

Price: $1695

Supplier's comments: Textbook Plus is designed to manage the circulation of textbooks. It utilizes barcodes and a barcode scanner. Data fields are tailored specifically for textbooks.

TEXTDBMS

Data Retrieval Corporation
11801 West Silver Spring Drive
Milwaukee, WI 53225-3042
800-421-3282
414-536-1984 - fax
Contact: Rob Schaefer

Hardware: IBM 370/30/XX/43XX; DEC MicroVAX, 8200 series & up

System Requirements: MVS or MVS/XA. CICS/VS release 1.6.1 or 1.7. PL/1 libraries, release 4.0 or 5.1. VMS (DEC)

Programming Language: PL/1

Components & Applications:

acquisitions	yes	catalog (batch)	yes
catalog (online)	yes	cataloging	yes
CD-ROM interface	no	circulation	yes
formatting bibliographies	no	index of keywords	yes
inter-library loan	no	interface for MARC records	no
media booking	no	reserve room	no
serials	yes	thesaurus	no

Updating Modes:

batch update	yes	dynamic update	yes

Features:

Boolean logic searchable	yes	full text searchable	yes
record fields	256	record size	230 char
statistical & math capabilities	yes	wholesale change capability	yes

Support:

application consulting	yes	maintenance and updates	yes
time share available	no	user training	yes

Recommended for:

Corporate & govt libraries	yes	Media center management	no
Public libraries	no	Records & files management	no
School libraries	no	University libraries	no

Installations:

Initial installation date   1969   Total number of installed sites   no info
Sampling of current clients: Florida Power & Light; Aetna Insurance; ManTech; NASA Johnson Space Center

Price: IBM-base Product: $155,000 and up plus $19,800 annual maintenance
DEC-base Product: $ 84,000 and up plus $18,000 annual maintenance

Monthly lease for in-house use:
IBM-based Product: $5,160 per month plus $1,500 maintenance
DEC-based Product: $2,820 per month plus $1,500 maintenance

Published articles and reviews:

Supplier's comments: TextDBMS manages all elements needed to create and maintain a centralized text resource, including full integration of:

TextSEARCHER, an online search and retrieval system with online update of information for immediate access;
TextBUILDER, a text application language facility, including Screen Management to define and create fixed
video screen formats, and Data Management to establish priority of information for searching;
TextCOMPOSER, for type composition of final output.

The TextDBMS system provides an array of comprehensive text tools. These tools provide the capability to: define, create, manipulate, and manage documents; create and define document databases; provide utilities for maintaining and protecting the database. It is integrated with an Application Language Facility for customization of the text application.

TRACS

Casher Associates, Inc.
1371 Beacon St.
Brookline, MA 02146
Contact: Richard Carlson
(617) 232-9111 or (212) 757-2868

Hardware: DEC PDP 11, VAX

System Requirements: no info

Programming Language: BASIC

Components & Applications:

acquisitions	no	catalog (batch)	yes
catalog (online)	yes	cataloging	yes
CD-ROM interface	no	circulation	yes
formatting bibliographies	no	index of keywords	yes
inter-library loan	no	interface for MARC records	no
media booking	no	reserve room	no
serials	no	thesaurus	no

Updating Modes:

batch update	no	dynamic update	yes

Features:

Boolean logic searchable	yes	full text searchable	no
record fields	variable	record size	variable
statistical & math capabilities	yes	wholesale change capability	yes

Support:

application consulting	yes	maintenance and updates	yes
time share available	negotiable	user training	yes

Recommended for:

Corporate & govt libraries	yes	Media center management	no
Public libraries	no	Records & files management	no
School libraries	no	University libraries	no

Installations:

Initial installation date	1977	Total number of installed sites	no info
Sampling of current clients:	no info		

Price: $40,000 for software

Supplier's comments: TRACS is a complete computerized system to help manage an archival storage facility and administer a records management program. TRACS was designed by records managers for records management. It includes all the features needed to customize the system to your specific needs. In the archive, TRACS improves logging, retrieving, dunning for borrowed files, and report creation. It optimizes archival space and automatically and accurately provides records retention and disposal information. An interface to bar code readers is provided.

ULISYS INTEGRATED LIBRARY SYSTEM

JES Library Automation Consulting Services, Inc.
#104-221 Blue Mountain Street
Coquitlam, BC, V3K 4H3 Canada
604-939-6775; fax 604-939-9970
Contact: Peter Smode

Hardware: DEC VAX

System Requirements: VAX/VMS

Programming Language: VAX BASIC

Components & Applications:

acquisitions	yes	catalog (batch)	yes
catalog (online)	yes	cataloging	yes
CD-ROM interface	yes	circulation	yes
formatting bibliographies	no	index of keywords	yes
inter-library loan	yes	interface for MARC records	yes
media booking	no	reserve room	yes
serials	no	thesaurus	yes

Updating Modes:

batch update	yes	dynamic update	yes

Features:

Boolean logic searchable	yes	full text searchable	no
record fields	MARC format	record size	MARC format
statistical & math capabilities	yes	wholesale change capability	yes

Support:

application consulting	yes	maintenance and updates	yes
time share available	no	user training	yes

Recommended for:

Corporate & govt libraries	yes	Media center management	no
Public libraries	yes	Records & files management	yes
School libraries	yes	University libraries	yes

Installations:

Initial installation date	1980	Total number of installed sites	14

Sampling of current clients: Carnegie Library of Pittsburgh (PA); Eugene Public Library (OR); Burnaby Public Library (BC); Bucks County Library Co-operative (PA).

Published reviews & articles:

Price: $30,000 to $1,000,000 (hardware and software), depending upon system size, options, etc. Software-only systems are available as well. Custom pricing information is available upon request.

Supplier's comments: The ULISYS library system delivers superior price/performance for both public and academic libraries. With the advent of new low-cost computer systems from DEC, small libraries can now enjoy the features of a large library system at a small system price. Smooth hardware upgrade paths are available for the library as their needs grow.

With powerful, consistent and easy to use software, ULISYS is currently supporting systems with up to 8,000,000 circulations per year.

Simple to learn and use commands make the ULISYS OPAC sub-system one of the best in the industry for public users at the library, or dialing in from home. A version optimized for talking terminal operation is also available.

Acquisitions system interfaces are available for Bibbase, INNOVACQ, or our very own ACQ. Numerous cataloguing interfaces are available for tape, PC and CD-ROM based cataloging sub-systems.

JES Library Automation prides itself on its flexibility and willingness to work with our clients to suit a system to their needs. Client suggestions and concerns are always a part of our ongoing development efforts.

ULTRACARD

Small Library Computing, Inc.
619 Mansfield Road
Willow Grove PA 19090
(215) 657-8472

Hardware: IBM PC with 512K RAM

System Requirements: DOS 2.0

Programming Language: no info

Components & Applications:

acquisitions	no	catalog (batch)	yes
catalog (online)	no	cataloging	yes
CD-ROM interface	no	circulation	no
formatting bibliographies	no	index of keywords	no
inter-library loan	no	interface for MARC records	yes
media booking	no	reserve room	no
serials	no	thesaurus	no

Updating Modes:

batch update	yes	dynamic update	yes

Features:

Boolean logic searchable	no	full text searchable	no
record fields	MARC	record size	MARC
statistical & math capabilities	no	wholesale change capability	no

Support:

application consulting	no	maintenance and updates	yes
time share available	no	user training	no

Recommended for:

Corporate & govt libraries	yes	Media center management	no
Public libraries	yes	Records & files management	no
School libraries	yes	University libraries	yes

Installations:

Initial installation date	1984	Total number of installed sites	no info
Sampling of current clients: no info			

Price: $395   software & documentation
        $ 30   demo disk and manual

Supplier's comments: Ultracard (UC) is a sophisticated, flexible, and easy-to-use program for the production of catalog cards and book labels (card, pocket, and spine). You input cataloging data on the screen with a full-screen editor. UC then, at your option, formats and prints a single card, a complete set of ready-to-file cards, and/or book labels. Virtually no limit on the number of subject, author, and title tracings. Includes numerous formatting options.

ULTRACARD/MARC

Small Library Computing, Inc.
619 Mansfield Road
Willow Grove PA 19090
(215) 657-8472

Hardware: IBM PC

System Requirements: DOS 2.0

Programming Language: no info

Components & Applications:

acquisitions	no	catalog (batch)	yes
catalog (online)	no	cataloging	yes
CD-ROM interface	no	circulation	no
formatting bibliographies	no	index of keywords	no
inter-library loan	no	interface for MARC records	yes
media booking	no	reserve room	no
serials	no	thesaurus	no

Updating Modes:

batch update	yes	dynamic update	yes

Features:

Boolean logic searchable	no	full text searchable	no
record fields	MARC	record size	MARC
statistical & math capabilities	no	wholesale change capability	no

Support:

application consulting	no	maintenance and updates	yes
time share available	no	user training	no

Recommended for:

Corporate & govt libraries	yes	Media center management	no
Public libraries	yes	Records & files management	no
School libraries	yes	University libraries	yes

Installations:

Initial installation date	1986	Total number of installed sites	no info
Sampling of current clients: no info			

Price: $595   software & documentation
$ 45   demo disk and manual

Supplier's comments: Ultracard/Marc (UCM) is a sophisticated, flexible, and easy-to-use program for the creation of MARC-format records and the printing of catalog cards and book labels (card, pocket, and spine). You input cataloging data on the screen with a full-screen editor and UCM stores this information on disk in a MARC-format file. UCM then, at your option, formats and prints a single card, a complete set of ready-to-file cards, and/or book labels. Virtually no limit on the number of subject, author, and title tracings. Includes numerous formatting options.

ULTRACARD/MARC PRINT-ONLY

Small Library Computing, Inc.
619 Mansfield Road
Willow Grove PA 19090
(215) 657-8472

Hardware: IBM PC

System Requirements: DOS 2.0

Programming Language: no info

Components & Applications:

acquisitions	no	catalog (batch)	yes
catalog (online)	no	cataloging	yes
CD-ROM interface	no	circulation	no
formatting bibliographies	no	index of keywords	no
inter-library loan	no	interface for MARC records	yes
media booking	no	reserve room	no
serials	no	thesaurus	no

Updating Modes:

batch update	yes	dynamic update	yes

Features:

Boolean logic searchable	no	full text searchable	no
record fields	MARC	record size	MARC
statistical & math capabilities	no	wholesale change capability	no

Support:

application consulting	no	maintenance and updates	yes
time share available	no	user training	no

Recommended for:

Corporate & govt libraries	yes	Media center management	no
Public libraries	yes	Records & files management	no
School libraries	yes	University libraries	yes

Installations:

Initial installation date	1989	Total number of installed sites	no info

Sampling of current clients: no info

Price: $295   software & documentation
         $ 30   demo disk and manual

Supplier's comments: Ultracard/Marc Print-Only (UCM-PO) reads the MARC records created in other library systems and prints catalog cards and book labels (card, pocket, and spine) from them. UCM-PO reads each record and, at your option, formats and prints a single card, a complete set of ready-to-file cards, and/or book labels. Supports both the full MARC and the MicroLIF formats. Virtually no limit on the number of subject, author, and title tracings. Includes numerous formatting options.

ULTRACAT

Library Systems and Services, Inc.
200 Orchard Ridge Drive
Gaithersburg, MD 20878
301-975-9800 or 800-638-8725
Attn: Marketing

Hardware: IBM compatibles; one or more floppy drives and one hard drive; 640K memory, & CD-ROM drive(s) if CD database is utilized.

System Requirements: DOS

Programming Language: Microsoft "C"

Components & Applications:

acquisitions	no	catalog (batch)	yes
catalog (online)	yes	cataloging	yes
CD-ROM interface	yes	circulation	no
formatting bibliographies	no	index of keywords	yes
inter-library loan	no	interface for MARC records	yes
media booking	no	reserve room	no
serials	no	thesaurus	no

Updating Modes:

batch update	yes	dynamic update	no

Features:

Boolean logic searchable	no	full text searchable	no
record fields	MARC format	record size	MARC format
statistical & math capabilities	no	wholesale change capability	no

Support:

application consulting	yes	maintenance and updates	yes
time share available	no	user training	no

Recommended for:

Corporate & govt libraries	yes	Media center management	yes
Public libraries	yes	Records & files management	no
School libraries	yes	University libraries	yes

Installations:

Initial installation date	1991	Total number of installed sites	n/a
Sampling of current clients:			

Published reviews & articles:

Price: $695; $100/year annual maintenance fee

Supplier's comments: ULTRACAT provides an economical, efficient, stand-alone cataloging support system for libraries, It may be used for retrieval and modification of data on CD-ROM databases (which LSSI can generate for a library or group of libraries) and for entry of original records.

UNICORN

Sirsi Corporation
110 Walker Ave.
Huntsville, AL 35801
(205) 536-5881
Contact: Sales/Marketing Dept.

Hardware: Any computer running UNIX operating systems

System Requirements: UNIX operating system; disk and memory requirements vary with collection size and library requirements

Programming Language: C

Components & Applications:

acquisitions	yes	catalog (batch)	yes
catalog (online)	yes	cataloging	yes
CD-ROM interface	yes	circulation	yes
formatting bibliographies	no	index of keywords	yes
inter-library loan	yes	interface for MARC records	yes
media booking	yes	reserve room	yes
serials	yes	thesaurus	yes

Updating Modes:

batch update	yes	dynamic update	yes

Features:

Boolean logic searchable	yes	full text searchable	yes
record fields	no info	record size	unlimited
statistical & math capabilities	yes	wholesale change capability	yes

Support:

application consulting	yes	maintenance and updates	yes
time share available	no	user training	yes

Recommended for:

Corporate & govt libraries	yes	Media center management	yes
Public libraries	yes	Records & files management	yes
School libraries	yes	University libraries	yes

Installations:

Initial installation date	1982	Total number of installed sites	175

Sampling of current clients:

Published reviews & articles:
"Introducing the Redstone Scientific Information Center", *DIGEST*, Volume 92, Number 2, April, 1992, p.4;
"Local Company Holds First International Users Group", DIRECTIONS, Volume 2, Issue 12, May, 1992, p.6;
"Companies in the News", *Wilson Library Bulletin*, June, 1992, p.17;
"Insider Report", *Media & Methods*, May/June, 1992, p.36;
"News Briefs", *Academic and Library Computing, Vol 9/No.5, May, 1992, p.8.*

Price: Each software module is priced separately.

Supplier's comments: Sirsi's Unicorn is a fully integrated UNIX-based library system which automates all aspects of a library's operation: cataloging (any format), authority control, public access, circulation, academic reserves, acquisitions, reference database manager, serials control, and electronic mail modules. The Retrieval Interface Manager module even connects the user automatically to multiple remote data bases and lets the user search them with Unicorn commands. Modules can be configured according to need. All types of libraries can benefit from Unicorn. Sirsi's customer base includes public, academic, school, government research, corporate and law libraries.

Unicorn's unique, user friendly user interface makes menus obsolete, giving simultaneous access to all system commands. Unicorn can be purchased for single or multiple access locations. Cooperating libraries can also network.

A variety of peripherals, including laser, bar code and OCR readers, receipt and screen printers, can be connected optionally to Unicorn workstations.

Sirsi is a full-service company, providing conversion services, training and support. Direct interfaces to laser disk, OCLC and other cataloging sources are available to enable the librarian to transfer records from these sources directly to Unicorn. Unicorn host computers range from 386 PCs to mainframes, making Unicorn fit any budget.

UNION CAT

Winnebago Software Company
310 West Main Street
Caledonia, MN 55921
(800) 533-5430; (507) 724-5411
Contact: Telesales

Hardware: IBM or compatible hardware

System Requirements: Internal or external hard disk drive, bar wand

Programming Language: Turbo PASCAL

Components & Applications:

acquisitions	no	catalog (batch)	yes
catalog (online)	yes	cataloging	yes
CD-ROM interface	yes	circulation	no
formatting bibliographies	no	index of keywords	yes
inter-library loan	yes	interface for MARC records	yes
media booking	no	reserve room	no
serials	no	thesaurus	no

Updating Modes:

batch update	yes	dynamic update	yes

Features:

Boolean logic searchable	yes	full text searchable	yes
record fields	MARC	record size	MARC
statistical & math capabilities	yes	wholesale change capability	yes

Support:

application consulting	yes	maintenance and updates	yes
time share available	no	user training	yes

Recommended for:

Corporate & govt libraries	yes	Media center management	yes
Public libraries	yes	Records & files management	yes
School libraries	yes	University libraries	yes

Installations:

Initial installation date	1989	Total number of installed sites	no info
Sampling of current clients: no info			

Published reviews & articles:

Price: $1,995

Supplier's comments: Union Cat is a district-level card catalog for the PC. The UNION CAT provides a means of centralized record keeping for all the library materials in a school district. This unique tool can handle hundreds of thousands of different titles at an unlimited number of locations. And all this regardless if the individual libraries are automated!

UNION CD PLUS

Follett Software Company
809 North Front Street
McHenry, IL 60050-5589
(815) 344-8700 or (800) 323-3397
FAX (815) 344-8774
Contact: Joy Danley

Hardware: IBM PC or compatible; CD-ROM drive (ISO 9660 format compatible); 20MB hard disk drive recommended

System Requirements: 640K RAM; MS-DOS 3.3 or higher, Microsoft Extensions 2.2 or higher

Programming Language: C

Components & Applications:

acquisitions	no	catalog (batch)	no
catalog (online)	no	cataloging	no
CD-ROM interface	yes	circulation	no
formatting bibliographies	no	index of keywords	yes
inter-library loan	no	interface for MARC records	yes
media booking	no	reserve room	no
serials	no	thesaurus	no

Updating Modes:

batch update	yes	dynamic update	yes

Features:

Boolean logic searchable	no	full text searchable	no
record fields	no info	record size	no info
statistical & math capabilities	no	wholesale change capability	no

Support:

application consulting	no	maintenance and updates	yes
time share available	no	user training	no

Recommended for:

Corporate & govt libraries	no	Media center management	no
Public libraries	no	Records & files management	no
School libraries	yes	University libraries	no

Installations:

Initial installation date	1991	Total number of installed sites	no info

Sampling of current clients: References available.

Published reviews & articles:

Price: $375/application software; $.04/per incoming record (This is the data processing charge)

Supplier's comments: Union CD Plus application software is designed to search a CD-ROM which contains a database of multiple libraries' holdings. A district or group of participating libraries will submit their individual records to Follett to be merged, deduplicated, indexed and pressed to a CD-ROM. Each of the libraries will receive a copy of the CD-ROM to search for items in other collections within their district or participating group of libraries.

VTLS

VTLS, Inc.
1800 Kraft Drive
Blacksburg, VA 24060
(703) 231-3605
Contact: Deveron Milne

Hardware: HP 3000 series including SPECTRUM models; IBM 370-architecture; and the ES/9000 family of mainframes.

System Requirements: IBM VM/SP, VM/IS, VM/XA, VM/ESA with SQL/DS and HP 3000 MPe/XL, MPe with IMAGE

Programming Language: COBOL

Components & Applications:

acquisitions	yes	catalog (batch)	yes
catalog (online)	yes	cataloging	yes
CD-ROM interface	yes	circulation	yes
formatting bibliographies	yes (VTLS-IW)	index of keywords	yes
inter-library loan	yes	interface for MARC records	yes
media booking	no	reserve room	yes
serials	yes	thesaurus	yes

Updating Modes:

batch update	yes	dynamic update	yes

Features:

Boolean logic searchable	yes	full text searchable	yes
record fields	MARC	record size	MARC
statistical & math capabilities	yes	wholesale change capability	yes

Support:

application consulting	yes	maintenance and updates	yes
time share available	no	user training	yes

Recommended for:

Corporate & govt libraries	yes	Media center management	no
Public libraries	yes	Records & files management	no
School libraries	yes	University libraries	yes

Installations:

Initial installation date	1975	Total number of installed sites	158

Sampling of current clients: Newman Library, Virginia Tech (VA); The University of New England (New South Wales); Capricornia Institute of Advanced Education (Australia); West Virginia Library Commission (WV); Hartnell College (CA); Mountain View Public Library (CA); Virginia State Library (VA); Pasadena City College (CA); University of Tennessee (TN); Marshall University (WV); National Center for Financial and Economic Information (Saudi Arabia); Singapore Polytechnic (Singapore); Pepperdine University (CA); Federal Energy Regulatory Commission (DC); Supreme Court of the United States (DC); Newberry Library (IL); National Agricultural Library (MD); National Library of Scotland (Scotland); National Gallery of Art (DC); Agricultural University of Malaysia (Kuala Lampur); Russian State Library (Moscow); Universitat Politecnica de Catalunya (Barcelona); Lund University Library (Sweden); Automation Unit of Finnish Research Libraries (Finland); Cumberland College of Health Sciences (Australia)

Published reviews & articles:

Crowder, Murray A. and Goetz, Robert P. "Cooperation, Conflict, and Compromises: Networking Multiple Institutions with a Common IOLS." *Proceedings of the 7th Integrated Online Library Systems Meeting, New York.* Medford, NJ, Learned Information, Inc., May 1992, p. 91-97

Boucher, Rick and Frank R. Bridge, Vinod Chachra, Jane R. Ryland, Peter R. Young, and Barbara L. Scheid, editors. "Proceedings of the 1st Annual VTLS Library Directors' Conference — Linking Multimedia Digital Libraries: Where We Are, Where We're Going, Blacksburg, Virginia." *Information Technology and Libraries*, March 1992, p. 40-61.

Chickering, S. and T. Strozik and G. Gulbenkian. "A Conversion of Serials Records: OCLC LDR to VTLS USMARC Format." *Information Technology and Libraries,* v.9, no.3, 1990, p. 263-271.

Guy, R.F. "Evolution of Automation in a National Library: the Experience of the National Library of Scotland from 1978-1989." *Program*, v. 24, no.1, 1990, p. 1-19.

Hafli, E. "Retrospective Conversion of Catalogues in Helsinki University Library." *International Cataloguing and Bibliographic Control,* April-June, 1990, p. 27-29.

VTLS continued

Lee, Newton S. "InfoStation: A Multimedia Access System for Library Automation." *The Electronic Library,* v.8, no. 6, 1990, p. 415-421.

Lee, Newton S. "Hypermedia Authoring and Annotation in InfoStation." *The Electronic Library,* v.9, no. 6, December, 1991, p. 337-341.

Litchfield, C.A., & D.H. McGrath. "VTLS Serials Control: Using the USMARC Format for Holdings and Locations in an Integrated, Online System." In B.B. Baker (ed), *The USMARC Format for Holdings and Locations: Development, Implementation and Use* (Technical Services Quarterly Monograph Series, v.1), Binghamton, NY, Haworth Press, 1988, p. 123-135.

McGrath, D.H., & C.R. Lee. "The Virginia Tech Library System (VTLS)." *Library Hi Tech,* v.7, no. 1, 1989, p. 17-26.

Arneson, R.H. "The VANILLA Network: Something is Better than Nothing." *Library Hi Tech,* v.7, no. 1, 1989, p. 20-21.

Soini, A & V. Chachra. "LINNEA — Library Information Network for Finnish Academic Libraries." *Library Hi Tech,* v.7, no.1, 1989, p.23.

Roberts-Buchanan, F & J. K. Rule. "The Statewide Information and Referral Service at Cabell County Public Library." *Library Hi Tech,* v.7, no.1, 1989, p. 26-28.

Price:

License fee (priced by CPU size)	$25,000 - $ 100,000
Maintenance	$ 8,000 - $ 24,000
Training fee and installation	$14,000 (3 phases of training are provided)
TOTAL	$47,000 - $138,000

Supplier's comments: VTLS Inc. provides turnkey, integrated library solutions for public, academic and special libraries. VTLS maintains its headquarters in Blacksburg, Virginia, with offices in Finland and Spain and sales offices in New York, Texas, Georgia, and California. VTLS also has distribution centers in Australia, Malaysia, Switzerland, and the West Indies.

VTLS has over 230 clients in 16 countries, and excels in network planning. The VTLS OPAC supports 16 languages concurrently, access to external data sources and multimedia information. The functionality of the VTLS software is versatile. The software is designed to include over 300 parameters to meet the special needs of academic, public, special and school libraries. The basic VTLS software is based on national and international standards and includes ten subsystems: OPAC, keyword and Boolean searching, circulation, reserve room control, cataloging, authority control, serials control, status monitoring, reporting and collection management, and parameters and library profiling. Specialized software options are available with the basic VTLS software to satisfy special library needs. These include: Acquisitions and Fund Accounting, Document Delivery, Journal Indexing, Cataloging Enhancer, Network Intelligent Link, VTLS InfoStation, VTLS Intelligent Workstation, and Locally-mounted databases.

WILSEARCH

The H.W. Wilson Company
950 University Avenue
Bronx, NY 10452
718-588-8400 or 800-367-6770
Fax 718-590-1617
Contact: Jon Clayborne

Hardware: IBM PC; Apple IIe

System Requirements: DOS; on Apples 128K of RAM; floppy disk drive, modem, super serial card.

Features:

Boolean logic searchable	yes	full text searchable	yes
record fields	no info	record size	no info
statistical & math capabilities	yes	wholesale change capability	no

Support:

application consulting	no	maintenance and updates	yes
time share available	no	user training	no

Recommended for:

Corporate & govt libraries	yes	Media center management	no
Public libraries	yes	Records & files management	no
School libraries	yes	University libraries	yes

Installations:

Initial installation date	no info	Total number of installed sites	no info
Sampling of current clients:			

Published reviews & articles:

Price: $150 per workstation plus prepaid subscription which ranges in costs from $750 for 250 prepaid searches to $2,000 for 2,000 prepaid searches.

Supplier's comments: Easy to use and inexpensive, WILSEARCH provides instantaneous online access to the same data available through the WILSONLINE system, but while WILSONLINE is designed for experienced sarches, WILSEARCH requires no search experience or training. Virtually anyone can use the menu-driven WILSEARCH to search its nineteen databases, which provide a direct line to more than three million records to date. Easy to use and inexpensive, WILSEARCH is a practaical reference tool for both patrons and staff in public, school, and college libraries.

    WILSEARCH users pay only for searches conducted. A search is defined as delivery of 10 references or any part thereof during any one WILSEARCH logon. If no references are found, there will be no charge.

WINNEBAGO CAT

Winnebago Software Company
310 West Main Street
Caledonia, MN 55921
(800) 533-5430; (507) 724-5411
Contact: Telesales

Hardware: IBM or compatible hardware, Macintosh

System Requirements: Internal or external hard disk drive, bar wand

Programming Language: Turbo PASCAL (IBM); C (Macintosh)

Components & Applications:

acquisitions	no	catalog (batch)	yes
catalog (online)	yes	cataloging	yes
CD-ROM interface	yes	circulation	no
formatting bibliographies	yes	index of keywords	yes
inter-library loan	no	interface for MARC records	yes
media booking	no	reserve room	no
serials	no	thesaurus	no

Updating Modes:

batch update	yes	dynamic update	yes

Features:

Boolean logic searchable	yes	full text searchable	yes
record fields	MARC	record size	MARC
statistical & math capabilities	yes	wholesale change capability	no

Support:

application consulting	yes	maintenance and updates	yes
time share available	no	user training	yes

Recommended for:

Corporate & govt libraries	yes	Media center management	yes
Public libraries	yes	Records & files management	yes
School libraries	yes	University libraries	yes

Installations:

Initial installation date 1987 - IBM; 1991 - Mac	Total number of installed sites	no info
Sampling of current clients: no info		

Published reviews & articles:
"A Primer on Automating the School Library Media Center." *Electronic Learning* , May 1989, pp. 34-37.
"Winnebago CIRC/CAT." *Media Evaluation Services* , January 1989, pp. 11-12.

Price: $1295 IBM; $1495 Macintosh

Supplier's comments: Winnebago CAT is an on-line public access catalog which allows patrons to search the catalog by subject, title, author, or note field using keyword, keyphrase, and Boolean logic search capabilities. System fully integrated with Winnebago CIRC.

WINNEBAGO CIRC

Winnebago Software Company
310 West Main Street
Caledonia, MN 55921
(800) 533-5430; (507) 724-5411
Contact: Telesales

Hardware: IBM or compatible hardware; Macintosh

System Requirements: Internal or external hard disk drive, bar wand

Programming Language: Turbo PASCAL (IBM); C (Macintosh)

Components & Applications:

acquisitions	no	catalog (batch)	yes
catalog (online)	no	cataloging	yes
CD-ROM interface	yes	circulation	yes
formatting bibliographies	yes	index of keywords	yes
inter-library loan	no	interface for MARC records	yes
media booking	no	reserve room	yes
serials	no	thesaurus	yes

Updating Modes:

batch update	yes	dynamic update	yes

Features:

Boolean logic searchable	yes	full text searchable	yes
record fields	MARC	record size	MARC
statistical & math capabilities	yes	wholesale change capability	yes

Support:

application consulting	yes	maintenance and updates	yes
time share available	no	user training	yes

Recommended for:

Corporate & govt libraries	yes	Media center management	yes
Public libraries	yes	Records & files management	yes
School libraries	yes	University libraries	yes

Installations:

Initial installation date 1986 - IBM; 1991 - Mac	Total number of installed sites	no info
Sampling of current clients: no info		

Published reviews & articles:
"A Primer on Automating the School Library Media Center." *Electronic Learning*, May 1989, pp. 34-37.
"Winnebago CIRC/CAT." *Media Evaluation Services,* January 1989, pp. 11-12.
"Circulation System Tracks What's Overdue." *T.H.E. Journal*, Dec/Jan 1987/88, p.32.

Price: $1295 IBM; $1495 Macintosh

Supplier's comments: Winnebago CIRC is a full circulation management program designed for the multimedia library using IBM or compatible hardware. All data is stored on either an internal or external hard disk drive. 300 different user defined material categories are recognized, each with its own number of hours or days out, renewal times, grace period and fine rate. 99 different user defined patron categories are recognized, each with its own privileges granted to it; ability to check out with overdues or outstanding fines, renew overdue materials, set their own due dates and also set the maximum number of items that one can check out. Also has an on-line catalog module which allows patrons to search by subject, author or title. Includes an inventory routine. Can handle a collection up to 300,000 items and 100,000 patrons. See also COMPUTER CAT.

ZYINDEX

Zylab Corporation
3105-T N. Wilke
Arlington Heights, IL 60004
(312) 632-1100
Contact: Ms Beth Harvey

Hardware: IBM PC or compatible

System Requirements: 448K RAM; hard disk, DOS 2.0 or later

Programming Language: no info

Components & Applications:

acquisitions	no	catalog (batch)	no
catalog (online)	no	cataloging	no
CD-ROM interface	no	circulation	no
formatting bibliographies	no	index of keywords	yes
inter-library loan	no	interface for MARC records	no
media booking	no	reserve room	no
serials	no	thesaurus	no

Updating Modes:

batch update	no	dynamic update	yes

Features:

Boolean logic searchable	yes	full text searchable	yes
record fields	variable	record size	variable
statistical & math capabilities	no	wholesale change capability	no

Support:

application consulting	no	maintenance and updates	yes
time share available	no	user training	no

Recommended for:

Corporate & govt libraries	yes	Media center management	yes
Public libraries	no	Records & files management	yes
School libraries	no	University libraries	no

Installations:

Initial installation date	no info	Total number of installed sites	no info
Sampling of current clients:	no info		

Published reviews & articles:

Blodgett, Nancy. "Freeborn & Peters, One of Chicago's Most Automated Law Firms." *Computer Counsel*, v.1, n.1, December 1988.
"ZyIndex Professional." *PC Magazine*, December 13, 1988.

Price:

ZyINDEX Server Version	$2,595
ZyINDEX Personal	95
ZyINDEX Professional	295
ZyINDEX Plus	695
ZyFEATURES	95

Supplier's comments: A microcomputer-based index and text retrieval system for files created with most of the popular word processors. Several versions are available.

RETROSPECTIVE CONVERSION SERVICES & PRODUCTS

ALLIANCE PLUS

Follett Software Company
809 North Front Street
McHenry, IL 60050-5589
(815) 344-8700 or (800) 323-3397
FAX (815) 344-8774
Contact: Joy Danley

Retrospective conversion of:

bibliographic records	yes	non-bibliographic records	yes
local data fields	yes	item level information	no
serials records	yes	classified accountability	no
circulation records	no	patron files	no
bar coding	no	authority files	yes

Record formats:

key to disk	yes	full MARC records	yes
convert tape files	no	partial MARC records	no
convert disk files	no	non-MARC records	no
convert OCLC holdings	no	convert RLIN holdings	no

Authority control services:

LC subject headings	yes	Sears subject headings	yes
corporate author	no	personal author	no
series	no	document number	no
local authority records	no		

Searches of following databases

OCLC databases	no	RLIN databases	no
LCMARC database	yes	REMARC database	no
CONSER database	no	our proprietary database	yes

Database formats:

floppy disk product	no	optical disk	yes
online	no	searches by staff	no
key to disk	no		

Output media:

Tape	no	Optical disk	no
Diskette	yes	Microfilm	no
Catalog cards	no	Book catalogs	no

Sold for installation in libraries   yes

Clients include:

Corporate & govt libraries	no	Media centers	no
Public libraries	no	Records & files mgmt	no
School libraries	yes	University libraries	no

Published articles and reviews:

Price: $250   application software
          $350   single CD-ROM disc
          $450   quarterly CD-ROM discs

Supplier's comments: Alliance Plus consists of application software and a specialized CD-ROM database, based on Library of Congress MARC records. The CD contains book, audio-visual, and serial records spanning years from 1901 to present. Many of which have been enhanced with: reading levels, interest levels, review sources, annotations, and LC, LC Children's and Sears subject headings. This product is a tool for library cataloging, etc. CardMaster Plus also works with the Alliance Plus CD-ROM MARC Database.

AMIGOS

AMIGOS Bibliographic Council, Inc.
12200 Park Central Drive, Suite 500
Dallas, TX 75251
(214) 851-8000 or (800) 843-8482
Fax (214) 991-6061
Internet: AMIGOS@UTDALLAS.EDU
Contact: Vandolyn Savage

Retrospective conversion of:

bibliographic records	yes	non-bibliographic records	no
local data fields	yes	item level information	yes
serials records	yes	classified accountability	no
circulation records	yes	patron files	no
bar coding	yes	authority files	no

Record formats:

key to disk	no	full MARC records	yes
convert tape files	yes	partial MARC records	no
convert disk files	yes	non-MARC records	no
convert OCLC holdings	yes	convert RLIN holdings	no

Authority control services:

LC subject headings	yes	Sears subject headings	yes
corporate author	yes	personal author	yes
series	yes	document number	no
local authority records	yes		

Searches of following databases

OCLC databases	yes	RLIN databases	no
LCMARC database	yes	REMARC database	no
CONSER database	yes	our proprietary database	yes

Database formats:

floppy disk product	no	optical disk	no
online	no	searches by staff	yes
key to disk	no		

Output media:

Tape	yes	Optical disk	no
Diskette	yes	Microfilm	no
Catalog cards	no	Book catalogs	no

Sold for installation in libraries	no

Clients include:

Corporate & govt libraries	yes	Media centers	yes
Public libraries	yes	Records & files management	no
School libraries	yes	University libraries	yes

Published articles and reviews:

Price: Pricing upon request - based on test of sample records.

Supplier's comments: AMIGOS Bibliographic Council, Inc. provides libraries implementing local automation systems with a complete database, ready to load into the new system. AMIGOS offers several retrospective conversion options, all of which can be customized to the library's specifications, including online conversion and batch conversion. AMIGOS' MARC Record Upgrade Service will convert your non-MARC bibliographic records to OCLC MARC format. Local holdings information can be merged into your new system without re-keying data.

AMIGOS can create a master file of holdings from MARC tapes ready to load into your local online system. Duplicate records can be identified and deleted or merged; item information can be automatically generated in local system format; filing indicator review can check and correct filing indicators in the titles fields of MARC records; and custom processing of union list of serials tapes converts union list local data records into a format that can be loaded into your local system. AMIGOS offers custom programming to ensure data is accepted by your local system. Authority control services and barcoding services are offered via subcontracts with other vendors.

AUTO-GRAPHICS

Auto-Graphics, Inc.
3201 Temple Avenue
Pomona, CA 91768-3200
Contact: Sales/Marketing Dept.
(714) 595-7204; (800) 776-6939

Retrospective conversion of:

bibliographic records	yes	non-bibliographic records	yes
local data fields	yes	item level information	yes
serials records	yes	classified accountability	no
circulation records	yes	patron files	no
bar coding	yes	authority files	yes

Record formats:

key to disk	yes	full MARC records	yes
convert tape files	yes	partial MARC records	no
convert disk files	yes	non-MARC records	no
convert OCLC holdings	yes	convert RLIN holdings	yes

Authority control services:

LC subject headings	yes	Sears subject headings	yes
corporate author	yes	personal author	yes
series	yes	document number	no
local authority records	yes		

Searches of following databases

OCLC databases	no	RLIN databases	no
LCMARC database	yes	REMARC database	no
CONSER database	yes	our proprietary database	yes

Database formats:

floppy disk product	no	optical disk	no
online	yes	searches by staff	yes
key to disk	no		

Output media:

Tape	yes	Optical disk	yes
Diskette	yes	Microfilm	yes
Catalog cards	no	Book catalogs	yes

Sold for installation in libraries   no

Clients include:

Corporate & govt libraries	yes	Media centers	no
Public libraries	yes	Records & files mgmt	no
School libraries	yes	University libraries	yes

Published articles and reviews: no info

Price: no info

Supplier's comments: Optionally the AGILE III online system may be installed in a local site.

BIBLIOFILE CATALOGING

The Library Corporation
Research Park
Inwood, WV 25428
304-229-0100 or 800-624-0559
Fax 304-229- 0295
Contact: Peggy Rulton

Retrospective conversion of:

bibliographic records	yes	non-bibliographic records	yes
local data fields	yes	item level information	yes
serials records	yes	classified accountability	yes
circulation records	yes	patron files	yes
bar coding	yes	authority files	yes

Record formats:

key to disk	yes	full MARC records	yes
convert tape files	yes	partial MARC records	yes
convert disk files	yes	non-MARC records	yes
convert OCLC holdings	yes	convert RLIN holdings	yes

Authority control services:

LC subject headings	yes	Sears subject headings	yes
corporate author	yes	personal author	yes
series	no	document number	yes
local authority records	yes		

Searches of following databases

OCLC databases	no	RLIN databases	no
LCMARC database	yes	REMARC database	no
CONSER database	no	our proprietary database	yes

Database formats:

floppy disk product	no	optical disk	yes
online	no	searches by staff	yes
key to disk	yes		

Output media:

Tape	yes	Optical disk	yes
Diskette	yes	Microfilm	yes
Catalog cards	yes	Book catalogs	yes

Sold for installation in libraries	yes

Clients include:

Corporate & govt libraries	yes	Media centers	yes
Public libraries	yes	Records & files mgmt	yes
School libraries	yes	University libraries	yes

Published articles and reviews:

The American Library Association's *Library Technology Reports* ranked automation products by performance, features, ease of use, customer support, data storage and documentation in the recently released twin issues for March-April and May-June, 1990. On a 1 to 10 scale, TLC's *BiblioFile* family of products received an "Excellent" 9 or 10 in every category. TLC's composite score of 9.5 outranked all 28 other suppliers.

The Library Corporation was listed in the May 1992 issue of *LAN* magazine's LAN 100. TLC was among the top 100 PC-based network integrators in North America; and was the only library automation vendor on the list.

Price: $2,250, plus subscription of choice (see vendor's comments below).

BIBLIOFILE CATALOGING continued

Supplier's comments: Over 8,000,000 MARC records are now available on our CD-ROM databases: the full LC MARC database (all Library of Congress cataloging in English), the LC MARC Foreign database, the Catalog Card Corporation's SEARS/Dewey database, special databases such as the BiblioFile Contributed MARC discs with records contributed by BiblioFile users in school, public, research and academic libraries, and Canadian MARC records. We have just added three new databases: A/V ACCESS with MARC records for current and popular audio-visual materials. A-V ONLINE MARC with individual MARC records representing more than 340,000 titles from the National Information Center for Education Media's (NICEM) A-V Online database, and DOCUFILE with government publications from a wide range of nations.

Costs for available databases are:

LC MARC English weekly	$ 2,995
LC MARC English monthly	$ 1,690
LC MARC English quarterly	$ 1,090
LC MARC Foreign quarterly	$ 800
Sears/Dewey quarterly	$ 850
Contributed Cataloging School & Public quarterly	$ 240
Contributed Cataloging Research & Academic quarterly	$ 180
Canadian MARC quarterly	$ 445
A/V Access quarterly	$ 995

BRCON 2

Research Libraries Group
1200 Villa Street
Mountain View, CA 94041
(800) 537-7546 FAX (415) 964-0943
Internet Address: BL.RIC@RLG.STANFORD.EDU
Contact: RLIN Information Center

Retrospective conversion of:

bibliographic records	yes	non-bibliographic records	no
local data fields	no	item level information	no
serials records	yes	classified accountability	no
circulation records	no	patron files	no
bar coding	no	authority files	no

Record formats:

key to disk	yes	full MARC records	yes
convert tape files	yes	partial MARC records	yes
convert disk files	no	non-MARC records	yes
convert OCLC holdings	no	convert RLIN holdings	yes

Authority control services:

LC subject headings	no	Sears subject headings	no
corporate author	no	personal author	no
series	no	document number	no
local authority records	no		

Searches of following databases

OCLC databases	no	RLIN databases	yes
LCMARC database	no	REMARC database	no
CONSER database	no	our proprietary database	no

Database formats:

floppy disk product	no	optical disk	no
online	yes	searches by staff	no
key to disk	yes		

Output media:

Tape	yes	Optical disk	no
Diskette	no	Microfilm	no
Catalog cards	yes	Book catalogs	no

Sold for installation in libraries   yes

Clients include:

Corporate & govt libraries	yes	Media centers	no
Public libraries	no	Records & files mgmt	no
School libraries	no	University libraries	yes

Published articles and reviews: no info

Price: $0.65 per hit; pay only for hits. Startup fee: $200 for first-time RLIN users; $50 for current RLIN users

Suppllier's comments: Free reports detail multiple hits. Files can be edited and re-uploaded. Menu-driven and simple to use. BRCON2 will derive CJK and Hebrew vernacular records. Uploaded records are matched against the entire RLIN bibliographic database.

BRODART

Brodart Automation (a division of Brodart Co.)
522 Arch Street
Williamsport, PA 17705
(800) 233-8467, ext. 522 FAX (717) 326-6769
Contact: Tom Sumpter, National Sales Manager

Retrospective conversion of:

bibliographic records	yes	non-bibliographic records	yes
local data fields	yes	item level information	yes
serials records	yes	classified accountability	no
circulation records	yes	patron files	yes
bar coding	yes	authority files	no

Record formats:

key to disk	yes	full MARC records	yes
convert tape files	yes	partial MARC records	no
convert disk files	yes	non-MARC records	no
convert OCLC holdings	yes	convert RLIN holdings	yes

Authority control services:

LC subject headings	yes	Sears subject headings	no
corporate author	yes	personal author	yes
series	yes	document number	no
local authority records	yes		

Searches of following databases

OCLC databases	no	RLIN databases	no
LCMARC database	yes	REMARC database	no
CONSER database	yes	our proprietary database	yes

Database formats:

floppy disk product	no	optical disk	yes
online	yes	searches by staff	yes
key to disk	yes		

Output media:

Tape	yes	Optical disk	yes
Diskette	yes	Microfilm	yes
Catalog cards	yes	Book catalogs	yes

Sold for installation in libraries: yes

Clients include:

Corporate & govt libraries	yes	Media centers	yes
Public libraries	yes	Records & files mgmt	no
School libraries	yes	University libraries	yes

Published articles and reviews: n/a

Price: Call for quote.

Supplier's comments: Brodart Automation is committed to providing products that meet all of the standards for open communication. We abide by the *Guidelines for the Retrospective Conversion for Bibliographic Records* proposed by the Association of Research Libraries, as printed in the March 2, 1985, issue of the Library of Congress Information Bulletin. Your database will be stored in an internal MARC format and may be readily output in either MARC II, OCLC MARC or US MARC MicroLif Protocol. A Brodart Automation Vendor Conversion ensures the quality of future database applications will not be compromised by the library's retrospectively converted database.

CAT ME PLUS

OCLC Online Computer Library Center, Inc.
6565 Frantz Road
Dublin, OH 43017-3395
(614) 764-6000
Contact: Marketing

Retrospective conversion of:

bibliographic records	yes	non-bibliographic records	no
local data fields	yes	item level information	no
serials records	yes	classified accountability	no
circulation records	no	patron files	no
bar coding	no	authority files	no

Record formats:

key to disk	yes	full MARC records	yes
convert tape files	no	partial MARC records	no
convert disk files	no	non-MARC records	no
convert OCLC holdings	yes	convert RLIN holdings	no

Authority control services:

LC subject headings	yes	Sears subject headings	no
corporate author	no	personal author	no
series	no	document number	no
local authority records	no		

Searches of following databases

OCLC databases	yes	RLIN databases	no
LCMARC database	yes	REMARC database	yes
CONSER database	yes	our proprietary database	yes

Database formats:

floppy disk product	no	optical disk	no
online	no	searches by staff	yes
key to disk	no		

Output media:

Tape	no	Optical disk	no
Diskette	yes	Microfilm	no
Catalog cards	no	Book catalogs	no

Sold for installation in libraries   yes

Clients include:

Corporate & govt libraries	yes	Media centers	yes
Public libraries	yes	Records & files mgmt	no
School libraries	yes	University libraries	yes

Published articles and reviews:

Price: no info

Supplier's comments: The microcomputer-based, batch-processing capabilities of the Cataloging Micro Enhancer Plus (CAT ME Plus) will give your library:

    Cost savings by letting you produce or update records in batch mode after hours to take advantage of OCLC's nonprime time charges. Dial-access users can reduce telecommunications charges by cataloging and editing records offline). Increased productivity through batch online searching and processing to reduce staff and workstation time for routine cataloging.

    NEW - Not previously available in the Cataloging MicroEnhancer package - an easy method of transferring records to local systems, in OCLC-MARC format, via the export function.

    Flexibility and convenience by letting you edit bibliographic information offline.

    Compatibility with the PRISM service (replaces the Cataloging Micro Enhancer package), including the ability to search records interactively using PASSPORT Software and transfer them to CAT ME Plus for editing and online processing.

    Training and ongoing support from your Regional Network and OCLC.

    CAT ME Plus dials up and logs on to the PRISM service automatically. It retrieves records from the PRISM service and downloads them to your microcomputer hard disk automatically.

CATALOG CARD COMPANY

Catalog Card Company
4401 West 76th Street
Edina, Minnesota 55435
(800) 328-2923 or (612) 893-8390
FAX (612) 893-8380
Contact: Customer Service Department

Retrospective conversion of:

bibliographic records	yes	non-bibliographic records	yes
local data fields	yes	item level information	no
serials records	no	classified accountability	no
circulation records	no	patron files	no
bar coding	yes	authority files	no

Record formats:

key to disk	yes	full MARC records	yes
convert tape files	no	partial MARC records	no
convert disk files	no	non-MARC records	no
convert OCLC holdings	no	convert RLIN holdings	no

Authority control services:

LC subject headings	no	Sears subject headings	no
corporate author	no	personal author	no
series	no	document number	no
local authority records	no		

Searches of following databases

OCLC databases	no	RLIN databases	no
LCMARC database	yes	REMARC database	no
CONSER database	no	our proprietary database	yes

Database formats:

floppy disk product	no	optical disk	yes
online	no	searches by staff	yes
key to disk	no		

Output media:

Tape	n/a	Optical disk	n/a
Diskette	n/a	Microfilm	n/a
Catalog cards	n/a	Book catalogs	n/a

Sold for installation in libraries   yes

Clients include:

Corporate & govt libraries	yes	Media centers	yes
Public libraries	yes	Records & files mgmt	yes
School libraries	yes	University libraries	yes

Published articles and reviews: n/a

Price: $.46/record; $.03/barcode label

Supplier's comments: Catalog Card Company offers two types of catalog cards: Abridged Dewey Classification with Sears subject headings or Library of Congress (LC) cataloging with LC subject headings and either LC or unabridged Dewey Classification. Numerous formatting options are available. A card set includes a main entry card, shelf list card, and all necessary added entry cards. A complete kit includes the book card, date due card, and spine labels.

     MARC records for new acquisitions or retrospective conversion are also available from either CCC's Dewey/Sears database or Library of Congress database. Library of Congress MARC records are also available with Sears subject headings for those entries our two databases have in common. For retrospective conversions, either database can be searched by author and title, so LCCN or ISBN numbers are not necessary. In addition, CCC's Dewey/Sears database is available on CD-ROM through either Bibliofile or CASPR, Inc.

     Having pioneered in the cataloging business in 1965, we are confident you will be satisfied with CCC's printed cards or the services of our Automation Division.

EKI

EKI, Inc.
145 Weldon Parkway
St. Louis, MO 63043-3148
(314) 567-1780, (800) 325-4984
FAX: (314) 567-5196
Contact: Larry Covington

Retrospective conversion of:

bibliographic records	yes	non-bibliographic records	yes
local data fields	yes	item level information	yes
serials records	yes	classified accountability	no
circulation records	yes	patron files	yes
bar coding	yes	authority files	yes

Record formats:

key to disk	yes	full MARC records	yes
convert tape files	yes	partial MARC records	yes
convert disk files	yes	non-MARC records	no
convert OCLC holdings	yes	convert RLIN holdings	yes

Authority control services:

LC subject headings	yes	Sears subject headings	yes
corporate author	yes	personal author	yes
series	yes	document number	no
local authority records	yes		

Searches of following databases

OCLC databases	yes	RLIN databases	yes
LCMARC database	yes	REMARC database	yes
CONSER database	yes	our proprietary database	no

Database formats:

floppy disk product	no	optical disk	no
online	no	searches by staff	no
key to disk	no		

Output media:

Tape	yes	Optical disk	no
Diskette	yes	Microfilm	no
Catalog cards	no	Book catalogs	no

Sold for installation in libraries — no

Clients include:

Corporate & govt libraries	yes	Media centers	yes
Public libraries	yes	Records & files mgmt	yes
School libraries	yes	University libraries	yes

Published articles and reviews: None

Price: Varies collection to collection

Supplier's comments: All of the services answered "yes" above are provided by EKI directly or are subcontracted as part of the complete retrospective conversion project.

FULLMARC SERVICES

OCLC Online Computer Library Center, Inc.
6565 Frantz Road
Dublin, OH 43017-3395
(614) 764-6000
Contact: Marketing

Retrospective conversion of:

bibliographic records	yes	non-bibliographic records	no
local data fields	yes	item level information	yes
serials records	yes	classified accountability	no
circulation records	no	patron files	no
bar coding	no	authority files	yes

Record formats:

key to disk	no	full MARC records	yes
convert tape files	no	partial MARC records	no
convert disk files	yes	non-MARC records	no
convert OCLC holdings	no	convert RLIN holdings	no

Authority control services:

LC subject headings	yes	Sears subject headings	no
corporate author	no	personal author	no
series	no	document number	no
local authority records	no		

Searches of following databases

OCLC databases	yes	RLIN databases	no
LCMARC database	yes	REMARC database	yes
CONSER database	yes	our proprietary database	yes

Database formats:

floppy disk product	no	optical disk	no
online	no	searches by staff	yes
key to disk	no		

Output media:

Tape	yes	Optical disk	no
Diskette	yes	Microfilm	no
Catalog cards	yes	Book catalogs	no

Sold for installation in libraries	no

Clients include:

Corporate & govt libraries	yes	Media centers	yes
Public libraries	yes	Records & files mgmt	no
School libraries	yes	University libraries	yes

Published articles and reviews:

Price: no info

Supplier's comments: If your machine-readable records lack access points, like subject headings, that your patrons want, these TAPECON and FULLMARC services can help. Both provide an efficient, inexpensive batch tape conversion option for upgrading your records into a full OCLC-MARC record format that takes advantage of your local system's capabilities. These tape conversion services are particularly beneficial if your library is part of a state-supported, resource sharing initiative or needs full OCLC-MARC records for a local system upgrade. Use TAPECON if your records do not now conform to MARC format standards; use FULLMARC if you have minimal MARC or better records.

GAYLORD

Gaylord Information Systems
P.O. Box 4901
Syracuse, NY 13221
(315) 457-5070 or 800-962-9580
FAX: 800-272-3412 or (315) 457-8387
Contact person: Lonnie Sirois

Retrospective conversion of:

bibliographic records	yes	non-bibliographic records	no
local data fields	yes	item level information	yes
serials records	yes	classified accountability	no
circulation records	yes	patron files	yes
bar coding	yes	authority files	no

Record formats:

key to disk	yes	full MARC records	yes
convert tape files	yes	partial MARC records	yes
convert disk files	yes	non-MARC records	yes
convert OCLC holdings	yes	convert RLIN holdings	yes

Authority control services:

LC subject headings	no	Sears subject headings	no
corporate author	no	personal author	yes
series	no	document number	yes
local authority records	no		

Searches of following databases

OCLC databases	no	RLIN databases	no
LCMARC database	yes	REMARC database	no
CONSER database	no	our proprietary database	yes

Database formats:

floppy disk product	no	optical disk	yes
online	no	searches by staff	yes
key to disk	no		

Output media:

Tape	yes	Optical disk	no
Diskette	yes	Microfilm	no
Catalog cards	no	Book catalogs	no

Sold for installation in libraries   yes, SuperCat

Clients include:

Corporate & govt libraries	yes	Media centers	yes
Public libraries	yes	Records & files mgmt	no
School libraries	yes	University libraries	yes

Published articles and reviews:

Price:

Supplier's comments:

LASERQUEST CD-ROM CATALOGING SYSTEM

General Research Corporation, Library Systems
5383 Hollister Avenue
Santa Barbara, CA 93111
(800) 933-5383 or (805) 964-7724
FAX (805) 967-7094
Contact: Darcy Cook

Retrospective conversion of:

bibliographic records	yes	non-bibliographic records	yes
local data fields	yes	item level information	yes
serials records	yes	classified accountability	no
circulation records	no	patron files	no
bar coding	no	authority files	no

Record formats:

key to disk	no	full MARC records	yes
convert tape files	no	partial MARC records	yes
convert disk files	no	non-MARC records	no
convert OCLC holdings	no	convert RLIN holdings	no

Authority control services:

LC subject headings	no	Sears subject headings	no
corporate author	no	personal author	no
series	no	document number	no
local authority records	no		

Searches of following databases

OCLC databases	no	RLIN databases	no
LCMARC database	yes	REMARC database	no
CONSER database	no	our proprietary database	yes

Database formats:

floppy disk product	no	optical disk	yes
online	no	searches by staff	no
key to disk	no		

Output media:

Tape	no	Optical disk	no
Diskette	yes	Microfilm	no
Catalog cards	yes	Book catalogs	no

Sold for installation in libraries: yes

Clients include:

Corporate & govt libraries	yes	Media centers	yes
Public libraries	yes	Records & files mgmt	no
School libraries	yes	University libraries	yes

Published articles and reviews: Supplied upon request.

Price: $4300 first year; $2600 second and subsequent years.

Supplier's comments: LaserQuest is the world's largest CD-ROM cataloging workstation for libraries for retrospective conversion and for on-going cataloging. The GRC Resource Database of over 7 million MARC records is recorded on six CD-ROM laser discs. Records for books, serials, computer files, music, visual materials, maps and manuscripts are included. Access is numeric and by title.

Title searches provide full MARC records which can be optionally modified. The record is then saved to diskette. These diskettes then can be: 1) sent to an "on-line" system via an RS232C port; 2) used to produce catalog cards; 3) sent to GRC for creation and maintenance of the library's database; or 4) instantly uploaded to LaserGuide, CD-ROM PAC. Network licenses available.

MARCIVE CATALOGING INPUT SYSTEM

Marcive Inc.
P.O. Box 47508
San Antonio, TX 78265
(800) 531-7678
FAX (210) 646-0167
Internet address: INFO@MARCIVE.MHS.COMPUSERVE.COM.
Contact person: Rose Marie McElfresh

Retrospective conversion of:

bibliographic records	yes	non-bibliographic records	no
local data fields	yes	item level information	yes
serials records	yes	classified accountability	no
circulation records	yes	patron files	no
bar coding	yes	authority files	no

Record formats:

key to disk	yes	full MARC records	yes
convert tape files	no	partial MARC records	yes
convert disk files	no	non-MARC records	no
convert OCLC holdings	no	convert RLIN holdings	no

Authority control services:

LC subject headings	yes	Sears subject headings	yes
corporate author	yes	personal author	yes
series	yes	document number	no
local authority records	yes		

Searches of following databases

OCLC databases	no	RLIN databases	no
LCMARC database	yes	REMARC database	no
CONSER database	no	our proprietary database	yes

Database formats:

floppy disk product	yes	optical disk	no
online	no	searches by staff	no
key to disk	yes		

Output media:

Tape	yes	Optical disk	yes
Diskette	yes	Microfilm	yes
Catalog cards	yes	Book catalogs	yes

Sold for installation in libraries	yes

Clients include:

Corporate & govt libraries	yes	Media centers	yes
Public libraries	yes	Records & files mgmt	no
School libraries	yes	University libraries	yes

Published articles and reviews: n/a

Price: $149.00 plus $.17 per record found (Call for quote)

Supplier's comments: MARCIVE offers two approaches to conversion: the library sends its shelflist to MARCIVE for keying or the library keys it using the Cataloging Input System (CIS). A CIS conversion is economical, keeps the shelflist in the library, and can be performed as time permits. The library keys the LCCN or ISBN as a search, and can add any number of local data fields to be appended to the MARC record at no additional cost.

The library's CIS diskettes are searched against the LC, National Library of Medicine, National Library of Canada, and Government Printing Office databases as well as records keyed from previous retros. Resulting records are in full MARC format and have had authorities checked at no additional cost.

MARCIVE KEYED CONVERSION

Marcive Inc.
P.O. Box 47508
San Antonio, TX 78265
(800) 531-7678 FAX (210) 646-0167
Internet address: INFO@MARCIVE.MHS.COMPUSERVE.COM
Contact person: Rose Marie McElfresh

Retrospective conversion of:

bibliographic records	yes	non-bibliographic records	no
local data fields	yes	item level information	yes
serials records	yes	classified accountability	no
circulation records	yes	patron files	no
bar coding	yes	authority files	no

Record formats:

key to disk	yes	full MARC records	yes
convert tape files	no	partial MARC records	yes
convert disk files	no	non-MARC records	no
convert OCLC holdings	no	convert RLIN holdings	no

Authority control services:

LC subject headings	yes	Sears subject headings	yes
corporate author	yes	personal author	yes
series	yes	document number	no
local authority records	yes		

Searches of following databases

OCLC databases	no	RLIN databases	no
LCMARC database	yes	REMARC database	no
CONSER database	no	our proprietary database	yes

Database formats:

floppy disk product	no	optical disk	no
online	no	searches by staff	yes
key to disk	no		

Output media:

Tape	yes	Optical disk	yes
Diskette	yes	Microfilm	yes
Catalog cards	yes	Book catalogs	yes

Sold for installation in libraries   no

Clients include:

Corporate & govt libraries	yes	Media centers	yes
Public libraries	yes	Records & files mgmt	no
School libraries	yes	University libraries	yes

Published articles and reviews: n/a

Price: $.45 per record found (call for quote)

Supplier's Comments: MARCIVE offers two approaches to conversion: the library sends its shelf list to MARCIVE for keying or the library keys it using the Cataloging Input System (CIS). A MARCIVE-Keyed Conversion is easy, fast, and reasonably priced. The library simply boxes up its shelf list, ships it to MARCIVE, and, within six to eight weeks, the conversion is complete.

  The library's shelf list cards are searched against the LC, National Library of Medicine, National Library of Canada, and Government Printing Office databases as well as records keyed from previous retros. For libraries which choose the 100% Conversion, a MARC records is also keyed for any no-hits. All records are in full MARC format and have had authorities checked at no additional cost.

MICROCON SERVICE

OCLC Online Computer Library Center, Inc.
6565 Frantz Road
Dublin, OH 43017-3395
(614) 764-6000
Contact: Marketing

Retrospective conversion of:

bibliographic records	yes	non-bibliographic records	no
local data fields	yes	item level information	yes
serials records	yes	classified accountability	no
circulation records	no	patron files	no
bar coding	no	authority files	yes

Record formats:

key to disk	no	full MARC records	yes
convert tape files	no	partial MARC records	no
convert disk files	yes	non-MARC records	no
convert OCLC holdings	no	convert RLIN holdings	no

Authority control services:

LC subject headings	yes	Sears subject headings	no
corporate author	no	personal author	no
series	no	document number	no
local authority records	no		

Searches of following databases

OCLC databases	yes	RLIN databases	no
LCMARC database	yes	REMARC database	yes
CONSER database	yes	our proprietary database	yes

Database formats:

floppy disk product	no	optical disk	no
online	no	searches by staff	no
key to disk	yes		

Output media:

Tape	yes	Optical disk	no
Diskette	yes	Microfilm	no
Catalog cards	yes	Book catalogs	no

Sold for installation in libraries   yes

Clients include:

Corporate & govt libraries	yes	Media centers	yes
Public libraries	yes	Records & files mgmt	no
School libraries	yes	University libraries	yes

Published articles and reviews:

Price: no info

Supplier's comments: The MICROCON Service is a low-cost, batch conversion service. With MICROCON, your staff enters search keys on diskettes, which are mailed to OCLC for machine-matching against the Online Union Catalog. MICROCON is a fast, easy, cost-effective way to convert your records when little or no editing is needed.

MITINET/MARC

Information Transform, Inc.
502 Leonard St.
Madison, WI 53711
(608) 253-4800; (800) TAG-Marc
FAX: (608) 255-4800
Contact Person: Hank Epstein

Retrospective conversion of:

bibliographic records	yes	non-bibliographic records	no
local data fields	yes	item level information	yes
serials records	yes	classified accountability	yes
circulation records	no	patron files	no
bar coding	yes	authority files	no

Record formats:

key to disk	yes	full MARC records	yes
convert tape files	no	partial MARC records	yes
convert disk files	no	non-MARC records	no
convert OCLC holdings	no	convert RLIN holdings	no

Authority control services:

LC subject headings	no	Sears subject headings	no
corporate author	no	personal author	no
series	no	document number	no
local authority records	no		

Searches of following databases

OCLC databases	no	RLIN databases	no
LCMARC database	no	REMARC database	no
CONSER database	no	our proprietary database	no

Database formats:

floppy disk product	no	optical disk	no
online	no	searches by staff	no
key to disk	no		

Output media:

Tape	no	Optical disk	no
Diskette	yes	Microfilm	no
Catalog cards	no	Book catalogs	no

Sold for installation in libraries	yes

Clients include:

Corporate & govt libraries	yes	Media centers	yes
Public libraries	yes	Records & files mgmt	no
School libraries	yes	University libraries	yes

Published articles and reviews:

Cibbarelli, Pamela R., "Modern Times: User Ratings of MITINET/marc Software" in *OASIS: Observations of the American Association for Information Science, Los Angeles Chapter*. (March 1992): 4.

Deacon, Jim, "MITINET/marc Software Review" in *CMC News*, Summer 1991, p. 6.

Epstein, Hank, "Creating Original MARC Records on a Mac - the Easy Way" in *Apple Library Users Group Newsletter* 9:2 (April 1991): 87-89.

Johnson, Susan W., "MITINET/marc: Easy Does It" in *Information Retrieval & Library Automation*, 26:9 (February 1991): 1-3.

Matthews, Joseph, "MITINET/marc (Macintosh Version)" (software review) in *Library Technology Reports*, 27:3 (May/June 1991): 341-346.

Matthews, Joseph, "MITINET/marc" (software review) in *Library Technology Reports*, 27:3 (May/June 1991): 335-340.

Price: $399.00 Same price in U.S., Canada & overseas

Supplier's comments: MITINET/marc enables you to create full MARC records from your original cataloging. A library clerk can learn to use the system to create MARC records for storage on floppy or hard disk. These MARC records can be imported into more than 60 automated library systems. Does not require the knowledge of MARC terminology.

OCLC CAT CD450 SYSTEM

OCLC Online Computer Library Center, Inc.
6565 Frantz Road
Dublin, OH 43017-3395
(614) 764-6000
Contact: Marketing

Retrospective conversion of:

bibliographic records	yes	non-bibliographic records	no
local data fields	yes	item level information	no
serials records	yes	classified accountability	no
circulation records	no	patron files	no
bar coding	no	authority files	no

Record formats:

key to disk	yes	full MARC records	yes
convert tape files	no	partial MARC records	no
convert disk files	no	non-MARC records	no
convert OCLC holdings	yes	convert RLIN holdings	no

Authority control services:

LC subject headings	yes	Sears subject headings	no
corporate author	no	personal author	no
series	no	document number	no
local authority records	no		

Searches of following databases

OCLC databases	yes	RLIN databases	no
LCMARC database	yes	REMARC database	yes
CONSER database	yes	our proprietary database	yes

Database formats:

floppy disk product	no	optical disk	yes
online	no	searches by staff	no
key to disk	no		

Output media:

Tape	no	Optical disk	no
Diskette	yes	Microfilm	no
Catalog cards	no	Book catalogs	no

Sold for installation in libraries	yes

Clients include:

Corporate & govt libraries	yes	Media centers	yes
Public libraries	yes	Records & files mgmt	no
School libraries	yes	University libraries	yes

Published articles and reviews:

Price: no info

Supplier's comments: The OCLC CAT CD450 system combines offline cataloging with batch processing to decrease costs and increase cataloging options in your library. As an OCLC member library, you contribute to the growth of an international database by adding records to the OCLC Online Union Catalog (OLUC). The OLUC includes over 23 million bibliographic records, representing items in over 370 languages, and covering a wider range of subjects and formats than is available from any other bibliographic source. Because OCLC membership is a prerequisite for purchase, the CAT CD450 system is the only compact disc cataloging system that gives you access to such a large and diverse database. You also enjoy the many benefits of being part of OCLC's vast resource sharing network, including acess to a growing international database and a comprehensive Union Listing Subsystem.

OCLC TECHPRO SERVICE

OCLC Online Computer Library Center, Inc.
6565 Frantz Road
Dublin, OH 43017-3395
(614) 764-6000
Contact: Marketing

Retrospective conversion of:

bibliographic records	yes	non-bibliographic records	no
local data fields	yes	item level information	no
serials records	yes	classified accountability	no
circulation records	no	patron files	no
bar coding	no	authority files	no

Record formats:

key to disk	yes	full MARC records	yes
convert tape files	no	partial MARC records	no
convert disk files	no	non-MARC records	no
convert OCLC holdings	yes	convert RLIN holdings	no

Authority control services:

LC subject headings	yes	Sears subject headings	no
corporate author	no	personal author	no
series	no	document number	no
local authority records	no		

Searches of following databases

OCLC databases	yes	RLIN databases	no
LCMARC database	yes	REMARC database	yes
CONSER database	yes	our proprietary database	yes

Database formats:

floppy disk product	no	optical disk	no
online	no	searches by staff	yes
key to disk	no		

Output media:

Tape	yes	Optical disk	no
Diskette	yes	Microfilm	no
Catalog cards	yes	Book catalogs	no

Sold for installation in libraries	yes

Clients include:

Corporate & govt libraries	yes	Media centers	yes
Public libraries	yes	Records & files mgmt	no
School libraries	yes	University libraries	yes

Published articles and reviews:

Price: no info

Supplier's comments: The TECHPRO service can clear your cataloging backlog, help you keep up with current acquisitions, or reclass your entire collection. And, all this can be done to conform with your current cataloging practices - just as if you were doing it yourself.

    The TECHPRO service at OCLC is your personalized cataloging service, offering off-site, short-and-long-term customized technical-processing functions, tailored to meet your special needs. It is available to all libraries - OCLC membership is not required. Over 170,000 titles have already been processed for more than 80 libraries using the TECHPRO service.

ONLINE RETROSPECTIVE CONVERSION

OCLC Online Computer Library Center, Inc.
6565 Frantz Road
Dublin, OH 43017-3395
(614) 764-6000
Contact: Marketing

Retrospective conversion of:

bibliographic records	yes	non-bibliographic records	no
local data fields	yes	item level information	yes
serials records	yes	classified accountability	no
circulation records	no	patron files	no
bar coding	no	authority files	yes

Record formats:

key to disk	no	full MARC records	yes
convert tape files	no	partial MARC records	no
convert disk files	no	non-MARC records	no
convert OCLC holdings	no	convert RLIN holdings	no

Authority control services:

LC subject headings	yes	Sears subject headings	no
corporate author	no	personal author	no
series	no	document number	no
local authority records	no		

Searches of following databases

OCLC databases	yes	RLIN databases	no
LCMARC database	yes	REMARC database	yes
CONSER database	yes	our proprietary database	yes

Database formats:

floppy disk product	no	optical disk	no
online	yes	searches by staff	no
key to disk	no		

Output media:

Tape	yes	Optical disk	no
Diskette	yes	Microfilm	no
Catalog cards	yes	Book catalogs	no

Sold for installation in libraries   no

Clients include:

Corporate & govt libraries	yes	Media centers	yes
Public libraries	yes	Records & files mgmt	no
School libraries	yes	University libraries	yes

Published articles and reviews:

Price: no info

Supplier's comments: Your staff uses the OCLC Online Union Catalog to convert your records at reduced rates. Online conversion gives you direct, in-house control of your project.

QUIKCAT

Library Systems & Services, Inc.
200 Orchard Ridge Drive
Gaithersburg, MD 20878
(301) 975-9800
FAX: (301) 975-9844
Contact person: Marketing Department

Retrospective conversion of:

bibliographic records	yes	non-bibliographic records	yes
local data fields	yes	item level information	yes
serials records	yes	classified accountability	no
circulation records	yes	patron files	yes
bar coding	yes	authority files	yes

Record formats:

key to disk	yes	full MARC records	yes
convert tape files	yes	partial MARC records	yes
convert disk files	yes	non-MARC records	yes
convert OCLC holdings	yes	convert RLIN holdings	yes

Authority control services:

LC subject headings	yes	Sears subject headings	no
corporate author	yes	personal author	yes
series	yes	document number	yes
local authority records	yes	MESH subject headings	yes

Searches of following databases

OCLC databases	yes	RLIN databases	yes
LCMARC database	yes	REMARC database	yes
CONSER database	yes	our proprietary database	yes

Database formats:

floppy disk product	no	optical disk	yes
online	no	searches by staff	yes
key to disk	yes		

Output media:

Tape	yes	Optical disk	yes
Diskette	yes	Microfilm	yes
Catalog cards	yes	Book catalogs	yes

Sold for installation in libraries: yes; A/V Image

Clients include:

Corporate & govt libraries	yes	Media centers	yes
Public libraries	yes	Records & files mgmt	yes
School libraries	yes	University libraries	yes

Published articles and reviews: no info

Price: no info

Supplier's comments: Library Systems & Services, Inc. (LSSI) has been in the business of providing high quality retrospective conversion services to libraries for over twelve years. In this capacity, LSSI has served hundreds of libraries of all types including: universities, colleges, public schools, government, law, and special libraries. During this time, LSSI has accumulated a comprehensive database of over 6.8 million records. This proprietary database, known as QUIKCAT, is added to on a regular basis through our ongoing retrospective conversion efforts.

A breakdown of the QUIKCAT database is as follows. Please note that the counts are approximate and some of the categories below do overlap.   Over 2.4 million records are for materials published prior to 1968.

Monographs	6,298,350	Maps	41,700
Serials	515,850	Archival, Manuscripts	19,850
Sound Recordings	216,175	Machine Readable	8,150
A/V Material	142,500	Kits & Instructional Material	4,650
Music	88,625	Microforms	2,400

RETRO LINK ASSOCIATES

Retro Link Associates
175 N. Freedom Blvd.
Provo, UT 84601
(801) 375-6508 FAX (801) 374-6975
Contact: Christine L. Kirby

Retrospective conversion of:

bibliographic records	yes	non-bibliographic records	yes
local data fields	yes	item level information	yes
serials records	yes	classified accountability	no
circulation records	yes	patron files	yes
bar coding	yes	authority files	yes

Record formats:

key to disk	yes	full MARC records	yes
convert tape files	yes	partial MARC records	yes
convert disk files	yes	non-MARC records	yes
convert OCLC holdings	yes	convert RLIN holdings	yes

Authority control services:

LC subject headings	yes	Sears subject headings	no
corporate author	yes	personal author	yes
series	yes	document number	no
local authority records	yes		

Searches of following databases

OCLC databases	no	RLIN databases	yes
LCMARC database	yes	REMARC database	no
CONSER database	no	our proprietary database	yes

Database formats:

floppy disk product	no	optical disk	no
online	no	searches by staff	no
key to disk	no		

Output media:

Tape	yes	Optical disk	yes
Diskette	yes	Microfilm	yes
Catalog cards	yes	Book catalogs	no

Sold for installation in libraries   no

Clients include:

Corporate & govt libraries	yes	Media centers	yes
Public libraries	yes	Records & files mgmt	yes
School libraries	yes	University libraries	yes

Published articles and reviews: n/a

Price: Individual by Library. Call for quote.

Supplier's comments: Retro Link Associates (RLA) provides retrospective conversions (using LC and other specialized databases), LC authority control and other custom database services for libraries. RLA provides retrocon services using the RLIN database. RLA also provide machine up-grading to full MARC records from non-MARC sources.

RETROCON SERVICE

OCLC Online Computer Library Center, Inc.
6565 Frantz Road
Dublin, OH 43017-3395
(614) 764-6000
Contact: Marketing

Retrospective conversion of:

bibliographic records	yes	non-bibliographic records	no
local data fields	yes	item level information	yes
serials records	yes	classified accountability	no
circulation records	no	patron files	no
bar coding	no	authority files	yes

Record formats:

key to disk	yes	full MARC records	yes
convert tape files	yes	partial MARC records	no
convert disk files	yes	non-MARC records	no
convert OCLC holdings	yes	convert RLIN holdings	no

Authority control services:

LC subject headings	yes	Sears subject headings	no
corporate author	no	personal author	no
series	no	document number	no
local authority records	no		

Searches of following databases

OCLC databases	yes	RLIN databases	no
LCMARC database	yes	REMARC database	yes
CONSER database	yes	our proprietary database	yes

Database formats:

floppy disk product	no	optical disk	no
online	no	searches by staff	yes
key to disk	no		

Output media:

Tape	yes	Optical disk	no
Diskette	yes	Microfilm	no
Catalog cards	yes	Book catalogs	no

Sold for installation in libraries   yes

Clients include:

Corporate & govt libraries	yes	Media centers	yes
Public libraries	yes	Records & files mgmt	no
School libraries	yes	University libraries	yes

Published articles and reviews:

Price: no info

Supplier's comments: The RETROCON Service is an online service where OCLC staff search for and customize matching records, accommodating more individualized specifications than batch services. When you consider personnel, workflow, and equipment needs, RETROCON can be faster, less expensive, and more convenient than managing your own online, inhouse conversion.

SAZTEC

Saztec International, Inc.
975 Oak Street, Suite 615
Eugene, OR 97401
(503) 343-8640 FAX: (503) 343-8726
Contact Person: Rod Slade

Retrospective conversion of:

bibliographic records	yes	non-bibliographic records	yes
local data fields	yes	item level information	yes
serials records	yes	classified accountability	no
circulation records	yes	patron files	yes
bar coding	no	authority files	yes

Record formats:

key to disk	yes	full MARC records	yes
convert tape files	no	partial MARC records	yes
convert disk files	no	non-MARC records	yes
convert OCLC holdings	yes	convert RLIN holdings	yes

Authority control services:

LC subject headings	no	Sears subject headings	no
corporate author	no	personal author	no
series	no	document number	no
local authority records	no		

Searches of following databases

OCLC databases	no	RLIN databases	no
LCMARC database	yes	REMARC database	yes
CONSER database	no	our proprietary database	yes

Database formats:

floppy disk product	no	optical disk	no
online	no	searches by staff	no
key to disk	no		

Output media:

Tape	yes	Optical disk	no
Diskette	yes	Microfilm	no
Catalog cards	no	Book catalogs	no

Sold for installation in libraries	no

Clients include:

Corporate & govt libraries	yes	Media centers	no
Public libraries	no	Records & files mgmt	yes
School libraries	no	University libraries	yes

Published articles and reviews: no info

Price: Varies by project, custom bid.

Suppliers comments: SAZTEC International offers a variety of services for the conversion of print information to machine-readable databases. In addition to experience in some of the largest bibliographic conversions in the world, SAZTEC has broad experience in the conversion of image databases, full-text databases, and a variety of support services for information processing.

For bibliographic data, SAZTEC's Tag & Key Service provides a solution to converting catalog records not currently available in the MARC format on magnetic tape. Database "misses", special collections, or special cataloging can be coded, captured via keyboarding and processed by SAZTEC to any version of MARC required for loading to a local system, a regional database, or a bibliographic utility. SAZTEC can produce all varieties of MARC records used worldwide, or can adapt to your local requirements.

SOLINET

SOLINET
1438 W. Peachtree NW, Suite 200
Atlanta, GA 30309-2955
(404) 892-0943 or (800) 999-8558
FAX (404) 892-7879
Contact: Cheryl Rogers

Retrospective conversion of:

bibliographic records	yes	non-bibliographic records	no
local data fields	yes	item level information	yes
serials records	yes	classified accountability	no
circulation records	no	patron files	no
bar coding	yes	authority files	no

Record formats:

key to disk	yes	full MARC records	yes
convert tape files	yes	partial MARC records	no
convert disk files	yes	non-MARC records	no
convert OCLC holdings	yes	convert RLIN holdings	no

Authority control services:

LC subject headings	yes	Sears subject headings	no
corporate author	yes	personal author	yes
series	yes	document number	no
local authority records	yes		

Searches of following databases

OCLC databases	yes	RLIN databases	no
LCMARC database	yes	REMARC database	no
CONSER database	yes	our proprietary database	yes

Database formats:

floppy disk product	no	optical disk	no
online	no	searches by staff	no
key to disk	no		

Output media:

Tape	yes	Optical disk	no
Diskette	yes	Microfilm	no
Catalog cards	yes	Book catalogs	no

Sold for installation in libraries	no

Clients include:

Corporate & govt libraries	yes	Media centers	yes
Public libraries	yes	Records & files mgmt	no
School libraries	yes	University libraries	yes

Published articles and reviews: n/a

Price: Individual by Library. Starts at $.65 per record

Supplier's comments: n/a

TAPECON SERVICE

OCLC Online Computer Library Center, Inc.
6565 Frantz Road
Dublin, OH 43017-3395
(614) 764-6000
Contact: Marketing

Retrospective conversion of:

bibliographic records	yes	non-bibliographic records	no
local data fields	yes	item level information	yes
serials records	yes	classified accountability	no
circulation records	no	patron files	no
bar coding	no	authority files	yes

Record formats:

key to disk	no	full MARC records	yes
convert tape files	no	partial MARC records	no
convert disk files	yes	non-MARC records	no
convert OCLC holdings	no	convert RLIN holdings	no

Authority control services:

LC subject headings	yes	Sears subject headings	no
corporate author	no	personal author	no
series	no	document number	no
local authority records	no		

Searches of following databases

OCLC databases	yes	RLIN databases	no
LCMARC database	yes	REMARC database	yes
CONSER database	yes	our proprietary database	yes

Database formats:

floppy disk product	no	optical disk	no
online	no	searches by staff	yes
key to disk	no		

Output media:

Tape	yes	Optical disk	no
Diskette	yes	Microfilm	no
Catalog cards	yes	Book catalogs	no

Sold for installation in libraries   no

Clients include:

Corporate & govt libraries	yes	Media centers	yes
Public libraries	yes	Records & files mgmt	no
School libraries	yes	University libraries	yes

Published articles and reviews:

Price: no info

Supplier's comments: If your machine-readable records lack access points, like subject headings, that your patrons want, these TAPECON and FULLMARC services can help. Both provide an efficient, inexpensive batch tape conversion option for upgrading your records into a full OCLC-MARC record format that takes advantage of your local system's capabilities. These tape conversion services are particularly beneficial if your library is part of a state-supported, resource sharing initiative or needs full OCLC-MARC records for a local system upgrade. Use TAPECON if your records do not now conform to MARC format standards; use FULLMARC if you have minimal MARC or better records.

LIBRARY AUTOMATION
CONSULTANTS

ATHENAEUM CONSULTATION

4155 Louisiana Street
San Diego, CA 92104
619-297-4558
Contact: Patricia Pierce

Library automation services:

Cataloging & classification	no	CD-Rom network installation	no
Consortiums	no	Database editing	no
Funding	yes	Grant writing	no
Hardware design and development	no	Hardware sales	no
Interface design	yes	Interfacing automation products	no
International and transnational issues	no	Internet, NREN, & e- mail systems	no
Negotiation of contracts and licenses	no	Network installation and management	no
Open systems architecture and interface	no	Procurement management	no
Publications	no	Retrospective conversion	no
RFPs	no	Seminars	yes
Serials automation	yes	Software design and development	yes
Software evaluation and selection	yes	Software sales	yes
Standards	no	Systems analysis and design	no
Systems testing	no	Thesaurus development	no
Training	no	Transitioning from one IOLS to another	no
Vendor support services	yes		

Areas of expertise

Archives	no	Automation vendors	yes
Community college libraries	no	Consortia	no
Corporate & govt libraries	yes	Law libraries	yes
Media center management	no	Medical libraries	yes
Museum libraries	no	Newspaper libraries	yes
Public libraries	no	Records & files management	no
School libraries	no	University libraries	yes

Geographical areas of service:

Africa	no	Australia & South Pacific	no
Canada	no	Eastern Europe	no
Far East	no	Middle East	no
Regional (please specify)	no	South & Central America	no
State (please specify)	no	United Kingdom	no
United States	yes	Western Europe	no

Recent publications:
Fund Raising Opportunities for Librarians, 1992.
Vendor/Librarian Communications: Allies, Adversaries, Aliens. 1990.
Operations Costs Reductions in an Automated Environment, 1989.

Consultant's comments:

After receiving an MLS from UCLA, I worked for about ten years as a reference librarian, systems administrator and manager in medical, legal, and corporate libraries including UCLA, Merck, Sharpe and Dohme, and Scripps Hospitals. During the last five years, I worked as an employee and consultant for Data Trek, Geac, Library Automation Products, Inlex, Autographics, Information Dimension, Advanced Information Management and others, doing software design and development, sales, management and marketing.

C. BERGER AND COMPANY

327 East Gundersen Drive
Carol Stream, IL 60188
(709) 653-1115   Fax (708) 653-1691
Contact: Carol Berger

Library automation services:

Cataloging & classification	yes	CD-Rom network installation	no
Consortiums	no	Database editing	yes
Funding	no	Grant writing	no
Hardware design and development	no	Hardward sales	no
Interface design	no	Interfacing autation products	no
International and transnational issues	no	Internet, NREN, & e-mail systems	no
Negotiation of contracts and licenses	no	Network installation & management	no
Open systems architecture and interface	no	Procurement management	no
Publications	yes	Retrospective conversion	yes
RFPs	yes	Seminars	yes
Serials automation	yes	Software design and development	no
Software evaluation and selection	yes	Software sales	no
Standards	no	Systems analysis and design	yes
Systems testing	no	Thesaurus development	yes
Training	yes	Transitioning from one IOLS to another	no
Vendor support services	yes		

Areas of expertise:

Archives	yes	Automation vendors	yes
Community college libraries	no	Consortia	yes
Corporate & govt libraries	yes	Law libraries	yes
Media center management	no	Medical libraries	yes
Museum libraries	yes	Newspaper libraries	yes
Public libraries	yes	Records & files management	yes
School libraries	no	University libraries	yes

Geographical areas of service:

Africa	no	Australia & South Pacific	no
Canada	no	Eastern Europe	no
Far East	no	Middle East	no
Regional (please specify)	no	South & Central America	no
State (please specify)	no	United Kingdom	no
United States	yes	Western Europe	no

Recent Publications:

"Alternative Staffing Practices in the USA," by Carol A. Berger. *Infomediary* 6(1992).

"Consultants: An Essential Tool or a Luxury," by Carol A. Berger, *Bottomline* (Fall 1992).

Library Lingo: a glossary of library terms for non-librarians, 2nd ed., CBC, 1989.

Consultant's comments:

C. Berger and Company has provided library and information management consulting and project support services for Midwest institutions since 1982. CBC directs and staffs large and small projects and will organize, inventory, and catalog collections of files, books and other materials; design and produce directories and indexes; install microcomputer databases; evaluate or set up libraries and develop customized records management programs. Personnel support services include conducting executive searches for library supervisors, managers and subject specialists, and supplying temporary library professional and clerical information workers and loose-leaf filers for short-or-long-term assignments.

CD CONSULTANTS, INC.

4404 Keswick Road
Baltimore, MD 21210
410-243-2755   Fax410-243-9419
Contact: Howard McQueen

Library automation services:

Cataloging & classification	no	CD-Rom network installation	yes
Consortiums	no	Database editing	no
Funding	no	Grant writing	no
Hardware design and development	no	Hardware sales	no
Interface design	no	Interfacing automation products	no
International and transnational issues	no	Internet, NREN, & e- mail systems	yes
Negotiation of contracts and licenses	yes	Network installation and management	yes
Open systems architecture and interface	no	Procurement management	no
Publications	no	Retrospective conversion	no
RFPs	yes	Seminars	yes
Serials automation	no	Software design and development	no
Software evaluation and selection	yes	Software sales	no
Standards	no	Systems analysis and design	yes
Systems testing	no	Thesaurus development	no
Training	yes	Transitioning from one IOLS to another	no
Vendor support services	no		

Areas of expertise

Archives	no	Automation vendors	no
Community college libraries	yes	Consortia	yes
Corporate & govt libraries	yes	Law libraries	yes
Media center management	no	Medical libraries	yes
Museum libraries	yes	Newspaper libraries	yes
Public libraries	yes	Records & files management	no
School libraries	yes	University libraries	yes

Geographical areas of service:

Africa	no	Australia & South Pacific	no
Canada	yes	Eastern Europe	no
Far East	no	Middle East	no
Regional (please specify)	no	South & Central America	no
State (please specify)	no	United Kingdom	no
United States	yes	Western Europe	no

Recent publications:
"Implementing CD-ROM Applications on a Local Area Network." in *Managing LANs*. Datapro, January 1992.
"Networking CD-ROMs: Implementation Consideration." *CD-ROM Professional*, March 1990.
"Remote Dial-In: Patron Access to CD-ROM LANs." *CD-ROM Professional*, July 1990.
"Accessing Databases." *CD-ROM EndUser*, September 1990.
"Considering a CD-ROM Network?" *CD-ROM EndUser*, April 1990.
"Minimizing Ongoing Operating Costs." *CD-ROM EndUser*, June 1990.
"Networking CD-ROMs." *CD-ROM EndUser*, March 1990.

Consultant's comments:
　　CDC has assisted more libraries implement CD-ROM over LAN/WAN than any other independent consulting firm in the U.S.

Editor's note: TELNET/FTD Internet training is also offered by CD Consultants.

CIBBARELLI'S

419 Main Street #82
Huntington Beach, CA 92648
714-969-8358   FAX 714-960-5454
Contact: Pamela R. Cibbarelli

Library automation services:

Cataloging & classification	no	CD-Rom network installation	no
Consortiums	yes	Database editing	yes
Funding	no	Grant writing	yes
Hardware design and development	no	Hardware sales	no
Interface design	no	Interfacing automation products	yes
International and transnational issues	no	Internet, NREN, & e- mail systems	yes
Negotiation of contracts and licenses	yes	Network installation and management	no
Open systems architecture and interface	no	Procurement management	yes
Publications	yes	Retrospective conversion	yes
RFPs	yes	Seminars	yes
Serials automation	no	Software design and development	yes
Software evaluation and selection	yes	Software sales	no
Standards	no	Systems analysis and design	yes
Systems testing	yes	Thesaurus development	yes
Training	yes	Transitioning from one IOLS to another	yes
Vendor support services	yes		

Areas of expertise

Archives	yes	Automation vendors	yes
Community college libraries	yes	Consortia	yes
Corporate & govt libraries	yes	Law libraries	yes
Media center management	yes	Medical libraries	yes
Museum libraries	yes	Newspaper libraries	yes
Public libraries	yes	Records & files management	yes
School libraries	yes	University libraries	yes

Geographical areas of service:

Africa	no	Australia & South Pacific	no
Canada	no	Eastern Europe	no
Far East	no	Middle East	no
Regional (please specify)	no	South & Central America	no
State (CALIFORNIA)	yes	United Kingdom	no
United States	yes	Western Europe	no

Recent publications:

"Automation in Review: CIBBARELLI'S Surveys," a column in *Computers in Libraries* providing User-Ratings of Library Automation Products, Sep 1992 - present.

IOLS '93 Proceedings of the Eighth Integrated Online Library Systems Meeting. Compiler and Editor. Medford, NJ, Learned Information, (in prep).

"Modern Times: User Ratings of (various) Software," a column appearing in *OASIS: Observations of the American Society for Information Science, Los Angeles Chapter,* January 1990 - present.

Directory of Library Automation Software, Systems, and Services. Compiler and Editor. Medford, NJ, Learned Information, 1992.

Information Management Software for Libraries, Information Centers, Record Centers: A Directory. Principal editor and author: 1989-1990; 1987-1988; Rev. ed 1985; Addendum 1984; 1983 (1st) edition. Published by Pacific Information. Distributed by The American Library Association

Off-the-Shelf Software Options for Information Management Workshop. Organizer & Key Speaker. American Society for Information Science Annual Conferences 1981, 1982, 1983, 1984, and 1985. Medical Library Association Annual Conferences 1984, 1987. Cal-Tech 1981. University of Hawaii 1981.

Consultant's comments: CIBBARELLI'S provides consulting services for:
- design and implementation of LIBRARY AUTOMATION SYSTEMS,
- design and implementation of INFORMATION RETRIEVAL SYSTEMS, and
- marketing and product support for LIBRARY AUTOMATION SOFTWARE VENDORS.

EMBAR INFORMATION CONSULTANTS

1234 Folkstone Ct.
Wheaton, IL 60187
(708) 668-1742
Contact: Indrani Embar

Library automation services:

Cataloging & classification	no	CD-Rom network installation	no
Consortiums	no	Database editing	no
Funding	no	Grant writing	no
Hardware design and development	yes	Hardware sales	no
Interface design	yes	Interfacing automation products	no
International and transnational issues	no	Internet, NREN, & e- mail systems	no
Negotiation of contracts and licenses	no	Network installation and management	no
Open systems architecture and interface	no	Procurement management	no
Publications	no	Retrospective conversion	no
RFPs	no	Seminars	no
Serials automation	yes	Software design and development	yes
Software evaluation and selection	yes	Software sales	no
Standards	no	Systems analysis and design	no
Systems testing	no	Thesaurus development	no
Training	no	Transitioning from one IOLS to another	no
Vendor support services	no		

Areas of expertise

Archives	no	Automation vendors	yes
Community college libraries	no	Consortia	no
Corporate & govt libraries	yes	Law libraries	yes
Media center management	yes	Medical libraries	yes
Museum libraries	no	Newspaper libraries	no
Public libraries	no	Records & files management	no
School libraries	no	University libraries	no

Geographical areas of service:

Africa	no	Australia & South Pacific	no
Canada	no	Eastern Europe	no
Far East	no	Middle East	no
Regional (please specify)	no	South & Central America	no
State	no	United Kingdom	no
United States	yes	Western Europe	no

Recent publications:

Consultant's comments:

Embar Information Consultants provide consulting services and microcomputer software products to businesses and libraries. Services include data gathering, information research, document order and delivery, consulting in library automation, management, organization, and planning.

FRANK R. BRIDGE CONSULTING, INC.

4412 Spicewood Springs Road, Suite 1006
Austin, TX 78759
512-346-9226   FAX 512-346-8207
Contact: Frank R. Bridge

Library automation services:

Cataloging & classification	no	CD-Rom network installation	yes
Consortiums	yes	Database editing	no
Funding	yes	Grant writing	yes
Hardware design and development	no	Hardware sales	no
Interface design	no	Interfacing automation products	no
International and transnational issues	no	Internet, NREN, & e- mail systems	no
Negotiation of contracts and licenses	yes	Network installation and management	no
Open systems architecture and interface	yes	Procurement management	yes
Publications	yes	Retrospective conversion	yes
RFPs	yes	Seminars	yes
Serials automation	yes	Software design and development	no
Software evaluation and selection	yes	Software sales	no
Standards	yes	Systems analysis and design	no
Systems testing	yes	Thesaurus development	no
Training	yes	Transitioning from one IOLS to another	yes
Vendor support services	no		

Areas of expertise

Archives	yes	Automation vendors	yes
Community college libraries	yes	Consortia	yes
Corporate & govt libraries	yes	Law libraries	yes
Media center management	no	Medical libraries	yes
Museum libraries	yes	Newspaper libraries	no
Public libraries	yes	Records & files management	no
School libraries	yes	University libraries	yes

Geographical areas of service:

Africa	no	Australia & South Pacific	no
Canada	no	Eastern Europe	no
Far East	no	Middle East	no
Regional (please specify)	no	South & Central America	no
State (please specify)	no	United Kingdom	no
United States	yes	Western Europe	no

Recent publications:
"Library Automation Marketplace Annual Survey," *Library Journal*, April 1, 1992.

Consultant's comments:
   Library managers, not consultants, should make decisions about the direction of library automation and the appropriate levels of library automation. The role of automation consultants has been, too often, to prescribe what and how libraries should automate. The role of a consultant instead should be to assist the management team in the process of analyzing automation options; and, guiding the staff in the selection, contracting, installation, implementation, and operation of the automated library system. Our consulting goal is to provide a project management method whereby library managers gain those skills necessary to be in control of the automation project, not to be controlled by it.
   Our philosophy is to encourage an open and honest procurement. We have a proven history in fairness towards different library vendors. We therefore suggest that you not only contact our client references, but also call the vendors. They will tell you that our clients conduct successful library automation projects because we have worked to achieve an equitable balance between them and their vendors.
   Frank R. Bridge Consulting, Inc. offers a "cafeteria-style" consulting service. This affords the client the greatest budget flexibility, with clearly delineated tasks having pre-defined prices. Although each proposal contains numbered tasks and "optional" tasks, all tasks are actually optional.

GENAWAY & ASSOCIATES, INC.

530 West Regency Circle
Canfield, OH 44406-0477
216-533-2194
Contact: David C. Genaway

Library automation services:

Cataloging & classification	no	CD-Rom network installation	no
Consortiums	no	Database editing	no
Funding	no	Grant writing	no
Hardware design and development	no	Hardware sales	no
Interface design	no	Interfacing automation products	no
International and transnational issues	no	Internet, NREN, & e- mail systems	no
Negotiation of contracts and licenses	yes	Network installation and management	no
Open systems architecture and interface	no	Procurement management	yes
Publications	yes	Retrospective conversion	no
RFPs	no	Seminars	no
Serials automation	no	Software design and development	no
Software evaluation and selection	no	Software sales	no
Standards	no	Systems analysis and design	no
Systems testing	no	Thesaurus development	no
Training	no	Transitioning from one IOLS to another	yes
Vendor support services	no		

Areas of expertise

Archives	no	Automation vendors	no
Community college libraries	no	Consortia	no
Corporate & govt libraries	yes	Law libraries	no
Media center management	no	Medical libraries	no
Museum libraries	no	Newspaper libraries	no
Public libraries	yes	Records & files management	no
School libraries	no	University libraries	yes

Geographical areas of service:

Africa	no	Australia & South Pacific	no
Canada	no	Eastern Europe	no
Far East	no	Middle East	no
Regional (please specify)	no	South & Central America	no
State (please specify)	no	United Kingdom	no
United States	yes	Western Europe	no

Recent publications:

IOLS '89-'91: Integrated Online Library Systems. Proceedings. 4th-6th national conference. New York, NY. Three vols.
Conference on Integrated Online Library Systems. Proceedings. 1st-3rd. 1983-1986. Columbus; Atlanta, St. Louis. Three vols.
Integrated Online Library Systems: Principles, Planning and Implementation. 1984.

Consultant's comments:

Our specialty is saving you money.
We will provide a common, plain language basis for comparison.
We will negotiate for you.
We will assist in planning for site preparation, wiring, HVAC, line conditioning, etc.
We will develop criteria for record conversion from cards to tape, from one system to another.
We will provide least cost networked options for regional access.
We will recommend compatible low-cost terminals or workstations.
We will identify and install CD-ROM network links to your system.
We will assist in selecting the best mix of hardware and software and/or turnkey system.
In short, we will help you save money on your integrated library system.

INFORMATION SYSTEMS CONSULTANTS, INC.

1711 P. Street NW
Washington, DC 20036
202-745-1952 Fax 202-745-2528
Contact: Richard W. Boss

Library automation services:

Cataloging & classification	no	CD-Rom network installation	no
Consortiums	no	Database editing	no
Funding	no	Grant writing	no
Hardware design and development	no	Hardware sales	no
Interface design	no	Interfacing automation products	no
International and transnational issues	no	Internet, NREN, & e- mail systems	no
Negotiation of contracts and licenses	yes	Network installation and management	no
Open systems architecture and interface	no	Procurement management	yes
Publications	no	Retrospective conversion	no
RFPs	yes	Seminars	yes
Serials automation	no	Software design and development	no
Software evaluation and selection	yes	Software sales	no
Standards	yes	Systems analysis and design	yes
Systems testing	yes	Thesaurus development	no
Training	no	Transitioning from one IOLS to another	yes
Vendor support services	no		

Areas of expertise

Archives	no	Automation vendors	yes
Community college libraries	yes	Consortia	yes
Corporate & govt libraries	yes	Law libraries	yes
Media center management	yes	Medical libraries	yes
Museum libraries	yes	Newspaper libraries	no
Public libraries	yes	Records & files management	no
School libraries	no	University libraries	yes

Geographical areas of service:

Africa	no	Australia & South Pacific	no
Canada	yes	Eastern Europe	no
Far East	no	Middle East	no
Regional (please specify)	no	South & Central America	no
State (please specify)	no	United Kingdom	yes
United States	yes	Western Europe	yes

Recent publications:
"Technical Services Functionality in Integrated Library Systems." *Library Technology Reports*, January - February 1992.

Consultant's comments:
   ISCI's 15 senior consultants, consultants, and adjunct consultants have completed over 900 projects on four continents since 1978. The company undertakes needs assessments, writes specifications, evaluates bid, negotiates contracts, and conducts tests on a wide range of information technologies: automated systems, CD-ROM, imaging systems, LANs, telefacsimile, etc. It also assists in strategic planning and facilities planning.

INFORMATION TECHNOLOGY CONSULTING

67 Old North Road
Carlisle, MA 01741
508-369-1981
Contact: Fae Hamilton

Library automation services:

Cataloging & classification	yes	CD-Rom network installation	no
Consortiums	yes	Database editing	yes
Funding	no	Grant writing	no
Hardware design and development	no	Hardware sales	no
Interface design	yes	Interfacing automation products	no
International and transnational issues	no	Internet, NREN, & e- mail systems	no
Negotiation of contracts and licenses	no	Network installation and management	no
Open systems architecture and interface	no	Procurement management	no
Publications	no	Retrospective conversion	yes
RFPs	no	Seminars	no
Serials automation	yes	Software design and development	no
Software evaluation and selection	no	Software sales	no
Standards	no	Systems analysis and design	yes
Systems testing	yes	Thesaurus development	no
Training	yes	Transitioning from one IOLS to another	yes
Vendor support services	no		

Areas of expertise

Archives	no	Automation vendors	yes
Community college libraries	yes	Consortia	yes
Corporate & govt libraries	yes	Law libraries	yes
Media center management	no	Medical libraries	yes
Museum libraries	no	Newspaper libraries	no
Public libraries	yes	Records & files management	no
School libraries	no	University libraries	yes

Geographical areas of service:

Africa	no	Australia & South Pacific	no
Canada	no	Eastern Europe	no
Far East	no	Middle East	no
Regional (please specify)	no	South & Central America	no
State (please specify)	no	United Kingdom	no
United States	yes	Western Europe	no

Recent publications:
Book reviews in *Information Technology and Libraries*.

Consultant's comments:
    Technical projects in library automation, particularly database design and conversion, system implementaion and training. My expertise is in building and converting bibliographic databases, system analysis and design, and the MARC format. I have in-depth knowledge of a variety of automated cataloging systems and integrated library systems.

INFORMATION TRANSFORM, INC.

502 Leonard St.
Madison, WI 53711
(608) 255-4800 Fax (608) 255-2082
Contact: Hank Epstein

Library automation services:

Cataloging & classification	no	CD-Rom network installation	yes
Consortiums	no	Database editing	no
Funding	no	Grant writing	no
Hardware design and development	no	Hardware sales	no
Interface design	yes	Interfacing automation products	yes
International and transnational issues	no	Internet, NREN, & e-mail systems	no
Negotiation of contracts and licenses	yes	Network installation & management	yes
Open systems architecture and interface	no	Procurement management	no
Publications	no	Retrospective conversion	yes
RFPs	yes	Seminars	yes
Serials automation	no	Software design and development	yes
Software evaluation and selection	yes	Software sales	yes
Standards	no	Systems analysis and design	yes
Systems testing	yes	Thesaurus development	no
Training	yes	Transitioning from one IOLS to another	yes
Vendor support services	no		

Areas of expertise:

Archives	yes	Automation vendors	yes
Community college libraries	yes	Consortia	no
Corporate & govt libraries	yes	Law libraries	yes
Media center management	yes	Medical libraries	yes
Museum libraries	yes	Newspaper libraries	yes
Public libraries	yes	Records & files management	no
School libraries	yes	University libraries	yes

Geographical areas of service:

Africa	no	Australia & South Pacific	yes
Canada	yes	Eastern Europe	no
Far East	yes	Middle East	no
Regional (please specify)	no	South & Central America	yes
State (please specify)	no	United Kingdom	yes
United States	yes	Western Europe	yes

Recent publications:

Consultant's comments:

     Information Transform, Inc. (ITI) has been providing library automation consulting for academic, government, national, public, school, and special libraries and computing centers since 1977. ITI supports all phases of automated systems selection and migration to new systems. Clients include small, medium, and large libraries, including the two largest automated US libraries and national libraries. ITI provides computing automation support to corporate, research, academic, and government computing centers. ITI staff have designed, developed, and implemented MARC-based systems for mainframe and microcomputers, and have implemented commercial data base management systems (DBMS) tailored to clients needs.

PACIFIC INFORMATION CONSULTING

4844 Escobedo Dr.
Woodland Hills, CA 91364
(818) 347-4357
Contact: Ed Kazlauskas

Library automation services:

Cataloging & classification	no	CD-Rom network installation	no
Consortiums	no	Database editing	no
Funding	no	Grant wrting	no
Hardware design and development	no	Hardware sales	no
Interface design	no	Interfacing automation products	no
International and transnational issues	no	Internet, NREN, & e-mail systems	no
Negotiation of contracts and licenses	no	Network installation & management	no
Open systems architecture and interface	no	Procurement management	no
Publications	no	Retrospective conversion	no
RFPs	no	Seminars	no
Serials automation	no	Software design and development	yes
Software evaluation and selection	yes	Software sales	no
Standards	no	Systems analysis and design	yes
Systems testing	no	Thesaurus development	yes
Training	yes	Transitioning from one IOLS to another	no
Vendor support services	no		

Areas of expertise:

Archives	no	Automation vendors	no
Community college libraries	yes	Consortia	no
Corporate & govt libraries	yes	Law libraries	yes
Media center management	yes	Medical libraries	yes
Museum libraries	no	Newspaper libraries	no
Public libraries	yes	Records & files management	yes
School libraries	yes	University libraries	yes

Geographical areas of service:

Africa	no	Australia & South Pacific	yes
Canada	no	Eastern Europe	no
Far East	no	Middle East	yes
Regional (please specify)	no	South & Central America	no
State (please specify)	no	United Kingdom	no
United States	yes	Western Europe	no

Recent publications: Senior Partner, Ed Kazlauskas, is the author of over 50 publications, including the following:

Administrative Uses of Computers in Schools: A Systems Analysis Approach to Selection, Design, and Implementation. Reston VA: Association of School Business Officials International (ASBO), 1991.

"Review and Exploratory Investigation of Instructional Design Strategies Relevant to Library and Information Management Software, " in *Information Technology and Libraries*, 9, No.2 (June 1990) 121-134

Management of Information Systems and Technologies, New York: Neal-Schuman Publishers, 1986, (179p.)

Consultant's comments:

Pacific Information is a firm of library and information management consultants specializing in the design and implementation of cost-effective library, records management, and information retrieval systems. Since 1982 we have had experience in a wide range of public and private organizations, with considerable experience in designing and organizing library and record systems. Other services include analysis of training needs and the development of training programs.

Editor's note: Consulting in the following areas is also available:

Instructional use of computers
Computer-based training
Administrative use of computers

PALINET

3401 Market St., Suite 262
Philadelphia, PA 19104
(215) 382-7031 Fax (215) 382-0022
Contact: James E. Rush, Executive Director

Library automation services:

Cataloging & classification	yes	CD-Rom network installation	yes
Consortiums	no	Database editing	no
Funding	no	Grant writing	no
Hardware design and development	no	Hardware sales	yes
Interface design	no	Interfacing automation products	no
International and transnational issues	no	Internet, NREN, & e-mail systems	yes
Negotiation of contracts and licenses	yes	Network installation & management	yes
Open systems architecture and interface	no	Procurement management	no
Publications	no	Retrospective conversion	no
RFPs	yes	Seminars	yes
Serials automation	no	Software design and development	no
Software evaluation and selection	yes	Software sales	yes
Standards	yes	Systems analysis and design	no
Systems testing	no	Thesaurus development	no
Training	yes	Transitioning from one IOLS to another	no
Vendor support services	no		

Areas of expertise:

Archives	no	Automation vendors	yes
Community college libraries	yes	Consortia	yes
Corporate & govt libraries	yes	Law libraries	yes
Media center management	yes	Medical libraries	yes
Museum libraries	no	Newspaper libraries	no
Public libraries	yes	Records & files management	no
School libraries	yes	University libraries	yes

Geographical areas of service:

Africa	no	Australia & South Pacific	no
Canada	no	Eastern Europe	no
Far East	no	Middle East	no
Regional (Mid Atlantic region)	yes	South & Central America	no
State	no	United Kingdom	no
United States	no	Western Europe	no

Recent publications:

Consultant's comments:

PALINET is a cooperataive membership organization of more than 350 libraries and information centers in Delaware, Maryland, New Jersey and Pennsylvania. PALINET offers a full range of consulting services to both member and nonmember libraries and information centers. Consulting is performed by PALINET staff and by carefully selected independent consultants in particular areas of expertise.

RICHARD W. MEYER

Trinity University
715 Stadium Drive
San Antonio, TX 78212
512-736-8121
Contact: Richard W. Meyer

Library automation services:

Cataloging & classification	no	CD-Rom network installation	no
Consortiums	no	Database editing	yes
Funding	no	Grant writing	no
Hardware design and development	no	Hardware sales	no
Interface design	no	Interfacing automation products	yes
International and transnational issues	no	Internet, NREN, & e- mail systems	yes
Negotiation of contracts and licenses	no	Network installation and management	no
Open systems architecture and interface	no	Procurement management	yes
Publications	no	Retrospective conversion	no
RFPs	no	Seminars	no
Serials automation	no	Software design and development	no
Software evaluation and selection	yes	Software sales	no
Standards	no	Systems analysis and design	yes
Systems testing	no	Thesaurus development	no
Training	no	Transitioning from one IOLS to another	no
Vendor support services	no		

Areas of expertise

Archives	no	Automation vendors	no
Community college libraries	no	Consortia	no
Corporate & govt libraries	yes	Law libraries	no
Media center management	no	Medical libraries	no
Museum libraries	no	Newspaper libraries	no
Public libraries	no	Records & files management	no
School libraries	no	University libraries	yes

Geographical areas of service:

Africa	no	Australia & South Pacific	no
Canada	no	Eastern Europe	no
Far East	no	Middle East	no
Regional (please specify)	no	South & Central America	no
State (please specify)	no	United Kingdom	no
United States	yes	Western Europe	no

Recent publications:

Meyer, Richard W., "The Affect of a Transition in Intellectual Property Rights Caused by Electronic Media on the Human Capital of Librarians." In *Technical Services: a Quarter of a Century of Change: a Look to the Future.* (Binghamton, NY: Haworth Press, in press).

Meyer, Richard W., "Locally Mounted Databases...Making Information as Close to Free as Possible." *Online* 16/1:15, 17-24 (January 1992).

Meyer, Richard W., "Management, Cost and Behavioral Issues with Locally Mounted Databases." *Information Technology and Libraries* 9/3:226-241 (September 1990)

Meyer, Richard W., "Earnings Gains Through the Institutionalized Standard of Faculty Status." *Library Administration and Management* 4/4:184-193 (Fall 1990)

Meyer, Richard W., "Librarians Salaries: Paid What We're Worth?" *College and Research Libraries News* 51/6:504-509 (June 1990)

Consultant's comments:

Richard W. Meyer has been a consultant to Harris Corporation, The Chemists Club, and others on library management, organization, automation support and cost containment. He specializes in analysis of corporate library and information center operations. Mr. Meyer is Director of the Library at Maddux Library, Trinity University, San Antonio. Mr. Meyer previously held positions as Associate Director of Libraries at Clemson University, Director of Library Technical Services at Indiana State University and Assistant Director of the Library at the University of Texas at Dallas. He has presented a variety of papers and published many articles related to technical and management issues of libraries, particularly regarding costs and automation.

RINGGOLD MANAGEMENT SYSTEMS, INC.

Box 368
Beaverton, OR 97006-5507
503-645-3507 Fax 503-690-6642
Contact: Dr. Ralph M. Shoffner

Library automation services:

Cataloging & classification	no	CD-Rom network installation	no
Consortiums	no	Database editing	no
Funding	no	Grant writing	no
Hardware design and development	no	Hardware sales	yes
Interface design	no	Interfacing automation products	no
International and transnational issues	no	Internet, NREN, & e- mail systems	no
Negotiation of contracts and licenses	no	Network installation and management	yes
Open systems architecture and interface	no	Procurement management	no
Publications	no	Retrospective conversion	no
RFPs	no	Seminars	no
Serials automation	no	Software design and development	yes
Software evaluation and selection	no	Software sales	yes
Standards	no	Systems analysis and design	no
Systems testing	no	Thesaurus development	no
Training	no	Transitioning from one IOLS to another	no
Vendor support services	no		

Areas of expertise

Archives	no	Automation vendors	no
Community college libraries	yes	Consortia	yes
Corporate & govt libraries	yes	Law libraries	yes
Media center management	yes	Medical libraries	no
Museum libraries	no	Newspaper libraries	no
Public libraries	yes	Records & files management	no
School libraries	no	University libraries	yes

Geographical areas of service:

Africa	no	Australia & South Pacific	no
Canada	yes	Eastern Europe	no
Far East	no	Middle East	no
Regional (please specify)	no	South & Central America	no
State (please specify)	no	United Kingdom	no
United States	yes	Western Europe	no
Carribean	yes		

Recent publications:

Consultant's comments:
Nonsuch Systems - Acquisitions, circulation and catalog; LAN & UNIX based.

RMG CONSULTANTS, INC.

333 West North Avenue, Suite F
Chicago, IL 60610
(312) 321-0432
Fax (312) 321-9594
Contact: Rob McGee

Offices in:
Bethesda MD
phone 301-469-5900
Richmond, Victoria, Australia
phone 03-427-1288

Library automation services:

Cataloging & classification	no	CD-Rom network installation	yes
Consortiums	yes	Database editing	no
Funding	yes	Grant writing	no
Hardware design and development	no	Hardware sales	no
Interface design	no	Interfacing automation products	no
International and transnational issues	yes	Internet, NREN, & e- mail systems	no
Negotiation of contracts and licenses	yes	Network installation & management	yes
Open systems architecture and interface	yes	Procurement management	yes
Publications	yes	Retrospective conversion	yes
RFPs	yes	Seminars	yes
Serials automation	no	Software design and development	no
Software evaluation and selection	yes	Software sales	no
Standards	yes	Systems analysis and design	no
Systems testing	yes	Thesaurus development	no
Training	no	Transitioning from one IOLS to another	yes
Vendor support services	no		

Areas of expertise:

Archives	yes	Automation vendors	no
Community college libraries	yes	Consortia	yes
Corporate & govt libraries	yes	Law libraries	yes
Media center management	no	Medical libraries	yes
Museum libraries	yes	Newspaper libraries	yes
Public libraries	yes	Records & files management	no
School libraries	yes	University libraries	yes
State Libraries	yes		

Geographical areas of service:

Africa	no	Australia & South Pacific	yes
Canada	yes	Eastern Europe	no
Far East	no	Middle East	no
Regional (please specify)	no	South & Central America	no
State (please specify)	no	United Kingdom	no
United States	yes	Western Europe	no

Recent publications:

Consultant's comments:

     RMG Consultants, Inc. was founded in 1980 to assist libraries to plan, procure and implement computer-based systems and services. RMG's five consultants and six support staff serve clients from our main office in Chicago and our offices in Bethesda, Maryland and Melbourne, Australia.

     RMG offers proven approaches to library automation. We are specialists with an unmatched track record in helping librarians to plan soundly and "buy right". Our consultants are professional librarians with extensive experience in the design, implementation, and management of library information systems. We actively track new products and trends, and issues in the library automation marketplace.

     RMG brings an objective, unbiased perspective to the process of evaluating and selecting automated library systems. We know from our constant involvement in competitive procurements that RMG's impartiality is vital to the financial interests of our clients. Our methodologies are tried, proven, and accurate. They reduce the time and effort required to collect and analyze data, prepare system requirements and RFP's and evaluate proposals. Our techniques for soliciting the best prices from vendors can result in measurable, bottom-line savings. We have prepared and successfully negotiated contracts with all the major vendors of automated systems. The goals of RMG's competitive procurements and negotiated contracts are to help clients make sound choices and "buy right".

SAVAGE INFORMATION SERVICES

2510 West 237th Street
Suite 200
Torrance, CA 90505-5235
310-530-4747 Fax 310-530-0049
Contact: Sue Savage

Library automation services:

Cataloging & classification	yes	CD-Rom network installation	no
Consortiums	no	Database editing	yes
Funding	no	Grant writing	no
Hardware design and development	no	Hardware sales	no
Interface design	no	Interfacing automation products	no
International and transnational issues	no	Internet, NREN, & e- mail systems	no
Negotiation of contracts and licenses	no	Network installation and management	no
Open systems architecture and interface	no	Procurement management	no
Publications	no	Retrospective conversion	yes
RFPs	no	Seminars	yes
Serials automation	no	Software design and development	no
Software evaluation and selection	yes	Software sales	yes
Standards	no	Systems analysis and design	yes
Systems testing	no	Thesaurus development	yes
Training	yes	Transitioning from one IOLS to another	no
Vendor support services	yes	Personnel Placement	yes

Areas of expertise

Archives	yes	Automation vendors	no
Community college libraries	yes	Consortia	yes
Corporate & govt libraries	yes	Law libraries	yes
Media center management	no	Medical libraries	yes
Museum libraries	yes	Newspaper libraries	yes
Public libraries	yes	Records & files management	yes
School libraries	yes	University libraries	yes

Geographical areas of service:

Africa	no	Australia & South Pacific	no
Canada	no	Eastern Europe	no
Far East	no	Middle East	no
Regional (please specify)	no	South & Central America	no
State (CALIFORNIA)	yes	United Kingdom	no
United States	yes	Western Europe	no

Recent publications:

Custom Online Guide (COG) - The Custom Online Guide is a database search tool that keeps track of changes in the databases and
vendor systems your organization accesses, and ONLY those you access.

Consultant's comments:

Savage Information Services's special expertise lies in the design, implementation and management of records management and information storage and retrieval systems. We also design databases; automate library systems; provide indexing, cataloging, vocabulary control and thesaurus development; provide research, database searching, and acquisition services; and place temporary and permanent information personnel.

Located in a suite of offices in Torrance, the company employs a staff of librarians, records managers, researchers, database searchers, lexicographers, indexers, and catalogers as well as information systems analysts and designers. SIS also employs on-call consultants for special projects.

Since its organization in 1977, SIS has successfully performed a large number of projects which span the range of information systems applications. Clients have included government agencies, engineering firms, aerospace companies, health care organizations, educational institutions, public utilities, accounting firms, law offices and public libraries.

SKP ASSOCIATES

160 Fifth Avenue
New York, NY 10010
212-675-7804 Fax 212-989-7542
Contact: Sandra K. Paul

Library automation services:

Cataloging & classification	no	CD-Rom network installation	no
Consortiums	no	Database editing	no
Funding	no	Grant writing	no
Hardware design and development	no	Hardware sales	no
Interface design	yes	Interfacing automation products	yes
International and transnational issues	no	Internet, NREN, & e- mail systems	yes
Negotiation of contracts and licenses	no	Network installation and management	no
Open systems architecture and interface	no	Procurement management	yes
Publications	yes	Retrospective conversion	no
RFPs	yes	Seminars	yes
Serials automation	yes	Software design and development	yes
Software evaluation and selection	yes	Software sales	no
Standards	yes	Systems analysis and design	yes
Systems testing	yes	Thesaurus development	no
Training	yes	Transitioning from one IOLS to another	yes
Vendor support services	no		

Areas of expertise

Archives	yes	Automation vendors	yes
Community college libraries	yes	Consortia	yes
Corporate & govt libraries	yes	Law libraries	yes
Media center management	yes	Medical libraries	yes
Museum libraries	yes	Newspaper libraries	yes
Public libraries	yes	Records & files management	yes
School libraries	yes	University libraries	yes

Geographical areas of service:

Africa	yes	Australia & South Pacific	yes
Canada	yes	Eastern Europe	yes
Far East	yes	Middle East	yes
Regional (please specify)	no	South & Central America	yes
State (please specify)	no	United Kingdom	yes
United States	yes	Western Europe	yes

Recent publications:

Consultant's comments:

SKP Associates serves those in the library, publishing, bookselling, recording, and related industries. SKP Associates specializes in automated and manual systems analysis and development, electronic publishing and the application of computer-based techniques. Sandra K. Paul, President of SKP Associates, was the primary force in the establishment and growth of the Book and Serials Industry Systems Advisory Committees (BISAC and SISAC). BISAC was the first organization in the country to develop industry-wide standards for electronic data interchange of order, payment and fulfillment-related information. She later designed comparable communication formats for the recorded music industry. She played a major role in the implementation of the International Standard Book Number and was the catalyst in BISAC's and SISAC's adoption of bar code standards. She was also instrumental in the formation and growth of the National Information Standards Organization, which develops and maintains standards for libraries, information science and publishing, and she represents their interests at ANSI and internationally.

TECHNOLOGY MANAGEMENT, INC.

101 West Washington Street, Suite 1110E
Indianapolis, IN 46204
317-686-5000
Vincent K. Roach

Library automation services:

Cataloging & classification	no	CD-Rom network installation	no
Consortiums	no	Database editing	no
Funding	no	Grant writing	no
Hardware design and development	no	Hardware sales	no
Interface design	no	Interfacing automation products	yes
International and transnational issues	no	Internet, NREN, & e- mail systems	no
Negotiation of contracts and licenses	yes	Network installation and management	yes
Open systems architecture and interface	yes	Procurement management	yes
Publications	no	Retrospective conversion	no
RFPs	yes	Seminars	no
Serials automation	no	Software design and development	yes
Software evaluation and selection	yes	Software sales	no
Standards	no	Systems analysis and design	yes
Systems testing	yes	Thesaurus development	no
Training	no	Transitioning from one IOLS to another	yes
Vendor support services	no		

Areas of expertise

Archives	no	Automation vendors	yes
Community college libraries	no	Consortia	no
Corporate & govt libraries	no	Law libraries	no
Media center management	no	Medical libraries	yes
Museum libraries	no	Newspaper libraries	no
Public libraries	yes	Records & files management	yes
School libraries	yes	University libraries	no

Geographical areas of service:

Africa	no	Australia & South Pacific	no
Canada	no	Eastern Europe	no
Far East	no	Middle East	no
Regional (please specify)	no	South & Central America	no
State	no	United Kingdom	no
United States	yes	Western Europe	no

Recent publications:

Consultant's comments:

   TMI provides management services related to information technology issues. We have worked on a number of library assignments, including the entire scope of automation activities for the Indianapolis-Marion County Public Library, the Franklin/Johnson County Library, and a number of special libraries.

   Unlike most consultants servicing the library market, TMI works with clients in all industries, which gives us a much broader management and system perspective. We view each client engagement as unique, and we tailor our methodologies and deliverables to the client's specific need. To ensure objectivity, we maintain no relationships with any hardware or software vendors. Some examples of services we have performed in the past include: long term strategic planning, capacity planning, hardware and software evaluations, conversion planning, procurement, contract negotiation, and implementation management.

TODD ENTERPRISES, INC.

224-49 67th Avenue
Bayside, NY 11364
(800) 445-TODD; (718) 343-1040
Fax (718) 343-9180
Contact person: Bob Bell, General Manager

Library automation services:

Cataloging & classification	no	CD-Rom network installation	yes
Consortiums	no	Database editing	no
Funding	no	Grant writing	no
Hardware design and development	yes	Hardware sales	yes
Interface design	no	Interfacing automation products	no
International and transnational issues	no	Internet, NREN, & e- mail systems	no
Negotiation of contracts and licenses	no	Network installation and management	yes
Open systems architecture and interface	no	Procurement management	no
Publications	no	Retrospective conversion	no
RFPs	no	Seminars	no
Serials automation	no	Software design and development	no
Software evaluation and selection	yes	Software sales	no
Standards	no	Systems analysis and design	no
Systems testing	no	Thesaurus development	no
Training	no	Transitioning from one IOLS to another	no
Vendor support services	yes		

Areas of expertise

Archives	no	Automation vendors	no
Community college libraries	yes	Consortia	no
Corporate & govt libraries	yes	Law libraries	yes
Media center management	no	Medical libraries	yes
Museum libraries	yes	Newspaper libraries	no
Public libraries	yes	Records & files management	no
School libraries	yes	University libraries	yes

Geographical areas of service:

Africa	no	Australia & South Pacific	no
Canada	no	Eastern Europe	no
Far East	no	Middle East	no
Regional (please specify)	no	South & Central America	no
State (please specify)	no	United Kingdom	no
United States	yes	Western Europe	no

Recent publications:

Consultant's comments:

     Custom design CD-ROM networks from four to 64 drives to interface with your existing computer environments using LOTUS CD-Networker software.

VENDOR RELATIONS

P.O. Box 40
Annandale, NJ 08801
908-730-9688
Contact: Ernest A. Muro

Library automation services:

Cataloging & classification	yes	CD-Rom network installation	yes
Consortiums	yes	Database editing	yes
Funding	no	Grant writing	no
Hardware design and development	yes	Hardware sales	yes
Interface design	yes	Interfacing automation products	yes
International and transnational issues	yes	Internet, NREN, & e- mail systems	no
Negotiation of contracts and licenses	yes	Network installation and management	yes
Open systems architecture and interface	yes	Procurement management	yes
Publications	yes	Retrospective conversion	yes
RFPs	yes	Seminars	no
Serials automation	yes	Software design and development	yes
Software evaluation and selection	yes	Software sales	yes
Standards	yes	Systems analysis and design	yes
Systems testing	yes	Thesaurus development	no
Training	yes	Transitioning from one IOLS to another	no
Vendor support services	yes		

Areas of expertise

Archives	no	Automation vendors	yes
Community college libraries	yes	Consortia	yes
Corporate & govt libraries	yes	Law libraries	yes
Media center management	yes	Medical libraries	yes
Museum libraries	yes	Newspaper libraries	no
Public libraries	yes	Records & files management	no
School libraries	yes	University libraries	yes

Geographical areas of service:

Africa	no	Australia & South Pacific	yes
Canada	yes	Eastern Europe	yes
Far East	yes	Middle East	yes
Regional (please specify)	no	South & Central America	yes
State (please specify)	no	United Kingdom	yes
United States	yes	Western Europe	yes

Recent publications:
ASLJ - Automation Services for Libraries.

Consultant's comments:

DATABASE HOSTS

DATABASE HOSTS

This section is new to the *Directory of Library Automation: Software, Systems, and Services*. It includes contact information and a brief description of the online services available which may be of interest to library automation. This is a selective listing, and is not intended to be a comprehensive listing of all online search services. Included here are a variety of database hosts whose services include subject-specific databases as well as large bibliographic citation databases, many in MARC format, available for retrospective conversion.

Auto-Graphics, Inc.

3201 Temple Avenue
Pomona, CA 91768-3200
714-595-7204 or 800-776-6939
Contact: Sales/Marketing Dept.

AGILE III

Supplier's comments: AGILE III is an online database management system and bibliographic utility supporting online cataloging and interlibrary loan. A shared resource approach provides access to MARC records as well as individual customer and regional databases for retrospective conversion, current acquisitions cataloging, interlibrary loan and upgrading of brief circulation records to full MARC. Dedicated line via US Sprint or dial access to AGILE III is available.

Brodart Automation (a division of Brodart Co.)

500 Arch Street
Williamsport, PA 17705
800-233-8467
Contact: Tom Sumpter, National Sales Manager

INTERACTIVE ACCESS SYSTEM™

Supplier's comments: The Interactive Access System™ (IAS) is an easy, efficient way to catalog and maintain a bibliographic database. Over 12 million records are available as a cataloging resource database. The cataloging module can interface with the public access and interlibrary loan modules to provide continuous, up-to-date information. Even though IAS operates in a time-share environment, each library's database is maintained as a separate and unique file.

CARL Systems, Inc.

3801 E. Florida Avenue, Bldg. D, Suite 300
Denver, CO 80210
303-758-3030
Contact: Martha Whittaker

CARL Systems

Supplier's comments: CARL'S stated mission is to promote the progress and advancement of research in Colorado through more effective sharing of resources. Today, the CARL System supports more than 1000 dedicated terminals and over 5 million bibliographic records from its Denver site. Replications of the System serve single institutions as well as consortia, with a total of 75 libraries presently supported on the system from eleven interconnected CPU locations linking 3500 dedicated terminals reaching from Hawaii to Boston and Maryland. In addition, approximately 150 libraries access the CAR System databases via gateway connections. And virtually every university campus in the United States has access to the CARL System through the national Internet.

UnCover

CARL Systems has provided gateway access to UnCover and a wide variety of union lists since the Spring of 1989; and today, over 150 libraries use UnCover through gateway agreements.

CompuServe, Inc.

5000 Arlington Centre Blvd.
Columbus, OH 43220
800-848-8990

Education Forums
Supplier's comments: Education forums are available on half a dozen topics including Computer Training Forum.

Hardware Forums
Supplier's comments: You'll find Forums run by manufacturers and devotees of different computer makes and peripherals including DEC Users Network, Hewlett-Packard Forum, Macintosh Forums, IBM Users Network, Intel Corporation, and Practical Peripherals Forum.

Magazines/Electronic Newsstand
Supplier's comments: The Electronic Newsstand has almost a dozen electronic issues awaiting your perusal including *InfoWorld On-Line, MacUser/MacWeek, and PC Magazine/PC Week/PC Computing.*

Reference Databases
Supplier's comments: Reference databases include Academic American Encyclopedia, Books in Print, Computer Database Plus, Computer Directory, and Newspaper Library.

Software Forums
Supplier's comments: CompuServe offers dozens of Forums that focus on software, either by manufacturer or generic type including: Autodesk Forum, IBM Desktop Software, Microsoft Connection, Novell NetWire, Symantec Forum, and UNIX Forum.

Data-Star

485 Devon Park Drive Suite 110
Wayne, PA 19087
800-221-7754
Contact: Louise M. Dagit

Data Star
Supplier's comments: DataStar provides access to a variety fo biomedical and business databases.

Dialog Information Services, Inc.

3460 Hillview Avenue
Palo Alto, CA 94304
415, 858-2700
Contact: Donna Hurwitt

Dialog Information Retrieval Service
Supplier's comments: The DIALOG Information Retrieval Service has been serving users since 1972. With nearly 400 databases from a broad scope of disciplines available on the system, the DIALOG Service offers unequaled subject balance and variety. The coverage, combined with the DIALOG searching capabilities, make it the most powerful online system of its type. Databases of particular interest to library automation include: AMERICAN LIBRARY DIRECTORY, BOOK REVIEW INDEX, BOOKS IN PRINT, BRITISH BOOKS IN PRINT, BUSINESS SOFTWARE DATABASE, BUYER'S GUIDE TO MICRO SOFTWARE, COMPUTER ASAP, COMPUTER DATABASE, COMPUTER NEWS FULLTEXT, COMPUTER-READABLE DATABASES, CONFERENCE PAPERS INDEX, ERIC, EVERYMAN'S ENCYCLOPEDIA, FINDEX, GALE DIRECTORY OF PUBLICA-TIONS, INFORMATION SCIENCE ABSTRACTS, LC MARC - BOOKS, LIBRARY AND INFORMATION SCIENCE AB-STRACTS, MICROCOMPUTER SOFTWARE GUIDE, MICROCOMPUTER INDEX, ONLINE/CD-ROM DATABASE NEWS, REMARC.

EBSCO

P.O. Box 1943
Birmingham, AL 35201-1943
205-991-6600
Contact: Joe Weed

EBSCONET Online Subscription Service

EBSCONET was created by librarians at EBSCO in response to customer demand to find a better way to process subscriptions. This online system linking our Regional Offices and International Headquarters with libraries and information centers was the answer. Today, hundreds of customers throughout the world are online with EBSCONET for their subscription service.

EBSCONET operates through a computer terminal at your library or information center. You're linked to our host computer in Birmingham for direct transmission of subscription information. It helps speed up subscription transactions that otherwise would require paperwork, mail and phone calls.

> With EBSCONET you will be able to:
> - transmit claims
> - make interim orders
> - access EBSCO's title file
> - use the EBSCO missing copy bank
> - review your summary of publications ordered
> - use TELMAIL, EBSCO's electronic mail service

The H.W. Wilson Company

950 University Avenue
Bronx, NY 10452
800-367-6770 or 718-588-8400

Wilsonline Online Retrieval System

The award-winning WILSONLINE Online Retrieval System offers online access to twenty-seven specialized databases. The most economical search system on the market today, WILSONLINE has no start-up fee, no charge for saved searches, and no royalty charges added to connect-time rates. WILSONLINE can also be accessed on a "pay as you go" basis—without maintaining a subscription.

Databases of particular interest to automation librarians include:

> LC/MARC file
> LC/Non-English MARC file
> Book Review Digest
> Cumulative Book Index
> Library Literature
> Wilson Business Abstracts
> Name Authority File

Marcive, Inc.

P.O. Box 47508
San Antonio, TX 78265
800-531-7678; Fax 512-646-0167

Shared cataloging service

Editor's comments: see detailed information about MARCIVE services in the SOFTWARE and RETROSPECTIVE CONVERSION sections of this directory.

Mead Data Central

9443 Springboro Pike
P.O. Box 933
Dayton, OH 45401
513-865-6800 or 800 543-6862

THE LEXIS SERVICE
Supplier's comments: Includes over 60 legal databases

THE LEXIS PUBLIC RECORDS ONLINE SERVICE
Supplier's comments: Includes 4 databases

THE MEDIS SERVICE
Supplier's comments: Includes MEDLINE

THE NEXIS SERVICE
Supplier's comments: Includes 16 additional databases on a variety of topics

OCLC Online Computer Library Center, Inc.

6565 Frantz Road
Dublin, OH 43017-3395
614-764-6000

The EPIC Service
Designed for the skilled searcher, the EPIC service gives you the tools you need: complete subject and keyword access to the OLUC;
a growing collection of databases at affordable rates; and sophisticated system capabilities—offline prints, current awareness profiles ,
extensive record sorting. EPIC provides quality indexing, access to unique databases, and free Internet usage.

The FirstSearch Catalog
An end-user online information service designed for library patrons, FirstSearch provides access to the databases patrons want,
including WorldCat (The OCLC Online Union Catalog). It's easy enough to use without training and is priced by the search, not by
connect hour. Eventually, most First Search databases will include OCLC holdings data. This, plus future links to OCLC Interlibrary
Loan and document suppliers, will enable patrons to request and receive the information they need.

Group Resource Sharing
Geographic or type-of-library groups can create a group database on OCLC to be used for resource sharing by all members of the
group, regardless of whether they are OCLC members. Access to the wider OCLC ILL network is provided to the nonmember
libraries by the member libraries in the group.

Interlibrary Loan
Multiply your resources and lower your borrowing costs with the vast resources of OCLC's online network:
    - 4,500 resource sharing libraries
    - 25 million bibliographic records
    - 400 million location symbols
    - 5 million serials union list holdings
One transaction fee covers sending a request to as many as five lenders of your choice. To help offset borrowing costs, lending credits
are given for each item you loan through the OCLC system. In December 1992, Interlibrary Loan moved to PRISM, enabling you to
take advantage of new PRISM search capabilities like title browse, combined search keys, and full-screen editing. Once PRISM ILL
is implemented, a link will be established between OCLC's reference systems—EPIC and FirstSearch—that will facilitate placing ILL
requests from the same system used to locate unowned items for patrons.

OCLC Document Delivery
In 1992 OCLC introduced on FirstSearch the first phase of a comprehensive document ordering and delivery program. Eventually
OCLC Document Delivery on FirstSearch and EPIC will include end-user document ordering for journal articles from a variety of
suppliers; mediated ILL, facilitated by a link from EPIC and First Search to OCLC Interlibrary Loan; and mediated requests for
documents from suppliers who participate in OCLC's Document Supply Program.

OCLC continued

OCLC Online Union Catalog
The OLUC includes over 23 million bibliographic records, representing items in over 370 languages, and covering a wider range of subjects and formats than is available from any other bibliographic source.

Union List Subsystem
Economically share up-to-date serials holdings with your library group to facilitate resource sharing, acquisition planning, collection management, and preservation.

Orbit Search Service

8000 Westpark Drive
McLean, VA 22102
800-955-0906 or 703-442-0900

Orbit Search Service
Supplier's comments: The primary object of ORBIT Search Service is to provide immediate, accurate, and uncompromising access to the world's technical information resources. ORBIT provides access to more than 100 databases on a variety of subjects. Of particular interest to automation librarians are: NATIONAL UNION CATALOG CODES, MICROSEARCH, POWER, and SCIENTIFIC & TECHNICAL BOOKS & SERIALS IN PRINT.

Research Libraries Group

1200 Villa Street
Mountain View, CA 94041-1100
800-537-RLIN   Fax 415-964-0943
Contact: RLIN Information Center

BRCON 2
BRCON 2 is a shared cataloging system providing access to MARC records.

CITADEL
CitaDel is the new, full-service citation and document-delivery service from the Research Libraries Group (RLG). With CitaDel, you can make a wide range of popular and scholarly citation databases available to your users — with none of the overhead of loading and maintaining large files locally.

STN International

c/o CAS
2540 Olentangy River Road
P.O. Box 3012
Columbus, OH 43210-0012
800-848-6533 or 614-447-3698
Fax 614-447-3713

STN International
Supplier's comments: STN International, the scientific and technical information network is an online system that provides direct access to over 100 scientific and technical databases. Databases of particular interest to automation librarians include: CJACS, COMPUSCIENCE, CONF, INFODATA, and NTIS.

WLN

P.O. Box 3888
Lacey, WA 98503-0888
800-DIALWLN or 206-459-6518
Fax 206-459-6341
Contact: Rushton Brandis

WLN Online System
Supplier's comments: New! WLN Easy Access via Internet. 7.5 million MARC bibliographic records; powerful searching; full authority control; dial-up, leased line, Internet access; full-feature ILL and Acquisitions Systems; and MARC record download to local systems.

CD-ROM
DISTRIBUTORS

CD-ROM DISTRIBUTORS

This section of the *Directory of Library Automation Software, Systems, and Services* includes contact information and brief product descriptions for a variety of the CD-ROM products and services which are most actively marketed to the library automation marketplace. Because there are literally thousands of database products available on CD-ROM, this listing is not intended to be comprehensive.

Included are a variety of CD-ROM database distributors as well as CD-ROM vendors who will create custom CD-ROMs of your library records.

American Library Association

50 East Huron St.
Chicago, IL 60611
312-944-6780 or 800-545-2433

DIRECTORY OF LIBRARY AND INFORMATION PROFESSIONALS
Supplier's comments: CD-ROM database.

Auto-Graphics

3201 Temple Avenue
Pomona, CA 91768
714-595-7204 or 800-776-6939
Fax 714-595-3506
Contact: Sales/Marketing Dept.

IMPACT GOVERNMENT DOCUMENTS DATABASE
Supplier's comments: IMPACT provides access to citations included in the Monthly Catalog.

IMPACT™ CD-ROM PUBLIC ACCESS CATALOG SYSTEM
Supplier's comments: IMPACT CD-ROM PUBLIC ACCESS CATALOG SYSTEM operates with the IBM/PC and compatibles. Cost is dependent on size of collection and frequency of update and remastering. Especially well suited to union database applications for multi-branch libraries and multi-library consortia, state and regional networks, etc. The IMPACT CD-ROM based public access catalog system provides sophisticated indexing techniques, simple screen designs, access levels ranging from browsing, to simple searching, to more complex searching. Special features include update capability through the cataloging module, locations handling for multi-branch systems and consortia, profile flexibility, and access to local files such as Information and Referral. The electronic interlibrary loan module is file server based, and features automatic dial-up and store-and-forward functions.

Bowker Electronic Publishing

121 Chanlon Road
New Providence, NJ 07974

BOOKS IN PRINT, BOOKS IN PRINT PLUS; BOOKS IN PRINT/OUT OF PRINT PLUS; REVIEWS PLUS, ULRICH'S PLUS
Supplier's comments: Bowker has the products and services that can make your library more productive, efficient, and exciting.

Brodart Automation (a division of Brodart Co.)

500 Arch Street
Williamsport, PA 17705
800-233-8467 ext. 522
Contact: Tom Sumpter, National Sales Manager

Brodart Automation continued

LE PAC®
Supplier's comments: Le Pac® is a microcomputer/CD-ROM-based public access catalog. Each client library's catalog is recorded on one (or more) compact discs. Searches access the data via author, title, and subject fields. Additional parts of the record may be indexed and used as access points in the ANYWORD field. Further options include the ability to combine catalogs and do interlibrary loan.

P1 INTEGRATED SYSTEM®
Supplier's comments: Brodart Automation's microcomputer, CD-ROM-based P1 Integrated System® provides automated management for libraries from the planning of the collection to circulating the material. Designed for operation in a Local Area Network (LAN) environment, the system allows libraries wishing to share resources efficiently the ability to manage and automate many library functions.

PRECISION ONE®
Supplier's comments: Precision One is a compact disc-based retrospective conversion/cataloging tool. Brodart Automation developed Precision One to offer school and public libraries an affordable, efficient, and accurate method of converting their records to MARC format.

CD Plus

333 Seventh Ave.
New York, NY 10001
800-950-2035 or 212-563-3006
Fax 212-563-3784

OVID
Supplier's comments: A breakthrough in searching bibliographic and text databases: OVID provides one Common User Interface to accommodate all users and environments. Feature-rich search software includes mapping to controlled vocabularies; limits to local journal holdings; and search modes for users with any level of experience. Available for Windows, DOS, and UNIX. Databases available include: ERIC, PSYCINFO, READER'S GUIDE ABSTRACTS, WILSON BUSINESS ABSTRACTS, MEDLINE, CURRENT CONTENTS, INDEX TO LEGAL PERIODICALS, AIDSLINE, CANCERLIT, CINAHL, and EMBASE

Catalog Card Company

4401 West 76th Street
Edina, Minnesota 55435
800-328-2923 or 612-893-8390
Fax 612-893-8380
Contact: Customer Service Department

CATALOG CARD COMPANY
Vendor's comments: CCC's Dewey/Sears database is available on CD-ROM through either Bibliofile or CASPR, Inc.

Columbia University Press

Dept E88
136 South Broadway
Irvington, NY 10533
800-844-UNIV; Fax 800-844-1844

Granger's on CD-ROM
Supplier's comments: More than just an index! Granger's on CD-ROM includes 8,500 poems in full text fully searchable by keyword as well as 3,000 quotations from 1,500 additional poems; citations for 90,000 poems by 15,000 poets, author, title, first line, subject and keyword access; indexing for 550 anthologies.

Compact Cambridge

7200 Wisconsin Avenue
Bethesda, MD 20814-4823
800-843-7751

Biomedical Reference Center
Supplier's comments: The Compact Cambridge Biomedical Reference Center is an economically priced collection of five leading biomedical databases on CD-ROM. It includes the Life Sciences Collection, CANCERLIT, HEALTH: PLANNING AND ADMINISTRATION; CINAHL: THE CUMULATIVE INDEX TO NURSING AND ALLIED HEALTH LITERATURE; and, MEDLINE.

Life Sciences Collection on CD-ROM
Supplier's comments: Life Sciences Collection is a CD-ROM database containing all 20 of Cambridge Scientific Abstracts' leading-edge life sciences journals. It gives you broad coverage of the key disciplines that impact on your research at far less cost than comparable life sciences databases.

Congressional Information Services, Inc.

4520 East-West Hwy, Suite 800
Bethesda, MD 20814-3389
301-654-1550; Fax 301-657-3203

Congressional Information Services
Supplier's comments: Congressional Information is now available on CD-ROM.

DIALOG Information Services, Inc.

3460 Hillview Avenue
Palo Alto, CA 94304
415-858-2700; Fax 415-858-7069
Contact: Bonnie Zelter

DIALOG ON DISC
Supplier's comments: Many of the same databases available online through DIALOG are now available on CD-ROM. Titles include ERIC, MEDLINE, STANDARD AND POOR'S CORPORATIONS.

Disclosure, Inc.

5161 River Road
Bethesda, MD 20816
800-945-3647 or 301-951-1300
Fax 301-657-1962

Disclosure
Supplier's comments: We offer information on over 11,000 U.S. and 8,000 non-U.S. companies in a wide variety of formats including image-based CD-ROM and text-based CD-ROM.

EBSCO

P.O. Box 1943
Birmingham, AL 35201-1943
205-991-6600
Contact: Joe Weed

CD-ROM SUBSCRIPTION SERVICE
EBSCO Subscription Services can handle the subscription for any serial or database produced on CD-ROM by others unless restricted by the publisher. CD-ROM subscribers can expect to receive the same quality service on these products that they receive when placing a printed periodical subscription order through EBSCO.

Encyclopaedia Britannica Educational Corporation

310 South Michigan Avenue
Chicago, IL 60604-9839
800-554-9862

Compton's MultiMedia Encyclopedia
Supplier's comments: With CMME you can use your Mac to access a rich pool of research information, bringing together your choice of text, illustrations, animation, and even sound.

Facts on File, Inc.

460 Park Ave S.
New York, NY 10016
212-683-2244 or 800-322-8755
Fax 212-6783-3633 or 800-678-3633

Facts on File News Digest CD-ROM
Supplier's comments:

Follett Software Company

809 North Front Street
McHenry, IL 60050-5589
815-344-8700 or 800-323-3397
Fax 815-344-8774
Contact: Joy Danley

ALLIANCE PLUS
Supplier's comments: Alliance Plus consists of application software and a specialized CD-ROM database, based on Library of Congress MARC records. The CD contains book, audio-visual, and serial records spanning years from 1901 to present. Many of which have been enhanced with: reading levels, interest levels, review sources, annotations, and LC, LC Children's and Sears subject headings. This product is a tool for library cataloging, etc. CardMaster Plus also works with the Alliance Plus CD-ROM MARC Database.

Gale Research, Inc.

835 Penobscot Bldg.
Detroit, MI 48226-4094
800-877-GALE; Fax 313-961-6083

DISCovering Authors
Supplier's comments: This all-new CD-ROM provides full biographical and critical coverage of 300 of the most-studied authors of all time. Search by author, title, or subject term.

Gaylord Information Systems

Box 4901
Syracuse, NY 13221
315-457-5070 or 800-962-9580

SUPERCAT
Supplier's comments: SuperCAT is a complete cataloging support system for libraries of all types and sizes. The complete Library of Congress database, of over 4 million bibliographic records, is available on three CD-ROM discs. Additionally, SuperCat accesses the National Library of Medicine's medical bibliographic records, Cassidy Cataloging Services law and business records, Hennepin County's audio-visual records as well as nearly 100,000 a/v records from Professional Media Services, Inc. The full ALA character

General Research Corporation, Library Systems

5383 Hollister Avenue
Santa Barbara, CA 93111
800-235-6788 or 805-933-5383
Fax 805-967-7094
Contact: Darcy Cook

LASERGUIDE

Supplier's comments: LaserGuide is a CD-ROM Patron Access Catalog for libraries. The library's own data is stored on CD-ROM discs. LaserGuide meets all of the usual requirements of searching and accessing cataloging information, using authors, titles, and subjects. Both Keyword and Boolean searching are available. LaserGuide provides simple and attractive screens for search requests, and suggests additional topics to be searched. Subjects and authors are extracted from the results of previous searches. These new items also can be quickly searched. Optionally, cross-references from the Library of Congress files, supplemented with local records, can be added to a LaserGuide catalog to provide even more suggestions for searching. A shelf list browse is also included and floor plans may be incorporated to locate books. LaserGuide can be updated in the library using LaserMerge and the LaserQuest CD-ROM Cataloging system.

LASERQUEST CD-ROM CATALOGING SYSTEM

Supplier's comments: LaserQuest is the world's largest CD-ROM cataloging workstation for libraries for retrospective conversion and for on-going cataloging. The GRC Resource Database of over 7 million MARC records is recorded on six CD-ROM laser discs. Records for books, serials, computer files, music, visual materials, maps and manuscripts are included. Access is numeric and by title.

    Title searches provide full MARC records which can be optionally modified. The record is then saved to diskette. These diskettes then can be: 1) sent to an "on-line" system via an RS232C port; 2) used to produce catalog cards; 3) sent to GRC for creation and maintenance of the library's database; or 4) instantly uploaded to LaserGuide, CD-ROM PAC. Network licenses available.

Grolier Educational Corporation

Sherman Turnpike
Danbury, CT 06816
800-243-7256; Fax 203-797-3285

Grolier Encyclopedia
Supplier's comments: Grolier Encyclopedia is now available full text on CD-ROM.

H.W. Wilson Company

950 University Avenue
Bronx, NY 10452
800-367-6770

Wilson Business Abstracts
Suppliers Comments: This remarkable new reference tool lets you cut right to the answers to business questions with full, informative abstracts. WILSONDISC contains 130,000 abstracts from the 345 most demanded journals on a single disc.

Wilson Information System
Suppliers comments: Turn to Wilson for the most comprehensive and affordable electronic retrieval system on the market—an integrated system of services unmatched in quality and ease of use by any other system. 27 databases are available including BIBLIOGRAPHIC INDEX, BIOGRAPHY INDEX, BOOK REVIEW DIGEST, BUSINESS PERIODICALS INDEX, CUMULATIVE BOOK INDEX, LIBRARY LITERATURE, LC/MARC FILE, LC/NON-ENGLISH MARC FILE

Information Access Company

352 Lakeside Drive
Foster City, CA 94404
800-226-8431; Fax 415-378-5369

Information Access Company continued

INFOTRAC
Suppliers comments: With over 15 million people using our databases, Information Access has become the world standard in the delivery of information systems. In fact, there are more InfoTrac reference systems installed than all our competitors combined. Infotrac CD-ROM databases include InfoTrac, Expanded Academic Index, Government Publications Index, LegalTrac, and the Wall Street Journal Database

The Library Corporation

Research Park
Inwood, WV 25428
304-229-0100 or 800-624-0559
Fax 304-229- 0295
Contact: Peggy Rulton

BIBLIOFILE CATALOGING
Vendor's comments: Over 8,000,000 MARC records are now available on our CD-ROM databases: the full LC MARC database (all Library of Congress cataloging in English), the LC MARC Foreign database, the Catalog Card Corporation's SEARS/Dewey database, special databases such as the BiblioFile Contributed MARC discs with records contributed by BiblioFile users in school, public, research and academic libraries, and Canadian MARC records. We have just added three new databases: A/V ACCESS with MARC records for current and popular audio-visual materials: A-V ONLINE MARC with individual MARC records representing more than 340,000 titles from the National Information Center for Education Media's (NICEM) A-V Online database, and DOCUFILE with government publications from a wide range of nations.

Available databases include:
>   LC MARC English weekly
>   LC MARC English monthly
>   LC MARC English quarterly
>   LC MARC Foreign quarterly
>   Sears/Dewey quarterly
>   Contributed Cataloging School & Public quarterly
>   Contributed Cataloging Research & Academic quarterly
>   Canadian MARC quarterly
>   A/V Access quarterly
>   NICEM A-V MARC
>   DocuFile quarterly (government documents database)

Marcive, Inc.

P.O. Box 47508
San Antonio, TX 78265
800-531-7678; Fax 512-646-0167

CD-ROM PAC
Supplier's comments: Your library MARC records can be output to CD-ROM to serve as a public access catalog.

Enhanced GPO catalog database on CD-ROM
Supplier's comments:

National Gallery of Art

Department of Extension Programs
4th Street and Constitution Avenue S.W.
Washington, CD 20565
202-842-6263

National Gallery of Art Videodisc
Supplier's comments:

NewsBank, Inc.

58 Pine Street
New Canaan, CT 06840
800-243-7694 or 203-966-1100

NewsBank Electronic Index
Supplier's comments: Current issues and events reference service, delivered monthly on CD-ROM.

OCLC Online Computer Library Center, Inc.

6565 Frantz Road
Dublin, OH 43017-3395
614-764-6000
Contact: Marketing

OCLC CAT CD450 SYSTEM
Supplier's comments: The OCLC CAT CD450 system combines offline cataloging with batch processing to decrease costs and increase cataloging options in your library. As an OCLC member library, you contribute to the growth of an international database by adding records to the OCLC Online Union Catalog (OLUC). The OLUC includes over 23 million bibliographic records, representing items in over 370 languages, and covering a wider range of subjects and formats than is available from any other bibliographic source. Because OCLC membership is a prerequisite for purchase, the CAT CD450 system is the only compact disc cataloging system that gives you access to such a large and diverse database. You also enjoy the many benefits of being part of OCLC's vast resource sharing network, including access to a growing international database and a comprehensive Union Listing Subsystem.

Oxford University Press

200 Madison Ave.
New York, NY 10016
212-679-7300; Fax 212-725-2972

The Oxford English Dictionary
Supplier's comments: The Oxford English Dictionary is now available on CD-ROM.

Public Affairs Information Service, Inc.

11 W. 40th Street
New York, NY 10018-2693
212-736-6629 or 800-841-2693

PAIS on CD-ROM
Supplier's comments: PAIS provides the most comprehensive index to literature on national and international economic, political, and social issues available. Within seconds, you can locate periodicals, books, specialized journals, government documents, legislative handbooks, and more from all over the world. And PAIS covers a vast range of subjects: international relations, education, environmental issues, social problems, business, and finance, just to name a few.

Research Publications International

12 Lunar Drive
Woodbridge, CT 06525
800-444-0799 or 203-397-2600
Fax 203-397-3893

PatentView
Supplier's comments: U.S. Patent Information on CD-ROM

Silver Platter

100 River Ridge Drive
Norwood, MA 02062
800-343-0064 or 617-769-2599
Fax 617-769-8563

Academic Reference Center
Supplier's comments: In the seven years since SilverPlatter first introduced the world to CD-ROM searching, we've earned a reputation as the foremost supplier of high quality CD-ROM titles. At the heart of the Academic Reference Center is a powerful technology that lets you network SilverPlatter's databases. With hard disk or CD-ROM options, this unique system affords libraries these important advantages: extremely fast searching; selection from SilverPlatter's library of 80+ databases; ability to add non-SilverPlatter titles.

SoftLine Information, Inc.

P.O. Box 16845
Stamford, CT 06905
203-968-8878; Fax 203-968-2370

ETHNiC NewsWatch
Supplier's comments: Until now, no one had collected the significant body of newspapers and magazines published by the ethnic and minority press in America. ETHNiC NewsWatch is a new multicultural database with full text on CD-ROM.

UMI

300 N. Zeeb Road
Ann Arbor, MI 48106
800-521-0600

UMI General Reference Databases
Supplier's comments: Full-text images and abstract databases on CD-ROM including Newspaper Abstracts Ondisc, Periodical Abstracts Ondisc, and ProQuest Newspapers/Full Text.

UMI Full-Image Databases
Supplier's comments: Full-image databases are available on CD-ROM including General Periodicals Ondisc, Magazine Express, and Social Sciences Index/Full text.

WLN

P.O. Box 3888
Lacey, WA 98503-0888
800-DIALWLN or 206-459-6518
Fax 206-459-6341

LaserCat CD-ROM Catalog
Supplier's comments: 3.8 million MARC records; catalog cards, label, bibliographies; powerful searching; MARC record download; original cataloging; retrospective conversion.

LaserPac CD-ROM Catalog
Supplier's comments: Public access catalogs with cross references.

World Book Educational Products

101 Northwest Point Blvd.
Elk Grove Village, IL 60007
708-290-5338; Fax 708-290-5403

The World Book Encyclopedia on CD-ROM
Supplier's comments: The World Book Encyclopedia is now available full-text on CD-ROM.

CONFERENCES AND MEETINGS

CONFERENCES AND MEETINGS
1993

1993 Jan

13-15	South Carolina Association of School Librarians	Charleston, SC
14-18	Association for Educational Communication & Technology	New Orleans, LA
19-22	Association for Library and Information Science Education	Denver, CO
22-28	American Library Association Midwinter	Denver, CO
24-26	Special Libraries Association Winter Education Conference	Los Angeles, CA
27-29	Special Libraries Association Mid Year	Los Angeles, CA
28-2/3	Art Libraries Society of North America	San Francisco, CA

1993 Feb

03-06	Music Library Association	San Francisco, CA
22-24	Computers in Libraries	London

1993 Mar

01-03	Computers in Libraries	Washington, DC
05-07	Michigan Association for Media Education	Sugar Loaf, MI
06-08	Alaska Library Association	Nome, AK
09-13	Texas Library Association	San Antonio, TX
17-20	New Mexico Library Association	Las Vegas, NV
17-21	ALA/Public Library Association cluster	Chicago, IL
22-26	Louisiana Library Association	Shreveport, LA
24-27	Kansas Library Association	Overland Park, KS
26-27	Hawaii Library Association	Kohala District, HI
30-4/3	Oklahoma Library Association	Oklahoma City, OK
TBA	Delaware Library Association	TBA

1993 Apr

01-03	Oregon Library Association	Eugene, OR
04-06	Missouri Assn. of School Librarians	Lake Ozark, MO
05-08	Association for Information and Image Management	Chicago, IL
12-15 Joint conf.	Catholic Library Association National Catholic Education Association	New Orleans, LA
13-16	Alabama Library Association	Huntsville, AL
14-15	Connecticut Library Association	Cromwell, CT
21-23	New Jersey Library Association	Long Branch, NJ
21-24	Washington Library Association	Tacoma, WA
27-5/01	Tennessee Library Association	Nashville, TN
28-5/01	Illinois Library Association	Springfield, IL
29-30	Wisconsin Educational Media Association	Appleton, WI
29-5/2	Alberta Library Association	Jasper, AB, Canada
30-5/3 Joint conf.	Council of Planning Librarians American Planning Association	Chicago, IL

CONFERENCES AND MEETINGS 1993 continued

1993 May

04-06	Indiana Library Association	Indianapolis, IN
05-06	IOLS '93	New York, NY
06-07	Solinet	Atlanta, GA
10-12	New Hampshire Library Association	Waterville Valley, NH
10-13	Florida Library Association	Daytona Beach, FL
11-15	School Library Media Div., Montana Lib. Association	Kalispell, MT
12-14	Utah Library Association	Cedar City, UT
13-14	Maryland Library Association	Pikesville, MD
14-20	Medical Library Association	Chicago, IL
16-18	Maine Library Association	Orona, ME
19-20	Vermont Library Association	Fairlee, VT
21-27	American Society for Information Science Mid-Year Meeting	Knoxville, TN

1993 Jun

05-10	Special Libraries Association	Cincinnati, OH
15-17	Campus Wide Information Systems	Cleveland, OH
24-7/1	American Library Association	New Orleans, LA
28	Theatre Library Association	New Orleans, LA

1993 Jul

08-11	Canadian Library Association	Toronto, ON
11-13	Church & Synagogue Library Association	Houston, TX
17-22	American Association of Law Libraries	Boston, MA

1993 Aug

22-28	International Federation of Library Associations	Barcelona, Spain
11-14 Joint conf.	Pacific Northwest Library Association Montana Library Association	Kalispell, MT

1993 Sep

02-05	Society of American Archivists	New Orleans, LA
22-24	Computers in Libraries	Toronto, Ontario
23-25	School Library Media Section, North Dakota Library Association	Williston, ND
26-28	New England Library Association	Burlington, VT
26-29	Pennsylvania Library Association	Philadelphia, PA
30-10/2	Nevada Library Association	Elko, NV
30-10/4 Joint conf.	Mountain Plains Library Association Colorado Library Association	Aspen, CO

1993 Oct

06-08	Minnesota Library Association	Rochester, MN
01-04 Joint conf.	Mountain Plains Library Association Colorado Library Association	Aspen, CO
06-08	Idaho Library Association	Moscow, ID
06-09	South Dakota Library Association	Brookings, SD

CONFERENCES AND MEETINGS 1993 continued

11-13	Arkansas Library Association	Hot Springs, AR
13-15	Iowa Library Association	Ames, IA
14-16	West Virginia Library Association	Huntington, WV
18-22	Association of Records Managers and Administrators	Seattle, WA
19-22	North Carolina Library Association	Winston-Salem, NC
18-22	Michigan Library Association	Lansing, MI
20-23	Michigan Association for Media in Education	Kalamazoo, MI
27-29	Missouri Library Association	Natchez, MO
27-30 Joint conf.	Ohio Library Association OELMA	Cleveland, OH
TBA	American Society for Information Science	Columbus, OH
TBA	Illinois School Library Media Association	Effingham, IL
TBA	Georgia Library Association	Jekyll Island, GA

1993 Nov

01-03	Online/CD-ROM '93	Washington, DC
03-05	Wisconsin Library Association	Green Bay, WI
03-07 Joint conf.	New York Library Association Ontario Library Association	Niagra Falls, NY
08-10	Document Delivery for Libraries	Philadelphia, PA
13-15	California Library Association	Oakland, CA
14-17	Information Industry Association	Washington, DC
19-21	Theatre Library Association	New Orleans, LA

1993 Dec

04-06	Electronic Publishers/Internet Publishers	New York, NY

CONFERENCES AND MEETINGS
1994

1994 Jan

14-20	American Library Association Midwinter	Los Angeles, CA
26-28	Special Libraries Association Winter Meeting	Dallas, TX
TBA	Art Libraries Society of North America	Providence, RI

1994 Feb

09-13	Association for Educational Communication & Technology	Anaheim, CA
TBA	South Carolina Association of School Librarians	Hilton Head, SC

1994 Mar

15-18	Louisiana Library Association	Baton Rouge, LA
23-26	ALA/Public Library Association	Atlanta, GA
TBA	Alaska Library Association	Anchorage, AK

CONFERENCES AND MEETINGS 1994 continued

1994 Apr

04-07 Joint conf.	Catholic Library Association National Catholic Education Association	Anaheim, CA
06-08	Kansas Library Association	Wichita, KA
12-16	Texas Library Association	Corpus Christi, TX
27-29	Washington Library Association	Yakima, WA
27-30	Oklahoma Library Association	Tulsa, OK
TBA	Montana Library Association	Butte, MT
TBA Joint conf.	Council of Planning Librarians American Planning Association	San Francisco, CA

1994 May

03-07 Joint conf.	Florida Library Association School & Children's Division, SELA	Orlando, FL
04-07	Illinois Library Association	Chicago, IL
TBA	Medical Library Association	TBA
TBA	Middle Atlantic Regional Library Federation	Baltimore, MD
TBA	American Society for Information Science	TBA

1994 Jun

11-16	Special Libraries Association	Atlanta, GA
16-19	Canadian Library Association	Quebec City, PQ
23-30	American Library Association	Miami, FL
27	Theatre Library Association	Miami, FL

1994 Jul

09-14	American Assoc. of Law Libraries	Seattle, WA

1994 Aug

TBA	International Federation Library Associations	Havana, Cuba

1994 Sep

05-11	Society of American Archivists	Indianapolis, IN
25-27	New England Library Association	Sturbridge, MA
24-28	Pennsylvania Library Association	Harrisburg, PA

1994 Oct

05-07	Minnesota Library Association	Duluth, MN
05-08	Idaho Library Association	Sun Valley, ID
12-14	Iowa Library Association	Davenport, IA
24-26	Online/CD-ROM '93	San Francisco, CA
25-29	Southeastern Library Association	Charlotte, NC
26-29 Joint conf.	Mountain Plains Library Association Nevada Library Association	No. Lake Tahoe, CO
27-29	Wisconsin Library Association	Oshkosh, WI

1994 Nov

12-15	California Library Association	Anaheim, CA

1994 Dec

SELECTED BIBLIOGRAPHY
OF
RECENT LIBRARY AUTOMATION BOOKS
AND PERIODICALS

SELECTED BIBLIOGRAPHY
OF
RECENT LIBRARY AUTOMATION BOOKS

Alberico, Ralph, and Mary Micco. *Expert Systems for Reference and Information Retrieval.* Westport, CT: Meckler, Inc., 1990. Supplement to Computers in Libraries, Number 10.

American Society for Information Science. Jose-Marie Griffiths, editor. *Proceedings of the 54th Annual Meeting of the American Society for Information Science,* 27 October 1991, Medford, NJ: Learned Information, Inc.

Anders, Vicki. *Automated Information Retrieval in Libraries: A Management Handbook.* Greenwood Publishing, July 1992.

Barry, Janice R. *Data Base Ownership and Copyright Issues among Automated Library Networks: An Analysis and Case Study.* 208p Ablex Pub, 1991.

Basch, N. Bernard, and Judy McQueen. *Buying Serials.* 198p Neal-Schuman, September 1990.

Beaument, Jane, and Joseph P. Cox. *Retrospective Conversion: A Practical Guide for Libraries.* Westport, CT: Meckler, Inc., 1989. Supplement to Computers in Libraries, Number 7.

Beiser, Karl. *DOS 5.0 for Libraries.* Westport, CT: Meckler, Inc., 1992. Supplement to Computers in Libraries, Number 57.

___. *Essential Guide to the Library IBM PC.* Westport, CT: Meckler, Inc., 1989. Volume 14: The Operating System: PC-DOS.

___. *Essential Guide to dBase IV in Libraries.* Westport, CT: Meckler, Inc., 1991.

Boss, Richard. *The Library Manager's Guide to Automation.* 3d ed. Macmillan, 1 June 1990.

Brandt, D. Scott, editor. *Computers in Libraries, 1990: Buyer's Guide & Consultant Directory.* 64p Westport, CT: Meckler Corp, June 1990.

Brandt, D. Scott. *UNIX and Libraries.* Westport, CT: Meckler, Inc., 1991. Supplement to Computers in Libraries, Number 20.

Breeding, Marshall. *Integrated Library Systems.* Westport, CT: Meckler, Inc., 1992. Essential Guide to the Library IBM PC: Volume 13.

___, editor. *Library LANs: Case Studies in Practice and Application.* Westport, CT: Meckler, Inc., 1992. Supplement to Computers in Libraries, Number 39.

Brenner, Ev. *Information Insights.* Medford, NJ: Learned Information, Inc., 1992.

Buckland, Michael and Susan Stone, editors. *Multimedia Information Systems. Based on the Proceedings of the 1991 ASIS Mid-Year Meeting.* Medford, NJ: Learned Information, Inc., 1991.

Carande, Robert. *Automation in Library Reference Services: A Handbook.* Greenwood, December 1992.

Cargill, Jennifer, editor. *Integrated Online Library Catalogs.* 160p Meckler Corp, March 1990.

Clayton, Marlene, and Chris Batt. *Managing Library Automation.* 2nd ed., Ashgate Pub Co, September 1992.

Computers in Libraries International 1990: Proceedings of the Fourth Annual Computers in Libraries Conference. Westport, CT: Meckler, Inc., 1990.

Computers in Libraries Index: 1985-1990. Westport, CT: Meckler, Inc., 1991.

Computers in Libraries International 1991: Proceedings of the Fifth Annual Computers in Libraries Conference. Westport, CT: Meckler, Inc., 1991.

Corbin, John. *Corbin's Library Automation Handbook.* 224p Oryx Pr, January 1993.

Davies, Peter. *Artificial Intelligence, Its Role in the Information Industry.* Medford, NJ: Learned Information, Inc., 1991.

Davis, Trisha, and James Huesmann. *Serials Control Systems for Libraries.* Westport, CT: Meckler, Inc., 1992. Essential Guide to the Library IBM PC: Volume 12.

Dempsey, Lorcan. *Libraries, Networks and OSI: A Review, with a Report on North American Developments, 1992 edition.* Westport, CT: Meckler, Inc., 1992. Supplement to Computers in Libraries, Number 49.

Desmarais, Barbara, and Norman Desmarais. *Library Computer and Technology Specialists: A Directory.* Westport, CT: Meckler, Inc., 1990.

SELECTED BIBLIOGRAPHY OF RECENT LIBRARY AUTOMATION BOOKS continued

Dewey, Patrick R. *FAX for Libraries*. Westport, CT: Meckler, Inc., 1990. Supplement to Computers in Libraries, Number 13.

___. *One Hundred One Microcomputer Projects to Do in Your Library: Putting Your Micro to Work*. 176p Chicago, IL: ALA, 1990.

Dillion, Martin. *Interfaces for Information Retrieval and Online Systems: The State of the Art*. Westport, CT: Greenwood Publishing, 1991.

Document Image Automation 1991: Proceedings of the First Annual Conference on Document Image Automation. Westport, CT: Meckler, Inc., 1991.

Duval, Beverly K., and Linda Main. *Automated Library Systems: A Librarian's Guide & Teaching Manual*. 275p Meckler Corp, June 1992.

Dyer, Hilary, and Anne Morris. *Human Aspects of Library Automation*. 250p Ashgate Pub Co, April 1990.

Dykhuis, Randy. *Template Directory for Libraries*. Westport, CT: Meckler, Inc., 1990.

European Foundation for Library Cooperation Staff, editor. *Library Automation & Networking: First European Conference, May 1990*. 600p K G Saur, 1991.

Evans, John Ross. *Serials Control Systems for Libraries*. Westport, CT: Meckler, Inc., 1991. Essential Guide to the Library IBM PC: Volume 12: .

Eyre, John editor. *Computers in Libraries International 1990: Proceedings of the Fourth Annual Computers in Libraries Conference*. Westport, CT: Mecker, Inc., 1990.

___. *Computers in Libraries International 1991: Proceedings of the Fifth Annual Computers in Libraries Conference*. Westport, CT: Meckler, Inc., 1991.

___. *Computers in Libraries International 1992: Proceedings of the Sixth Annual Computers in Libraries Conference*. Westport, CT: Mecker, Inc., 1992.

Godden, Irene P., editor. *Library Technical Services: Operations & Management*. 2d ed. Academic Press, 1991.

Grundner, Thomas M., and Susan E. Anderson. *The Infosphere Project: Public Access to Computer-Mediated Communication and Information Resources*. Westport, CT: Meckler, Inc., 1992. Supplement to Computers in Libraries, Number 60.

Hagler, Ronald. *The Bibliographic Record & Information Technology*, 2d ed. Chicago, IL: American Library Association, distributor, 1991.

Haynes, David. *Information Sources in Information Technology*. New Providence, NJ: K.G. Saur, 1990.

Hayman, Lynne editor. *101 Uses of dBase in Libraries*. Westport, CT: Meckler, Inc., 1990. Supplement to Computers in Libraries, Number 12.

Henry, Marcia K., Linda Keenan, and Michael Reagan. *Search Sheets for OPACs on the Internet: A Selective Guide to U.S. OPACs Utilizing VT100 Emulation*. Westport, CT: Meckler, Inc., 1991. Supplement to Computers in Libraries, Number 32.

Johnson, Peggy. *Automation & Organizational Change in Libraries*. 245p Macmillan, March 1991.

Johnson, Richard D., and Harriett H. Johnson. *The Macintosh Press: Desktop Publishing for Libraries*. Westport, CT: Meckler, Inc., 1989. Supplement to Computers in Libraries, Number 9.

Kehoe, Brendan P. *Zen & the Art of the Internet: A Beginner's Guide*. 2d ed. Prentice Hall, January 1993.

Kershner, Lois M. *Forms for Automated Library Systems: An Illustrated Guide for Selection, Design, & Use*. New York, NY: Neal-Schuman Publishers, Inc., 1988.

Kessler, Jack. *Directory to Fulltext Online Resources 1992*. Westport, CT: Meckler, Inc., 1992. Supplement to Computers in Libraries, Number 55.

Kranch, Douglas A. *Automated Media Management Systems*. New York, NY: Neal-Schuman Publishers, Inc., 1991.

Krol, Ed, and Mike Loukides, editor. *The Whole Internet Users Guide and Catalog*. 400p O'Reilly & Assocs, September 1992.

Lane, Elizabeth S. *Microcomputer Management and Maintenance for Libraries*. Westport, CT: Meckler, Inc., 1990. Supplement to Computers in Libraries, Number 16.

SELECTED BIBLIOGRAPHY OF RECENT LIBRARY AUTOMATION BOOKS continued

Lane, Elizabeth, and Craig Summerhill. *An Internet Primer for Librarians and Educators: A Basic Guide to Internet Networking Technology.* Westport, CT: Meckler, Inc., 1992. Supplement to Computers in Libraries, Number 54.

LaPier, Cynthia B. *The Librarian's Guide to WordPerfect 5.0.* Westport, CT: Meckler, Inc., 1990. Supplement to Computers in Libraries, Number 14.

Learned Information, Inc. David C. Genaway, editor. *IOLS '90: Proceedings of the 5th Integrated Online Library Systems Meeting, New York, NY, 1990.* Medford, NJ: Learned Information, Inc., 1990.

___. David C. Genaway, editor. *IOLS '91: Proceedings of the 6th Integrated Online Library Systems Meeting, New York, NY, 8 May 1991.* Medford, NJ: Learned information, Inc., 1991.

Library Association Publishing, Ltd. *The Basics of Systems Analysis and Design for Information Managers.* Lanham, MD: UNIPUB, 1990.

___. *Expert Systems and Artificial Intelligence: An Information Manager's Guide.* Lanham, MD: UNIPUB, 1991.

___. *New Horizons in Information Retrieval.* Lanham, MD: UNIPUB, 1990.

Lynch, Daniel C., and Marshall T. Rose. *Internet System Handbook.* 900p Addison-Wesley, October 1992.

MacDonald, Linda B., Mara R. Saule, Margaret W. Gordon, and Craig A. Robertson. *Teaching Technologies in Libraries.* 198p Macmillan, December 1990.

Main, Linda, and Char Whitaker. *Automating Literacy: A Challenge for Libraries.* Greenwood, April 1991.

Malamud, Carl. *Exploring the Internet: A Technical Travelogue.* Prentice Hall, January 1993.

Mandelbaum, Jane. *Small Project Automation for Libraries and Information Centers.* Westport, CT: Meckler, Inc., 1992. Supplement to Computers in Libraries, Number 28.

Marks, Kenneth E., Steven Nielsen, and Gary Wethersbee. *Electronic Collection Maintenance and Video Archiving.* Westport, CT: Meckler, Inc., 1993. Supplement to Computers in Libraries, Number 53.

Marks, Kenneth, and Steven Nielsen. *Local Area Networks in Libraries.* Westport, CT: Meckler, Inc., 1991. Supplement to Computers in Libraries, Number 27.

Markuson, Barbara Evans and Elaine W. Woods, editors. *Networks for Networkers II: Critical Issues for Libraries in the National Network Environment.* New York, NY: Neal-Schuman Publishers, Inc., 1992.

Marmion, Dan. *Integrated Library Systems.* Westport, CT: Meckler, Inc., 1991. Essential Guide to the Library IBM PC. Volume 13

___. *Windows for Libraries.* Westport, CT: Meckler, Inc., 1992. Supplement to Computers in Libraries, Number 47.

Mates, Barbara T. *Library Technology for Visually and Physically Impaired Patrons.* Westport, CT: Meckler, Inc., 1991. Supplement to Computers in Libraries, Number 26.

McClure, Charles R. *The Role of Libraries in a National Research and Education Network.* Westport, CT: Meckler, Inc., 1992. Supplement to Computers in Libraries, Number 51.

Metz, Roy. *Directory of Directories on the Internet.* Westport, CT: Meckler, Inc., 1992. Supplement to Computers in Libraries, Number 33.

Miller, Mark A. *Troubleshooting TCP - IP: Analyzing the Protocols of the Internet.* 450p M&T Books, July 1992.

Morrow, Blaine Victor. *CD-ROM Retrieval Software: An Overview.* Westport, CT: Meckler, Inc., 1991. Supplement to Computers in Libraries, Number 22.

___. *Utility Software.* Westport, CT: Meckler, Inc., 1990. Essential Guide to the Library IBM PC: Volume 15.

Moulton, Lynda W. *Data Bases for Special Libraries: A Strategic Guide to Information Management.* Westport, CT: Greenwood Publishing, 1991.

Muro, Ernest A. *Automation Services for Libraries: A Resource Handbook of Marketing & Sales.* Vendor Relations, January 1991.

Murphy, Catherine. *Automating School Library Catalogs: A Reader.* 200p Libraries Unlimited, March 1992.

SELECTED BIBLIOGRAPHY OF RECENT LIBRARY AUTOMATION BOOKS continued

Nelson, Nancy Melin, editor. *Computers in Libraries; Canada '90: Proceedings of the 1st Annual Computers in Libraries Canada Conference.* Westport, CT: Meckler, Inc., 1990.

___. *Computers in Libraries 1990: Proceedings of the 5th Annual Computers in Libraries Conference.* Westport, CT: Meckler, Inc., 1990.

___. *Computers in Libraries; Canada '91: Proceedings of the 2nd Annual Computers in Libraries Canada Conference.* Westport, CT: Meckler, Inc., 1991.

___. *Computers in Libraries 1991: Proceedings of the 6th Annual Computers in Libraries Conference.* Westport, CT: Meckler, Inc., 1991.

___. *Computers in Libraries; Canada '92: Proceedings of the 3rd Annual Computers in Libraries Canada Conference.* Westport, CT: Meckler, Inc., 1992.

___. *Computers in Libraries 1992: Proceedings of the 7th Annual Computers in Libraries Conference.* Westport, CT: Meckler, Inc., 1992.

___. *Library Technology 1970-1990: Shaping the Library of the Future.* Westport, CT: Meckler, Inc., 1991. Supplements to Computers in Libraries, Number 25.

___. *Serials Management in an Automated Age.* Westport, CT: Meckler, Inc., 1981. Proceedings of the First Annual Serials Conference.

___. *Technology for the '90's.* Westport, CT: Meckler, Inc., 1990. Supplement to Computers in Libraries, Number 15.

Nelson, Nancy Melin, and Eric Flower, editors. *Electronic Information Networking.* Westport, CT: Meckler, Inc., 1992. Supplement to Computers in Libraries, Number 45.

___. *Library Computing in Canada: Bilingualism, Multiculturalism, and Transborder Connections.* Westport, CT: Meckler, Inc., 1991. Supplement to Computers in Libraries, Number 41.

Pitkin, Gary M. , editor. *Cost-Effective Technical Services: How to Track, Manage, and Justify Internal Operations.* New York, NY: Neal-Schuman Publishers, Inc., 1989.

___. *The Evolution of Library Automation: Management Issues and Future Perspectives.* Westport, CT: Meckler, Inc., 1991. Supplement to Computers in Libraries, Number 44.

___. *Information Management and Organizational Change in Higher Education: The Impact on Academic Libraries.* Westport, CT: Meckler, Inc., 1992. Supplement to Computers in Libraries, Number 59.

___. *Library Systems Migration: Changing Automated Systems in Libraries and Information Centers.* Westport, CT: Meckler, Inc., 1991. Supplement to Computers in Libraries, Number 30.

Ra, Marsha editor. *Advances in Online Public Access Catalogs, Vol. 1.* Westport, CT: Meckler, Inc., March 1992.

RMG Consultants, Inc Staff. *Plans and Recommendations for Linking Automated Systems in Long Island Libraries.* 84p LI Lib Resources, March 1991.

Roth, Judith Paris , editor. *Converting Information for WORM Optical Storage: A Case Study Approach.* Westport, CT: Meckler, Inc., 1990.

Saffady, William. *Automating the Small Library.* 16p ALA, 1991.

___. *Electronic Document Imaging Systems: Design, Evaluation, and Implementation.* Westport, CT: Meckler, Inc., 1992.

___. *Text Storage and Retrieval Systems: A Technology Survey and Product Directory.* Westport, CT: Meckler, Inc., 1989.

Schuyler, Michael. *Dial In: An Annual Guide to Library Online Public Access Catalogs.* Westport, CT: Meckler, Inc., 1992.

SELECTED BIBLIOGRAPHY OF RECENT LIBRARY AUTOMATION BOOKS continued

___. *The Systems Librarian Guide to Computers.* Westport, CT: Meckler, Inc., 1990. Supplement to Computers in Libraries, Number 18.

Schuyler, Michael, and Jake Hoffman. *PC Management: A How-To-Do-It Manual for Librarians.* New York, NY: Neal-Schuman Publishers, Inc., 1990.

Sloan, Bernard G. *Linked Systems for Resource Sharing.* Boston, MA: G.K. Hall & Co., 1990.

Talley, Marcia D., and Virginia McNitt. *Automating the Library with AskSam: A Practical Handbook.* 165p Meckler Corp, November 1991.

Tapper, Garry, and Ken Tombs. *The Legal Admissibility of Document Imaging Systems.* Westport, CT: Meckler, Inc., 1992.

Warwick, Robert T., and Patricia E. Jensen. *Using OCLC: A How-To-Do-It Manual for Libraries.* New York, NY: Neal-Schuman Publishers, Inc., 1990.

Wasserman, Ellen S. , editor. *Software Publishers' Catalogs Annual.* Westport, CT: Meckler, Inc., 1991.

Williams, Brian. *Directory of Computer Conferencing in Libraries.* Westport, CT: Meckler, Inc., 1992. Supplement to Computers in Libraries, Number 36.

Williams, Martha E. , editor. *ARIST 26 Annual Review of Information Science and Technology.* Medford, NJ: Learned Information, Inc., 1991.

Woodsworth, Anne. *Patterns and Options for Managing Information Technology on Campus.* Chicago, IL: American Library Association, 1991.

Wright, Keith C. *Workstations and Local Area Networks for Librarians.* Chicago, Il: American Library Association, 1990.

Zuck, Gregory and Bruce Flanders. *Wide-Area Network Applications in Libraries.* Westport, CT: Meckler, Inc., 1992. Supplement to Computers in Libraries, Number 58.

SELECTED BIBLIOGRAPHY
OF
LIBRARY AUTOMATION PERIODICALS

Academic & Library Computing. Westport, CT: Meckler, Inc. 10 issues/year; $95. (School rate $33.)

ASLIB Proceedings. Medford, NJ: Learned Information, Inc. (U.S. Distributor). 10 issues/year; $220.

C L S I Newsletter of Library Automation. Newtonville, MA: C L S I, Inc. 2/year; free.

Computers in Libraries. Westport, CT: Meckler, Inc. 12 issues/year; $77. (School Rate $35.)

Corporate Library Update. Brewster, NY: Corporate Library Update. 26/year; $62.

D L A Bulletin. Oakland, CA: University of California Division of Library Automation. 4 issues/year; free.

Document Image Automation Update. Westport, CT: Meckler, Inc. 11 issues/year; $297.

Document Image Automation. Westport, CT: Meckler, Inc. 4 issues year; $115. (School Rate: $35.)

The Electronic Library. Medford, NJ: Learned Information, Inc. Bimonthly; $99.

Electronic Networking; Research, Applications and Policy. Westport, CT: Meckler, Inc. 4 issues/year; $95. (School rate: $35.)

Information Retrieval & Library Automation. Mt. Airy, MD: Lomond Publications, Inc. 12/year; $66.

Information Technology and Libraries. Chicago, IL: American Library Association Library and Information Technology Association. 4/year; $45.

Information Today. Medford, NJ: Learned Information, Inc. 11 issues/year; $39.95.

Information World Review, The Information Community Newspaper. Medford, NJ: Learned Information, Inc. 11 issues/year; $69.

Journal of the American Society for Information Science. New York, NY: John Wiley & Sons, Inc. 10/year; $375.

Legal Information Management Index. Newton Highlands, MA: Legal Information Services. 4 issues/year; $50.

Library Computer Systems and Equipment Review. Westport, CT: Meckler, Inc. 2 issues/year; $225.

Library Hi Tech Journal. Ann Arbor, MI: Pierian Press. 4 issues/year; $65.

Library Hi Tech News. Ann Arbor, MI: Pierian Press. 4 issues/year; $65.

Library Hotline. New York, NY: Cahners Publishing Co. 50/year; $74.

Library Journal. Marion, OH: Cahners Publishing. 21/year; $74.

Library Software Review. Westport, CT: Meckler, Inc. 6 issues/year; $125. (School Rate: $35.).

Library Systems Newsletter. Chicago, IL: American Library Association. $35.

Library Technology Reports. Chicago, IL: American Library Association. $35.

LISA; Library & Information Science Abstracts. Folkstone, Kent, England: Bowker-Saur. 12 issues/year; $499.

MeckJournal: An Electronic Monthly. Westport, CT: Meckler, Inc. 12 issues/year; no charge.

Multimedia Review. Westport, CT: Meckler, Inc. 4 issues/year; $97. (School rate: $35.)

OCLC Micro. Westport, CT: Meckler, Inc. 6 issues/year; $50. (School rate: $35.)

ON CARL: The Newsletter of the Colorado Alliance of Research Libraries. Denver, CO: CARL. Free.

Research & Education Networking. Westport, CT: Meckler, Inc. 9 issues/year; $97. (School rate: $35.)

BRIEF INFO

BRIEF INFO

Brief information is provided about library automation software for which it was not appropriate or not possible to provide detailed information. The reasons for not including full information are specified for each product.

- A -

25:02, Information Research Corp.
name changed to OFFICE LIBRARIAN; no response to requests for info
A V INVENTORY, D and H Software
no response to requests for info
A-V CATALOG WRITER, Follett Software
not included in current catalog
A-V MANAGER, Moorpark College
no response to requests for info
A/VION, Cambridge Documentary Films, Inc.
no response to requests for info
ADVANCED LIBRARY INFORMATION SYSTEMS, Systems Control, Inc.
no response to requests for info
ALI'I, Advanced Libraries and Information, Inc.
see ADVANCE (GEAC Computer Corporation)
ALIS II, Data Phase
product rights transferred to OCLC
ALIS III, Data Phase
product rights transferred to UTLAS
ALLIED INSTRUCTIONAL MEDIA, Allied Instructional Media Company
no response to requests for info
ALOHA, ALI'I
name changed to ADVANCE (GEAC Computer Corporation)
AMI, RTI
no response to requests for info
AMMS-CATALOG SYSTEM, Tek Data Systems Company
product discontinued
AMMS-MEDIA SYSTEM, Tek Data Systems Company
product discontinued
ARMS, Automated Records Management, Inc.
name changed to ACTIVE RECORDS SOFTWARE
AS/TECH, Administrative Software Technology
no response to requests for info
ASPENSEARCH, Aspen Systems Corporation
no response to requests for info
ASSISTANT, Library Automation Products, Inc.
product rights transferred to INLEX, Inc.
ATLAS, Data Research Associates, Inc.
name changed to DATA RESEARCH SYSTEM
AUDIO VISUAL CARD/DIRECTORY
name changed to LIBRARY PROCESSES SYSTEM
AUTOMATED BOOKING AND CATALOG, VIS Consultants, Inc.
name changed to MEDIA MANAGER
AUTOMATED CATALOGING SERVICES, The Computer Company
Library Services Division discontinued

AUTOMATED LIBRARY INFORMATION SYSTEM, Dataphase
product rights transferred to OCLC and UTLAS
AUTOMATED MEDIA LIBRARY CIRCULATION AND SCHEDULING SYSTEM, Tek Data Systems Company
no response to requests for info
AUTOMATIC INDEXING, AT&T Technology Licensing
no response to requests for info
AV CATALOG WRITER, Library Software Company
no response to requests for info
AVPATH, Alpine Data Services
name changed to FILMPATH

- B -

Battelle Software Products Center
name changed to Information Dimensions, Inc.
BEST SELLER, Infocentre Library Mgt, Inc.
no response to requests for info
BIBLIO
see INMAGICPLUS
BIBLIOFILE: CATALOG PRODUCTION, Library Corporation
available as part of BIBLIOFILE "TLC" (TOTAL LIBRARY COMPUTING) SYSTEM
BIBLIOFILE: LASERSEARCH BOOK ACQUISITIONS, Library Corporation
available as part of BIBLIOFILE "TLC" (TOTAL LIBRARY COMPUTING) SYSTEM
BIBLIOGRAPHY, Pro-Tem Software
no response to requests for info
BIBLIOGRAPHY GENERATOR, Educational Activities Inc.
product discontinued
BIBLIOGRAPHY WRITER, Follett Software Company
product discontinued
BIBLIOTEK, Scientific Software Products, Inc.
no response to requests for info
BIBPRO IV, Information General Corporation
no response to requests for info
BLIS, Bibliotechniques
product discontinued
BOOKDEX, Capital Systems Group
no current contact info
BOOKLINE, CLSI
available as part of LIBS 100PLUS
BOOKWORM, J.L. Hammett Company
no response to requests for info
BRIDGE-IT, Western Library Network
not included in current catalog

- C -

C & A MICRO/SYSTEM, Cibbarelli & Associates, Inc
product discontinued
CADMAC 410/STARS, Infodetics
product discontinued
CADMUS, ICL, Inc.
no response to requests for info
CAIRS, Info/Doc (Information/Documentation, Inc.)
no longer distributed by Info/Doc, no current contact info

CALIB, Calib Systems, Inc.
no response to requests for info

CALICO, Calico, Inc.
no response to requests for info

CARD CAT, Compu-tations Inc.
no current contact info

CARD DATALOG, Data Trek, Inc.
name changed to MANAGER SERIES

CARDPRO, Clinton-Essex-Franklin Library System
vendor requested deletion of product from Directory

CATALOG CARD ASSEMBLER II, Micro Tech Software Company
no response to requests for info

CATALOG CARD PROGRAM, Library Processes System, Educomp
no response to requests for info

CATALOGIT III, Right On Programs
not included in current catalog

CATALOGIT III AV, Right On Programs
not included in current catalog

CBLS, Cibbarelli & Associates, Inc.
product discontinued

CBMS, Cibbarelli & Associates, Inc.
product discontinued

CHECKMATE II, CLASS
product discontinued

CINCINNATI ELECTRONICS, Cincinnati Electronics
no response to requests for info

CIRCA II, MSC Computer Store
no response to requests for info

CIRCULATION MANAGEMENT SYSTEM, Orchard Systems
no response to requests for info

CIRCULATION MANAGER, Micro Solutions
no current contact info

CITY OF MIDLAND CIRCULATION SYSTEM, Grace A. Dow Memorial Library
no response to requests for info

CL-PERLINE, CLSI, Inc.
product discontinued

CLASS ON TYME, Class
product discontinued

CLASSIC, Dougherty County Public Library
no response to requests for info

CLSI
name changed to LIBS 100PLUS

Columbia Computing Services
name changed to CTB Macmillan/McGraw-Hill

Compel, Inc.
no current contact info

COMPU SYSTEM II, Compu System
no response to requests for info

COMPU-TATIONS, Compu-tations, Inc.
no response to requests for info

COMPUCIRC, Embar Information Consultants
product discontinued

COMPULOG, Embar Information Consultants
product discontinued

COMPUMEDIA, Embar Information Consultants
product discontinued

COMPUTER TRANSLATION, Computer Translation, Inc.
product discontinued

CORPORATE DOCUMENTS, Data Trek, Inc.
vendor requested deletion of product from Directory

CREATE, Microdex
no current contact info

CROSSTALK, Mead Data Central Ltd.
product discontinued

CSC SEARCH SOFTWARE, IIT Research Institute
no response to requests for info

- D -

DATA MANAGEMENT SYSTEM, Central Iowa Regional Library
no response to requests for info

DATA RECALL, Data Recall, Inc.
no response to requests for info

DISK-IT, Right On Programs
not included in current catalog

DM, Information Dimensions, Inc.
now part of BASISPLUS

DOBIS/LEUVEN, IBM Corporation
product rights transferred to ELIAS in Belgium who will be responsible for existing customers.

DOBIS/LIBIS, IBM Corporation
product rights transferred to ELIAS in Belgium who will be responsible for existing customers.

DRA, DRA, Inc.
name changed to DATA RESEARCH SYSTEM

- E -

EASY DATA SYSTEMS, Sydney Development Corporation
name changed to MICRO LIBRARY SYSTEM; company name change also from Sydney Dataproducts, Inc. to International Library Systems Corp.

ELOQUENT MM, Eloquent Systems Inc.
name changed to ELOQUENT MEDIA MANAGER

ELOQUENT RM, Eloquent Systems Inc.
name changed to GENCAT

ELOQUENT UC, Eloquent Systems Inc.
replaced by newer products ELOQUENT LIBRARIAN and GENCAT

EQUIPMENT INVENTORY, Right On Programs, Inc.
not included in current catalog

ERS, Infologics, Inc.
see INFOLOGICS/ERS II

ETTACQ , ETT Library Automations, Inc.
no response to requests for info

ETTACQ PC, ETT Library Automations, Inc.
no response to requests for info

EYRING LIBRARY SYSTEMS, Eyring Library Systems, Inc.
no response to requests for information

- F -

F.I.L.L.S., MacNeal Hospital Health Science Resource Center
product discontinued
FAMULUS, U.S. Department of Agriculture
product discontinued
FILESIFTER, M.B. Stevens
no response to requests for info
FILM BOOKING, Software Technology for Computers
no response to requests for info
FINAL RECORD, Palinet/ULC
product discontinued
FIRMS, Guy H. Thomas & Associates
no response to requests for info
FOLLETT UTILITY TRAK, Follett Software
not included in current catalog
FYI/3000+, FYI, Inc.
product discontinued

- G -

GEAC LIBRARY INFORMATION SYSTEM, Geac Computer Corporation
name changed to ADVANCE (GEAC Computer Corporation)
GMUtant SEARCH TRAINER, GMUtant Software
product discontinued; new product is BIBL
GOLDEN RETRIEVER, Class
product discontinued
GS-100 CIRCULATION CONTROL SYSTEM, Gaylord Brothers, Inc.
product discontinued
GS-3000, Gaylord Information Systems
no response to requests for info

- H -

H&P INTERACT, Harris & Paulson, Inc.
no response to requests for info

- I -

ILL FORMS PRINTER, Mack Memorial Health Sciences Library, Salem Hospital
vendor requested deletion of product from Directory
ILS, National Technical Information Service
name changed to INTEGRATED LIBRARY SYSTEM (ILS)
INCASE
see INMAGIC PLUS
INCHARGE
see INMAGIC PLUS
INDEXIT, Graham Conley Press
product discontinued
INFOQUEST, UTLAS, Inc.
name changed to M/SERIES 10
INFORM, Inform Software Inc.
name changed to RIM; company name changed to Records & Information Management Solutions

INFORONICS, Inforonics, Inc.
no response to requests for info
INFOSEL, InfoSel
no current contact info
INNOVACQ, Innovative Interfaces, Inc.
available as a part of INNOPAC
INNOVATION-45 PLUS, Scribe Software, Inc.
name changed to INNOVATION PLUS
INVENTORY-IT, Right On Programs
not included in current catalog
IRAS, IIT Research Institute
no response to requests for info
IZE, Persoft, Inc.
product discontinued

- J -

JSPACE, Information Access Systems
no response to requests for info

- K -

KAETZEL, GLASS, SMITH DATABASE (KGS), U.S. Department of Commerce
available as NBS Technical Note 1123, "A Computer Database System for Indexing Research Papers"
KEYWORD INDEXING PROGRAM, Cygnus, Inc.
no current contact
KWICKKWOC, M.B. Stevens
no response to requests for info
KWINDEX, Golden Gate Systems
vendor requested deletion of product from Directory

- L -

LABORATORY NOTEBOOK, Data Trek, Inc.
vendor requested deletion of product from Directory
LASERFILE, Library Systems & Services, Inc.
product discontinued
LIAS (LIBRARY INFORMATION ACCESS SYSTEM), Pennsylvania State University
product discontinued
LIBMAN, VTEC Pty. Ltd.
no U.S. distributor
Library Automation Products, Inc.
company acquired by INLEX, Inc.; product name continues to be THE ASSISTANT
LIBRARY BAR CODE SYSTEM, Computext Innovation in Communication
no response to requests for information
LIBRARY HELPER OVERDUES, Southern Micro Systems
no response to requests for information
LIBRARY INTERFACE SYSTEMS, Library Interface Systems, Inc.
no response to requests for info
LIBRARY MASTER, Clarion Computing
no current contact
LIBRARY MATE, Geoglobal
no response to requests for info

LIBRARY MICROTOOLS: OVERDUES, K-12 MicroMedia Publishing
    not included in current catalog
LIBRARY OVERDUE MATERIALS RECORD, Minnesota Computer
    no response to requests for info
LIBRARY PROCESSES SYSTEM, Educomp
    product rights transferred to Library Processes System
LIBRARY SKILLS, Micro Power & Light Co.
    no current contact info
LIBRARY SYSTEM, Verticon Computer Center
    no current contact info
LIBRARYBROWSER
    see LIBRARYWORKS in software section
LIBRARYDISC
    see LIBRARYWORKS in software section
LIFESAVER, Follett Software
    not included in current catalog
LISTMASTER, Master Software
    no current contact info
LMS - LIBRARY MANAGEMENT SYSTEM, AS/TECH, Inc.
    no current contact info
LS/2000, OCLC
    product discontinued

- M -

MAC LIBRARY SYSTEM (MLS), CASPR, Inc.
    name changed to LIBRARYWORKS
MACBOOK SERIES: LIBRARY MANAGEMENT, LISI, Library Interface Systems Inc
    no current contact info
MAG-IT, Right On Programs
    not included in current catalog
MAGGIE'S PLACE
    name changed to EYRING LIBRARY SYSTEMS; EYRING discontinued
MARCON PLUS, AIRS, Inc.
    no current contact info
MARVELIN, Marvelin Corp.
    no response to requests for info
MASTERING LIBRARY SKILLS, Educational Publishing Concepts, Inc.
    no current contact info
Maxwell Online Services, Inc.
    corporate name changed to BRS Software Products, Inc.
MB-RMS, McLeod-Bishop Systems Ltd.
    product discontinued
MEDIA AND EQUIPMENT MANAGEMENT, Educational Activities, Inc.
    product discontinued
MEDIACAT, Dymaxion Research Ltd.
    no response to requests for info
MEMORY LANE, Group L Corp
    no current contact info
MICRO INDEXING SYSTEM, Compugramma, Inc.
    no response to requests for info
MICRO MARC, Library Systems & Services, Inc.
    product discontinued

MICROCHECK, Brodart Automation
product discontinued

MICROCOMPUTERIZED PERIODICAL MANAGEMENT SYSTEM, Avery International
no response to requests for info

MICROLIAS (LIBRARY INFORMATION ACCESS SYSTEM), Pennsylvania State University
no response to requests for info

MICROLINX CHECK-IN, The Faxon Company, Inc.
no response to requests for info

MICROLS, Document Automation Corporation
no response to requests for info

MINI MARC, Library Systems & Services, Inc.
no response to requests for info

MINISIS, McLeod-Bishop Systems Ltd.
now distributed by International Development Research Centre

MISTRAL, Honeywell Bull Information Systems
no response to requests for info

- N -

NET-SEARCH, Informatics General Corporation
product rights transferred to Sterling, then ATLAS; product discontinued

NEW AGE SOFTWARE, New Age Software
no response to requests for info

NOTIS, Northwestern Library
now distributed by NOTIS Systems, Inc.

- O -

OCELOT LIBRARY SYSTEM
name changed to COLUMBIA LIBRARY SYSTEM

OCLC, LS/2000
product discontinued

OFFICE LIBRARIAN, Information Research Corp.
no response to requests for info

OFISFILE, Burroughs Corporation
no response to requests for info

OLIS, Republic Geothermal
no response to requests for info

ORCHARD SYSTEMS CIRCULATION MANAGEMENT SYSTEM, Orchard Systems
no response to requests for info

OUTPUTM, Center for the Study of Rural Librarianship, College of Library Science, Clarion University of Pennsylvania
no response to requests for info

OVERDUE COLLECTOR, Follett Software
not included in current catalog

OVERDUE MASTER, Master Software
no current contact info

OVERDUE WRITER, Follett Software
not included in current catalog

OVERNIGHT WRITER, Follett Software Company
product discontinued

- P -

PALS AUTOMATED LIBRARY SYSTEM, Sperry Corporation Computer System
no response to requests for info

PAPERBACK CATALOG CARDER, Right on Programs
not included in current product catalog

PC/NET-LINK, Informatics General Corporation
product discontinued

PC/PALS, Unisys Corporation
name changed to PALS

PCC/INFOMANAGER, Productivity Concepts Corp.
no response to requests for info

PCEMAS LIBRARY AUTOMATION SYSTEMS, Scholar Chips Software, Inc.
no response to requests for info

PEACH 3, City of Hayward CA Public Library
product discontinued

PERIODICAL ROUTER, Right On Programs
name changed to ROUTING MANAGER

PLESSEY, Plessey Marketing International
no response to requests for info

PLUS LINK NETWORK SYSTEM, Follett Software Company
product discontinued

PORTABLE SCAN PLUS, Follett Software Company
product discontinued

PRO-SEARCH, Menlo Corporation
no current contact info

ProData Computer Services
no longer sells any software or service to libraries

PROFESSIONAL BIBLIOGRAPHIC SYSTEM, Professional Bibliographic Software
name changed to PRO-CITE 2.0

PUBLICATION INDEXER, Right On Programs
name changed to PERIODICAL INDEXING MANAGER

PUBLISH OR PERISH, Park Row Software
no current contact info

- Q -

QUICK SEARCH LIBRARIAN, Interactive Microwave
company acquired by another; all library automation products discontinued

- R -

RANGEFINDER, University of Rhode Island
no response to requests for info

RICHMOND LIBRARY MANAGEMENT SYSTEM, Follett
not included in current catalog

RILEY'S CATALOG CARDS, Riley's Catalog Cards
no response to requests for information

- S -

SAILS, Swets North America, Inc.
no response to requests for info

SCHOOL LIBRARY MANAGEMENT SYSTEMS, Data Trek, Inc.
vendor requested deletion of product from Directory

SCI, System Control, Inc.
no response to requests for info

SCI-MATE, Institute of Scientific Information
product discontinued

SCS, SCS Engineers
no response to requests for info

SERIAL CONTROL, Right On Programs
product discontinued

SERIALS CONTROL SYSTEM, Meta Micro Library Systems, Inc.
no response to requests for info

SIMS-1, Sedna Corporation
no current contact info

SIRE, Cucumber Information Systems
name changed to PERSONAL LIBRARIAN

SKILLS MAKER, Follett Software
not included in current catalog

SOFTWARE LIBRARIAN, Educational Activities, Inc.
product discontinued

SON OF OVERDUE BOOKS, Right On Programs
not included in current catalog

SPINDEX II, National Archives Services
no response to requests for info

SPINE/POCKET/CARD/LABELS PROGRAM, EDUCOMP, Inc
product discontinued

STACS, Information Dimensions
available as part of TECHLIBPLUS

SUBJECT LIST, Right On Programs
product discontinued

SUBSCRIPTION CONTROL, Right On Programs
name changed to SUBSCRIPTION MANAGER

SYDNEY'S MICRO LIBRARY SYSTEM, Sydney Dataproducts, Inc.
name changed to MICRO LIBRARY SYSTEM, then discontinued; company name changed also from **Sydney Dataproducts, Inc.** to International Library Systems Corp.

- T -

T/SERIES 50, UTLAS International
product rights transferred to CARL Systems; being phased out by CARL

TABLE OF CONTENTS ROUTER, Right On Programs
product discontinued

TANDY LIBRARY SOLUTIONS, Radio Shack
no response to requests for info

TELEMARC III, Gaylord Bros.
product discontinued

TEQLIB, Software Consulting Services
no response to requests for info

TERMMARC, Small Library Computing, Inc.
product discontinued

TEXTBANK/PC, Group L Corp
no response to requests for info

TINLIB, Information Management & Engineering Ltd.
name changed to INFORMATION NAVIGATOR (IME Systems, Inc.)

TOTAL LIBRARY SYSTEM - product rights transferred to Honnold Service Group, Claremont Colleges
product discontinued
TOTAL RECALL, Packet Press
vendor requested deletion of product from Directory

- U -

ULTIMATE LIBRARY SYSTEM, Data Trek, Inc.
name changed to PROFESSIONAL SERIES
ULTRACARD/CDROM, Small Library Computing, Inc.
product discontinued
UNIVERSAL SEARCH MODULE (USM), Data Trek, Inc.
name changed to GOPAC
URICA, McDonnell Douglas Computer Systems Co.
vendor discontinued U.S. distribution
UTLAS
this is a bibliographic utility, not a software package; software packages available from UTLAS are listed in the Directory by name, e.g., M/Series 10 and T/Series 50

- V -

VERTICAL FILE LOCATER, Right On Programs
name changed to MAGAZINE ARTICLE FILER
VIDEO RESERVE CONTROL, Right On Programs
product discontinued
VIRGINIA TECH LIBRARY SYSTEM
name changed to VTLS

- W -

WESTERN LIBRARY NETWORK SOFTWARE, Western Library Network
no longer available for license; see WLN
WORDCRUNCHER, Electronic Text Corporation
no current contact info

INDEX

HOUGHTON MIFFLIN HARCOURT

MATH Expressions
Common Core

Dr. Karen C. Fuson

GRADE
4
Volume 1

This material is based upon work supported by the
National Science Foundation
under Grant Numbers
ESI-9816320, REC-9806020, and RED-935373.

Any opinions, findings, and conclusions, or recommendations expressed in this material
are those of the author and do not necessarily reflect the views of the National Science Foundation.

 HOUGHTON MIFFLIN HARCOURT

Printed in the U.S.A.

ISBN: 978-0-547-82424-6

18 19 20 21 22   0304   21 20 19 18 17

4500675361   C D E F G

Homework

Read and write each number in standard form.

1. 90 + 2 _____

2. 600 + 80 + 9 _____

3. 2,000 + 800 + 50 + 7 _____

4. 3,000 + 80 + 5 _____

Read and write each number in expanded form.

5. 48 _____

6. 954 _____

7. 6,321 _____

8. 4,306 _____

9. 1,563 _____

10. 2,840 _____

Read and write each number in word form.

11. 300 + 20 + 5 _____

12. 5,000 + 700 + 40 + 8 _____

13. 9,000 + 400 + 6 _____

Read and write each number in standard form.

14. seventy-six _____

15. three hundred one _____

16. four thousand, two hundred sixteen _____

17. five thousand, one hundred forty-two _____

Write the value of the underlined digit.

18. 2<u>8</u>7 _____

19. <u>8</u>,792 _____

20. 7,<u>8</u>12 _____

Remembering

Multiply or divide.

1. $6 \times 4 = $ _____

2. $56 \div 8 = $ _____

3. $45 \div 9 = $ _____

4. $6 \times 6 = $ _____

5. $3 \times 7 = $ _____

6. $48 \div 6 = $ _____

7. Grace read six books over the summer. Her sister read three times that number. How many books did Grace's sister read over the summer?

_____

Write the number of thousands and the number of hundreds in each number.

8. 5,812

_____ thousands

_____ hundreds

9. 7,026

_____ thousands

_____ hundreds

Make a place value drawing for each number, using ones, quick tens, hundred boxes, and thousand bars.

10. 603

11. 3,187

12. **Stretch Your Thinking** Mr. Thomas writes 4,<u>9</u>64 on the board. Amy says the value of the underlined digit is 9. Chris said the value is 900. Which student is correct? Explain.

_____

_____

Name _____ **Date** _____

Homework

Round each number to the nearest ten.

1. 46 _____   **2.** 381 _____   **3.** 4,175 _____   **4.** 5,024 _____

Round each number to the nearest hundred.

5. 789 _____   **6.** 971 _____   **7.** 2,759 _____   **8.** 3,148 _____

Round each number to the nearest thousand.

9. 6,578 _____   **10.** 4,489 _____   **11.** 8,099 _____   **12.** 2,761 _____

Compare using >, <, or =.

13. 4,538 ◯ 4,835   **14.** 3,554 ◯ 3,449   **15.** 1,289 ◯ 1,298

16. 7,235 ◯ 6,987   **17.** 4,004 ◯ 4,034   **18.** 5,609 ◯ 5,059

Solve.

19. When you round a number, which digit in the number helps you decide to round up or round down? Explain your answer.

_____

_____

_____

_____

20. When you round a number, what should you do with the digits to the right of the place to which you are rounding?

_____

_____

_____

Remembering

Find the unknown number.

1. $4 \times 8 =$ _____

2. $42 \div 7 =$ _____

3. $63 \div$ _____ $= 9$

4. _____ $\times 5 = 40$

5. $9 \times$ _____ $= 81$

6. _____ $\div 6 = 10$

7. $21 \div 7 =$ _____

8. $10 \times$ _____ $= 100$

Write the number of tens and the number of ones in each number.

9. 607

_____ tens

_____ ones

10. 9,324

_____ tens

_____ ones

Read and write each number in standard form.

11. $40 + 3$ _____

12. $500 + 70 + 9$ _____

13. $1,000 + 200 + 50 + 8$ _____

14. $8,000 + 70 + 7$ _____

15. **Stretch Your Thinking** Sara is thinking of a number. When she rounds her number to the nearest hundred, she gets 700. What is the greatest number Sara can be thinking of? Explain.

_____

_____

_____

Name _____ **Date** _____

Read and write each number in expanded form.

1. 39,012 _____ **2.** 640,739 _____

3. 102,453 _____ **4.** 460,053 _____

Read and write each number in word form.

5. 1,000,000

_____

6. 730,812

_____

7. 45,039

_____

8. 600,439

_____

Read and write each number in expanded form.

9. nine hundred twenty-three thousand, nine hundred twenty-three

_____

10. one hundred forty thousand, one hundred four

_____

11. seventy-six thousand, five

_____

12. fifty-nine thousand, two hundred sixty-one

_____

13. seven hundred thousand, four hundred thirty

_____

14. thirty-one thousand, two hundred seventy-nine

_____

Remembering

Use the numbers 7, 9, and 63 to complete the related equations.

1. 7 × _____ = _____

2. 9 × _____ = _____

3. _____ ÷ _____ = 7

4. _____ ÷ _____ = 9

Solve.

5. Aileen made 36 mini muffins for the school bake sale. Each bag holds four mini muffins. How many bags of mini muffins will she have for the bake sale?

_____

Read and write each number in expanded form.

6. 86 _____

7. 421 _____

8. 7,915 _____

9. 3,402 _____

Write the value of the underlined digit.

10. 4<u>8</u>9 _____

11. <u>7</u>,493 _____

12. 1,50<u>6</u> _____

Round each number to the nearest ten.

13. 47 _____

14. 6,022 _____

Round each number to the nearest hundred.

15. 672 _____

16. 3,940 _____

17. **Stretch Your Thinking** How many zeros are in the standard form of six hundred thousand, twenty? Explain.

_____

_____

Compare using >, <, or =.

1. 57,068 ◯ 57,860

2. 24,516 ◯ 24,165

3. 154,424 ◯ 145,424

4. 836,245 ◯ 683,642

5. 89,175 ◯ 89,175

6. 100,000 ◯ 1,000,000

Round to the nearest ten thousand.

7. 11,295 _____

8. 82,964 _____

9. 97,079 _____

Round to the nearest hundred thousand.

10. 153,394 _____

11. 410,188 _____

12. 960,013 _____

13. 837,682 _____

Solve.

14. What would 672,831 be rounded to the nearest:

   a. ten? _____

   b. hundred? _____

   c. thousand? _____

   d. ten thousand? _____

   e. hundred thousand? _____

15. Compare the number 547,237 rounded to the nearest hundred thousand and 547,237 rounded to the nearest ten thousand. Which is the greater number? Write a comparison statement and explain your answer.

   _____

   _____

   _____

   _____

Name _____ **Date** _____

Remembering

Find the unknown value in the number sentence.

1. $8 \times k = 16$ $k =$ _____
2. $n \times 9 = 90$ $n =$ _____
3. $35 \div t = 5$ $t =$ _____
4. $p \div 6 = 9$ $p =$ _____

Solve.

5. In an arcade game, Nick can earn up to 10 tickets, depending on which slot his coin goes through. If he plays the game six times, what is the greatest number of tickets Nick could earn?

_____

Round each number to the nearest thousand.

6. 2,950 _____
7. 4,307 _____

Read and write each number in word form.

8. 16,977 _____

9. 403,056 _____

10. **Stretch Your Thinking** Leon says that he can compare numbers in the same way that he alphabetizes words. For example, since the first two letters of *cat* and *cane* are the same, he goes to the next letter to compare. Since *n* comes before *t* in the alphabet, the word *cane* comes first in a dictionary. To compare 64,198 with 641,532, he knows that the first three digits 641 are the same. Then he compares the next digit in each number. Since 9 is greater than 5, the number 64,198 must be greater. Is Leon's way of thinking correct? Explain.

_____

_____

_____

_____

_____

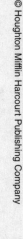

    Compare and Round Greater Numbers

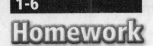

Name _____   Date _____

Use the information in the table to answer the questions.

Driving Distances (in miles) between Various Cities in the United States

	New York, NY	Chicago, IL	Los Angeles, CA
Atlanta, GA	886	717	2,366
Dallas, TX	1,576	937	1,450
Nashville, TN	914	578	2,028
Omaha, NE	1,257	483	1,561
Seattle, WA	2,912	2,108	1,141
Wichita, KS	1,419	740	1,393

1. If you drive from New York to Dallas and then from Dallas to Chicago, how many miles would you drive?

_____

2. Which two cities are farther apart in driving distance: Seattle and Los Angeles or Wichita and New York? Use place value words to explain your answer.

_____

_____

Use any method to add. On another sheet of paper, make a drawing for exercise 5 to show your new groups.

3.　1,389
　　+ 5,876

4.　3,195
　　+ 2,674

5.　1,165
　　+ 7,341

6.　2,653
　　+ 4,908

7.　3,692
　　+ 7,543

8.　8,598
　　+ 5,562

9.　4,295
　　+ 8,416

10.　6,096
　　+ 9,432

Name _____ **Date** _____

Remembering

Multiply or divide.

1. $81 \div 9 =$ _____

2. $7 \times 4 =$ _____

3. $9 \times 3 =$ _____

4. $24 \div 4 =$ _____

5.
$$\begin{array}{r} 7 \\ \times\ 8 \\ \hline \end{array}$$

6.
$$\begin{array}{r} 5 \\ \times\ 7 \\ \hline \end{array}$$

7. $10\overline{)80}$

8. $7\overline{)42}$

Read and write each number in expanded form.

9. eighty-six thousand, nine hundred twenty-one

_____

10. nine hundred twenty thousand, four hundred thirteen

_____

Compare using >, <, or =.

11. 36,290 ◯ 36,290

12. 438,000 ◯ 43,800

13. 298,150 ◯ 298,105

14. 999,999 ◯ 1,000,000

15. **Stretch Your Thinking** Find the unknown digits in the following addition problem.

$$\begin{array}{r} 3,\ \square\ 6\ \square \\ +\ 4,\ 9\ \square\ 2 \\ \hline \square,\ 5\ 3\ 6 \end{array}$$

Make New Groups for Addition

Copy each exercise, lining up the places correctly. Then add.

1. 51,472 + 7,078

2. 94,280 + 56,173

3. 1,824 + 36,739

4. 372,608 + 51,625

5. 314,759 + 509,028

6. 614,702 + 339,808

7. 493,169 + 270,541

8. 168,739 + 94,035

The table shows the surface area of each of the Great Lakes.

Use the data in the table to help answer the following questions.

Lake	Surface Area (square miles)
Erie	9,906
Huron	22,973
Michigan	22,278
Ontario	7,340
Superior	31,700

9. Which is greater, the surface area of Lake Superior, or the sum of the surface areas of Lake Michigan and Lake Erie?

Show your work.

_____

10. Which two lakes have a combined surface area of 30,313 square miles?

_____

Remembering

Multiply or divide.

1. $30 \div 5 =$ _____

2. $8 \times 7 =$ _____

3. $4 \times 6 =$ _____

4. $70 \div 7 =$ _____

5. $3 \times 9 =$ _____

6. $36 \div 6 =$ _____

Compare using >, <, or =.

7. $6,299 \bigcirc 62, 990$

8. $389,151 \bigcirc 394,027$

9. $134,657 \bigcirc 134,257$

10. $93,862 \bigcirc 93,862$

Use any method to add.

11.
$$\begin{array}{r} 1,362 \\ + 6,509 \\ \hline \end{array}$$

12.
$$\begin{array}{r} 3,893 \\ + 5,245 \\ \hline \end{array}$$

13.
$$\begin{array}{r} 6,399 \\ + 7,438 \\ \hline \end{array}$$

14. Stretch Your Thinking Peter adds $245,936 + 51,097$ as follows. Explain his error. What is the correct sum?

$$\begin{array}{r} \overset{1\overset{1}{}}{2\,4\,5,9\,3\,6} \\ +\ 5\,1,0\,9\,7 \\ \hline 7\,5\,6,9\,0\,6 \end{array}$$

_____

_____

_____

Name _____ **Date** _____

Homework

Write a number sentence that shows an estimate of each answer. Then write the exact answer.

1. 69 + 25 _____

2. 259 + 43 _____

3. 2,009 + 995 _____

4.	5	5.	38	6.	28	7.	243	8.	154
	3		54		44		625		131
	7		+ 52		32		+387		204
	+ 4				+46				+179

Solve.   *Show your work.*

9. Paul's stamp collection includes 192 domestic and 811 foreign stamps.

   About how many domestic and foreign stamps does Paul have altogether?

   _____

   Exactly how many domestic and foreign stamps does Paul have altogether?

   _____

10. Plane A travels 102,495 miles. Plane B travels 91,378 miles. How many miles in all do the two planes travel?

    _____

    Explain how you can use estimation to check that your answer is reasonable.

    _____

    _____

Name _____   Date _____

Remembering

What is 362,584 rounded to the nearest:

1. hundred? _____   2. thousand? _____

3. ten thousand? _____   4. hundred thousand? _____

Use any method to add.

5.	2,938	6.	8,305	7.	8,074
	+ 4,271		+ 1,467		+ 3,552

Copy each exercise, lining up the places correctly. Then add.

8. 45,296 + 38,302   9. 293,017 + 58,226

10. **Stretch Your Thinking** Luanne estimates the sum of 39 + 15 is about
    40 + 15, or 55. Jacob estimates the sum of 39 + 15 is about 40 + 20,
    or 60. Which estimate is closer to the exact sum? Explain.

    _____

    _____

    _____

    _____

Subtract. Show your new groups.

1. 7,000
    − 3,264

2. 9,632
    − 3,785

3. 8,054
    − 1,867

4. 4,000
    − 2,945

5. 8,531
    − 7,624

6. 8,006
    − 4,692

7. 9,040
    − 5,712

8. 6,000
    − 5,036

9. 7,180
    − 4,385

10. 6,478
    − 3,579

11. 9,490
    − 5,512

12. 5,000
    − 3,609

Solve.

Show your work.

13. A cross-country automobile rally is 1,025 kilometers long. At a stopping place, the leader had traveled 867 kilometers. How far away was the finish line?

14. A census counted 5,407 people in Marina's home town. If 3,589 are males, how many are females?

15. A construction company is building a stone wall. The finished wall will contain 5,000 stones. So far, 1,487 stones have been placed. How many stones have not been placed?

Name _____ Date _____

Remembering

Use any method to add.

1.   6,022
  + 1,988

2.   4,586
  + 1,693

3.   8,374
  + 3,707

The table shows the amount of litter collected from parks across a city on Earth Day each year. Use the data in the table to help answer the following questions.

4. How much litter was collected altogether in 2007 and 2008?

_____

5. Which two years had a combined litter collection of 23,456 pounds?

_____

Litter Collected on Earth Day

Year	Pounds of Litter
2007	8,293
2008	12,104
2009	15,877
2010	11,352

Write an equation that shows an estimate of each answer. Then write the exact answer.

6. 495 + 812 _____

7. 7,203 + 299 _____

8. 2,859 + 6,017 _____

9. **Stretch Your Thinking** Bridget ungrouped 5,000 as shown. Use your understanding of place value to explain how the ungrouped number is equal to 5,000.

    4 9 9 10
    5,000
   − 2,896

_____

_____

_____

Subtract from Thousands

Subtract. Then use addition to check the subtraction.
Show your work.

1. 1,400 − 238 = _____

2. 1,900 − 1,238 = _____

Check: _____

Check: _____

3. 4,620 − 1,710 = _____

4. 5,243 − 2,454 = _____

Check: _____

Check: _____

5. 3,142 − 1,261 = _____

6. 2,375 − 896 = _____

Check: _____

Check: _____

Solve.

Show your work.

7. A school library has 1,058 books in its collection.
The town library has 4,520 books in its collection.
How many books are there altogether?

_____

8. A town official knows how many books the town
library has and how many books both libraries have
altogether. She wants to know how many books the
school library has. How can she use subtraction
to find the answer?

_____

Name _____ **Date** _____

Remembering

Copy each exercise, lining up the places correctly. Then add.

1. 32,418 + 508,182

2. 734,150 + 60,382

Solve.

Show your work.

3. The entire fourth grade is made up of 102 boys and 86 girls. *About* how many students are in the fourth grade altogether?

_____

Exactly how many students are in the fourth grade altogether?

_____

Subtract. Show your new groups.

4. 5,000
     − 2,583
   ‾‾‾‾‾‾‾

5. 8,259
     − 3,716
   ‾‾‾‾‾‾‾

6. 2,081
     − 1,733
   ‾‾‾‾‾‾‾

7. Stretch Your Thinking What is the unknown number in this break-apart drawing? List all the addition and subtraction problems for the drawing.

_____

_____

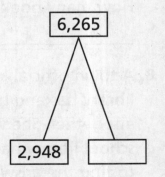

Subtraction Undoes Addition

Homework

Subtract.

1. 71,824
    − 36,739

2. 960,739
    − 894,045

3. 665,717
    − 82,824

4. 372,608
    − 57,425

5. 597,603
    − 404,980

6. 614,702
    − 539,508

7. 724,359
    − 99,068

8. 394,280
    − 56,473

In an experiment, a scientist counted how many bacteria
grew in several labeled dishes. The table shows how
many bacteria were in each dish.

Dish	Number of Bacteria
A	682,169
B	694,154
C	57,026
D	150,895
E	207,121

Solve. Estimate to check.   *Show your work.*

9. What was the difference between the greatest
   number of bacteria and the least number of bacteria?

   _____

10. How many more bacteria were in dish A than in dish D?

   _____

11. How many fewer bacteria were in dish E than
    in the combined dish C and dish D?

   _____

Write an equation that shows an estimate of each answer. Then write the exact answer.

1. 503 + 69 _____

2. 2,825 + 212 _____

3. 6,190 + 3,858 _____

Subtract. Show your new groups.

4. 8,760	**5.** 6,000	**6.** 5,060
− 1,353	− 5,258	− 2,175

Subtract. Then use addition to check the subtraction. Show your work.

7. 6,355 − 891 = _____ 　　**8.** 8,326 − 1,425 = _____

Check: _____ 　　　　**Check:** _____

9. Stretch Your Thinking Write an addition word problem in which the estimated sum is 14,000.

_____

_____

_____

Homework

Solve each problem.   *Show your work.*

1. Mr. Chase is ordering 249 pencils, 600 sheets of paper, and 190 erasers. How many more sheets of paper than pencils and erasers altogether is Mr. Chase ordering?

   _____

2. There were 623 people at the concert on Friday. On Saturday, 287 more people attended the concert than attended on Friday. How many people in all attended the concert on Friday and Saturday?

   _____

Add or subtract.

3.	695 + 487	4.	8,452 − 5,938	5.	5,895 + 9,727

6.	49,527 − 26,088	7.	86,959 − 38,486	8.	39,458 + 98,712

9.	286,329 + 394,065	10.	708,623 − 421,882	11.	952,774 − 613,386

Remembering

Add or subtract.

1. 7,982
    − 3,517
    _____

2. 600,000
    − 399,410
    _____

3. 138,925
    + 47,316
    _____

Subtract. Then use addition to check the subtraction. Show your work.

4. 4,652 − 1,593 =
   _____

5. 30,000 − 26,931 =
   _____

6. 896,581 − 355,274 =
   _____

Check:
_____

Check:
_____

Check:
_____

Subtract.

7. 731,285 − 369,114 = _____

8. 645,803 − 52,196 = _____

9. **Stretch Your Thinking** Write a two-step problem in
   which the answer is 130.

   _____

   _____

   _____

   _____

Practice Addition and Subtraction

Name _____   **Date** _____

Add or subtract.

1. $12,673 - 9,717 =$ _____   **2.** $8,406 + 45,286 =$ _____   **3.** $2,601 - 1,437 =$ _____

Answer each question about the information in the table.

Area of the Countries of Central America

Country	Area (square miles)
Belize	8,867
Costa Rica	19,730
El Salvador	8,124
Guatemala	42,042
Honduras	43,278
Nicaragua	49,998
Panama	30,193

4. What is the total area of Guatemala and Honduras?   *Show your work.*

_____

5. Which two countries have the least area? What is
the sum of their areas?

_____

6. Which is greater: the area of Nicaragua or the total
area of Costa Rica and Panama?

_____

7. How much greater is the area of Honduras than
the area of Guatemala?

_____

Remembering

Subtract. Then use addition to check the subtraction.

1. $1,500 - 705 = $ _____

2. $9,523 - 8,756 = $ _____

Check: _____

Check: _____

The table shows how many fans attended a team's
baseball games at the start of the season. Solve.
Estimate to check.

3. How many fewer people attended Game 4
than Game 5?

_____

_____

4. What was the difference between the
greatest number of fans and the least
number at a game?

_____

_____

Game	Fans
1	68,391
2	42,908
3	9,926
4	35,317
5	46,198

Add or subtract.

5.　 $7,452$
　　 $+\ 3,801$

6.　 $2,155$
　　 $+\ 5,890$

7.　 $293,635$
　　 $-\ 178,098$

8. Stretch Your Thinking The equation $32,904 + m = 61,381$
shows that the number of females plus the number of
males, m, living in a certain city equals the total population.
Write a subtraction equation that represents the same
situation. How many males live in this city?

_____

_____

Problem Solving with Greater Numbers

Homework

Companies often use bar graphs to present information to the media or stockholders. Data may show how attendance or profits vary at different times of the year, or compare the successes of different divisions or quarters of the year.

1. Research attendance numbers for your favorite amusement park, sporting team, or movie during five different periods of time. Complete the table with your information.

2. Use the grid below to graph the data in your table.

Remembering

Subtract.

1. 958,299 − 63,419 = _____

2. 9,523 − 8,756 = _____

Add or subtract.

3. 5,191
     + 273

4. 13,687
     + 25,137

5. 758,194
     −   6,029

Answer each question about the information in the table.

6. What is the total number of miles the trucker drove in the last 2 years?

_____

7. Which is greater, the increase in miles driven between 1998 and 1999 or between 1999 and 2000? What is that increase?

_____

Miles Driven by a Trucker

Year	Miles
1998	75,288
1999	117,391
2000	126,304
2001	87,192
2002	94,386

8. Stretch Your Thinking Look at the trucking data in the table for Exercises 6 and 7. How would you round the data to make a bar graph? What scale would you use?

_____

_____

Focus on Mathematical Practices

Homework

1. Label the sides of each rectangle.

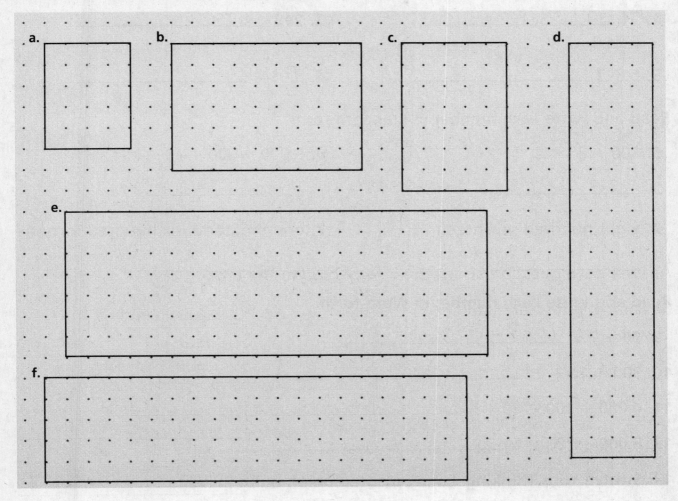

2. Write the equation representing the area of each rectangle shown above.

a. _____   b. _____   c. _____

d. _____   e. _____   f. _____

Find the area (in square units) of a rectangle with the given dimensions.

3. 3×5 _____   **4.** 3×50 _____   **5.** 30×5 _____

Remembering

Read and write each number in expanded form.

1. 71 _____

2. 298 _____

3. 5,627 _____

4. 3,054 _____

Read and write each number in standard form.

5. $500 + 80 + 3$

_____

6. $9,000 + 200 + 40 + 1$

_____

7. eight hundred seventeen

_____

8. one thousand, six hundred forty-six

_____

Read and write each number in word form.

9. $90 + 7$ _____

10. $300 + 10 + 2$ _____

11. $4,000 + 100 + 80 + 5$ _____

12. $8,000 + 700 + 6$ _____

13. Stretch Your Thinking Emmy planted onion bulbs in her backyard garden, giving each bulb one square foot of space. She arranged the onion bulbs in a rectangular array of 4 rows with 5 in each row. Make a sketch of Emmy's onion patch. How many onion bulbs did she plant? What is the area of the onion patch? Identify three other rectangular arrangements Emmy could have used to plant these onion bulbs.

_____

_____

_____

_____

Arrays and Area Models

Solve each problem.

1. $10 \times$ _____ $= 3$ tens

2. 10×6 tens $=$ _____

Follow the directions.

3. Divide the 30×40 rectangle into 10-by-10 squares of 100 to help find the area.

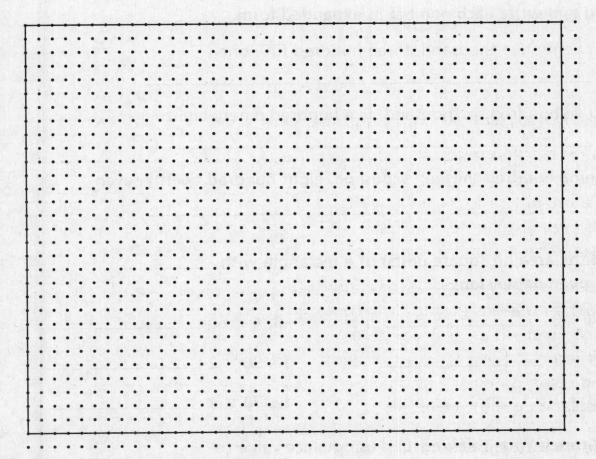

4. Complete the steps to factor the tens.

$30 \times 40 = ($ _____ $\times 10) \times ($ _____ $\times 10)$

$= ($ _____ $\times$ _____ $) \times (10 \times 10)$

$=$ _____ $\times 100$

$=$ _____

5. What is the area of the 30×40 rectangle, in square units?

_____

Name _____ **Date** _____

Remembering

Write the number of thousands and the number of hundreds in each number.

1. 4,672

_____ thousands

_____ hundreds

2. 1,023

_____ thousands

_____ hundreds

3. 610

_____ thousands

_____ hundreds

Read and write each number in expanded form.

4. twenty-five thousand, three hundred fifty-one

_____

5. five hundred six thousand, five hundred ninety-eight

_____

6. nine hundred thirteen thousand, eight hundred twenty-seven

_____

Find the area (in square units) of a rectangle with the given dimensions.

7. 4×6 _____

8. 4×60 _____

9. 9×2 _____

10. 90×2 _____

11. 3×7 _____

12. 70×3 _____

13. Stretch Your Thinking Li is using place value to multiply 90×30.

$$90 \times 30 = (9 \times 10) \times (3 \times 10)$$
$$= (9 \times 3) \times (10 \times 10)$$
$$= 27 \times 10$$
$$= 270$$

Is Li's answer correct? Explain.

_____

_____

Connect Place Value and Multiplication

Find each product by factoring the tens. Draw rectangles if you need to.

1. 6×2, 6×20, and 6×200

_____

_____

2. 4×8, 4×80, and 4×800

_____

_____

3. 5×5, 5×50, and 5×500

_____

_____

4. 5×9, 50×9, and 500×9

_____

_____

5. 6×5, 60×5, and 60×50

_____

_____

6. 7×6, 70×6, and 70×60

_____

_____

On a sheet of grid paper, draw two different arrays of connected squares for each total. Label the sides and write the multiplication equation for each of your arrays.

7. 18 squares

_____

_____

8. 20 squares

_____

_____

9. 24 squares

_____

_____

Name _____ **Date** _____

Remembering

Add or subtract.

1.	2,728	2.	83,054	3.	27,300
	+ 7,245		+ 1,496		− 9,638

Use any method to add.

4.	4,335	5.	3,806	6.	6,401	7.	9,826
	+ 2,694		+ 8,129		+ 7,763		+ 8,531

Solve each problem.

8. 10 × _____ = 6 tens   9. 10 × 9 = _____

10. _____ × 10 = 2 tens   11. _____ × 10 = 5 tens

12. 10 × 4 tens = _____   13. 10 × _____ = 7 hundreds

14. 10 × _____ = 8 tens   15. _____ × 10 = 3 tens

16. **Stretch Your Thinking** Lucas says that since 40 × 70 and 60 × 50 both have factors with a total of two zeros, they will both have products with a total of two zeros. Is he correct? Explain.

_____

_____

_____

Homework

Draw a rectangle. Find the tens product, the ones product,
and the total product. The first one is done for you.

1. 5 × 39

```
39 =        30           +   9
   ┌─────────────────┬────────┐      150
 5 │  5 x 30 = 150   │ 5 x 9  │    + 45
   │                 │  = 45  │    ─────
   └─────────────────┴────────┘      195
```

2. 7 × 32

3. 9 × 54

4. 3 × 47

Solve each problem.

Show your work.

5. Maria's flower garden is 14 feet long and 3 feet
wide. How many square feet is her garden?

_____

6. Maria planted 15 trays of flowers. Each tray had
6 flowers in it. How many flowers did she plant?

_____

7. Write and solve a multiplication word problem
about your family.

_____

_____

_____

_____

_____

Remembering

Round each number to the nearest hundred.

1. 283 _____   **2.** 729 _____   **3.** 954 _____

Round each number to the nearest thousand.

4. 4,092 _____   **5.** 6,550 _____   **6.** 5,381 _____

Compare using >, <, or =.

7. 92,800 _____ 92,830   **8.** 165,000 _____ 156,000

9. 478,390 _____ 478,390   **10.** 736,218 _____ 89,479

Find each product by factoring the tens. Draw rectangles if you need to.

11. 3×2, 3×20, and 3×200 **12.** 7×3, 7×30, and 7×300

_____   _____

_____   _____

13. Stretch Your Thinking Write a word problem that could be solved using the rectangle model shown. Then solve the problem by finding the tens product, the ones product, and the total product.

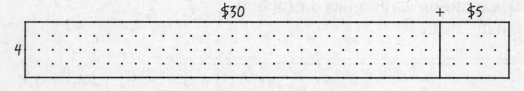

_____

_____

_____

Estimate each product. Solve to check your estimate.

1. 4 × 26

2. 5 × 63

3. 7 × 95

_____

_____

_____

_____

_____

_____

4. 4 × 84

5. 2 × 92

6. 3 × 76

_____

_____

_____

_____

_____

_____

Estimate the answers. Then solve each problem.

Show your work.

7. The Bicycling Club is participating in a cycling event.
   There are 65 teams registered for the event.
   Each team has a total of 8 cyclists. How many cyclists
   will participate in the event?

   _____

8. The theater group is making costumes for their play.
   There are 9 costume changes for each of the 23 performers.
   How many costumes does the theater group need?

   _____

9. The town library shows 6 different books each day in the
   display case. The library is open 27 days in one month.
   How many books does the library need for the display?

   _____

Write and solve a multiplication word problem.

10. _____

    _____

    _____

Remembering

Estimate each sum. Then solve to check your estimate.

1. $288 + 609$ _____

Solve.   *Show your work.*

2. During one weekend, a museum had 7,850 visitors on Saturday and 5,759 visitors on Sunday.

About how many visitors were there that weekend?

_____

Exactly how many visitors were there that weekend?

_____

Draw a rectangle model. Find the tens product, the ones product, and the total product.

3. 7×42 **4.** 5×67

5. Stretch Your Thinking Marcia says she can use *rounding* to find the *exact* product of 6×75. She says that since 75 is halfway between 7 tens and 8 tens, the exact product of 6×75 must be halfway between 6×70 and 6×80. Is she correct? Explain.

_____

_____

_____

_____

_____

                                   Estimate Products

2-6

Homework

Use the Place Value Sections Method to solve
the problem. Complete the steps.

1. 9 × 86 _____

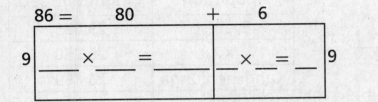

86 =   80   +   6

9 | ___ × ___ = ___ | __ × __ = __ | 9

+ _____
  _____

Use the Expanded Notation Method to solve
the problem. Complete the steps.

2. 4 × 67 _____

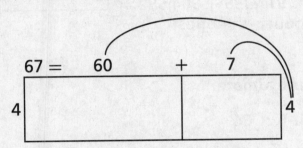

67 =   60   +   7

4 | | 4

67 = _____ + _____
× 4 = _____
_____ × _____ = _____
_____ × _____ = _____
              _____

Use any method to solve. Draw a rectangular
model to represent the problem.

Show your work.

3. Natalia read her new book for 45 minutes each
day for one week. How many minutes did she
read after 7 days?

_____

© Houghton Mifflin Harcourt Publishing Company

Name _____ **Date** _____

Remembering

The table shows the approximate height of the world's five tallest mountain peaks. Use the data in the table to help answer the following questions.

1. How tall are the two tallest mountain peaks combined?

_____

2. Which two mountain peaks combined are 56,190 feet tall?

_____

Mountain	Height (in feet)
Everest	29,035
K2	28,250
Kangchenjunga	28,169
Lhotse	27,940
Makalu	27,766

Subtract.

3. $586,720 - 293,415 =$ _____

4. $917,336 - 904,582 =$ _____

Estimate each product. Solve to check your estimate.

5. 5×39

_____

_____

6. 6×64

_____

_____

7. 9×23

_____

_____

8. 7×48

_____

_____

9. Stretch Your Thinking Explain how the Expanded Notation Method is used to multiply 82×3.

_____

_____

_____

_____

Use Place Value to Multiply

Homework

Use the Algebraic Notation Method to solve each problem. Complete the steps.

1. $7 \cdot 53$ _____

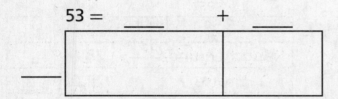

$53 =$ _____ $+$ _____

$7 \cdot 53 =$ _____ $\cdot ($ _____ $+$ _____ $)$

$= 350 + 21$

$= 371$

2. $4 \cdot 38$ _____

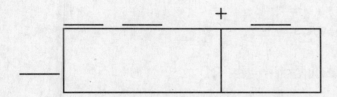

$4 \cdot 38 =$ _____ $\cdot ($ _____ $+$ _____ $)$

$=$ _____ $+$ _____

$=$ _____

Draw an area model and use the Algebraic Notation Method to solve the problem.

Show your work.

3. Mr. Henderson needs to get plywood to build his flatbed trailer. The flatbed is 8 feet by 45 feet. What is the area of the flatbed Mr. Henderson needs to cover with plywood?

_____

Remembering

Subtract. Show your new groups.

1. 4,000
   − 1,946

2. 8,441
   − 7,395

3. 9,340
   − 8,614

4. 1,587
   − 1,200

5. 6,193
   − 3,295

6. 4,006
   − 2,631

**Use the Expanded Notation Method to solve the problem.
Complete the steps.**

7. 5×68 _____

8. Stretch Your Thinking Jenna made 6 bracelets using
32 beads each. Kayla made 7 bracelets using 29 beads
each. Who used more beads? Use the Distributive
Property to solve the problem.

_____

_____

_____

_____

_____

Algebraic Notation Method

Homework

Use any method to solve. Sketch a rectangle model, if you need to.

1. 7 × 62 _____

2. 6 × 63 _____

3. 6 × 82 _____

4. 57 × 7 _____

5. 5 × 76 _____

6. 4 × 65 _____

7. 7 × 83 _____

8. 36 × 9 _____

9. 27 × 8 _____

Solve each problem.

Show your work.

10. 94 people are sitting down to a fancy six-course meal. The first course is soup, which only needs a spoon. The rest of the courses each need fresh forks. How many forks will be used?

_____

11. Leo uses plastic letters to make signs. A chain store asks Leo to put signs in front of their 63 stores that say "SALE: HALF PRICE ON ALL DRESSES." How many plastic "S" letters will Leo need?

_____

Name _____ Date _____

Remembering

Subtract. Then use addition to check the subtraction. Show your work.

1. 6,459 − 921 = _____

Check: _____

2. 5,603 − 3,284 = _____

Check: _____

3. 7,863 − 2,734 = _____

Check: _____

4. 9,582 − 1,447 = _____

Check: _____

Use the Algebraic Notation Method to solve each problem. Complete the steps.

5. 4 · 93 _____

6. 3 · 78 _____

7. Stretch Your Thinking Xander says that the Place Value Sections Method, the Expanded Notation Method, and the Algebraic Notation Method of multiplying a one-digit number by a two-digit number are pretty much the same. Do you agree or disagree? Explain.

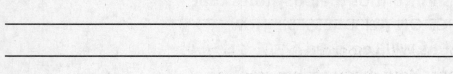

_____

_____

_____

_____

_____

　　　　Compare Methods of One-Digit by Two-Digit Multiplication

Homework

Solve, using any numerical method. Use rounding and estimating to see if your answer makes sense.

1. 35
    × 9

2. 79
    × 5

3. 56
    × 3

4. 94
    × 2

5. 68
    × 4

6. 27
    × 8

7. 82
    × 6

8. 43
    × 7

Solve each problem.

Show your work.

9. Describe how you solved one of the exercises above. Write at least two sentences.

_____

_____

_____

_____

_____

10. Mariko wrote the full alphabet (26 letters) 9 times. How many letters did she write?

_____

11. Alan has 17 packs of bulletin-board cutouts. Each one contains 9 shapes. How many shapes does he have altogether?

_____

Remembering

Add or subtract.

1. 6,095
    + 2,382

2. 53,894
    − 12,914

3. 629,137
    − 508,978

Solve each problem.

Show your work.

4. During the first half of a college basketball game, 24,196 people entered the athletic center. During the second half, 2,914 people left and 4,819 people entered. How many people were in the athletic center at the end of the game?

_____

5. Miles had three sets of building blocks. His first set had 491 pieces. His second set had 624 pieces. Miles combined his three sets for a total of 1,374 pieces. How many pieces had been in his third set?

_____

Use any method to solve. Sketch a rectangle model if you need to.

6. 6 × 23 _____   7. 8 × 44 _____   8. 3 × 95 _____

9. **Stretch Your Thinking** A bookcase has 3 shelves with 38 books each and 4 shelves with 29 books each. How many books are in the bookcase? Use any method to solve. Show your work.

_____

Discuss Different Methods

Homework

Cross out the extra numerical information and solve.   *Show your work.*

1. A gymnastic meet is 2 hours long. It has 8 competitors and each competes in 4 events. How many events will be scored?

   _____

2. George makes $20 doing lawn work for 4 hours each week. He wants to buy a $2,500 used car from his grandmother. He has been saving this money for 30 weeks. How much has he saved?

   _____

Tell what additional information is needed to solve the problem.

3. Michelle is saving $20 each week for the bike of her dreams. How long until she can purchase her bike?

   _____

4. A teacher sees a sale on packages of pencils. She wants to give each of her students a pencil. How many packages should she buy?

   _____

Solve each problem and label your answer. Write hidden questions if you need to.

5. There are 18 windows on each side of a rectangular building. It takes the window washer 3 minutes to wash each window. How many minutes will it take to finish the job?

   _____

6. The school office prints a newsletter every month that uses 2 pieces of paper. They make 35 copies for each room. How many pieces of paper do they need to print copies for 10 rooms?

   _____

Remembering

Add or subtract.

1. $\begin{array}{r} 5,900 \\ -\ 1,386 \\ \hline \end{array}$

2. $\begin{array}{r} 54,371 \\ +\ 12,703 \\ \hline \end{array}$

3. $\begin{array}{r} 800,000 \\ -\ 753,192 \\ \hline \end{array}$

Solve using any numerical method. Use rounding and estimating to check your work.

4. $\begin{array}{r} 83 \\ \times\ 5 \\ \hline \end{array}$

5. $\begin{array}{r} 36 \\ \times\ 2 \\ \hline \end{array}$

6. $\begin{array}{r} 94 \\ \times\ 6 \\ \hline \end{array}$

7. $\begin{array}{r} 44 \\ \times\ 8 \\ \hline \end{array}$

Draw a rectangle model. Solve using any method that relates to the model.

8. $6 \times 358 =$ _____

9. $4 \times 692 =$ _____

10. **Stretch Your Thinking** Write a word problem that involves multiplication and addition. Include extra numerical information. Solve the problem, showing your work.

_____

_____

_____

_____

_____

_____

Sketch an area model for each exercise. Then find the product.

1. 74×92 _____

2. 65×37 _____

3. 55×84 _____

4. 49×63 _____

5. 34×52 _____

6. 24×91 _____

7. Write a word problem for one exercise above.

_____

_____

_____

_____

_____

_____

_____

_____

_____

_____

Remembering

What is 851,632 rounded to the nearest:

1. hundred? _____

2. thousand? _____

3. ten thousand? _____

4. hundred thousand? _____

Compare using >, <, or =.

5. 58,320 ◯ 58,320

6. 642,810 ◯ 64,281

7. 427,900 ◯ 428,000

8. 71,253 ◯ 409,135

Draw a rectangle model. Solve using any method that relates to the model.

9. $6 \times 358 =$ _____

10. $4 \times 692 =$ _____

Tell what additional information is needed to solve the problem.

11. Rosalina knitted 8 scarves for gifts. She used 38 feet of yarn for each scarf. How much did Rosalina spend on the yarn?

_____

12. Stretch Your Thinking How many smaller rectangles are there in an area model that represents 27×83? Why? What are their dimensions?

_____

_____

_____

_____

_____

Homework

Multiply using any method. If you use an area model to multiply, show your sketch.

1. 45 × 79

2. 88 × 29

3. 74 × 57

4. 84 × 68

_____ _____ _____ _____

Mr. Gomez's class is learning about multiplication. The class wants to see what multiplications they can find in their school. Solve each problem.

5. The class counts 37 tiles across the front of their room and 64 tiles down one side. How many floor tiles are in their classroom?

_____

6. The back of their classroom is a brick wall. Down one side, they count 26 rows of bricks. Across the bottom, they count 29 bricks. How many bricks make up the wall?

_____

7. In the school, there are 3 classrooms for each grade: kindergarten, 1, 2, 3, 4, 5, and 6. Each classroom has 32 lockers. How many lockers are there in the school building?

_____

8. The school auditorium has 69 rows of seats. Each row has 48 seats across. If 6,000 people want to see the school talent show, how many times do the students have to do the show?

_____

Write two multiplication word problems of your own. Then solve each problem.

9. _____

_____

_____

_____

10. _____

_____

_____

_____

Name _____ Date _____

Remembering

Estimate each sum. Then solve to check your estimate.

1. 289 + 503 _____

2. 4,199 + 684 _____

3. 8,128 + 895 _____

Cross out the extra numerical information and solve.   *Show your work.*

4. Marlene is making 4 batches of muffins for her drama
   party. Each batch requires 2 cups of flour and makes
   24 muffins. How many muffins will Marlene have
   for the party?

   _____

5. One pack of batteries costs $6 and contains 9 batteries.
   Trevor bought 3 packs of batteries. How much did
   Trevor spend on batteries?

   _____

Sketch an area model for each exercise. Then find the product.

6. 54 × 38 _____   7. 49 × 75 _____

8. **Stretch Your Thinking** Jackson used the Shortcut
   Method to multiply 84 × 37. Did he do it correctly?
   Explain.

   _____

   _____

   _____

   _____

1
2
84
× 37
588
+ 252
840

Different Methods for Two-Digit Multiplication

Homework

Solve each multiplication problem using any method. Use rounding and estimation to check your work.

1. 45×61 _____

2. 24×56 _____

3. 83×27 _____

4. 39×48 _____

5. 36×96 _____

6. 63×87 _____

7. 58×79 _____

8. 15×92 _____

9. 33×43 _____

10. 76×29 _____

11. 69×63 _____

12. 84×23 _____

Remembering

Subtract. Then use addition to check the subtraction. Show your work.

1. $8,960 - 1,238 =$ _____

2. $5,418 - 5,269 =$ _____

Check: _____

Check: _____

Sketch an area model for each exercise. Then find the product.

3. 28×94 _____

4. 63×88 _____

Use any method to solve. Sketch an area model if you need to.

5. 66×24 _____

6. 27×83 _____

7. 79×35 _____

8. **Stretch Your Thinking** Kia is printing packets of information. There are 23 pages in a packet, and she needs enough copies for 52 people. Each package of paper contains 200 sheets. She estimates she needs 5 packages of paper to print the packets. Will she have enough paper? Explain.

_____

_____

_____

_____

_____

Check Products of Two-Digit Numbers

Homework

Solve using any method and show your work.
Check your work with estimation.

1. 55 × 64   **2.** 42 × 67   **3.** 59 × 32   **4.** 78 × 44

_____   _____   _____   _____

5. 62 × 23   **6.** 53 × 28   **7.** 71 × 35   **8.** 22 × 66

_____   _____   _____   _____

Solve.   *Show your work.*

9. Keesha walks 12 blocks to school every day. One day, she counts 88 sidewalk squares in one block. If each block has the same number of sidewalk squares, how many squares does Keesha walk on as she walks *to* and *from* school each day?

_____

10. The Card Collector's Club is having a meeting. Each member brings 25 sports cards to show and trade. If 35 members attend, how many cards do they bring altogether?

_____

11. On a separate sheet of paper, write and solve your own multiplication word problem.

_____

Remembering

Add or subtract.

1.	4,659	2.	9,380	3.	248,266
	+ 2,047		+ 1,599		− 147,852

Use any method to solve. Sketch an area model if you need to.

4. 26 × 18   **5.** 35 × 64   **6.** 82 × 73   **7.** 91 × 23

_____   _____   _____   _____

Solve using any method. Use rounding and estimation to check your work.

8. 17 × 44   **9.** 62 × 74   **10.** 53 × 89   **11.** 32 × 96

_____   _____   _____   _____

12. Stretch Your Thinking Greyson is planning to lay a brick driveway which will be made up of 84 rows of 14 bricks per row. He will also lay a backyard patio with 25 rows of 31 bricks per row. How many pallets of bricks should Greyson order if each pallet has 1,000 bricks? Show your work.

_____

_____

_____

_____

Practice Multiplication

Homework

Sketch a rectangle for each problem and solve using any method that relates to your sketch.

1. 8 × 6,000

_____

2. 6 × 3,542

_____

3. 7 × 3,124

_____

4. 5 × 7,864

_____

Show your work

5. A school is participating in a pull tab program to raise money for a local organization. The school puts 1,295 pull tabs in each bag. The school has 7 bags of pull tabs. How many pull tabs has the school collected?

_____

6. A dance company has scheduled 4 performances at a theater. The theater has 2,763 seats. Every ticket has been sold for each of the performances. How many tickets were sold in all?

_____

7. An amusement park has about 3,600 visitors each day. About how many visitors does the amusement park have in one week?

_____

Name _____ Date _____

Remembering

Add or subtract.

1.	23,152	2.	308,000	3.	827,381
	− 10,894		− 175,296		+ 154,338

Solve each multiplication problem using any method. Use rounding and estimation to check your work.

4. 21 × 36   **5.** 48 × 16   **6.** 53 × 99   **7.** 64 × 72

_____   _____   _____   _____

Solve using any method and show your work. Check your work with estimation.

8. 45 × 91   **9.** 26 × 33   **10.** 47 × 52   **11.** 87 × 14

_____   _____   _____   _____

12. Stretch Your Thinking Lily says that 4 × 7,000 has the same product as 7 × 4,000. Is she correct? Explain using the Associative Property of Multiplication.

_____

_____

_____

_____

Multiply One-Digit and Four-Digit Numbers

Homework

On a separate sheet of paper, sketch a rectangle for each problem and solve using any method. Round and estimate to check your answer.

1. 5 × 4,751 _____

2. 7 × 6,000 _____

3. 6 × 5,214 _____

4. 8 × 3,867 _____

5. Describe the steps you used for one of your solutions to Exercises 1–4.

_____

_____

A fourth grade class is counting the supplies in the school's art closet. Help them to finish their count.   *Show your work.*

6. They have 6 rolls of white craft paper. The paper on the rolls is 1,275 feet long. How many feet of craft paper do they have altogether?

_____

7. They counted 592 boxes of color pencils and 468 boxes of markers. If each box holds 8 pencils or markers, how many color pencils and markers do they have altogether?

_____

8. They found 9 boxes of glass beads. There are 1,376 beads per box. How many glass beads do they have in all?

_____

9. They found 7 cases of sketching paper. If each case has 2,500 sheets of paper, how many sheets of sketching paper do they have in all?

_____

Remembering

Add or subtract.

1. 82,905
      − 81,927

2. 53,742
      + 93,587

3. 400,000
      − 162,947

Solve.   *Show your work.*

4. Marta bought 18 sheets of stickers for her sticker album.
Each sheet contained 32 stickers. How many stickers did
Marta buy for her sticker album?

_____

**Draw a rectangle model. Solve using any method that
relates to the model.**

5. 3 × 2,816 _____

6. 7 × 1,578 _____

7. Stretch Your Thinking Zoe rounded 6 × 8,493 to
6 × 8,000. Andrew rounded 6 × 8,493 to 6 × 9,000.
Who will have an estimate closer to the actual product?
How do you know? Explain another way to estimate
6 × 8,493 that would give a better estimate.

_____

_____

_____

_____

_____

_____

Use the Shortcut Method

Homework

Solve using any method and show your work. Check your work with estimation.

1. 6×88 _____

2. 62×32 _____

3. $3 \times 3,719$ _____

4. $\begin{array}{r} 63 \\ \times\ 4 \\ \hline \end{array}$

5. $\begin{array}{r} 523 \\ \times\ 8 \\ \hline \end{array}$

6. $\begin{array}{r} 39 \\ \times 19 \\ \hline \end{array}$

7. $\begin{array}{r} 84 \\ \times 47 \\ \hline \end{array}$

8. $\begin{array}{r} 2,858 \\ \times\ \ \ \ 9 \\ \hline \end{array}$

9. $\begin{array}{r} 541 \\ \times\ \ 6 \\ \hline \end{array}$

Solve.

10. Mr. Jackson goes on vacation for 22 days. He pays $17 each day he is gone for Holly's Home Service to get the mail, walk the dog, and water the plants. How much does Mr. Jackson pay Holly's Home Service for the time he is on vacation?

_____

11. A contractor needs to know the area of a sidewalk that is 2,381 feet long and 7 feet wide. What is the area of the sidewalk?

_____

Remembering

Add or subtract.

1.   38,560
     + 16,429

2.   272,311
     − 164,838

3.   815,007
     + 174,399

Draw a rectangle model. Solve using any method that relates to the model.

4. 9 × 4,572 _____

5. 4 × 8,386 _____

A grocery store clerk is ordering produce for the month. Help him find how many snap peas and garlic bulbs are in his order.

Show your work.

6. He orders 4 crates of snap peas. Each crate contains 3,275 snap peas. How many snap peas is he ordering?

_____

7. He orders 9 boxes of garlic bulbs. Each box contains 1,930 bulbs of garlic. How many garlic bulbs is he ordering?

_____

8. Stretch Your Thinking A videographer earns $485 for every wedding he records and $18 for every extra copy of the video his customers order. How much money does the videographer earn in a summer during which he records 34 videos and has 87 orders for extra copies? Show your work.

_____

_____

_____

Practice Multiplying

Homework

Solve using any method and show your work. Check your work with estimation.

1. 3×45 _____

2. 32×82 _____

3. $9 \times 2{,}477$ _____

4. $\begin{array}{r} 86 \\ \times\ 4 \\ \hline \end{array}$

5. $\begin{array}{r} 419 \\ \times\ 6 \\ \hline \end{array}$

6. $\begin{array}{r} 76 \\ \times\ 39 \\ \hline \end{array}$

7. $\begin{array}{r} 23 \\ \times\ 95 \\ \hline \end{array}$

8. $\begin{array}{r} 6{,}965 \\ \times\ 8 \\ \hline \end{array}$

9. $\begin{array}{r} 746 \\ \times\ 5 \\ \hline \end{array}$

Solve.

10. Simon makes an array that is 47 units wide and 33 units long. What is the area of Simon's array?

_____

11. A farmer plants vegetables in rows. He plants 36 rows of carrots with 13 carrot seeds in each row. How many carrot seeds did the farmer plant?

_____

Remembering

Add or subtract.

1.
$$563,902$$
$$-\ 153,884$$

2.
$$327,148$$
$$-\ 123,960$$

3.
$$650,295$$
$$+\ 101,586$$

Sketch a rectangle model and solve using any method.
Round and estimate to check your answer.

4. $6 \times 3,916$ _____

5. $7 \times 2,843$ _____

Solve using any method and show your work. Check your
work with estimation.

6. 7×43 _____

7. 48×26 _____

8. $4,715 \times 3$ _____

9.
$$62$$
$$\times\ 91$$

10.
$$849$$
$$\times\ \ 6$$

11.
$$5,293$$
$$\times\ \ \ \ 4$$

12. **Stretch Your Thinking** LaDonne has a budget of $240
for new school clothes. She needs at least two new
shirts, two new pairs of pants, and one new pair of
shoes. The shirts cost $18 each. The pants cost $32 each.
The shoes cost $49 per pair. Plan two different
combinations of numbers of shirts, pants, and shoes
that LaDonne could buy within her budget. What is the
total cost for each buying plan?

_____

_____

_____

Homework

Divide with remainders.

1. $5\overline{)29}$ **2.** $8\overline{)34}$ **3.** $9\overline{)75}$

4. $2\overline{)13}$ **5.** $4\overline{)39}$ **6.** $4\overline{)30}$

7. $7\overline{)45}$ **8.** $6\overline{)38}$ **9.** $5\overline{)39}$

10. $3\overline{)25}$ **11.** $4\overline{)31}$ **12.** $9\overline{)35}$

13. $4\overline{)27}$ **14.** $8\overline{)29}$ **15.** $7\overline{)22}$

16. $3\overline{)26}$ **17.** $6\overline{)37}$ **18.** $8\overline{)42}$

Remembering

Write the number of thousands and the number of hundreds in each number.

1. 4,128

_____ thousands

_____ hundreds

2. 8,395

_____ thousands

_____ hundreds

3. 612

_____ thousands

_____ hundreds

Read and write each number in expanded form.

4. 94 _____

5. 752 _____

6. 3,576 _____

7. 8,109 _____

Read and write each number in standard form.

8. $200 + 30 + 7$ _____

9. $5,000 + 800 + 60$ _____

10. four hundred sixty-three

_____

11. eight thousand, one hundred ten

_____

Find the area (in square units) of a rectangle with the given dimensions.

12. 5×7 _____

13. 20×3 _____

14. 3×8 _____

15. 4×90 _____

16. 4×4 _____

17. 30×6 _____

18. Stretch Your Thinking Three vocabulary terms for division are shown in the division model. Use these terms to complete the multiplication sentence.

$$\text{divisor} \overline{)\text{dividend}}^{\text{quotient}}$$

_____ $\times$ _____ = _____

Homework

Solve. Use the Place Value Sections Method for division.

Charlie has 944 baseball cards in his collection. He places the cards in an album with exactly 4 cards on each page. How many pages does Charlie fill in his baseball card album? __236 pages__

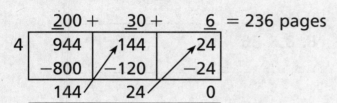

1. A hardware store has 834 planks of wood to deliver to 6 building sites. If each site gets the same number of planks, how many planks should each building site get? _____

   __00 + __0 + __ = ____

Solve. Use the Expanded Notation Method for division.

2. A park planner is designing a rectangular butterfly garden. The plan is for the garden to have an area of 1,917 square feet. If the garden is 9 feet wide, how long is it? _____

3. A family drives 1,498 miles from Boston, Massachusetts to Miami, Florida. If they drive the same number of miles each day for 7 days, how many miles will they drive each day? _____

Remembering

Round each number to the nearest hundred.

1. 591 _____   **2.** 827 _____   **3.** 457 _____

Round each number to the nearest thousand.

4. 7,129 _____   **5.** 6,742 _____   **6.** 1,028 _____

Draw a rectangle. Find the tens product, the ones product, and the total product.

7. 4×29

8. 8×36

Divide with remainders.

9. $7\overline{)38}$ **10.** $4\overline{)29}$ **11.** $3\overline{)14}$

12. Stretch Your Thinking Divide 594 by 3 using the Place Value Sections Method and Expanded Notation Method. Explain how you can check your answer using multiplication.

```
       __00   +  __0  +  __  =  __          3)594
  3 |  594  |      |      |
    |       |      |      |
```

_____

_____

_____

Relate 3-Digit Multiplication to Division

3-3

Homework

Solve. Use the Place Value Sections and the Expanded
Notation Methods for division.

1.   __0 + __ = ___

6	564

6)564

2.   __0 + __ = ___

7	245

7)245

3.   _,000 + __00 + __0 + __ = _____

5	9,675		

5)9,675

4.   _,000 + __00 + __0 + __ = _____

4	9,536		

4)9,536

Read and write each number in word form.

1. 73,894 _____

2. 220,508 _____

3. 1,000,000 _____

4. 915,007 _____

Estimate each product. Solve to check your estimate.

5. 6 × 42   **6.** 3 × 19   **7.** 5 × 78

_____   _____   _____

_____   _____   _____

Solve. Use the Place Value Sections Method and the Expanded Notation Method for division.

8. A ball pit at an entertainment center contains 2,120 balls. The balls are cleaned regularly by a machine which can hold a certain number of balls at once. If the machine must be run 8 times to clean all the balls, how many balls fit in the machine at one time?

_____

$8\overline{)2,120}$

	__ 00	+	__ 0	+	__	=	__
8	2,120						

9. Stretch Your Thinking How many digits will be in the quotient of 588 divided by 6? Use place value to explain.

_____

_____

_____

Discuss 2-Digit and 4-Digit Quotients

Homework

Divide.

1. $6\overline{)2,142}$

2. $4\overline{)886}$

3. $8\overline{)576}$

4. $5\overline{)8,265}$

5. $3\overline{)795}$

6. $9\overline{)2,664}$

7. $6\overline{)259}$

8. $7\overline{)952}$

9. $3\overline{)7,459}$

Solve.

Show your work.

10. For the school field day, students are divided into 5 same-size teams. Any extra students will serve as substitutes. If 243 students participate, how many students will be on each team? How many substitutes will there be?

_____

11. A fruit stand sells packages containing 1 peach, 1 pear, 1 apple, 1 banana, and 1 mango each. One week they sold a total of 395 pieces of fruit. How many packages did they sell?

_____

Digit-by-Digit Method **73**

Compare using >, <, or =.

1. 258,800 ◯ 258,700   **2.** 142,367 ◯ 342,367

Use the Algebraic Notation Method to solve the problem.
Complete the steps.

3. 7 · 28 _____

Solve. Use the Place Value Sections and the Expanded
Notation Methods for division.

4.   __ 00 + __ 0 + __ = _____   4)‾1,036

4	1,036		

5. Stretch Your Thinking Jenna divides 2,506 by 4.
Explain the error in Jenna's solution. Then show
the correct solution.

```
    604
 4)2,506
  -2 4
     1
   - 0
    16
  - 16
     0
```

_____

_____

_____

_____

_____

_____

Digit-by-Digit Method

Name _____ **Date** _____

Homework

Use any method to solve.

1. 5)652

2. 4)940

3. 6)840

4. 7)942

5. 5)6,502

6. 6)8,370

7. 4)5,267

8. 8)9,161

Solve.

9. Joe had 145 peanuts in a bag. He fed all of the peanuts to the 5 squirrels that he saw. If each squirrel got the same number of peanuts, how many peanuts did each squirrel get?

_____

10. There were 1,148 students at Jefferson High School who wanted to go on a field trip. Since they could not all go at the same time, they went in 7 equal groups. How many students were in each group?

_____

11. A printing company has 1,080 ink cartridges to be packed in 9 shipping boxes. If each box holds the same number of cartridges, how many ink cartridges will be packed in each box?

_____

Name _____

Date _____

Remembering

The table shows the water surface area of each of the Great Lakes. Use the data in the table to answer the following questions.

1. What is the combined surface area of the two Great Lakes with the greatest surface area?

   _____

2. Which is greater, the surface area of Lake Michigan or the sum of the surface areas of Lake Erie and Lake Ontario?

   _____

Lake	Surface Area (square kilometers)
Erie	25,655
Huron	59,565
Michigan	57,753
Ontario	19,009
Superior	82,097

Use any method to solve. Sketch a rectangle model, if you need to.

3. 4×39 _____

4. 3×71 _____

5. 7×62 _____

Divide. Show your work.

6. $5\overline{)1,985}$

7. $6\overline{)253}$

8. $7\overline{)1,477}$

9. **Stretch Your Thinking** Which method do you prefer for division: the Place Value Sections Method, Expanded Notation Method, or Digit-by-Digit Method? Explain. Then solve $6,583 \div 4$ using your preferred method.

   _____

   _____

   _____

Homework

Solve.

1. $3\overline{)21}$ $\qquad$ $3\overline{)22}$ $\qquad$ $3\overline{)23}$ $\qquad$ $3\overline{)24}$ $\qquad$ $3\overline{)25}$

2. $7\overline{)21}$ $\qquad$ $7\overline{)22}$ $\qquad$ $7\overline{)23}$ $\qquad$ $7\overline{)24}$ $\qquad$ $7\overline{)25}$

3. Describe how the repeating pattern in row 1 is different
from the pattern in row 2. Explain why.

_____

_____

_____

Use any method to solve.

4. $9\overline{)2,359}$ $\qquad\qquad$ **5.** $2\overline{)5,389}$ $\qquad\qquad$ **6.** $4\overline{)1,648}$

7. $5\overline{)1,456}$ $\qquad\qquad$ **8.** $8\overline{)2,506}$ $\qquad\qquad$ **9.** $6\overline{)8,473}$

Solve. $\qquad\qquad\qquad\qquad\qquad\qquad\qquad\qquad$ *Show your work.*

10. Mr. James arranged his collection of 861 baseball
cards in 7 equal rows. How many cards were in
each row?

_____

11. A shoe company has 9,728 pairs of shoes to be divided
equally among 8 stores. How many pairs of shoes will
each store get?

_____

Remembering

Write a number sentence that shows an estimate of
each answer. Then write the exact answer.

1. 413 + 382 _____

2. 880 + 394 _____

3. 7,056 + 798 _____

Sketch rectangles and solve by any method that
relates to your sketch.

4. 8 × 415 _____   5. 6 × 853 _____

Use any method to solve.

6. 7)‾3‾2‾5   7. 5)‾7‾,‾3‾9‾0   8. 6)‾9‾,‾3‾2‾9

9. **Stretch Your Thinking** Toby is choosing from two bead
   art projects. Project A uses equal numbers of red, black,
   and green beads totaling 825 beads. Project B uses equal
   numbers of black, blue, green, and yellow beads totaling
   1,020 beads. Toby has 260 green beads and doesn't want
   to purchase more green beads. Explain which of the two
   bead projects Toby should choose.

   _____

   _____

   _____

   _____

   _____

Homework

Solve.

1. $4\overline{)21}$　　$4\overline{)22}$　　$4\overline{)23}$　　$4\overline{)24}$　　$4\overline{)25}$

2. $6\overline{)21}$　　$6\overline{)22}$　　$6\overline{)23}$　　$6\overline{)24}$　　$6\overline{)25}$

3. Describe how the repeating pattern in row 1 is different from the pattern in row 2. Explain why.

_____

_____

Use any method to solve.

4. $8\overline{)6,726}$　　5. $7\overline{)9,259}$　　6. $3\overline{)1,504}$　　7. $2\overline{)8,037}$

8. $9\overline{)3,385}$　　9. $5\overline{)2,347}$　　10. $6\overline{)9,003}$　　11. $4\overline{)8,360}$

Solve.

12. Altogether, the members of an exercise club drink 840 bottles of water each month. Each member drinks 8 bottles. How many members are there?

_____

13. There are 7,623 pencils ready to be packaged in boxes at a factory. Each box holds 6 pencils. How many full boxes of pencils can be packaged?

_____

Name _____   Date _____

Remembering

Subtract. Show your new groups.

1.   5,267
   − 1,390
     _____

2.   9,000
   − 2,482
     _____

3.   6,129
   − 5,773
     _____

Cross out the additional numerical information and solve.   *Show your work.*

4. Rick is selling fresh-squeezed lemonade for $2 a serving. Rick makes each serving with 2 lemons and 4 tablespoons of sugar. If he sells 27 servings of lemonade, how much sugar does he use?

_____

5. An animal shelter receives 9 large bags of dog food every month for 14 years. Each bag weighs 55 pounds. How many pounds of dog food does the animal shelter receive each month?

_____

Solve using any method.

6. $3\overline{)452}$

7. $8\overline{)527}$

8. $4\overline{)3,693}$

9. **Stretch Your Thinking** What is the greatest remainder you could have with the divisor 3? With the divisor 8? With the divisor 5? Explain.

_____

_____

_____

_____

       Just-Under Quotient Digits

Name _____ **Date** _____

**Solve by any method on a separate sheet of paper.
Then check your answer by rounding and estimating.**

1. $3\overline{)246}$ **2.** $6\overline{)75}$ **3.** $7\overline{)60}$

4. $3\overline{)256}$ **5.** $4\overline{)805}$ **6.** $5\overline{)927}$

7. $4\overline{)325}$ **8.** $4\overline{)378}$ **9.** $6\overline{)432}$

10. $5\overline{)1,838}$ **11.** $4\overline{)2,715}$ **12.** $7\overline{)3,042}$

Solve. *Show your work.*

13. The area of Matt's rectangular bedroom is 96 square feet.
If the room is 8 feet wide, how long is it?

_____

14. The fourth-grade students at Lincoln Elementary
School are attending an assembly. There are 7 equal
rows of seats in the assembly hall. If there are
392 fourth-grade students, how many students will
sit in each row?

_____

15. Pablo is packing books into crates. He has 9 crates.
Each crate will contain the same number of books.
If he has 234 books, how many books can he put
into each crate?

_____

Remembering

Add or subtract.

1. 1,429
   + 3,882
	2. 28,178
	   − 13,428
		3. 500,000
		   − 61,835

Sketch an area model for each exercise. Then find the product.

4. 27 × 59 _____   **5.** 36 × 92 _____

Solve using any method.

6. 9)271   **7.** 6)2,436   **8.** 4)2,139

9. Stretch Your Thinking Katherine is considering two new cell phone plans. She doesn't want to spend more for minutes she won't use. One plan allows up to 250 minutes per month for $49, and the other plan allows up to 350 minutes per month for $65. In the last 6 months, she used 1,470 minutes. Use estimating and an exact answer to determine the best cell phone plan for Katherine.

_____

_____

_____

_____

Homework

Solve. Write the remainder as a whole number.

1. $7\overline{)7,012}$

2. $9\overline{)8,410}$

3. $2\overline{)7,825}$

4. $5\overline{)3,512}$

5. $6\overline{)6,618}$

6. $8\overline{)7,225}$

Solve. Then explain the meaning of the remainder.

7. Principal Clements wants to buy a pencil for each of the 57 fourth-graders in her school. The pencils come in packages of 6. How many packages does Principal Clements need to buy?

_____

_____

_____

_____

8. Tyler has 71 CDs in his collection. He places the CDs in a book that holds 4 CDs on each page. If Tyler fills each page, how many CDs will be on the last page?

_____

_____

_____

_____

9. Amanda and her family are hiking a trail that is 46 miles long. They plan to hike exactly 7 miles each day. How many days will they hike exactly 7 miles?

_____

_____

_____

_____

10. Cesar makes 123 ounces of trail mix. He puts an equal number of ounces in each of 9 bags. How many ounces of trail mix does Cesar have left over?

_____

_____

_____

_____

Remembering

The table shows the word count for each of five books in a series. Use the table to answer each question. Estimate to check.

1. How many more words are there in Book 2 than in Book 1?

   _____

   _____

2. What is the difference between the book with the greatest number of words and the book with the least number of words?

   _____

   _____

Book	Word Count
1	82,647
2	91,313
3	109,842
4	73,450
5	90,216

Solve each multiplication problem using any method. Use rounding and estimation to check your work.

3. 39×52 4. 81×76 5. 18×63 6. 45×91

_____   _____   _____   _____

Solve using any method. Then check your answer by rounding and estimating.

7. $7\overline{)65}$ 8. $3\overline{)289}$ 9. $8\overline{)5,024}$

10. **Stretch Your Thinking** Write a word problem that is solved by $43 \div 5 = 8$ R3, in which the remainder is the only part needed to answer the question.

    _____

    _____

    _____

Homework

When the Kent Elementary School fourth-grade classes were studying butterflies, they took a field trip to a butterfly garden.

Use the correct operation or combination of operations to solve each problem.

Show your work.

1. Nine buses of students, teachers, and parents went on the field trip. If 5 of the buses held 63 people each and the other buses held 54 people each, how many people went in all?

   _____

   _____

2. Some female butterflies lay their eggs in clusters. If one kind of butterfly lays 12 eggs at a time and another kind lays 18 eggs at a time, how many eggs would 8 of each kind of butterfly lay?

   _____

   _____

3. Teachers divided students into groups of 3. Each group of 3 wrote a report that had 9 pictures in it. The students used 585 pictures altogether. How many students were there in all?

   _____

4. Driving to and from the butterfly garden took 45 minutes each way. The students spent 3 hours in the garden and 30 minutes eating lunch. If the groups left the school at 9:00 A.M., what time did they get back?

   _____

   _____

   _____

Remembering

Add or subtract.

1.	5,833 − 2,159	2.	49,802 + 15,658	3.	98,139 − 27,345

Sketch rectangles and solve by any method that relates to your sketch.

4. 5 × 6,294 _____

5. 8 × 1,375 _____

Solve. Then explain the meaning of the remainder.

6. Vince has 138 artist trading cards. He is arranging them in an album that can hold 4 to a page. If Vince fills each page as he goes, how many cards are on the last page?

7. Amber is doing an online math drill program. She has exactly 300 seconds to complete as many problems as she can. If it takes Amber 7 seconds to do each problem, how many problems does she complete?

8. **Stretch Your Thinking** In the fall, Wesley swam a race in 58 seconds, and Aiden swam it in 54 seconds. In the spring, they swam the same race. Wesley did it in 53 seconds, and Aiden did it in 52 seconds. How much more of an improvement was one boy's race time over the other boy's race time? Explain.

Homework

Divide.   *Show your work.*

1. 5)456   **2.** 4)1,247   **3.** 7)829

4. 6)2,254   **5.** 3)729   **6.** 8)658

7. 9)4,437   **8.** 5)3,649   **9.** 6)875

Solve.   *Show your work.*

10. Sharon has 1,278 beads to make bracelets. She sorts them into 6 different containers so she can have an equal amount of beads in each container. How many beads will Sharon put in each container?

_____

11. Kyle collects baseball cards. He places his cards into an album that has 9 cards on each page. He has a total of 483 baseball cards. He fills each page before putting cards on the next page. How many cards will be on the last page?

_____

Remembering

Answer each question about the information in the table.

1. What was the total amount donated to the theatre in 2007 and 2009 combined?

   _____

2. How much more was donated in 2010 than in 2006?

   _____

Donations to a Children's Theatre

Year	Donations
2006	$26,304
2007	$28,315
2008	$63,418
2009	$53,237
2010	$86,061

Solve using any method and show your work.
Check your work with estimation.

3. 26×6 _____

4. 932×7 _____

5. $2,107 \times 8$ _____

Use the correct operation or combination of operations to solve the problem.

Show your work.

6. Selena sold 9 homemade bracelets for $12 each and 14 pairs of earrings for $8 each. How much did she make in sales?

   _____

7. **Stretch Your Thinking** At a skating rink, Emma makes 21 laps at a steady pace during a 5-minute song. She divided $21 \div 5 = 4$ R1 and says that means she did $4 + 1 = 5$ laps each minute. Explain Emma's error.

   _____

   _____

   _____

Homework

Simplify each expression.

1. $11m - 9m =$ ____   **2.** $y + 8y =$ ____   **3.** $13s - s =$ ____

4. $d + 2d + d =$ ____   **5.** $(9b - b) - 2b =$ ____   **6.** $104z + z =$ ____

7. $21 - (10 - 5) =$ ____   **8.** $(900 - 100) - 100 =$ ____   **9.** $90 - (50 - 1) =$ ____

10. $18 \div (27 \div 9) =$ ____   **11.** $(63 \div 7) \div 9 =$ ____   **12.** $40 \div (36 \div 9) =$ ____

13. $(48 \div 6) \cdot (11 - 9) =$ _____   **14.** $(3 + 17) \div (16 - 12) =$ _____

15. $(15 + 10) - (50 \div 10) =$ _____   **16.** $(19 + 11) \div (9 - 6) =$ _____

Evaluate.

17. $c = 3$

$4 \cdot (7 - c)$

_____

18. $r = 2$

$(42 \div 7) \cdot (r + 1)$

_____

19. $w = 7$

$(72 \div 9) \cdot w$

_____

20. $m = 0$

$(12 \div 3) \cdot (5 - m)$

_____

21. $h = 14$

$45 \div (h - 5)$

_____

22. $p = 19$

$(p + 1) \div (9 - 4)$

_____

23. $v = 6$

$(18 - 9) + (2 + v)$

_____

24. $t = 1$

$(7 \cdot 2) \div t$

_____

25. $g = 10$

$(g + 90) \div (17 - 13)$

_____

Solve for □ or n.

26. $7 \cdot (3 + 2) = 7 \cdot \square$

$\square =$ ____

27. $(9 - 1) \cdot 4 = \square \cdot 4$

$\square =$ ____

28. $8 \cdot (4 + 5) = \square \cdot 9$

$\square =$ ____

29. $6 \cdot (8 - 8) = n$

$n =$ ____

30. $(12 - 6) \div 3 = n$

$n =$ ____

31. $(21 \div 7) \cdot (5 + 5) = n$

$n =$ ____

Remembering

Read and write each number in expanded form.

1. ninety-six thousand, one hundred thirty-seven

_____

2. four hundred thirteen thousand, five hundred twenty-one

_____

3. seven hundred eight thousand, fifty-three

_____

4. six hundred thirty thousand, four hundred seventeen

_____

Find the area (in square units) of a rectangle with the given dimensions.

5. 4×6 _____

6. 4×60 _____

7. 5×9 _____

8. 50×9 _____

Divide with remainders.

9. $9\overline{)28}$

10. $3\overline{)17}$

11. $6\overline{)46}$

12. $7\overline{)54}$

13. **Stretch Your Thinking** Evaluate the expression
$(d - 10) + (d \div 3)$ for $d = 21$. Explain each step.

_____

_____

_____

_____

_____

Properties and Algebraic Notation

Homework

Write = or ≠ to make each statement true.

1. 5 + 2 + 6 ◯ 6 + 7   **2.** 90 ◯ 110 − 9   **3.** 70 ◯ 30 + 30

4. 70 ◯ 95 − 25   **5.** 2 + 8 + 10 ◯ 30   **6.** 27 − 10 ◯ 14 + 3

7. 51 + 99 ◯ 150   **8.** 35 ◯ 100 − 55   **9.** 50 ◯ 20 + 5 + 20

10. Write the eight related addition and subtraction equations for the break-apart drawing.

48
42   6

_____   _____

_____   _____

_____   _____

_____   _____

Write an equation to solve the problem. Draw a model if you need to.   *Show your work.*

11. There were some people at the arts and crafts fair. Then 347 people went home. Now 498 people are left at the fair. How many people were at the fair to start?

_____

_____

12. A group of scientists spends 3,980 hours observing the behavior of monarch butterflies. They spend some more hours recording their observations. Altogether, the scientists spend 5,726 hours observing the butterflies and recording their observations. How many hours do the scientists spend recording their observations?

_____

_____

Solve.

1. What is 538,152 rounded to the nearest:

a. hundred? _____

b. thousand? _____

c. ten thousand? _____

d. hundred thousand? _____

Draw a rectangle model. Find the tens product, the ones product, and the total product.

2. 3×65

3. 8×29

Evaluate each expression.

4. $(12 - 4) \cdot (6 + 3) =$ _____

5. $(8 \div 2) + (12 - 2) =$ _____

6. Stretch Your Thinking There were 381 books sold at a children's used book fair. At the end of the day, there were still 493 books remaining. Samantha says there were 112 books at the start of the book fair. Explain her error. How many books were there at the start of the book fair?

_____

_____

_____

_____

Situation and Solution Equations for Addition and Subtraction

1. Write the eight related multiplication and division equations for the rectangle model below.

```
     15
  ┌────────┐
6 │   90   │
  └────────┘
```

_____   _____

_____   _____

_____   _____

_____   _____

Solve each equation.

2. $r = 200 \div 5$

$r =$ _____

3. $12 \times d = 84$

$d =$ _____

4. $80 \div 10 = n$

$n =$ _____

5. $120 = 10 \times m$

$m =$ _____

6. $88 = 8 \times c$

$c =$ _____

7. $100 \div q = 20$

$q =$ _____

Write an equation to solve the problem. Draw a model if you need to.

8. Lucy bought some shrubs to plant in her garden. Each shrub cost $9. If Lucy spent $216 in all, how many shrubs did she buy?

Show your work.

_____

_____

9. Jeremiah has 592 flyers in stacks of 8 flyers each. How many stacks of flyers did Jeremiah make?

_____

_____

10. The apples from an average-sized tree will fill 20 baskets. If an orchard has 17 average-sized trees, how many baskets of apples can it produce?

_____

_____

Name _____ **Date** _____

Remembering

Use the Algebraic Notation Method to solve the problem. Complete the steps.

1. 5 · 68 _____

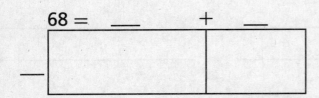

$5 \cdot 68 =$ ___ · (___ + ___)
$= 300 + 40$
$= 340$

Solve. Use the Place Value Sections and the Expanded Notation Methods for division.

2.　　　 ___0 + ___ =

3 | 234 |

3)234

3.　　　 ___0 + ___ =

9 | 468 |

9)468

Write = or ≠ to make each statement true.

4. 40 + 40 ◯ 90　　　5. 12 − 4 ◯ 12 + 4　　　6. 4 + 7 ◯ 4 + 2 + 5

7. 26 ◯ 30 − 4　　　8. 8 + 10 + 2 ◯ 20　　　9. 85 − 25 ◯ 65

10. **Stretch Your Thinking** Write a word problem about puzzle pieces using the equation $9 \times p = 450$. Then solve the equation.

_____

_____

_____

_____

　　　Situation and Solution Equations for Multiplication and Division

Homework

Use the shapes to answer Exercises 1–4.

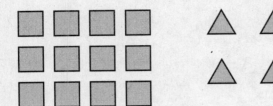

1. How many squares? How many triangles?
   Use multiplication to find the answers.

   _____

2. Because 4 × _____ = 12, there are _____ times
   as many squares as triangles.

3. Write a multiplication equation that compares
   the number of squares *s* to the number of
   triangles *t*.

   _____

4. Write a division equation that compares the
   number of triangles *t* to the number of
   squares *s*.

   _____

Solve each comparison problem.

5. Stephen and Rocco were playing a video game.
   Stephen scored 2,500 points which is 5 times as
   many points as Rocco scored. How many points
   did Rocco score?

   _____

6. Nick's dog weighs 72 pounds. Elizabeth's cat weighs
   9 pounds. How many times as many pounds does
   Nick's dog weigh as Elizabeth's cat weighs?

   _____

Name _____ Date _____

Remembering

Solve using any numerical method. Use rounding and estimating to see if your answer makes sense.

1. 71	**2.** 36	**3.** 94	**4.** 77
$\times$ 4	$\times$ 5	$\times$ 8	$\times$ 6

Divide.

5. $6\overline{)89}$ **6.** $5\overline{)485}$ **7.** $4\overline{)743}$

Solve each equation.

8. $9 \times n = 108$ **9.** $40 \div t = 10$ **10.** $r = 56 \div 7$

   $n =$ _____ $t =$ _____ $r =$ _____

11. Stretch Your Thinking Write and solve a word problem to match the comparison bars shown below.

Grandfather | 8 |

Grandmother | 8 | 8 | 8 |

m

_____

_____

_____

_____

_____

Multiplication Comparisons

Write and solve an equation to solve each problem. Draw comparison bars when needed.

Show your work.

1. This year, a business had profits of $8,040. This is 4 times as great as the profits that the business had last year. What were last year's profits?

_____

2. In July 74,371 people visited an art museum. In August 95,595 people visited the art museum. How many fewer people visited the art museum in July than in August?

_____

3. Drake has 36 animal stickers. Brenda has 9 animal stickers. How many times as many animal stickers does Drake have as Brenda has?

_____

4. A game is being watched by 60 adults and some children. If there are 20 more adults than children, how many children are watching the game?

_____

5. During the first lunch period, 54 students ate hot lunch. This is 9 fewer students than ate hot lunch during the second lunch period. How many students ate hot lunch during the second lunch period?

_____

6. The Jenkins Family traveled 750 miles by car during the summer. The Palmer Family traveled 3 times as many miles by car this summer. How many miles did the Palmer Family travel?

_____

Name _____ **Date** _____

Remembering

Copy each exercise, aligning the places correctly. Then add.

1. 11,931 + 3,428

2. 25,422 + 89,360

Draw a rectangle model. Solve using any method that relates to the model.

3. 3 × 428 _____

4. 7 × 519 _____

Write and solve an equation to solve the problem. Draw comparison bars if you need to.

5. Virginia sold 84 rolls of wrapping paper this year. She sold 3 times as many rolls of wrapping paper this year as she sold last year. How many rolls of wrapping paper did Virginia sell last year?

_____

6. Stretch Your Thinking There are 1,438 boys and 1,196 girls at a school. How many fewer girls are there than boys?

Write the comparison question for this problem in a different way. Then write and solve an equation to solve the problem. Draw comparison bars if you need to.

_____

_____

_____

Discuss Comparison Problems

Name _____ **Date** _____

Homework

The graph below shows the amount of snow recorded each month last winter. Use the graph for Problems 1–6.

1. During which month was the amount of snow recorded 12 inches greater than the amount of snow recorded in December?

   _____

2. How many fewer inches of snow were recorded in March than were recorded in February?

   _____

Snowfall Last Winter

Inches: 0, 4, 8, 12, 16, 20, 24, 28

Month: Nov. Dec. Jan. Feb. Mar.

3. The total amount of snow shown in the graph is 4 times as much snow as was recorded during the winter of 2004. How much snow was recorded during the winter of 2004?

   _____

4. Write an addition equation and a subtraction equation that compare the number of inches of snow recorded during December (d) to the number of inches of snow recorded during March (m).

   _____

5. Write a multiplication equation and a division equation that compare the number of inches of snow recorded during November (n) to the number of inches of snow recorded during January (j).

   _____

6. On a separate sheet of paper, write a sentence about the graph that contains the words _times as much_.

Remembering

Sketch an area model for each exercise. Then find the product.

1. 28 × 45 _____

2. 53 × 96 _____

Solve using any method.

3. 9)‾506‾

4. 2)‾538‾

5. 7)‾8,165‾

Write and solve an equation to solve each problem. Draw comparison bars when needed.

Show your work.

6. Benjamin received 52 emails at work today. This is 4 times as many emails as he received yesterday. How many emails did Benjamin receive yesterday?

_____

7. There are 327 third-grade students on a field trip at the history museum. There are 423 fourth-grade students on the same field trip. How many fewer third-grade students are there than fourth-grade students on the field trip?

_____

8. Stretch Your Thinking Look at the graph. Tatiana says there are 4 more dog owners than fish owners in the classroom. Explain Tatiana's error. Then write an equation that compares the numbers of dog owners and fish owners in the classroom.

Pet Owners in the Classroom	
Pet	
Cat	☺ ☺ ☺
Bird	☺
Dog	☺ ☺ ☺ ☺ ☺ ☺
Fish	☺ ☺

☺ = 2 students

_____

Homework

Use an equation to solve.

Show your work.

1. The soccer club has 127 members. The baseball club has 97 members. Both clubs will meet to discuss a fundraiser. The members will be seated at tables of 8 members each. How many tables will they use?

_____

2. A hardware store pays $3,500 for 42 lawnmowers. Then the store sells the lawnmowers for $99 each. How much profit does the store make from the lawnmower sales?

_____

3. George buys a set of 224 stamps. He gives 44 stamps to a friend. Then he places the remaining stamps into an album with 5 stamps on each page. How many pages does he fill in his album?

_____

4. Shane and his family go to the movie theater and buy 6 tickets for $12 each. Then they spend a total of $31 for popcorn and drinks. How much did Shane and his family spend for tickets, popcorn and drinks at the movie theater?

_____

5. Last year, 226 people attended the school graduation ceremony. This year, the school expects 125 more people than last year. The school has arranged for a van to transport people from the parking area to the ceremony. Each van holds 9 people. How many trips will the van make?

_____

Name _____ **Date** _____

Remembering

Solve each multiplication problem, using any method. Use rounding and estimation to check your work.

1. 22 × 58

2. 34 × 91

3. 63 × 72

4. 17 × 56

_____ _____ _____ _____

Solve by using any method. Then check your answer by rounding and estimating.

5. 9)‾39‾

6. 4)‾168‾

7. 5)‾4,204‾

The graph shows the number of points Derek scored during his first five basketball games.

8. Write a multiplication equation and a division equation that compare the number of points Derek scored during Game 1 (*x*) to the number of points Derek scored during Game 4 (*y*).

_____

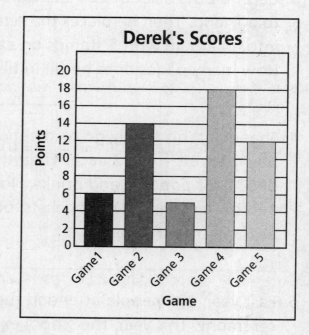

9. Stretch Your Thinking There will be 138 people at a fundraising auction. Each table seats six. An additional 3 tables are needed to display the auction items. What is the minimum number of tables that are needed for the fundraiser? Which equation *cannot* be used to answer this question? Explain.

$$138 \div (6 + 3) = t \qquad (138 \div 6) + 3 = t$$

_____

_____

_____

_____

Solve Two-Step Problems

Homework

Use an equation to solve.   *Show your work.*

1. Rosa and Kate both went shopping. Kate bought a jacket for $45 and boots for $42. Rosa bought jeans for $27, a sweater for $22, and sneakers. They both spent the same exact amount of money. How much were Rosa's sneakers?

   _____

2. Kyle works at a bakery on weekends. On Saturday, Kyle needs to make 120 muffins. Each recipe makes 8 muffins and uses 2 cups of flour. On Sunday, he needs to bake a large batch of cookies that uses 6 cups of flour. How many cups of flour will Kyle use to bake the muffins and the cookies?

   _____

3. A toy factory made 715 small stuffed bears and packed them in boxes with 5 bears in each box. Then they made 693 large stuffed bears and packed them in boxes with 3 bears in each box. All the boxes of small and large stuffed bears are loaded into a truck for delivery. How many boxes are loaded into the truck?

   _____

4. Last summer, Chris went to Europe and bought postcards from the cities he visited. In France, he visited 6 cities and bought 11 postcards in each city. In Italy, he visited 7 cities and bought 9 postcards in each city. In Spain, he visited 10 cities and bought 15 postcards in each city. How many postcards did Chris buy in Europe?

   _____

5. Three fourth grade classes went on a field trip to see a play. Each class had 19 students and 2 adults attending. The rows in the playhouse each seat 9 people. How many rows did the fourth grade classes and adults take up at the playhouse?

   _____

Name _____ **Date** _____

Remembering

Add or subtract.

1. 9,000
    − 5,613

2. 317,492
    + 36,057

3. 659,741
    − 652,438

Solve. Then explain the meaning of the remainder.

4. Jessica needs to bake 50 muffins.
   Her baking pan holds 12 muffins.
   How many rounds of baking will she
   need to do?

   _____

   _____

   _____

   _____

   _____

Use an equation to solve.

Show your work.

5. At the fair, Hannah bought her family 5 hot dogs for
   $3 each and a pitcher of lemonade for $6. How much
   money did she spend in all?

   _____

6. Reggie is keeping 7 of his 31 stuffed animals and splitting
   the remainder of his collection evenly among his 3 younger
   sisters. How many stuffed animals does each sister get?

   _____

7. **Stretch Your Thinking** Write a word problem using
   the equation ($60 + $3 − $15) ÷ $4 = w. Then solve
   the equation to solve the problem.

   _____

   _____

   _____

   _____

Solve Multistep Problems

4-9

Homework

Solve each problem.

1. $5 \times 7 + 9 = t$

_____

2. $9 \times (1 + 3) = m$

_____

3. $7 - 2 \times 2 = k$

_____

4. $(7 \times 2) + (4 \times 9) = w$

_____

5. $(7 - 2) \times (3 + 2) = r$

_____

6. $8 \times (12 - 7) = v$

_____

7. Whitney and Georgia are at the snack bar buying food for their family. Sandwiches cost $4 each. Salads cost $2 each. How much money will it cost them to buy 5 sandwiches and 7 salads?

_____

8. Lisa put tulips and roses into vases. Each vase has 12 flowers. The red vase has 7 tulips. The blue vase has twice as many roses as the red vase. How many roses are in the blue vase?

_____

9. Pam has 9 bags of apples. Each bag contains 6 apples. There are 3 bags of red apples and 1 bag of green apples. The rest of the bags contain yellow apples. How many more yellow apples are there than red apples?

_____

10. Clay works on a farm. He packaged eggs into containers that hold 1 dozen eggs each. He filled 4 containers with white eggs and 5 containers with brown eggs. How many eggs did Clay collect? Hint: one dozen eggs = 12 eggs

_____

Name _____ **Date** _____

Remembering

Subtract. Show your new groups.

1. 3,146
    − 1,960

2. 7,504
    − 2,738

3. 6,000
    − 5,241

Solve using any method and show your work.
Use estimation to check your work.

4. 23 × 88   5. 71 × 49   6. 62 × 67   7. 15 × 38

_____   _____   _____   _____

Use an equation to solve.

8. An audio book is made up of 8 CDs. Each of the first
   7 CDs is 42 minutes long and the final CD is 26 minutes
   long. Mark plans to listen to the book the same number
   of minutes for 8 days. How many minutes each day will
   Mark listen to the audio book?

   _____

9. **Stretch Your Thinking** A sign shows the price per
   pound for several bulk food items. Use the
   information to write a word problem that requires
   at least 3 steps to solve. Then solve your problem

Food Item	Cost per pound
mixed nuts	$5
dried fruit	$3
snack mix	$7
wild rice	$2
red lentils	$4

   _____

   _____

   _____

   _____

   _____

   _____

Practice with Multistep Problems

Name _____ **Date** _____

Homework

List all the factor pairs for each number.

1. 49

_____

2. 71

_____

3. 18

_____

4. 57

_____

Write whether each number is *prime* or *composite*.

5. 50

_____

6. 29

_____

7. 81

_____

8. 95

_____

9. 19

_____

10. 54

_____

Tell whether 6 is a factor of each number. Write *yes* or *no*.

11. 6

_____

12. 80

_____

13. 36

_____

14. 72

_____

Tell whether each number is a multiple of 8. Write *yes* or *no*.

15. 64

_____

16. 32

_____

17. 88

_____

18. 18

_____

Use the rule to complete the pattern.

19. Rule: skip count by 11

11, 22, _____, _____, 55, _____, _____, 88, 99

20. Rule: skip count by 9

9, _____, 27, _____, 45, _____, 63, _____, 81, _____

21. Rule: skip count by 8

8, 16, 24, _____, _____, _____, _____, 64, 72, _____

Name _____ **Date** _____

Remembering

Draw a rectangle model. Solve using any method that relates to the model.

1. $8 \times 1{,}593$ _____

2. $3 \times 6{,}247$ _____

Use the correct operation or combination of operations to solve the problem.

3. Melina has 4 sheets of wacky face stickers with 24 stickers on each sheet. Melina cuts each sticker individually from the sheet. She then divides them evenly into 3 piles to give to friends. How many stickers are in each pile?

_____

Solve.

4. $5 \times 4 + 7 = g$ _____

5. $(3 \times 7) + (2 \times 10) = h$ _____

6. $16 - (5 \times 3) = m$ _____

7. $(9 - 3) \times (2 + 7) = l$ _____

8. $(12 - 8) + (3 \times 3) = p$ _____

9. $(24 \div 4) + 19 = t$ _____

10. Stretch Your Thinking Use _prime_ or _composite_ to complete the sentence. Then explain your choice. All even numbers greater than 2 are _____.

_____

_____

_____

_____

Factors and Prime Numbers

Homework

Name _____   **Date** _____

Use the rule to find the next three terms in the pattern.

1. 2, 6, 18, 54, ...

Rule: multiply by 3

_____

2. 115, 145, 175, 205, 235, ...

Rule: add 30

_____

Use the rule to find the first ten terms in the pattern.

3. First term: 12   Rule: add 25

_____

Make a table to solve.

4. Jay saves $2 in June, $4 in July, $6 in August, and $8 in September. If the pattern continues, how much money will Jay save in December?

_____

Describe the next term of each pattern.

5.

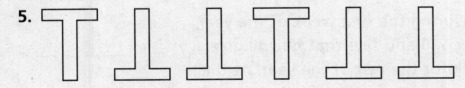

_____

_____

6.

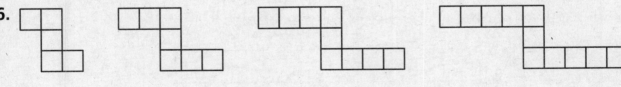

_____

_____

Name _____ **Date** _____

Remembering

Subtract.

1. 491,562
    − 208,723

2. 392,119
    − 48,319

Solve.   *Show your work.*

3. Sid unpacks 8 cartons of paper clips. Each carton contains 3,500 paper clips. How many paper clips is this altogether?

    _____

4. Camille unpacks 102 boxes of red pens and 155 boxes of blue pens. Each box contains 8 pens. How many pens does she unpack altogether?

    _____

List all of the factor pairs for each number.

5. 55 _____   6. 14 _____

7. **Stretch Your Thinking** During the first week of the year, Angelina's dad gives her $10 and says that he will give her $10 more each week for the rest of the year. At the end of the year, how much money will Angelina receive from her dad? (Hint: 1 year = 52 weeks) Make a table to show the pattern, and explain your answer.

_____

_____

_____

_____

Analyze Patterns

Homework

1. Design the blank pot below by drawing a pattern that meets the following conditions.

   ▸ At least three different shapes are used.

   ▸ The pattern begins with a square or a circle.

   ▸ The pattern is repeated at least two times.

   ▸ At least two different colors are used.

2. Describe your pattern.

   _____

   _____

3. Suppose 184 students from Wilson Middle School complete this page at home. If each student draws 9 shapes on his or her pot, how many shapes in all would be drawn?

   _____

Name _____   **Date** _____

Remembering

Add or subtract.

1.   8,500
    − 1,265

2.   24,187
    − 14,856

3.   683,519
    + 292,744

Solve using any method and show your work. Check your work with estimation.

4.   19
    × 82

5.   649
    ×   3

6.   2,934
    ×   8

Use the rule to find the next five terms in the pattern.

7. 3, 6, 12, 24, …

    Rule: multiply by 2

8. 25, 60, 95, 130, …

    Rule: add 35

_____   _____

Use the rule to find the first ten terms in the pattern.

9. First term: 18   Rule: add 12

_____

10. **Stretch Your Thinking** For a cookie exchange, Kaiya bakes 2 pans of 12 chocolate chip cookies each, 3 pans of 16 lemon drops each, and 4 pans of 10 peanut butter cookies each. She is dividing the cookies into 8 tins, with an equal number of each type of cookie in each tin. How many of each type of cookie will be in each tin? How many cookies in all will be in each tin? Explain.

_____

_____

_____

_____

Focus on Mathematical Practices